PERSONS IN CONTEXT

PERSONS
IN CONTEXT
Building a Science of the Individual

Edited by
Yuichi Shoda
Daniel Cervone
Geraldine Downey

THE GUILFORD PRESS
New York   London

© 2007 The Guilford Press
A Division of Guilford Publications, Inc.
72 Spring Street, New York, NY 10012
www.guilford.com

Printed in the United States of America

This book is printed on acid-free paper.

Last digit is print number: 9   8   7   6   5   4   3   2   1

Library of Congress Cataloging-in-Publication Data

Persons in context : building a science of the individual / edited by Yuichi
Shoda, Daniel Cervone, Geraldine Downey.
   p. cm.
  Includes bibliographical references and index.
  ISBN-10: 1-59385-567-2 ISBN-13: 978-1-59385-567-3 (cloth : alk. paper)
  1. Personality—Social aspects. 2. Personality and cognition. I. Shoda,
Yuichi. II. Cervone, Daniel. III. Downey, Geraldine.
  BF698.9.S63P473 2007
  155.2—dc22

                                           2007024870

About the Editors

Yuichi Shoda, PhD, is a Professor in the Department of Psychology at the University of Washington. After studying physics at Hokkaido University in Sapporo, Japan, he studied psychology at the University of California, Santa Cruz, and at Stanford University, and received his doctorate at Columbia University. Dr. Shoda's research is aimed at identifying and understanding stable and distinctive within-person patterns of variation in the ever-changing stream, over time and across situations, of an individual's cognition, affect, and behavior.

Daniel Cervone, PhD, is a Professor in the Department of Psychology at the University of Illinois at Chicago. He received his doctorate at Stanford University; has held visiting faculty positions at the University of Washington and the University of Rome, La Sapienza; has been a fellow at the Center for Advanced Study in the Behavioral Sciences; and has served as associate editor of the *Journal of Research in Personality*. Dr. Cervone's main work involves the development of a conceptual model of the architecture of personality systems and of idiographic, person-centered methods that follow from that model.

Geraldine Downey, PhD, is Vice Provost for Diversity Initiatives and a Professor in the Department of Psychology at Columbia University. She received her BS in psychology from University College, Dublin, and her MA and PhD in developmental psychology from Cornell University. Her work focuses on the personal and interpersonal costs of rejection by significant others and social groups. Dr. Downey is also interested in identifying personal and contextual resources that can ameliorate and remediate the harm of social rejection and marginalization.

Contributors

Susan M. Andersen, PhD, Department of Psychology, New York University, New York, New York

Ozlem Ayduk, PhD, Department of Psychology, University of California, Berkeley, Berkeley, California

Niall Bolger, PhD, Department of Psychology, Columbia University, New York, New York

Gordon H. Bower, PhD, Department of Psychology, Stanford University, Stanford, California

Daniel Cervone, PhD, Department of Psychology, University of Illinois at Chicago, Chicago, Illinois

Geraldine Downey, PhD, Department of Psychology, Columbia University, New York, New York

E. Tory Higgins, PhD, Department of Psychology, Columbia University, New York, New York

Alice M. Isen, PhD, Department of Psychology, Cornell University, Ithaca, New York

Jerome Kagan, PhD, Department of Psychology, Harvard University, Cambridge, Massachusetts

Christina S. Kooij, BA, Department of Psychology, New York University, New York, New York

Rodolfo Mendoza-Denton, PhD, Department of Psychology, University of California, Berkeley, Berkeley, California

Paul S. Mischel, MD, Department of Pathology and Laboratory Medicine, University of California, Los Angeles Medical School, Los Angeles, California

Walter Mischel, PhD, Department of Psychology, Columbia University, New York, New York

Richard E. Nisbett, PhD, Department of Psychology, University of Michigan, Ann Arbor, Michigan

Alexander O'Connor, MA, Department of Psychology, University of California, Berkeley, Berkeley, California

Sang Hee Park, MA, Department of Psychology, University of California, Berkeley, Berkeley, California

Rainer Romero-Canyas, PhD, Department of Psychology, Columbia University, New York, New York

Yuichi Shoda, PhD, Department of Psychology, University of Washington, Seattle, Washington

Richard A. Shweder, PhD, Department of Comparative Human Development, University of Chicago, Chicago, Illinois

Edward E. Smith, PhD, Department of Psychology, Columbia University, New York, New York

Robert J. Sternberg, PhD, Department of Psychology, Tufts University, Medford, Massachusetts

Jennifer S. Thorpe, MA, Department of Psychology, New York University, New York, New York

Preface

At a conference held in honor of Walter Mischel on June 11, 2005, scholars and researchers gathered in New York to discuss potential parallels among their diverse areas of research. As the day progressed, a common theme emerged: During the last half century or so, there appears to have been a fundamental shift in the understanding of human nature, from a focus almost exclusively on internal factors to a view of human behaviors as reflecting person–context systems. This theme was not surprising because Mischel's ideas, although originating in his effort to understand puzzling phenomena in personality and social psychology, address fundamental issues that cut across diverse research areas. The conference organizers felt that that theme was made particularly clear thanks to the diversity of the talks presented, ranging from psychology to cultural anthropology to cancer biology, and the extraordinary caliber of the minds gathered that day.

Seymour Weingarten, Editor in Chief of The Guilford Press, also witnessed the emergence of this theme, and offered to publish a volume that captured this rare moment of intersection among multiple fields and minds. This volume thus is a collection of essays by the conference participants. Each essay highlights the changes in how human beings are understood, seen by preeminent scholars and researchers from psychological, social, and biological sciences. Together, we believe the essays form a gestalt, through which one can see how a fundamental transformation in the view of human nature has been taking place in the last half century, likely to be the foundation of more specific changes to come.

YUICHI SHODA
DANIEL CERVONE
GERALDINE DOWNEY

Contents

I

INTRODUCTION

Construing Persons in Context
On Building a Science of the Individual

DANIEL CERVONE
YUICHI SHODA
GERALDINE DOWNEY

Ever since the Renaissance, people have constructed sciences: sciences of the natural world (Atkins, 2004); sciences of the social (Vico, 1744/ 1999), even sciences of the artificial (Simon, 1969). Of these efforts, people can be proud. Even the most skeptical observer must acknowledge that the body of ideas and discoveries that is the sciences constitutes one of humanity's greatest success stories.

Yet in at least one scientific arena our efforts cannot be character-ized as a string of successes. Somewhat ironically, it is one in which indi-viduals might be expected to be maximally expert: the science of individuals. Efforts to build a science of the psychological life of the whole, individual person have been marked by false starts, road-blocks, and flat-out breakdowns. Psychology's most intrepid investiga-tor, Sigmund Freud, was so thoroughly discouraged by his first major effort, the *Project for a Scientific Psychology,* that he not only aban-doned it but omitted mention of it in his autobiographical writings (Gay, 1988). Freud was proud of his later efforts, but subsequent scientists judged that the unique claims of psychoanalysis, the most renowned of all scientific models of the individual, are supported by few, if any, reli-able scientific findings (Kihlstrom, 1990). The 20th century's next guid-ing paradigm for a science of the individual, behaviorism, now appears

3

in the literature primarily as an introduction to a story about the cognitive revolution that supplanted it (e.g., Gardner, 1985). The cognitive revolution, in turn, was criticized by one of its primary founders as being so enamored with the information-processing capacities of intelligent machines that it failed to confront the meaning-making capacities of agentic persons (Bruner, 1990). In the psychology of personality, the Big Five model of personality traits energized the field in the 1980s and 1990s (e.g., Goldberg, 1993) but soon was shown to be limited as a model of the individual person in two significant respects: (1) the five factors, being merely latent variables that summarize variation in the population at large, could not be assumed to explain psychological functioning at the level of the individual (Borsboom, Mellenberg, & van Heerden, 2003; also see Sternberg, Chapter 14, this volume), and (2) the factor structure was found to replicate in populations of nonhuman animals (Gosling & John, 1999), which means that it did not capture unique psychological features of persons.

PERSONS OUT OF CONTEXT

The various efforts to build a science of persons reviewed in the paragraph above are so diverse that they may appear to have nothing in common, yet they share a notable quality. Each tended to study the individual by removing the person from the context of his or her life. Freud assessed persons as they lay on couches in his office. Rorschach supplemented these assessments by having them contemplate splotches of ink. Skinner took his research participants out of their environmental niches and put then into metal boxes. Cognitive psychologists investigated inner mental representations while devoting lesser attention to the outer social, cultural, and interpersonal contexts in which those representations develop and come into play (but cf. Clancey, 1994; Vygotsky, 1978; Rogoff, 1990). Trait-based personality psychologists posited global psychological tendencies—that is, average-level tendencies, with the averages computed by aggregating across, and thereby sacrificing information about, the contexts of people's lives.

Why would one do this? Why try to build a science of the individual by pulling individuals out of their life contexts? In part, this intellectual move may have reflected the scientific spirit of the day. Much of 20th-century scientific psychology was shaped by positivism. A positivistic search for generalizable laws may incline one to disregard the possibility that an individual's psychological functioning might vary qualitatively from one context to the next, rather than generalizing broadly across domains. In a "Humean positivistic methodology," one adopts concepts corresponding to "continuity in . . . behavior" and treats the supposed invariance as "something like a person's character, or personality" (Harré & Secord, 1973, p. 142).

A second possibility is that the notion of context-free psychological qualities is inherently alluring. Irrespective of the scientific zeitgeist of the day, the human mind may find it pleasing to suppose that the world consists of a small set of fixed essential properties that manifest themselves universally (Kagan, 1998 and Chapter 3, this volume). The intuitive plausibility of abstract essences fosters a mindset in which one construes average dispositional tendencies as foundational and deviations from the average as irrelevances. One treats "broad, nonconditional, decontextualized" qualities as "basic" (McAdams & Pals, 2006, p. 207, 208). Due to the attraction of abstract essences, investigators see "diversity as surface and universality as depth" (Geertz, 2000, p. 59).

A third factor has sustained interest in global, person-out-of-context variables specifically in the psychology of personality. It combines two aspects of the field's discourse. The first aspect is somewhat unusual for a scientific discipline: a recurring questioning of whether the discipline's central target of inquiry exists (cf. Goldberg, 1993; Perugini & DeRaad, 2001). Many writers read critiques of the field written in the 1960s (e.g., Mischel, 1968; Peterson, 1968) as questioning whether enduring, distinctive features of individuals existed—that is, whether personality existed (see Isen, Chapter 8, this volume). The second aspect is the nature of the existence proofs that investigators pursued in light of this reading. They relied, to an overwhelming degree, on the criterion of predictability (e.g., Wiggins, 1973). Textbooks instructed that "in psychology . . . our major concern is . . . estimation or prediction" (Horst, 1966, pp. 264–265).

These two lines of thinking combined in a manner that was counterproductive to the growth of personality science (Cervone & Mischel, 2002). The existence discourse made plausible an implausible null hypothesis: Maybe there is nothing out there. The prediction discourse provided a tool for refuting it: If measures of context-free attributes predict anything at all, to any nonzero degree, then the null hypothesis falls; "any nonzero effect of a personality characteristic" is judged "a large effect in practical terms" (Ozer & Benet-Martinez, 2006, p. 416). Since the people who are classified as high and low on global personality trait measures of course do differ from one another, the null hypothesis falls routinely. This rejection of the null, in this storyline of the field, contributed to exultation over the fact that personality exists and consists of global, context-free psychological attributes (see Goldberg, 1993).

This line of discourse is problematic in a number of ways (see Cervone, in press; Cervone, Caldwell, & Orom, in press). One is its excessive reliance on the criterion of predictability. Philosophers of science have long explained that the fundamental task for science is to explain phenomena and that prediction may be attained in the absence of explanatory understanding. Toulmin (1961), for example, noted that ancient Babylonians could predict eclipses while lacking any understanding of the nature of the cosmos. They merely calculated from numerical tables that described occurrences of past eclipses. The Babylonians had arithmetical tools that yielded prediction but no intellectual tools that yielded explanation; they "acquired great *forecasting-power*" (Toulmin, 1961, p. 30) but failed to achieve the "central aim of science," namely, the "intellectual creation . . . [of] explanatory ideas" (Toulmin, 1961, p. 38). Shweder (Chapter 5, this volume) explains that the decisive question in building a science of the individual is how best to formulate an explanatory model that might yield understanding of purposive human action.

The second curious feature of personality psychology's discourse is that the existence of significant, enduring differences among persons is so self-evident that one must wonder not only how anyone could question it, but if anyone actually did. Consider the critique generally seen as the most severe, that of Mischel (1968). Mischel did not question the existence of enduring personal qualities to be explained by a science of personality; he questioned the adequacy of the extant scientific strategies. The conclusion of his famed volume was that the research methods of the time were inadequate; they "[missed] both the richness and the uniqueness of individual lives" (Mischel, 1968, p. 301). The primary inadequacy was the inattention to context. "The notion of 'typical' behavior" led investigators to treat "situational variability as . . . 'error' " (Mischel, 1968, p. 296) and deflected attention from the essence of psychological functioning, which, "rather than being exclusively intrapsychic," involves dynamic relations between "behavior and the conditions in which the behavior occurs" (Mischel, 1968, p. 298).

PUTTING PERSONS IN THEIR PLACE

This book features contemporary efforts to build a science of the individual by studying persons in context. In some respects, such efforts are not new. Psychological scientists have long attended to questions of social context; "context makes no difference" is as much a strawman position as "personality does not exist." Within the psychology of personality, an important line of thinking in the past three to four decades has been interactionism (e.g., Magnusson & Endler, 1977). Interactionist investigators have long recognized that more of the variance in social behavior can be predicted if one takes a step beyond merely classifying persons according to global dispositional tendencies. The extra step is to observe the differentially classified persons in different settings. Measures of global dispositional constructs may predict more between-person variability in behavior or emotion in one setting than in another. For example, rank orderings of persons on a global trait such as neuroticism may predict more of the variability in emotional reactions in settings that feature threats than in stress-free contexts. Classifications on the global trait of extraversion might predict more of the variability in talking at large parties than in talking in small classroom discussion sections.

There can be no question that measures of context-free, average-level personality constructs often are correlated to a nonzero degree with measures of important psychosocial outcomes. There also is no question that such validity coefficients often vary across context (see Schmitt & Borkenau, 1992). The distinguishing feature of the present contributions is that they pose a deeper question—"deeper" in that the presuppositions made in computing such correlations are questioned. Contributors commonly do not accept a picture of the world in which context-free averages are what is basic. Instead, the statistical average is seen as just that: a statistic, a parameter computed by an investigator who, by dint of professional training, attraction to abstract essential qualities, or some combination of the two, is inclined to aggregate emotional experiences and social actions that occur in widely varying contexts. The aggregating has two costs. If one's goal is to describe the meaningful social behavior of the individual, much information is lost. Even a minimally adequate scientific description may need to include information about how the individual's behavior varies across context. If one's goal is to map the mental systems that make up the individual's personality, context-free averages may be an unsure guide. Affective systems of personality may be context linked in that they are activated by environmental cues present in some settings but not others (see Kagan, Chapter 3, this volume). Cognitive systems are context linked in that most cognition has the quality of intentionality (Searle, 1983); that is, cognitive content represents, and is directed to, particular aspects of the world. Contributors of the chapters that comprise the present volume, then, pursue the scientific goals of description and explanation by studying persons in context.

Overview of the Present Volume: Four Mischelian Themes

In some respects, the contributors to this volume are an exceptionally diverse group. Not only do they represent varied subfields of psychology—personality, social, cognitive, developmental, cultural—but one of them is not a psychologist at all but a cancer biologist (Paul Mischel). Despite this professional diversity, the volume as a whole possesses much substantive coherence. A common set of themes is sounded consistently across the chapters.

This substantive coherence stems in part from the book's origins. The contributors took part in a festschrift conference at Columbia University held to honor the career contributions and recent election to the U.S. National Academy of Sciences of Walter Mischel, the Robert Johnston Niven Professor of Humane Letters at Columbia University. Prior to the conference, participants were asked to consider the relationship between their own work and the ideas in a specific paper of Mischel's, namely his 1973 "reconceptualization" of personality that appeared in the *Psychological Review*; this citation classic is reprinted as Chapter 16, this volume. Four themes Mischel developed in this article can serve as a framework for an overview of the contributions to this volume:

1. *Ground a science of the individual on the study of basic psychological processes.* This idea, which may seem obvious in retrospect, needed to be stated because an alternative was—and, to a significant degree, still is—popular. The alternative is to base a science of persons on descriptive taxonomic constructs. One might describe individual differences in observable social behavior, use these descriptions to formulate a descriptive taxonomy of between-person differences, and treat the resulting taxonomy as foundational to a science of the individual. Mischel judged this strategy inadequate for at least two reasons: (a) One obtains little understanding of the psychological processes underlying the behaviors that are observed, and (b) the taxonomy might not even be a good first step in identifying those processes because different people may engage in the same observable actions for different reasons. He argued, then, that the field would best advance by treating as foundational the basic cognitive and affective processes underlying observed behavior. The goal was to specify psychological systems that give rise to the enduring observable qualities that are the basis of our intuitive inferences about an individual's personality. Mischel's argument had a huge pragmatic advantage. It placed personality psychologists into a partnership with investigators in the cognitive, social, developmental, and neural sciences, whose explorations of brain and mind contribute to an understanding of the development and functioning of the whole individual.

2. *Self-control.* Mischel's 1973 piece highlighted, as a central challenge for the field, the psychological systems that underlie people's

capacity to delay, suppress, modify, and, more generally, gain control over their impulsive emotions. Not only did Mischel's arguments draw needed attention to processes of self-control, but they also had the broader effect of highlighting the role of competencies in personality functioning. People's everyday social behavior often is well understood by analyzing the cognitive and behavioral competencies that they possess and the relation between those competencies and situational demands.

3. *Individual idiosyncracy.* A third theme is that a science of the person must grapple with the idiosyncracies of the individual. In accord with classic theorists such as Lewin (1935) and Murray (1938), Mischel argued that the personality psychologist's target of inquiry was not an abstract, prototypical person whose qualities could be discerned by averaging features displayed by a large sample of individuals. The target was the actual, concrete individual. For purposes both scientific and practical, the target of explanation for the personality scientist is the psychological life and social action of the potentially idiosyncratic individual.

4. *Persons in context.* The fourth theme is the one we have highlighted already: to build a science of the individual, one must study persons in context.

Each of these four themes is reflected, in distinctive ways, in the contributions to this volume. Regarding the first theme, that of grounding a science of the individual on the study of basic cognitive and affective processes, Smith (Chapter 9, this volume) reviews neuroimaging evidence of the activation of brain regions that mediate pain perception, particularly in the study of placebo effects. In so doing, he shows how contemporary evidence in cognitive neuroscience illuminates the functional role of expectancies—one of the five person variables proposed by Mischel (1973). Isen (Chapter 8, this volume) reviews research showing how the release of dopamine in frontal cortical regions underlies the influence of positive affect on personality functioning. Bower (Chapter 2, this volume) shows that the model of personality processes developed by Mischel and Shoda (1995) can be reconfigured as a feedforward connectionist model that can be "trained" across trials of social interaction and feedback. Bower's contribution illustrates how conceptual tools in cognitive science can directly inform the most basic task in the science of personality: developing a comprehensive model of the overall architecture of personality structures and processes. Shoda (Chapter 17, this volume) explicates a critical implication of a process-based approach to personality—namely, that it leads one to treat personality as a system. As he explains, a key implication of a systems perspective involves explanation. We may label an individual's overt tendencies with a natural-language term that corresponds to an average behavioral tendency (e.g., "conscientious") but in a systems perspective one would *not* expect to find an isomorphic structure (e.g., a structure "of conscientiousness"), in the psyche of the individual actor. Similarly, Higgins (Chapter 7, this volume) insightfully explains that Mischel's processing perspective moves beyond a simple "content-matching" assumption, or the assumption of a match between an intuitively constructed class of manifest social action and the mechanisms underlying that action. Finally, Mendoza-Denton, Park, and O'Connor (Chapter 12, this volume) provide a unique perspective on questions of basic personality processes. They review research showing that lay perceivers, when engaged in person perception, inherently become "Mischelian" in certain contexts. Rather then primarily inferring the existence of global personality traits, perceivers infer the presence of dynamic, contextualized cognitive and affective personality processes when they make inferences either about important, well-known targets or about targets whose trait-related behavior varies systematically across contexts.

A variety of chapters sound the second theme, that of self-control and personal competencies. Kagan (Chapter 3, this volume) addresses the development of personal competencies. He explains why competencies must be conceptualized not as abstract abilities that transcend time and place, but as capacities that manifest themselves in context and that can only be properly described and understood if one considers the context in which performance occurs. Sternberg (Chapter 14, this volume) addresses the nature of intelligence and emphasizes that the concept of intelligence incorporates a variety of capacities, some of which are basic to the solution of everyday problems of social behavior that are commonly seen as manifestations of personality. Higgins (Chapter 7) explores the phenomenological experiences associated with efforts to regulate one's actions by examining experiences of regulatory fit—that is, experiences that occur when individuals pursue a goal in a manner consistent with their goal orientation. Isen (Chapter 8) reviews research on the role of positive affect in self-control, which leads to the important conclusion that positive affect can promote self-control through its effect on the flexibility of thinking. Ayduk (Chapter 6) reviews the seminal research of Mischel and colleagues on children's capacity for delay of gratification. She explains how current research documents the importance of this self-control capacity to success in both achievement and interpersonal domains.

Various contributors highlight the theme of individual idiosyncrasy. Paul Mischel (Chapter 13) describes a paradigm shift in medicine that parallels the paradigm shift in psychology heralded by Walter Mischel (1973). Rather than fitting individual clients into generic classificatory schemes based on observable symptoms, the contemporary physician pursues individual care that is grounded in molecular classification. Sternberg, when explaining that successful intelligence must be assessed by gauging a person's actions in relation to his or her personal life pursuits, notes that such pursuits "can be astonishingly varied" (Sternberg, Chapter 14, this volume, p. xxx), an observation that inherently calls for an individual-centered approach to assessing successful intelligence. When reviewing and extending Mischel and Shoda's (1995) cognitive-affective personality systems (CAPS) model, Bower notes that the phenomenon being modeled is the behavioral profile exhibited by "a given individual" (Chapter 2, this volume, pp. 240–241); the explanandum is not variation in the population at large, but variability in the social actions of a given individual. Andersen and Thorpe explain that their groundbreaking work on social-cognitive processes in transference relies on idiographic assessments of both mental representations and the social contexts in which those representations are activated. Their combination of individual-centered methods with a nomothetic theory of psychological processes yields a "combined idiographic–nomothetic approach" (Andersen & Thorpe, Chapter 10, this volume, p. 178) that is sensitive to idiosyncracy in the activation of transference processes.

The fourth theme, the need to attend to context, is so pervasive in these chapters that we will only highlight a few cases in which contributors enunciate it with particular force. One important context for understanding the individual is the macro-context of culture. Nisbett (Chapter 4) reviews his landmark program of research on cultural (Eastern vs. Western world) variations in individuals' experiences of the world. In the West, perceivers tend to view entities as possessing encapsulated essential qualities. In the East, holistic thinking predominates; objects are perceived in relation to a broader contextual field within which they are embedded. The person-in-situation perspective of Mischel is seen as a natural conception of the individual from the Eastern perspective. Shweder draws upon concepts developed in cultural psychology and anthropology in arguing that the message "attend to context" is even deeper than it may at first appear, as it entails a "shift in metatheoretical assumptions" (Shweder, Chapter 5, this volume, p. 91) in which social action is no longer viewed as the product of separate person and situation variables. Instead, one views the person as an agent who constructs and acts upon meaning, and one adopts as core explanatory variables preference and constraints—variables that are inherently contextual.

Another important aspect of context is the more local, micro-environment of interpersonal relations. Andersen and Thorpe's (Chapter 10, this volume) review of the model of the relational self (Andersen &

Chen, 2002) highlights the fact that mental representations of significant others are activated only in particular interpersonal contexts. Attention to context, then, is necessary to understand the basic functioning of the underlying psychological systems. Ayduk's (Chapter 6) review of research on rejection sensitivity similarly highlights this theme.

The importance of context also is evident in investigators' careful attention to an aspect of personality long highlighted by Mischel and colleagues: *intra*individual variability across time and settings. The potential of studying intraindividual variability is illustrated particularly vividly by Bolger and Romero-Canyas (Chapter 11), who review advances in research methods (especially experience-sampling techniques) and data analysis that enable investigators to obtain intensive, detailed descriptions of the personality tendencies of a given individual as he or she confronts the varying everyday contexts of his or her life. Other contributions also speak eloquently to the question of intraindividual variability. Bower's (Chapter 2) analysis of production rules inherently addresses the topic in that a production rule has a "condition side"—that is, the action represented in the rule is enacted only when particular situational conditions are encountered. Sternberg's (Chapter 14) analysis of intelligence reveals the influence of situational contexts on performance on intelligence tests and, more generally, indicates that the specific capacities required to act in a manner that one may rightly call "intelligent" can vary dramatically from one social, cultural, or socioeconomic context to another. Mendoza-Denton, Park, and O'Connor (Chapter 12) show that lay perceivers spontaneously attend to context when making inferences about the psychological qualities of others. Finally, Paul Mischel's (Chapter 13) review of recent research in cancer biology documents remarkable parallels between Walter Mischel's contributions to the study of personality-in-context and advances in this branch of biomedicine. The search for mechanisms underlying sensitivity and resistance to drugs in cancer treatment is shown to be informed by a conditional *if . . . then . . .* analysis inspired by Mischel and colleagues' (Mischel & Shoda, 1995) analysis of *if . . . then . . .* behavioral signatures in the study of personality.

Organization of the Volume

This volume is not organized around these four thematic building blocks for a science of the individual—basic processes, self-control, individual idiosyncrasy, and context—for reasons that are apparent from the review above; each of a number of different chapters speaks to each of the themes. We thus have organized the contributions to the volume around three more general topics: Conceptualizing the Person, Self-Regulation, and Incorporating Situations into a Science of the Individual. The reader should recognize that this three-part organization, while useful, underestimates the coherent interrelations among the chapters that become apparent when considering the four Mischelian themes that appear throughout the book.

Finally, the concluding section of this book includes the piece that was the touchstone for contributors to the volume: Mischel's 1973 article in *Psychological Review*. It is preceded by a commentary prepared for this book by Mischel, who reflects on the spirit of the times in which that paper was written and the subsequent advances that fostered psychological science's ever-growing awareness of the need to understand the multiplicity of interactions between persons and the social contexts within which they live.

CONCLUSIONS AND THANKS

We conclude this chapter with a salute to our inspirational colleague Walter Mischel. This volume pays tribute to his scientific findings, his theoretical advances, his professional guidance, and his personal friendship. But we are indebted most of all to his intellectual courage. In 1968, in *Personality and Assessment,* Mischel had the courage to say—louder and more clearly and bluntly than anyone else—that personality psychology's standard operating procedures were substandard. They were, if not a dead end, then a road that no longer should be taken. Other paths, less traveled at that time, led more surely to a cumulative, integrative science of the individual.

Mischel prompted a crisis in the field in 1968. At a personal level, creating a crisis is not the easiest thing to do. It prompts attacks both substantive and ad hominem. Readers forget the lesson taught by Kuhn that it is "period[s] of pronounced professional insecurity" (Kuhn, 1962, pp. 67–68) that trigger periods of innovative scientific theory and research and misconstrue one's purposes as destructive rather than constructive.

Kuhn's lesson implies that for a field to advance, someone must be willing to create the crisis. Someone must have not only the intelligence but the fortitude to tell a field its problems and to weather the aftermath that follows. This burden fell primarily on Mischel, as he surely knew it would. The contributions to this volume attest to the scientific innovations that followed in *Personality and Assessment*'s wake.

REFERENCES

Andersen, S. M., & Chen, S. (2002). The relational self: An interpersonal social-cognitive theory. *Psychological Review, 109,* 619–645.

Atkins, P. (2004). *Galileo's finger.* New York: Oxford University Press.

Borsboom, D., Mellenbergh, G. J., & van Heerden, J. (2003). The theoretical status of latent variables. *Psychological Review, 110,* 203–219.

Bruner, J. (1990). *Acts of meaning.* Cambridge, MA: Harvard University Press.

Cervone, D. (in press). Explanatory models of personality: Social-cognitive theories and the knowledge-and-appraisal model of personality architecture. In G. Boyle, G. Matthews, & D. Saklofske (Eds.), *Handbook of personality and testing.* London: Sage.

Cervone, D., Caldwell, T. L., & Orom, H. (in press). Beyond person and situation effects: Intraindividual personality architecture and its implications for the study of personality and social behavior. In A. Kruglanski & J. Forgas (Series Eds.) & F. Rhodewalt (Vol. Ed.), *Frontiers of social psychology: Personality and social behavior.* New York: Psychology Press.

Cervone, D., & Mischel, W. (Eds.). (2002). *Advances in personality science.* New York: Guilford Press.

Clancey, W. J. (1994). Situated cognition: How representations are created and given meaning. In R. Lewis & P. Mendelsohn (Eds.), *Lessons from Learning* (pp. 231–242). Amsterdam: North Holland.

Gardner, H. (1985). *The mind's new science: A history of the cognitive revolution.* New York: Basic Books.

Gay, P. (1988). *Freud: A life for our times.* New York: Norton.

Geertz, C. (2000). *Available light: Anthropological reflections on philosophical topics.* Princeton, NJ: Princeton University Press.

Goldberg, L. R. (1993). The structure of phenotypic personality traits. *American Psychologist, 48,* 26–34.

Gosling, S. D., & John, O. P. (1999). Personality dimensions in nonhuman animals: A cross-species review. *Contemporary Directions in Psychological Science, 8,* 69–75.

Harré, R., & Secord, P. F. (1973). *The explanation of social behaviour.* Oxford, UK: Blackwell.

Horst, P. (1966). *Psychological measurement and prediction.* Belmont, CA: Wadsworth.

Kagan, J. (1998). *Three seductive ideas.* Cambridge, MA: Harvard University Press.

Kihlstrom, J. F. (1990). The psychological unconscious. In L. Pervin (Ed.), *Handbook of personality: Theory and research* (pp. 445–464). New York: Guilford Press.

Kuhn, T. S. (1962). *The structure of scientific revolutions.* Chicago: University of Chicago Press.

Lewin, K. (1935). *A dynamic theory of personality: Selected papers.* New York: McGraw-Hill.

Magnusson, D., & Endler, N. S. (Eds.). (1977). *Personality at the crossroads: Current issues in interactional psychology.* Hillsdale, NJ: Erlbaum.

McAdams, D. P., & Pals, J. L. (2006). A new Big Five: Fundamental principles for an integrative science of personality. *American Psychologist, 61,* 204–217.

Mischel, W. (1968). *Personality and assessment.* New York: Wiley.

Mischel, W. (1973). Toward a cognitive social learning reconceptualization of personality. *Psychological Review, 80,* 252–283.

Mischel, W., & Shoda, Y. (1995). A cognitive-affective system theory of personality: Reconceptualizing situations, dispositions, dynamics, and invariance in personality structure. *Psychological Review, 102,* 246–286.

Murray, H. A. (1938). *Explorations in personality.* New York: Oxford University Press.

Ozer, D. J., & Benet-Martinez, V. (2006). Personality and the prediction of consequential outcomes. *Annual Review of Psychology, 57,* 401–421.

Perugini, M., & DeRaad, B. (2001). Editorial: Personality and economic behaviour. *European Journal of Personality, 15,* S1–S4.

Peterson, D. R. (1968). *The clinical study of social behavior.* New York: Appleton-Century-Crofts.

Rogoff, B. (1990). *Apprenticeship in thinking: Cognitive development in social context.* New York: Oxford University Press.

Schmitt, M., & Borkenau, P. (1992). The consistency of personality. In G. V. Caprara & G. Van Heck (Eds.), *Modern personality psychology* (pp. 29–55). London: Harvester-Weatsheaf.

Searle, J. R. (1983). *Intentionality: An essay in the philosophy of mind.* New York: Cambridge University Press.

Simon, H. A. (1969). *The sciences of the artificial.* Cambridge, MA: MIT Press.

Toulmin, S. (1961). *Foresight and understanding: An enquiry into the aims of science.* Bloomington: Indiana University Press.

Vico, G. (1999). *New science: Principles of the new science concerning the common nature of nations* (3rd ed.). London: Penguin Books. (Original work published 1744)

Vygotsky, L. S. (1978). *Mind in society: The development of higher psychological processes.* Cambridge, MA: Harvard University Press.

Wiggins, J. S. (1973). *Personality and prediction: Principles of personality assessment.* Reading, MA: Addison-Wesley.

II

CONCEPTUALIZING THE PERSON

2

The Trait versus Situation Debate
A Minimalist View

GORDON H. BOWER

It has been my pleasure to participate in the conference and contribute to the book honoring the good works of my friend Walter Mischel. My invited participation arose largely from my long-term friendship with Walter, as my specialty is in cognitive psychology and decidedly not in personality psychology. Therefore, I must defer to the experts in this volume who have reviewed Walter's many contributions to personality psychology and personality assessment. I will try to honor Walter's work in a small way by recapitulating for myself the logic of his theoretical position on personality. Readers may view this exercise as a tutorial Walter has given me.

MY TRAINING BACKGROUND

I should tell readers a bit about myself, so they will know where I am coming from. I was trained in learning theory at Yale University, working primarily with Neal Miller and Frank Logan, who were eminent defenders of the behaviorist tradition of Clark Hull. I learned at Miller's side the canons of liberalized stimulus–response (S-R) reinforcement theory as illustrated in two famous books he coauthored with John Dollard, *Social Learning and Imitation* (1941) and *Personality and Psychotherapy* (1950). The latter book, which my class practically memorized in Miller's seminar (and I have kept my tattered copy as proof), was extremely important and influential in the 1950s. It attempted to show how a liberalized version of S-R reinforcement theory could be used to interpret many aspects of personality. In particular, it aimed to understand personality and psychoneuroses by interpreting in S-R terms many of the important concepts of Freudian psychoanalysis: unconscious contents and processes, motivational conflicts, symptom formation of "defenses" (e.g., repression, projection) that reduced anxiety, and the therapeutic value of "uncovering" unconscious conflicts in order to teach patients more adaptive, discriminating ways to interpret or resolve their conflicts. Like most graduate students, I thought my mentors' theories were eminently reasonable and powerful.

MY EARLY STANFORD YEARS

With this training in learning theory, I was ready to accept the social learning theory of my colleague, Albert Bandura (1969, 1977), when I arrived at Stanford in 1959. I had merely to widen my worldview to a few more liberalizing ideas about vicarious (imitative) learning and self-control. I was also influenced at this time by the work in behavior modification and behavior therapy done by Joseph Wolpe (1958) and the researchers collaborating with Hans Eysenck (e.g., Eysenck & Rachman, 1965). In fact, I spent part of my sabbatical leave year (1965–1966) in London becoming familiar with the works of the central figures of the British behavior therapy movement, most situated around Eysenck at the Maudsley Hospital.

I was in a highly prepared, receptive stage when Walter Mischel arrived at Stanford in the mid 1960s. Walter was just publishing *Personality and Assessment* (1968). I read it, as I recall, in one or two sittings because I found it so congruent with my skeptical views of personality tests. I agreed with his critiques of traditional trait theories of personality and personality tests and applauded his learning-oriented views of personality. Walter's move to Stanford coincided with his intellectual partnership with Al Bandura in supporting, extending, and publicizing the social learning theory orientation. Indeed, social learning theory was beginning to sweep the field of clinical psychology in the 1960s and 1970s. Inevitably, Walter was drawn into a long-running debate with traditional trait theorists (who were promoting personality tests) about the proper way to describe personality (e.g., Allport, 1937, 1961; Cattell, 1965; Exner, 1993; Norman, 1963). A central issue in that debate was whether the more important determiner of people's behavior was their enduring dispositions ("traits") or their current situation.

THE DISPOSITIONAL
VERSUS SITUATIONAL DEBATE

I had not really thought about the dispositional versus situational debate until I started preparing my paper for this conference. I had simply assumed that my friends, Walter, Al, Lee Ross (1977), and Philip Zimbardo (Zimbardo & Ebbeson, 1970), were right, that the situation usually trumps or overpowers people's dispositions in determining their behavior. After all, that is a corollary of "the fundamental attribution error" (Ross, 1977). People learn in what situations to exhibit more or less friendliness, open-mindedness, aggressiveness, or extroversion. They vary their behaviors in a manner attuned to the histories of their reinforcement contingencies that vary across social situations. For example, most of us know that Walter would be more extroverted at an artists' party than at a funeral. This variability of behavioral expressions is so obvious that the trait versus situation debate could not be about variability of a person's behaviors across situations. I knew I was missing something.

IF NOT VARIABILITY OF BEHAVIOR,
THEN WHAT IS IT?

In thinking about a psychological issue, I try to reduce the big issue to simple examples to clarify them. Using some examples of this type, I will reconstruct the logical steps by which I learned what the debate was all about. I also find that a useful strategy to understand an argument is to play devil's advocate and imagine what one might say to defend the position opposed to your own. In this case, given my bias toward the situational viewpoint, I tried to think of how I might defend a dispositional trait theory of behavior. I would begin by conceding that of course people respond discriminatively to different situations; cultural customs and norms practically guarantee it. So, variability of a given type of trait-related behavior (e.g., aggressiveness) across situations for an individual cannot possibly be what the debate is about. Such variability should not upset a trait theorist at all.

THE CRITICAL POINT:
CONSISTENT RANK ORDERING OF INDIVIDUALS

Rather, the critical point for the trait theorist is that the *rank ordering* of two or more individuals in the frequency of a given type of behavior

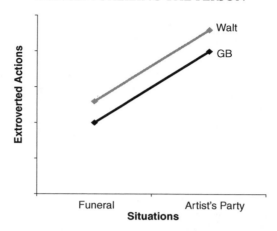

FIGURE 2.1. Trait consistency: Walter is more extroverted than I am at both an artist's party and a funeral. Traits imply consistent ranking of individuals across situations.

should remain fairly constant across situations that presumably tap into the same trait. Figure 2.1 shows the kind of evidence that would make a trait theorist happy: Walter is more extroverted than I across several different situations. Thus, traits are all about *consistency of rankings of individuals* on a given type of behavior across situations. This conclusion seems sort of plausible and not obviously wrong.

CHALLENGING TRAIT THEORY WITH SITUATION–BEHAVIOR INTERACTIONS

To challenge trait theory, one need only observe pairs of people and situations in which person A outranks person B on the frequency of some trait-related behavior X in situation 1, but person B outranks person A in situation 2. An interaction of this type is displayed in Figure 2.2. In other words, a situation–person interaction on trait-related behavior X would disconfirm the hypothesis that person A has (and will exhibit) more of trait X than person B in all situations—and that counterexample would weaken trait theory in general.

One has only to think for a minute to recognize that we all know many such situation–person interactions. Figure 2.2 shows a typical example. Perhaps that is the end of the matter: Frequently observed person–situation interactions obviously trump trait theories.

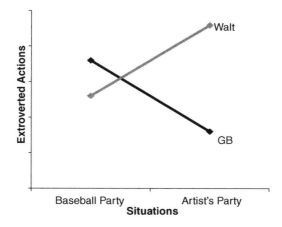

FIGURE 2.2. Situation–behavior interaction: Walter is more extroverted than I am at an artist's party, but I am more extroverted than he is at a party of baseball fans.

A REFORMULATION OF TRAIT THEORY

But is it the end of the matter? Let's abide with my trait theorist for another epicycle. He could argue that the situationalists erred in describing the social situations for the two individuals; they have stupidly taken the direct, nominal characterization of the two situations as both being just social parties. A trait theorist might propose that what is more important is the individual's subjective interpretations of the situations and argue that a more discerning way to characterize the situation is to notice whether it matches the individual's interests and knowledge or not. In this case the proper prediction of the trait theory is that Walter and I will both be more extroverted in situations that match our respective interests and knowledge (see Figure 2.3). But people's interests, motivations, and knowledge clearly differ according to their experiences. In this light, these situation–behavior interactions (as in Figure 2.2) might arise simply as an *artifact* of people differing in their interpretations of social situations.

PERHAPS TRAITS INFLUENCE PERCEPTION
OF SOCIAL SITUATIONS

This position is not unreasonable; psychologists recognize many cases in which individuals differ greatly in how they perceive and interpret social situations. For example, psychologists routinely claim that patients with

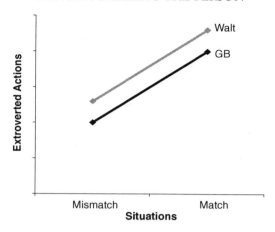

FIGURE 2.3. Second-level trait consistency: Walter might be more extroverted than I am even when the reinterpreted (functional) situations are chosen equally to match or mismatch our respective interests.

anxiety disorders perceive social situations as more threatening than do nonanxious folks and that depressed or paranoid individuals interpret ambiguous feedback as more negative than do nondepressed or nonparanoid people. It is plausible that Walter would be more extroverted in situations he perceives as calling forth his extroverted behaviors, whereas I would be more extroverted in those situations I perceive as calling forth my extroverted behaviors. Moreover, after equating Walter and me on our having similar interpretations of several situations, the trait theorist might further discover that Walter is indeed usually more extroverted than I am (as in Figure 2.3). In this manner, consistency of rank ordering of our extroverted behaviors across settings is restored for the trait theorist, albeit it is now mediated by how the two individuals (Walter and I) interpret the respective social situations.

This maneuver has rescued trait theory from the jaws of defeat.

HOW GOOD IS THE RESCUE?

But how valuable is the rescue? What kind of trait theory remains after the rescue?

It seems that this maneuver has rendered trait theory almost vacuous and impotent because the trait theorist can almost always appeal to individual differences in people's interpretations of social situations to explain away embarrassing situation–behavior interactions. If we ask how we can assess an individual's interpretation of a given nominal situation, the trait theorist can always say, "Well, let's first see how our subject behaves in that situation (his level of friendliness, aggressiveness, etc.) and that will tell us how he has interpreted the situation relevant to that trait-related behavior." Rather than inferring the strength of a person's trait from a behavioral frequency, the theorist is inferring the individual's perception of the situation as well as the strength of his trait to "explain" his behavior.

It takes only a moment's reflection to see the scam hidden in this card trick: the trait theorist now has two *unconstrained* intervening variables (the trait and the social perception) to explain one bit of behavior (in this social situation), and neither is measured independently of the behavior to be explained. This is the kind of circular theory that explains everything and nothing.

TESTING THE RESTRICTED TRAIT THEORY

Perhaps the nearest thing we can arrange to test this restricted trait theory would begin by finding some way to measure or estimate and then equate individuals' interpretations of several different situations. If we could do those measurements before observing the behaviors to be explained, then we would have a small chance of testing the restricted trait theory. In particular, if we could establish that two individuals interpret two situations approximately the same way, and if we then observe significant situation–behavior interactions, then such results would constitute a major blow to the restricted trait theory. The critical data would look like those shown in Figure 2.4. Such results, if observed in sufficient quantity, would seem to deliver the *coup de grace* to the restricted trait theory, but how can we find these test cases?

THE SHODA, MISCHEL, AND WRIGHT STUDIES

It was with these thoughts in mind that I returned to Mischel and Shoda's (1995) *Psychological Review* article, which I had skimmed through years ago. That article described their studies, begun with Jack Wright, of the behavior of delinquent boys in a summer residential camp (Shoda, Mischel, & Wright, 1994; Wright & Mischel, 1987). I was surprised and amazed. In designing and reporting these boys' camp studies, Mischel, Shoda, and Wright had anticipated and answered practically all the objections of my beleaguered trait theorist. I will list four critical parts of their design and analysis that responded to the hedges proffered by the hypothetical trait theorist.

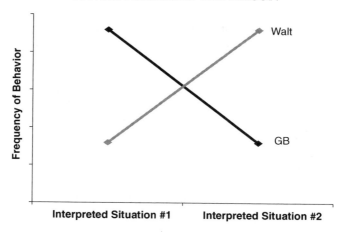

FIGURE 2.4. The killing field for trait theory: The situation–behavior interaction might still arise even when Walter and I have been equated on our perceptual interpretation of two different situations in which our behavior is observed.

First, and most critical, the investigators interviewed a large sample of young boys in the residential camp to obtain many descriptions of prototypical camp situations and their perceptions of and typical reactions to them. The investigators then carried out a cluster analysis on the content of the protocols to identify what, *in the children's perceptions,* were the critical features of the camp's social situations and the boys' interactions. These critical features proved to be whether the boys were interacting with an adult counselor or child peer and whether the interaction was positive or negative. There was almost universal agreement on which interaction situations were positive (e.g., getting an extra dessert) and which negative (e.g., being scolded by an adult counselor).

Having obtained the boys' perceptual ratings of a variety of camp interaction situations, the investigators then drew up a list of five social interactions that exemplified combinations of the features, namely, positive or negative interactions with a peer or an adult counselor. The five social situations in which behaviors were recorded are listed along the horizontal axis in Figure 2.5. Three classes of negative interaction situations (being teased by a peer, warned off by a threatening adult, and punished by an adult) and two classes of positive interaction situations (receiving a friendly overture from a peer and praise from an adult) were distinguished. These interaction situations were described in operational terms so that observers could reliably identify them and objectively code the behaviors of a child in social interactions of each type. Whenever any of these interaction situations occurred while the observer was watching a given child, the observer would classify and record the child's behaviors in one of five categories—as showing verbal aggression, physical aggression, whining, compliance/giving in, or talking prosocially.

A methodological refinement of their data analysis is shown in Figure 2.5. These graphs of verbal aggression (or other behaviors) plot the standardized z-score for each boy for each situation relative to the whole sample of boys. A boy's z-score is like his rank order in the group for that behavior in that situation. Z-scores remove the variability caused by some situations provoking more aggression than others for all the boys.

The behavior profiles for any children for each of the five behaviors mentioned above can thus be compared. For n children observed, there will be $5 \times n(n - 1)/2$ (e.g., 225 if $n = 10$) possible comparisons of behavior profiles. Figure 2.5 shows one such comparison for verbal aggression displayed by child #9, on the left, and child #28, on the right. In a plot of this type, any person–situation interactions can be seen directly. We can see that child #9 is less verbally aggressive than child #28 when a peer initiates a friendly overture, whereas child #9 is more verbally aggressive than child #28 when an adult warns or punishes him. Frequent interactions like this in the data (e.g., Shoda et al., 1994) constitute a major embarrassment of trait theory.

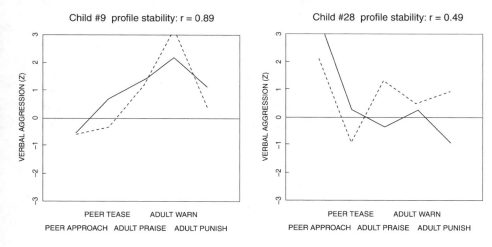

FIGURE 2.5. Observed verbal aggression profiles of two boys (plotted in normalized z-scores) across five camp interaction situations. The two lines in each panel are for the boys' profiles measured at two time periods several weeks apart. The stability of the profiles is the covariation between the five data points on the solid and dashed lines within each panel. From Mischel and Shoda (1995, p. 249). Copyright 1995 by the American Psychological Association. Reprinted by permission.

The individual zigzag plots (solid lines) in Figure 2.5 might reflect unreliable sampling variability and measurement error, so the investigators observed and rated the verbal aggressiveness of the boys during two time periods several weeks apart. The dashed lines in Figure 2.5 show the verbal aggression profile observed during this second period. The positive correlation between the two profile samples indicates that the profile is stable and does not reflect random errors of measurement. We can see that child #9 is more stable in his behavior profile (stability coefficient of .89) than is child #28 (stability coefficient of .49).

The importance of this investigation is that a thorough attempt was made first to assess the children's perception and interpretation of a variety of prototypical interaction situations in the camp. Following such assessment, the observation and recording of the situational profiles of five behaviors (verbal and physical aggression, prosocial talking, etc.) yielded a high percentage of person–situation interactions like those shown in Figure 2.5. The data seem to disconfirm the refined trait theory.

I had to think through these simple exercises regarding the fallback hedges of the trait theorist before I could fully appreciate how well designed those residential camp studies were. Their design and analyses fully responded to and undermined the excuses and counterarguments that trait theorists could provide for these data. It is rare that we can look back at an older study—this series actually began in 1988—and see it with new eyes, gathering a deeper appreciation for the ingenuity that went into it. *That* is the small epiphany, the sudden appreciation of beautiful minds at work, that I experienced in rereading Mischel and Shoda's article. I recognized for the first time that the answers to my concerns were right there in these writings, some nearly 20 years old (e.g., Wright & Mischel, 1987). For me, the experience was reminiscent of these lines from a well-known poem ("Little Gidding" in *Four Quartets*) by T. S. Eliot:

> We shall not cease from exploration,
> And the end of all our exploring
> Will be to arrive where we started
> And know the place for the first time.

CAN TRAIT THEORY BE RESURRECTED?

How might a sufficiently motivated trait theorist respond when confronted with person–situation interactions like those shown in Figure 2.5? A fallback position would be to question the abstractions that go into the investigators' composition of the situation categories (e.g., approach by a peer, warning by a threatening adult) and the abstractions used to categorize different behaviors (e.g., verbal aggression, prosocial talking). Such abstract categories aggregate what might be significantly different subclasses of situations and/or behaviors. Each child may be approached by many different peers in the camp and receive warnings from many different adult counselors. Some peers may be big bullies; others may be small and meek. Some may be friends, while others are long-term enemies. Some warning counselors may be harsh and well known to follow up their threats of punishment; others may be known to be lenient, basically friendly, and unlikely to follow up on punishment.

It takes only a little thought to see how such distinctions rescue trait theory. Consider the two situations of peer approach and adult warning for child #9 and child #28, which produce a large interaction in Figure 2.5. We can imagine that child #28 is a discriminating bully, aggressive with the smaller boys in his cabin with whom he primarily interacts (and is most frequently observed), but he slyly pretends to be passive and obsequious in interactions with his formidable camp counselor, who is a punitive disciplinarian. On the other hand, suppose child #9 is a puny runt who has often been beaten up when he has verbally aggressed against his larger peers, so he is passive and withdrawn with them; on the other hand, his most frequent encounters with a counselor is with the known "softie" of the group, one to whom the boys can be verbally aggressive. Moreover, suppose that this counselor and child #9 both understand that the boy's father is the employer of the counselor's mother outside the camp, so the power roles of the child and adult are reversed.

This set of imagined circumstances would produce the interaction shown in Figure 2.5: Child #28 would be verbally aggressive when a peer approaches but not when his big, stern counselor warns him off; child #9 would not be verbally aggressive when approached by his larger peers but would be when his counselor tries ineffectually to warn him away from some unruly behavior. Similar moderating circumstances might be conjectured to explain other situation–behavior interactions shown by other subjects and responses.

WHAT IS THIS SALVAGING MANEUVER?

The maneuver that perhaps saves the skin of the trait theorist is to recognize the adaptive and discriminative nature of each person's behaviors across situations. The same abstract situation can vary enormously according to the people and issues involved. The abstract category of "a conversation between persons *A* and *B*" may have different dynamics depending on the topic; person *A* may be verbally domineering when they are discussing company finances, but roles reverse when they are discussing vendors. Similarly, different instances of an "abstract response class" (e.g., verbal aggression) can vary contextually according to the actors: A profane slur against one's mother is considered humorous "bonding jive" among streetwise adolescents, but the same remark would get you fired if directed to a boss on the job.

SO, TRAIT THEORY DISAPPEARS INTO THE FOG OF IDIOSYNCRATIC HISTORIES

The simple fact of adaptive, discriminative, contextually appropriate behaviors would seem strongly to imply nominal person–situation interactions, but in the trait theorists' hedging we have for all practical purposes lost what little substance remains for the trait construct. After all, what is a personality trait? Gordon Allport (1937) defined a trait as "an enduring characteristic . . . distinctive to each person, that serves to unify many different stimuli by leading the person to generate consistent responses to them" (quoted in Mischel, Shoda, & Smith, 2004, p. 453). The quicksand under this construct is the contextually varying definitions of "stimuli" and "responses"; nominal descriptions just will not capture regularities in behavior. If followed to its end, this line of argument leads to a radical "idiographic characterization" of each person. For a personality theorist, that outcome is an admission that there are no predictive or explanatory generalizations that hold across people. Presumably, we would like to avoid that conclusion.

Surely, there is something bizarre about this conclusion of "nonpredictability," as it so grossly violates common experience. Everyone relies upon his or her commonsense understanding of the personalities of friends and uses it to predict their reactions with some success. Similarly, people rely upon each other to follow societal norms in their behavior (e.g., in the United States, we drive on the right side of the road). So, what creates the layperson's impression of the predictability of his or her friends?

Is belief in consistency an illusion? Walter has written extensively about how the apparent consistency (and predictability) in the behavior of our acquaintances could arise from biases in our samples of their behavior and from distortions in our inferences and judgments about them (Mischel, 1969, 1984). Nonetheless, underlying the inflated impressions of consistency is the collection of situation–behavior profiles of our acquaintances that we hold in memory. These "common-ground" profiles doubtless foster our belief that individuals are consistent within themselves. What is the nature of these profiles?

IF . . . THEN . . . CONDITIONAL RULES

Michael and Shoda (1995) argue that what we all have is an incomplete but nonetheless serviceable collection of "*if* condition, *then* action" conditional rules describing for us the behaviors of ourselves and acquaintances. Therefore, in place of trait descriptions, Mischel and colleagues want to substitute a collection of "*if* condition, *then* action" conditional rules for each target person. These rules are situation–action pairs of the form "*If* situation *S* occurs, *then* predict behavior B." Such rules can be used for summarizing and forecasting one's own behavior—for example, "*If* I'm in situation *S, then* I will (or am likely to) carry out behavior *B*"—and they can be used to predict others' behavior, as in "*If* person *P* is in situation *S**, *then* *P* will (or is likely to) carry out behavior *B.**" The behavioral profiles seen in Figure 2.5 are a small sample of such collections.

Although *if . . . then . . .* rules are similar to the traditional S-R associations, they really most resemble what cognitive scientists call "production rules" (or just "productions"). Starting with the seminal work on problem-solving programs by Newell and Simon (1972), production systems have become routine tools for use in computer programs that simulate cognitive processes. Such programs can simulate not only behaviors reflecting reasoning, problem solving, and decision making (see, e.g., Anderson, 1993; Anderson & Lebiere, 1998; Lovett & Anderson, 2005), but also emotional reactions (Bower & Cohen, 1982; Sloman, 1987), attitude consistency (Abelson, 1973; Carbonell, 1980), and personality dynamics (Colby, 1963, 1982; Dyer, 1987).

Productions are like steps in a computer program that move it forward in a manner resembling the sequential flow of thought, but they differ in several important respects from traditional S-R associations. Firstly, the *condition* and the *action* sides of a production can be reasonably abstract instead of the concrete specificity typically assumed by S-R associations. The rules are not just concrete ones like "*If* John Budue calls me a slacker, *then* I punch him." They can also be of the form "*If anyone insults* me, *then* I *do something* to harm that *anyone.*" Note the abstractions on both sides of the rule. It leaves for determination (by other productions) the classification of what constitutes an insult and leaves me to search for some action in my repertoire that will harm the target person. The use of "anyone" in the rule exemplifies an "abstract variable." It specifies whoever should fill that role; moreover, the "anyone" in the *condition* side is bound to the same "anyone" on the *action* side of the rule.

A second, powerful aspect of productions is that the *condition* side of the rule may consist of any logical (Boolean) combination of situational features, such as "*If* features 1 and 2 are present in the situation but not feature 3, *then* do such and such." Similarly, the *action* side of the rule may consist of a chain of behaviors, such as "*If* I hear my cell phone ring, *then* I locate the phone, open it, press the Listen button, and say "hello."

Third, the *condition* side and the *action* side of the rule need not respectively be external stimuli and overt responses. The condition can be internal feeling states (e.g., "*If* I'm feeling depressed") or memories (e.g., "*If* I just remembered my promise to call Mother"). Similarly, the *action* can be to fetch something from memory, to turn on an emotion, to take the next step in a chain of covert reasoning, or to transform the contents of short-term working memory to achieve some goal. Especially important *conditions* are the person's momentary low-level goals, such as "*If* I want to go to the airport, *then* hire a taxi."

The relevance of *if . . . then . . .* productions for capturing behavioral regularities and personality dynamics has been frequently noted (e.g., Bower & Cohen, 1982; Colby, 1963; Dyer, 1987). For example, in a speech at a convention of the Association for Advancement of Behavior Therapy (Bower, 1978), I proposed production systems as a way to characterize the automatic, unconscious inferences that all of us make about social situations and the people we meet. Relevant to cognitive-behavioral theorists would be the dysfunctional inferences and irrational thinking of some neurotic patients. Such automatic, irrational inferences that underlie and drive neurotic cognitions were called "thought schemas" by Aaron Beck (1964, 1976) and "irrational beliefs" by Albert Ellis (1958; Ellis & Harper, 1961). Several examples (Bower, 1978, Fig. 3, p. 127) were rules of the form "*If* person *P* disagrees with me, *then P* dislikes me" and "*If* anyone dislikes me, *then* I feel sad"; or "*If* I fail at task *T, then* I believe I fail at everything" and "*If* I fail at everything, *then* my life is hopeless"; or "*If* person *P* compliments me, *then* that means that person P pities me" and "*if* anyone pities me, *then* I am unlovable" and "*If* I am unlovable, *then* I feel sad and I don't deserve to live." It is obvious how habitual activation of unconscious rules such as these "could move the stream of thought along automatically to its inexorable, morbid conclusion" (Bower, 1978, p. 127).

This use of production rules to describe automatic inferences and thoughts was apparently not foremost in the thinking of Mischel and Shoda (1995). Rather, they were mainly interested in *if . . . then . . .* rules that referred to situations as interpreted by a person and overt behavioral actions taken in that situation. Such rules provide a fairly good description of interpersonal behaviors. Insofar as the situations and behaviors are characterized at the right level of abstraction and granularity, they are useful for making predictions of others' behaviors, allowing us to adjust our behavior toward them in light of our predictions. From a scientific perspective, it would be more satisfying to have a somewhat deeper understanding of the factors that generate the *if . . . then . . .* regularities for a given individual. It was that goal that motivated Mischel and Shoda (1995) to develop their Cognitive–Affective Processing System (CAPS) theory of personality. We turn to a discussion of it now.

THE CAPS THEORY

The CAPS theory was proposed for understanding the intrapersonal and interpersonal dynamics underlying the collection of *if . . . then . . .* regularities exhibited by a given individual. In so doing, CAPS could also explain how and why individuals may differ radically in their behavioral profiles. The authors propose a very complex system of interacting parts composed of cognitive–affective (CA) units that mediate between the nominal interpersonal situation and the person's response (see Mischel & Shoda, 1995, Table 1, p. 253). Some proposed CA mediating units encode and interpret the personal and social situation in terms of the person's categories for the self, other people, and events; some of these categories will be chronically more accessible than others, thus biasing the person's social perceptions. Other CA units represent the person's expectancies and beliefs about the world and about outcomes for behaviors in different situations (self-efficacy). Still other CA units represent affects (feelings, emotions), values, and goals that motivate the person's plans and life projects and the person's repertoire of behavioral competencies that can be performed as well as strategies the person uses to control and regulate his or her behavior.

The architecture of the overall system is shown in Figure 2.6. Situations are characterized by a collection of features, some of which are "turned on" by a given situation. When stimulated, these input features send "activation" into the CA mediating units to which they are connected. The amount of activation reaching a given CA mediating unit from an activated input feature is determined by the "weight" (importance) of that input feature's connection to that mediating unit. The aroused CA units pass this recent wave of activation around among themselves, eventually settling into some internal state that will cause a response to be emitted. That response may in turn change the external

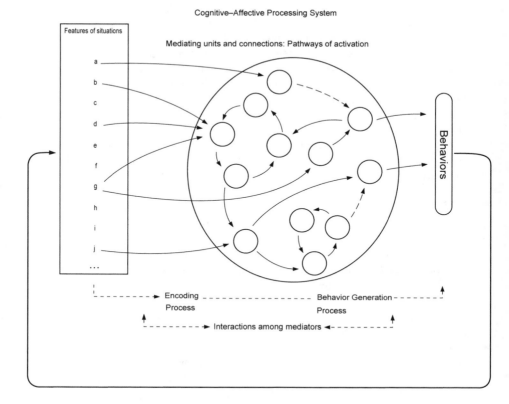

FIGURE 2.6. Illustration of the types of CA units that mediate behavior in a situation according to the CAPS model. Activation flows from the situational features (on the left) into the interassociated CA units, which pass the activation among themselves until they settle into a stable pattern, at which point some behavior is emitted. See text for details. From Mischel and Shoda (1995). Copyright 1995 by the American Psychological Association. Reprinted by permission.

situation, thus initiating the next cycle of responding. Each person has his or her own collection of cognitive–affective units and own set of connection weights, reflecting how his or her learning experiences have brought about particular CA units and their connection (importance) weightings.

To illustrate the operation of this system, Mischel and Shoda (1995) constructed a small computer simulation of CAPS for a single individual (see their Appendix, p. 267). The simulation is simple and concrete, affording better understanding of how the CAPS operates. Their illustration used six situational features, some two of which were turned on, thus allowing for 15 different situations (i.e., 6 × 5/2). Each feature was connected to the same four mediating units but with different connection weights. No connections were assumed to exist between the mediating units. The "response" of the system (say, the simulated subject's degree of "friendly behaviors") was generated from the weighted sum of the activation of the four CA mediating units. Different responses (friendliness, aggressiveness) would be characterized by different weights to the output units. As noted above, the differences between people would be represented in different connection weights to the mediating units and to the response units.

The authors ran the simulation model for a given individual twice through the 15 situations; for the second run, the connection weights were each perturbed a small random amount to reflect moment-by-moment variability of effective factors. The model produced variable situation–behavior profiles like those shown for three simulated individuals in the panels of Figure 2.7. The solid curve in each panel illustrates how this person's friendliness varies across the 15 situations; the dashed curve depicts the model's second run through these situations and illustrates the day-to-day variability in the individual's profile.

Examining these profiles, several patterns of interest stand out. First, the three individuals' behavior frequencies vary greatly across situations. Second, the individuals' profiles differ appreciably from one another, showing many person–situation interactions. Both of these effects were created, of course, by the different connection weights assigned to the three individuals by the authors. Third, these three indi-

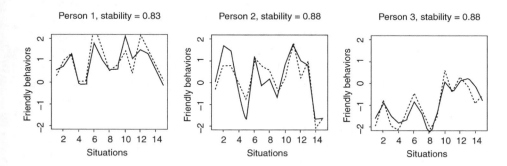

FIGURE 2.7. Three examples of friendly behavior profiles produced for 15 interaction situations as simulated by the CAPS theory. Each simulated individual corresponds to a table of different weights for the connections between the situational features and the CA units. From Mischel and Shoda (1995, p. 268). Copyright 1995 by the American Psychological Association. Reprinted by permission.

viduals are fairly stable from one to another time sample (simulation run). This stability depends, of course, on the size of the random "error" terms the theorist added to the weights from one run to the next. Fourth, averaging across situations, we can see that person 1 is usually above average in friendliness, person 2 is near the average of the population (i.e., z-score near zero), and person 3 is below average in friendliness.

These simulation results help us appreciate how the simulation model captures many behavioral facts that are central to the person versus situation controversy—that is, the model shows how individuals can vary their behavioral profiles across situations but in a pattern that is more or less stable. Moreover, the average of their behavior frequencies across situations can be considered as a composite index reflecting the individual differences that trait theorists emphasize.

A HOLE IN THE CAPS

How good is CAPS for predicting and explaining behavior? If the simulation model is to be taken seriously, then we must conclude that the model is egregiously underconstrained when we consider data from only a single response class. There are far too many unknown parameters (the weights) given the amount of data to be explained. For example, to produce one of the profile panels in Figure 2.7, containing its 15 behavior frequencies, the theorist needs to assign weights to the 24 connections for that subject, from the six stimulus features to the four mediating CA units. Then for each subject four more weights must be assigned to the connections from each mediating unit to each response-output unit. Thus, at a minimum, there are 28 arbitrary constants for fitting each subject's 15 data points. (I am ignoring the issue of transforming "response-output activation" into behavioral frequencies.) A stringent test of a model cannot be done unless there are at least more independent data points than unknown parameters of the model to be estimated.

The situation in this simulation could be rectified by including more data from other responses the model might be predicting. For each of R response classes, we would observe 15 response frequencies (for the 15 situations), comprising $15R$ data points in all; this number is to be compared to the number of unknown constants, which is $24 + 4R$, that is, four output weights for each of the R response classes. So the number of data points, $15R$, exceeds the number of parameters, $24 + 4R$, whenever the number of categories of responses, R, is more than 2.

TRAINING THE WEIGHTS

For toy-simulation purposes, the underconstraint problem can be relieved a little by training the model to learn weights that will produce adaptive responses to the 15 situations. The CAPS architecture in this illustration can be reconfigured into a simple connectionist (PDP) feedforward network model with one "hidden layer," such as shown in Figure 2.8 (see Rumelhart, McClelland, & the PDP Research Group, 1986).

The six input features are shown at the bottom of the net, each connected with a certain weight to the four hidden CA units, which in turn have weighted connections to the output units (only two are shown here, for friendliness and verbal aggression). The advantage of representing the CAPS architecture in this format is that there are well-known training methods for feedforward networks.

The training would proceed as follows: presented with a situation (i.e., "turn on" or activate some features of the input layer), the response made by the network is calculated at the output layer and then compared to the response the trainers want the learner to have for that situa-

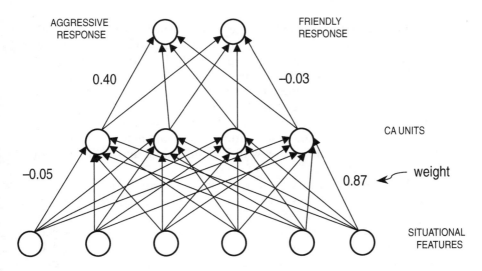

FIGURE 2.8. The CAPS theory reconfigured as a feedforward connectionist network. Activation flows from the bottom situational features up through the "hidden" CA units, and then into the behavioral output units, yielding either a friendly or aggressive response. Each connection has a weight or association strength attached to it. (Only a few are shown.)

tion. (The trainers could be the physical and social environments, parents and teachers, or the learner him- or herself.) Comparing the actual response to the trainers' desired response on a given trial, the weights on all the connections are then adjusted a small amount so as to bring the network's response closer to the desired response. The "back-propagation" learning algorithm (Rumelhart, Hinton, & Williams, 1986) adjusts these weights trial-by-trial in a manner that minimizes the expected errors of the network across the full range of situation–behavior pairings. By repeatedly cycling through the many stimulus patterns, reinforcing the trainer's desired response to each, the network eventually adjusts (or learns) those weights that will produce a close approximation to the desired response for each. In this way, the hidden mediating units can be trained to reflect a person's reinforcement history, and the CAPS theorist avoids the arbitrariness of assigning the connection weights for each simulated subject. This method does require, however, that a trainer know the desired response profiles.

WILL THIS MODEL SCALE UP TO MORE COMPLEX SITUATIONS?

Of course, even with the connection weights learned in this manner, this is still a toy simulation in a toy social world, well short of the reality in which we would like the theory to operate. Real situations differ in far more than six features; there will be far more than four CA units; and these units will probably interact among themselves in determining the output. We can imagine how much worse the underconstraint problem would become with these more realistic circumstances, having many more situations with many more features and many more CA units that interact with one another. How will the model scale up to situations of greater complexity?

I think Mischel and Shoda's response to this situation is well illustrated by the path they have followed in their several writings on the CAPS model. They use the model as an "in-principle" theoretical framework, showing how many different social behavior patterns can be generated from simple assumptions but without moving to the level of quantitative predictions. In applications of the theory to individual cases, they first gather many useful facts about an individual that they use to assess his or her expectancies, self-concepts, self-efficacy, habitual interpersonal strategies, values, goals, and motivations. The constructs of the theory guide the kind of data collected. They then use the theory as a framework for generating plausible explanations of an individual's behavior (see, e.g., the example of Gary in Mischel et al., 2004, pp. 284–

287). The theory enables them to construct plausible causal stories that help us understand why the individual behaved as he or she did in a given situation (e.g., Ayduck et al., 2000; Ayduk, Mischel, & Downey, 2002).

I view this level of understanding as an important advance, albeit short of the quantitative predictions so dear to the hearts of experimental psychologists. There are still many questions to be asked about the CAPS theory, and a lot of research work lies ahead to fashion it into a more satisfactory explanatory tool. One question, for example, arises when we notice that the CAPS theory is silent on the issue of which processes are available to consciousness; it makes no commitment about which CA units are conscious and which unconscious, or how unconscious CA units become conscious by virtue of exceeding some threshold of activation. Since much of modern social-cognitive research is aimed at uncovering automatic and nonconscious factors influencing judgment, motivation, mood, memory, and social behavior (e.g., Banaji, 2001; Bargh & Chartrand, 1999; Fazio & Olson, 2003), the CAPS theory should probably begin addressing this issue in the coming years.

CAPS IS A FITTING CAPSTONE TO WALTER'S CAREER

I believe that with his proposal of the CAPS theory, Walter has created a fitting CAPStone to his illustrious and productive career, a career that has years yet to run its course. CAPS is truly a social learning theory insofar as each individual acquires most of his or her CA units by virtue of an idiosyncratic and discriminative learning history. The idiosyncrasies of individual histories allow for the almost infinite variation we see in human personalities; CAPS uses principles that capture many of the stable regularities in a given individual's behavior. The theory provides a guiding light for researchers to follow in fleshing out the details of the relevant factors and their interactions. In that path to progress, filled with many eager researchers on personality, we can be sure that Walter and his collaborators will be pointing the way.

I will end with a few laudatory comments. For one who inveighs against behavioral consistency, Walter himself is amazingly consistent in his virtues. He has been a witty, generous, and constant friend of mine for 40 years. He writes with grace and elegance and makes a sincere effort to respond respectfully to his critics. He has been a master mentor to some of the leading investigators in the field of personality, including many who contributed to this volume. Moreover, he continues to generate original and creative ways of looking at personality, and, despite his many contributions, he continues as one of the leading innovators in the field of personality.

Perhaps that is why in a recent scientific survey focused on significant contributors (Haggbloom et al., 2002) Walter was recognized as one of the 100 most important psychologists of the 20th century. For all his many contributions, it is altogether proper and fitting that we honor him with our contributions to this volume.

REFERENCES

Abelson, R. P. (1973). The structure of belief systems. In R. C. Schank & K. M. Colby (Eds.), *Computer models of thought and language* (pp. 287–340). San Francisco: Freeman.

Allport, G. W. (1937). *Personality: A psychological interpretation.* New York: Holt, Rinehart & Winston.

Allport, G. W. (1961). *Pattern and growth in personality.* New York: Holt, Rinehart & Winston.

Anderson, J. R. (1993). *Rules of the mind.* Hillsdale, NJ: Erlbaum.

Anderson, J. R., & Lebiere, C. (1998). *The atomic components of thought.* Mahwah, NJ: Erlbaum.

Ayduk, O., Mendoza-Denton, R., Mischel, W., Downey, G., Peake, P. K., & Rodriguez, M. (2000). Regulating the interpersonal self: Strategic self-regulation for coping with rejection sensitivity. *Journal of Personality and Social Psychology, 79,* 776–792.

Ayduk, O., Mischel, W., & Downey, G. (2002). Attentional mechanisms linking rejection to hostile reactivity: The role of "hot" vs. "cool" focus. *Psychological Science, 13,* 443–448.

Banaji, M. R. (2001). Implicit attitudes can be measured. In H. L. Roediger III, J. S. Nairne, I. Neath, & A. Surprenant (Eds.), *The nature of remembering: Essays in honor of Robert G. Crowder* (pp. 117–150). Washington, DC: American Psychological Association.

Bandura, A. (1969). *Principles of behavior modification.* New York: Holt, Rinehart & Winston.

Bandura, A. (1977). *Social learning theory.* Englewood Cliffs, NJ: Prentice Hall.

Bargh, J., & Chartrand, T. (1999). The unbearable automaticity of being. *American Psychologist, 54,* 462–479.

Beck, A. T. (1964). Thinking and depression: II. Theory of therapy. *Archives of General Psychiatry, 10,* 561–571.

Beck, A. T. (1976). *Cognitive therapy and the emotional disorders.* New York: New American Library.

Bower, G. H. (1978). Contacts of cognitive psychology with social learning theory. *Cognitive Therapy and Research, 2,* 123–146.

Bower, G. H., & Cohen, P. R. (1982). Emotional influences on memory and thinking: Data and theory. In S. Fiske & M. Clark (Eds.), *Affect and cognition* (pp. 291–331). Hillsdale, NJ: Erlbaum.

Carbonell, J. G. (1980). Towards a process model of human personality traits. *Artificial Intelligence, 15,* 49–74.

Cattell, R. B. (1965). *The scientific analysis of personality.* Baltimore: Penguin.

Colby, K. M. (1963). Computer simulation of a neurotic process. In S. S. Tompkins & S. Messick (Eds.), *Computer simulation of personality* (pp. 163–179). New York: Wiley.

Colby, K. M. (1982). Modeling a paranoid mind. *Behavioral and Brain Sciences, 4,* 515–560.

Dollard, J., & Miller, N. E. (1950). *Personality and psychotherapy.* New York: McGraw-Hill.

Dyer M. G. (1987). Emotions and their computations: Three computer models. *Cognition and Emotion, 1,* 323–348.

Ellis, A. (1958). Rational psychotherapy. *Journal of General Psychology, 59,* 35–49.

Ellis, A., & Harper, R. A. (1961). *A guide to rational living.* New York: Institute for Rational Living.

Exner, J. E. (1993). *The Rorschach: A comprehensive system: Vol. 1. Basic foundations* (3rd ed.). New York: Wiley.

Eysenck, H. J., & Rachman, S. (1965). *The causes and cures of neurosis.* San Diego: Knapp.

Fazio, R., & Olson, M. (2003). Implicit measures in social cognition research. *Annual Review of Psychology, 54,* 297–327.

Haggbloom, S. J., Warnick, R., Warnick, J. E., Jones, V. K., Yarbrough, G. L., Russell, T. M., et al. (2002). The 100 most eminent psychologists of the 20th century. *Journal of General Psychology, 6,* 139–152.

Lovett, M. C., & Anderson, J. R. (2005). Thinking as a production system. In K. J. Holyoak & R. G. Morrison (Eds.), *The Cambridge handbook of thinking and reasoning* (pp. 401–430). New York: Cambridge University Press.

Miller, N. E., & Dollard, J. (1941). *Social learning and imitation.* New Haven, CT: Yale University Press.

Mischel, W. (1968). *Personality and assessment.* New York: Wiley.

Mischel, W. (1969). Continuity and change in personality. *American Psychologist, 24,* 1012–1018.

Mischel, W. (1984). Convergence and challenges in the search for consistency. *American Psychologist, 39,* 351–364.

Mischel, W., & Shoda, Y. (1995). A cognitive-affective system theory of personality: Reconceptualizing situations, dispositions, dynamics, and invariance in personality structure. *Psychological Review, 102,* 246–268.

Mischel, W., Shoda, Y., & Smith, R. E. (2004). *Introduction to personality: Towards an integration* (7th ed.). New York: Wiley.

Newell, A., & Simon, H. A. (1972). *Human Problem Solving.* Englewood Cliffs, NJ: Prentice Hall.

Norman, W. T. (1963). Toward an adequate taxonomy of personality attributes: Replicated factor structure in peer nomination personality ratings. *Journal of Personality and Social Psychology, 66,* 574–583.

Ross, L. (1977). The intuitive psychologist and his shortcomings. In L. Berkowitz (Ed.), *Advances in experimental social psychology* (Vol. 10, pp. 173–220). San Diego: Academic Press.

Rumelhart, D. E., McClelland, J. L., & the PDP Research Group (Eds.) (1986) *Parallel distributed processing: Explorations in the microstructure of cognition* (Vol 1). Cambridge, MA: MIT Press.

Rumelhart, D. E., Hinton, G. E., & Williams, R. J. (1986). Learning internal representations by error propagation. In D. E. Rumelhart, J. L. McClelland, & the PDP Research Group (Eds.) *Parallel distributed processing: Explorations in the microstructure of cognition* (Vol 1, pp. 318–362). Cambridge, MA: MIT Press.

Shoda, Y., Mischel, W., & Wright, J. C. (1994). Intra-individual stability in the organization and patterning of behavior: Incorporating psychological situations into the idiographic analysis of personality. *Journal of Personality and Social Psychology, 67,* 674–687.

Sloman, A. (1987). Motives, mechanisms, and emotions. *Cognition and Emotion, 1*(3), 217–233.

Wolpe, J. (1958). *Psychotherapy by reciprocal inhibition.* Stanford, CA: Stanford University Press.

Wright, J. C., & Mischel, W. (1987). A conditional approach to dispositional constructs: The local predictability of social behavior. *Journal of Personality and Social Psychology, 53,* 1159–1177.

Zimbardo, P. G., & Ebbeson, E. B. (1970). *Influencing attitudes and changing behavior.* Reading, MA: Addison-Wesley.

3

The Power of Context

JEROME KAGAN

Thomas Mann's gracefully phrased comment "For every great truth there is an equally great opposite truth" is an appropriate way to describe Walter Mischel's contribution to the social sciences. While most psychologists were confining their attention to the foreground, he appreciated that the meaning and consequences of the foreground event always depended on its background (Mischel, 1973). The problem with most terms for personality traits is a failure to specify the context in which a presumed characteristic is actualized. Walter Mischel is part of a grand tradition in biology. The significance of the ecological context is the central idea in Darwin's magnificent thesis. Hans Krebs, who discovered the citric acid cycle, told a journalist inquiring why he, rather than a more eminent European chemist, made this important discovery was that the chemist imagined the critical reaction occurring in a test tube, whereas Krebs imagined it occurring in a living person.

An individual is a worker and consumer in the context of the economy, a transmitter of genes in the context of evolutionary biology, and an agent with intentions in the context of psychology. When a professional football game is viewed on television, the players and their talents have psychological prominence. When the same contest is viewed from a seat high in the stadium, with attractive, gyrating cheerleaders, perceptually compelling advertisements, varied foods for purchase, and frequent, blaring announcements demanding attention, the players' physical size and psychological significance are reduced by so many orders of magnitude that they become merely one element in an extravagantly complex event serving commercial interests.

HOW CONSTRAINED IS A COMPETENCE?

The relevance of the context in psychology is inherent in the popular distinction between the hypothetical ability to deal with a large class of problems and actual performance in a specific situation. This tension can be stated succinctly. Is it useful to assume that a hypothetical capacity for a cognitive process, behavior, or emotional state inferred from a performance in a particular setting is preserved and potentially ready to be actualized in contexts in which the capacity should be, but is not, observed? There are many examples of limitations on the generality of a competence. For example, 3-month-olds can discriminate between a heavy and a light object when tested in the dark—they hold the lighter objects for a longer time—but, surprisingly, not if tested in a normally lit room (Striano & Bushnell, 2005). Fourteen-month-olds who had initially learned a name for a toy (e.g., Max) looked toward the toy when they heard its name in a story a minute or so later, even if the toy was several feet away and covered with a blanket. But infants did not look toward the toy if there was a 15-minute delay between learning its name and hearing it spoken (Ganea, 2005). The age when 9-to-12-month-olds can learn to select the novel of two objects in a delayed nonmatch-to-sample procedure is a function of small details in the testing. If the reward (e.g., a toy) is physically separate from the object that the infants must lift in order to obtain it, they do not learn to pick the novel familiar object; however, if the reward is attached to the object to be lifted, infants performed as expected because the reward and the object were perceived as a unity (Diamond, Lee, & Hayden, 2003). The probability that a 4-year-old will treat a round cookie as "more similar" to a coin rather than to a square piece of chocolate depends on whether the three objects in the array are presented without any context or as part of an ecologically natural scene (Cimpian & Markman, 2005). The features children select to categorize objects depend on the context in which they appear because children's perceptual schemas for many objects/events (in contrast to their semantic representations) represent the object together with its usual settings. That is why 1-year-olds are more likely to cry if their mother leaves them through an exit she rarely takes (e.g., the door to the attic) than if she leaves by the front door.

In each of the above cases, it is appropriate to ask whether the child possessed a broadly generalized ability (e.g., the ability to discriminate light from heavy objects) or whether the ability is limited to specific contexts. Should psychologists write that most humans have a general capacity for guilt, or should they always append a description of the classes of experiences capable of evoking guilt?

Contextual restraints on the generality of a competence also apply to social behavior. The stability of the rank structure among primate species influences the consequences of an encountered stress. High-ranking animals experience stress when the structure is unstable; low-ranking animals are maximally stressed when the rank is stable (Sapolsky, 2005). Whether one bonobo chimp dominates another depends on whether a third bonobo is present (Vervaecke, De Vries, & Van Elsacker, 1999). Young male elephants experience periodic surges in testosterone that are accompanied by increased aggressive behavior. This state, called "musth," can last as long as 6 months if no adult males are present but is much shorter if older males are introduced into groups of wild young males (Slotow, Vandyk, Poule, Page, & Klacke, 2000). Surprisingly, the color of the clothing opponents with equivalent athletic ability wear in two-person Olympic combat sports affects the outcome of the match. When one athlete wore blue and the other red, the former was less likely to win the competition (Hill & Barton, 2005).

The psychological state of "outsiders" whose beliefs, history, or physical features prevent them from being members of the majority holding power and privilege is always dependent on historical context. Change the time, setting, or values and the psychological state of shame disappears. Christians were outsiders in the 1st century C.E.; Jews were outsiders centuries later. Biological scientists were outsiders in the academic halls of 18th-century Oxford; humanists are outsiders today. Outsiders adopt one of three coping strategies. Some accept their diminished virtue passively and live with doubt. A much smaller number, usually better educated and from families with higher status, rebel aggressively (some Islamic terrorists illustrate this adaptation). A somewhat larger group mounts a criticism of the majority by constructing a different ethos that allows them to feel more virtuous. England's 17th-century Quakers, who exemplify this reaction, represent one of the advantages of outsider status. Because outsiders do not feel it necessary to conform to the premises of the majority, they are free to invent new ideologies. That is one reason a disproportionate number of Nobel laureates over the past century were Jews living in Christian countries. Einstein, siding with Schopenhauer, wrote that flight from the harshness of everyday life motivates many who choose art and science.

However, the contexts in which scientists work are changing. A major transformation in science began about three or four decades ago, when extraordinary advances in technology made it difficult for those who did not have access to expensive machines to participate fully in the excitement of significant discovery. In addition, because these machines require the skills of many scientists with different talents, this research typically is done by teams. The traits of those who are most effective in a team are not necessarily those traits most effective among those who prefer solitary inquiry. For example, among those who must work in teams, individuals who are comfortable in large groups and have the ability to organize others without threatening them will advance their careers more quickly than those who are shy and less able to recruit enthusiastic loyalty to their views.

Youths who enjoy the luxury of choosing a career imagine the activities and contexts of their future work rather than specific products. College seniors considering science are presented with Einstein and Darwin as mythical heroes sitting quietly in their studies reflecting on observations, whereas the current reality in experimental physics and neuroscience has a linear accelerator and a magnetic scanner in the foreground and the investigator and colleagues in the background, a scene reminiscent of the contrast between watching a quarterback on television versus from the top of a stadium. It is possible that one of the many reasons fewer talented American and European 20-year-olds are choosing science as a career is a suspicion that being a member of a large team of specialists dependent on a complicated machine operating on algorithms that spit out probabilities for each outcome, without requiring the judgment of an experienced eye or mind, seems less gratifying than an intellectual activity permitting a solitary, entrepreneurial style that does not demand cooperation and a compromise of one's ideas. Charles Townes, the inventor of the MASER—an acronym for microwave amplification by stimulated emission of radiation—that amplifies radio waves, was told by his elders in the 1950s to abandon his far-fetched ideas. This contrast between the lone scholar and the team member does not reflect a nostalgic wish for the past, but simply a description of how history has altered the nature of scientific activity in a few disciplines and the types of personalities that are likely to achieve eminence.

Contexts affect the meaning of biological variables. One significant context is a person's social class. The responsivity of the serotonergic system and the relation between the trait of novelty seeking and the presence of the 2 or 5 repeat of the allele for the type 4 dopamine receptor (DRD4) are influenced by an individual's social class (Manuck, Flory, Ferrell, & Muldoon, 2004; Lahti et al., 2006). Waveforms in the event-related potential to discrepant tones are affected by features of the stimulus. If the duration of a frequently presented standard tone is 1,600 milliseconds and the duration of the infrequent, deviant tone is 800 milliseconds, the resulting waveform at 250 milliseconds is smaller than when the duration of the standard tone is 200 milliseconds and that of the deviant tone 100 milliseconds (Naatanen, Fyssoeva, & Takegata, 2004). The power of a discrepant tone of a particular duration to evoke an event-related potential is not knowable until one specifies the larger context in which it appears. That is why the change in c-fos activity in the caudate–putamen of rats to an amphetamine challenge depends on whether the rat is in a familiar cage or a novel setting (Ferguson, Norton, Watson, Akil, & Robinson, 2003).

The increase in amygdalar activity produced by 2 minutes of pain (caused by placing a hand in very cold water) is muted if the subjects know what to expect (Petrovic, Carlsson, Petersson, Hansson, & Ingvar, 2004). The amygdalar response to erotic film clips that occurs when the scenes are shown with no instruction disappears when adult males are told to suppress their sexual arousal in response to the scenes (Beauregard, Levesque, & Bourgouin, 2001). The magnitude of sustained activation of dopamine-producing neurons in the ventral mid-brain areas of a monkey during the 2 seconds between the appearance of a cue that signals a liquid reward and the presentation of the reward is related to the probability that the reward will be delivered. Sustained neuronal reactivity was maximal when the probability was .5—that is, when the uncertainty was greatest (Fiorillo, Tobler, & Schultz, 2003); perhaps that is why the pursuit of an uncertain goal creates more pleasure than working for a certain one. Contemporary science has affirmed the many commentators on human nature who, based on subjective experience, suggested that the "joy is in the doing." The decreased tendency to pursue uncertain goals as one grows older might be due, in part, to a developmental compromise in dopamine functioning.

Context also affects the results of classical conditioning experiments with mice (Calandreau, Desmedt, Decorte, & Jaffard, 2005), and, in humans, the recovery of a classically conditioned skin conductance reaction depended on whether exposure to the unconditioned stimulus (following extinction trials) occurred in the room where the original conditioning occurred or in a different room (LaBar & Phelps, 2005). Many years ago, I developed a classically conditioned vasovagal reaction to the sight of blood on a person while watching the final scenes of the film *Bonnie and Clyde* about an hour after learning of the assassination of Martin Luther King, Jr. This reaction, which lasted 2 years, only occurred when the victim was on a movie or television screen, not when I saw blood on myself or another in a natural context.

This brief list, along with many other studies not cited, suggests that the validity of inferences regarding the presence of a state or ability is affected in a serious way by contextual factors that can include the age, class, gender, biology, past experience, and current mental set or state of the agent, as well as the source of evidence, the point in time when the measurement is made, and whether the test situation is familiar or unfamiliar, socially supportive or solitary. This claim would have provoked a smile on the faces of Kurt Koffka, Wolfgang Kohler, and Max Wertheimer. These three German psychologists who brought gestalt theory to the United States in the 1920s were unable to compete with the behaviorists for intellectual legitimacy because American psychologists, aping 19th-century physicists, wanted to analyze all events into their elemental components and designed their experiments to make this analysis possible. It would be almost 75 years before behaviorists acknowledged that the probability of an event functioning as a conditioned stimulus depended on its salience, or distinctiveness, which was influenced by the local context as well as by the biology and history of the organism.

THREE SOLUTIONS

The evidence invites three positions on the generality of a presumed competence that occurs in a limited number of settings. The first, and perhaps the most popular, is the assumption that the hypothetical competence is present even though it is not displayed in every theoretically appropriate context. This Platonic view treats a competence as an idealized but nonetheless real phenomenon in the natural world (e.g., self-esteem); however, Wittgenstein (1984) warned that we should never confuse a prototype with a specific object and should always ask, "What is actually true in this. . . . In what case is that actually true?" (p. 14).

A second, less popular position argues that the ability or state has special features when it is manifested in behavior or biology that it does not possess when it is not actualized. For example, most 4-year-olds answer correctly when shown a cow, cup, and car and asked to point to the animal. The correct response implies that 4-year-olds have some representation of the semantic form "animal," but most psychologists agree that the concept "animal" held by most adults is far more elaborate and perhaps qualitatively different from the one held by 4-year-olds. Some physicists, such as Niels Bohr, argue that the only reality scientists can ever know is defined by what is observed, and every observation is influenced by the machines and procedures employed.

The third, least popular solution urges scientists always to describe a competence together with the types of contexts in which it is observed. In this frame, the ability to remember seven unrelated events—words, numbers, designs, or familiar pictures—is an idealized, highly abstract conception and not a natural phenomenon. One solution to the problem of performance failure in settings in which a presumably broad competence should appear is to view every ability quantitatively, as varying in probability of occurrence, rather than qualitatively as present or absent. The image that illustrates this perspective is a plot with the ordinate representing the probability of a correct performance and the abscissa representing the number of different contexts in which the presumed competence is observed. This plot contains a very large number of functions; each represents the probability that a specific ability will appear in performance as a function of a number of different contexts in which it is measured. This function is likely to be a straight line for the ability to recall semantically coherent nine-word sentences composed of familiar words, such as "The capital of the state of California is Sacramento," but a set of decreasing functions when the information to be retrieved consists of nine unrelated or unfamiliar words. The ability to retrieve nine words heard 30 seconds earlier is not a Platonic competence waiting to be expressed; hence, investigators should describe the ability as a combination of the retrieval competence and the classes of contexts in which correct retrievals occur, a position advocated by Kurt Fischer (1980).

Of course, not all competences are restricted to a limited number of contexts. The sensory capacities for taste, smell, vision, hearing, and touch; the abilities to perceive motion, shape, and pattern; and the capacity to locomote, learn a language, and retrieve an object are more general, but this breadth does not characterize many competences that refer to conceptual structures, inferences, and emotional states. The differences between broad and contextually constrained competences remain fuzzy. Some clarity is gained by borrowing the physicists' distinction between potential and kinetic energy. A 2-kilogram log has the competence to emit a certain amount of heat but only when specific conditions are met.

A related perspective, which resembles physicists' concept of a phase space, treats a psychological or biological process as the foundation of an envelope of possible outcomes, with the immediate context selecting one outcome from the total number in the set. My representation of the concept "summer" consists of a network of schemata and semantic forms. One pattern is elicited as I watch snow fall on a January morning; a different pattern is evoked as I swelter in August's humid heat. Low levels of brain serotonin render individuals vulnerable to displaying violent aggression, anxiety, or depression, depending on their life contexts (Balaban, Alper, & Kasamon, 1996). A similar conclusion is likely for many biological measures, such as asymmetry of activation in an electroencephalogram (EEG) and cortisol level. Of course, genetic differences among humans can create brain states that produce variations in energy level, impulsivity, apathy, or uncertainty, but each of these psychological states is embedded in a particular person with a unique history living in a specific community. Adolescents who have difficulty moderating impulsive decisions because of their genome are at some risk for school failure and asocial behavior if they live with illiterate parents in a poor neighborhood in a large city but are at less risk if they live with an educated, affluent family in a town of 1,000 residents in rural Montana. A woodworker can make many different forms from the planks of a cherry tree.

Humans have the potential competence to be tolerant toward those holding different ethical beliefs, but that competence is only actualized under certain rearing conditions and applies to specific beliefs held by others. Many Christians who hold tolerant attitudes toward Muslims and Jews, for example, do not hold an equally tolerant attitude toward gays. Thus, it seems useful, as noted earlier, to treat every competence as varying in its probability of being actualized, with the context determining the probability value. I suspect that the number of psychological competences with probabilities less than 1 is far greater than the number of those with perfect probabilities. This conception is implicit in the psychiatric notion of diathesis, or a vulnerability to a disease.

It is not clear why Western minds are friendlier to locating all the conditions leading to an observed phenomenon in an object than recognizing that the object in a setting is the phenomenon to understand. The latter view is more common in Asian philosophies, which regard a person's social relationships as essential features of his or her personhood. The concept of creativity provides an example. Many American scholars write about creativity as if it were primarily a personal biological quality (Andreasen, 2005), rather than a concept defined by the relation between a community's evaluation of an idea, painting, musical composition, and a person's intellectual products. During the opening decades of the 20th century, Japanese and Germans did not regard Freud's ideas as creative because the former held a more favorable attitude toward carnality and the latter were bothered by a mechanistic analysis of human nature that celebrated the ego's rationality and, in so doing, robbed each person of his or her creativity and spirituality (Kauders, 2005). The suggestion that Goethe's poetry was a sublimation of sexuality struck Germans as ridiculous. Americans of the same era were more receptive to psychoanalytic ideas because of a more prudish stance toward sex and a friendlier attitude toward a mechanistic, materialistic conception of mind that celebrated the ego's accurate, pragmatic reality testing. It is interesting to note that a proportion of contemporary Americans who, like the Germans in 1920, are threatened by an increasingly popular unsentimental biological determinism that denies free will makes thought and emotion slaves of neuronal activity, and satirizes religious faith have become hostile to the claims of the biological sciences. Many psychological competences that are now regarded as "inside the person," such as creativity, are more properly viewed as capacities-cum-settings. Ivan Pavlov was lucky to be working in St. Petersburg because it had the only facility in Europe for performing surgery on dogs. Had Pavlov been located in Moscow he might not have discovered classical conditioning and would not have received the Nobel Prize in medicine.

CONTEXT AND TEMPERAMENT

My research on temperamental categories over the past 35 years illustrates the utility of treating all personality characteristics as contextually constrained. My colleagues and I have studied the temperamental biases that we call inhibited and uninhibited to the unfamiliar. These biases rest on the assumption that the familiarity of an incentive in a particular setting is a critical determinant of a child's initial behavioral reaction, a generalization that applies equally well to rats, cats, and monkeys. Each species inherits a susceptibility to treating certain classes of events as especially salient. Unexpected tactile sensations have primacy for sharks; unfamiliar smells play that role for gazelles; and unfamiliar people and settings possess this quality for humans.

The first question a brain asks of every event is whether it is expected or unexpected, familiar or unfamiliar, in the present setting. It answers that question by recruiting activity in more than half its neurons in less than 200 milliseconds and, having arrived at an answer, generates activity in circuits that become the foundation of varied emotions, cognitions, and behaviors. It is relevant that the onset of an unexpected, unfamiliar tone followed by the tingling sensations created by electric shock to a rat's paws is, first and foremost, an event that activates the many brain sites that are the foundation of a state one might call "alerted surprise"; whether it also creates a state called "fear" in the animal is a little less certain.

The concepts "inhibited" and "uninhibited" refer to two distinct behavioral reactions to unfamiliarity observed in children older than 1 or 2 years and defined by an initial reaction of caution and avoidance on the one hand or spontaneity and approach on the other (Kagan, 1994; Kagan & Snidman, 2004). The disposition to become quiet and apprehensive or excited and bold is only actualized in unfamiliar contexts and is not a trait seen in all settings. We have suggested, but not yet proved, that the bases for the differences between these two groups, which are partially heritable, are distinct neurochemistries in the amygdala and its multiple connections to many brain sites. Our colleague Carl Schwartz affirmed this idea by placing 20-year-olds, who had been classified as inhibited or uninhibited in their second year of age, in a magnetic scanner. The adults who had been inhibited 20 years earlier, compared with those who had been uninhibited, showed more sustained amygdalar activity when sets of unfamiliar faces with neutral expressions suddenly replaced sets of familiar ones (Schwartz, Wright, Shin, Kagan, & Rauch, 2003).

Nancy Snidman and I have been following a group of more than 400 healthy, middle-class, white children who were first observed when they were 4 months old. These infants were presented with unfamiliar visual, auditory, and olfactory stimuli, none of which was threatening or potentially harmful. Of this group, 20% showed high levels of vigorous motor activity and crying and 40% showed minimal motor activity and minimal crying. We call the former group "high reactive" and the latter "low reactive" and assume that the behavioral differences between them are due to differential excitability of the amygdala and its projections.

We expected that high reactives would be biased to develop an inhibited profile, whereas low reactives would develop an uninhibited persona. We observed these children at 14 and 21 months in a 2-hour laboratory session as they encountered unfamiliar settings, people, and objects. The children who had been high reactive were indeed more inhibited than those who had been classified as low reactive (Kagan, 1994). When they were 7½ years old, the high reactives were more likely than the low reactives to possess anxious symptoms, and they were quieter and smiled less often when interacting with an unfamiliar adult.

When they were 11 years old, the high reactives showed four biological signs that could be regarded as the product of greater amygdalar excitability (Kagan & Snidman, 2004). More adolescents who had been high reactive as infants and highly fearful in their second year showed greater EEG activity in the right frontal area than in the left. Because visceral feedback is more fully represented in the right amygdala, and this activity is transmitted to the frontal lobe ipsilaterally, it is possible that the greater desynchronization of alpha frequencies in the right frontal lobe, which results in greater right frontal activation, reflects greater activity in the right amygdala. However, the magnitude of right frontal activation is affected by the context and the person's momentary state and does not only index a stable trait (Hagemann et al., 2005).

The amygdala projects indirectly to the inferior colliculus; hence, it can enhance the excitability of the colliculus to produce a larger brainstem-evoked auditory potential to a series of click sounds. The evidence confirmed this expectation, as high reactives had larger evoked potential values than low reactives, implying a more excitable amygdala. The amygdala also sends projections to the locus ceruleus, ventral tegmentum, and nucleus basalis, which, in turn, project to the cortical pyramidal neurons that moderate the magnitude of the event-related potential. Hence, children with a more excitable amygdala should show larger P300 or N400 waveforms to unfamiliar events. High reactives sustained, over many trials, a larger N400 waveform to ecologically invalid scenes (e.g., a child's head on an animal's body) than low reactives.

Finally, the amygdala projects to the sympathetic nervous system. We measured the cardiac spectrum at rest and computed the proportion of low and high frequency power in that spectrum. The combination of greater power in the lower frequency band, which reflects sympathetic and parasympathetic activity, combined with a high resting heart rate, characterized one of every three high reactives, but only one of five low reactives.

We evaluated these participants when they were 15 to 16 years old. The consequences at age 16 of having been a high- or a low-reactive infant are more salient for private feelings and sources of worry than for social behavior, even though more high- than low-reactive adolescents were subdued or motorically tense when interacting with an unfamiliar adult. The differences in emotional state to the anticipation of un-wanted, unfamiliar events were more distinctive than the differences in social behavior because youth can regulate their behavior. Adolescents who had been high rather than low reactive were more likely to report feeling uneasy with strangers or in crowds, even though many reporting this tension were not exceptionally shy or subdued during an interview in their home with a woman they did not know. Three clinically depressed adolescents who had been high-reactive infants did not reveal excessively inhibited behavior in their interaction with the interviewer. A few high reactives, who appeared full of energy and vivacity, told the interviewer that they disliked being touched, could not sleep before school examinations, or experienced profound periods of sadness or worry (Kagan, Snidman, Kahn, and Towsley, in press). Their biology affected their feelings more than it affected their social behaviors. These data affirm the intuition that Howard Moss and I formed 40 years ear-lier when we wrote *Birth to Maturity*, a monograph summarizing the longitudinal data gathered on the population at the Fels Research Insti-tute (Kagan & Moss, 1962), but I have the illusion that I have a deeper understanding of these phenomena now than I did in 1962.

Carl Jung noted that each adult displays one psychological face to others, which he called the "persona," but another that represents pri-vate feelings, the "anima." A major change in development at puberty is the construction of a wall between the psychological face displayed to others and a person's inner life. This dissociation between public behav-ior and internal state is managed by sites in the prefrontal and anterior cingulate cortex, which, by placing a heavy hand on the amygdala, pre-vent it from disrupting well-practiced habits of social behavior.

One result gathered with the 15-year-olds supports Schwartz's finding of sustained amygdalar activity in the young adults who had been inhibited in their second year. The adolescents were shown six blocks of pictures, with 20 unique pictures in each block. Blocks 1, 3, and 5 consisted of familiar, ecologically valid scenes, whereas blocks 2, 4, and 6 consisted of ecologically invalid scenes (for example, a person with a slice of tomato for a head or a watch with snakes for the hour and minute hands). The high and low reactives displayed equal magnitude N100 and N400 waveforms, and similar rates of habituation of these waveforms, to the valid scenes. But more low than high reactives showed habituation of the two waveforms across the three blocks of invalid pictures, whereas about half of high reactives did not display habituation. This fact suggests that a continued biological reactivity to unfamiliarity remained a stable property for high reactives 15 years after their initial classification at 16 weeks of age. One adolescent, who was a prototypical high-reactive infant and a very inhibited 1-year-old, confessed that she does not like spring because April and May in New England are full of unpredictable changes, whereas the continuous cold of January and February contain few surprises. It remains a possibility that the special neurochemistry of high reactives, which remains unknown, interferes with the pleasure of exploring the novel.

A vulnerability to excessive guilt induced by one's thoughts is a consequence of a high-reactive temperamental bias because these adolescents attribute their frequent moments of tension to a violation of one of their ethical imperatives. In answer to the question "When was the last time you felt guilty?" most low reactives mentioned an act that actually hurt someone, such as a rude comment or a refusal to cooperate. Many more high than low reactives described violating a private standard that hurt no one (e.g., gossiping about a friend behind his or her back or having a racist thought). High reactives resemble Stephen Daedalus in James Joyce's *Portrait of the Artist as a Young Man*. Twice as many high- as low-reactive adolescents were deeply religious, and the satisfaction derived from their faith appeared to mute the more intense worry felt by the high reactives without any religious faith. The few high-reactive adolescents who were clinically depressed were most likely to have been girls who were skeptical of all formal religions.

A particular level of amygdalar excitability does not, by itself, create a specific emotional state or behavior. A brain state is linked to a symbolic network constructed over a lifetime that can produce a vulnerability to guilt, anxiety, loneliness, anger, or depression, depending on one's history. A brain state can be likened to verbs, such as *take, hit, give, kiss,* and *love* that can take different objects. Thus, anger or joy should not be described with the biological language of brain states, but as psychological states that combine brain profiles with the representations that history and the current setting evoke together.

Although variation in behavioral and biological reactions to unfamiliarity is a significant personality disposition, unfamiliarity is necessarily a contextually constrained concept. One must know an individual's past (distant and immediate) in order to know whether a particular event will be regarded as unfamiliar or unexpected. A novel, unexpected tone presented in a quiet environment and followed by electric shock is more likely to acquire the functions of a conditioned stimulus than one presented in a noisy environment.

THE ATTRACTION TO ESSENCES

If many actions, cognitive abilities, and emotional states are actualized in a limited number of settings, it is appropriate to ask why some psychologists describe these functions as potentially present, even though there is no sign of their presence in settings in which the behavior, ability, or feeling should be actualized. For example, scientists who assume the utility of the concept of fear in animals treat different behaviors displayed in varied contexts or activation of the amygdala to particular incentives as indices of the same essential fear state, even though the measured behaviors are often uncorrelated and the amygdala can be activated by events symbolic of pleasant states (LeDoux, 1996; Ohman & Mineka, 2001). If scientists first probed the conditions that produce conditioned freezing, potentiated startle, reluctance to explore an unfamiliar or brightly lit area, retreat from the sight or smell of a natural predator, along with activation of the amygdala, they would discover that the probability of each of the above reactions varies seriously with the species, the agent's state, the setting, and the integrity of the amygdala. As a result, they might have been reluctant to posit an abstract competence ("fear") that was manifest in all of these measurements.

Direct recordings from clusters of amygdalar neurons in monkeys watching film clips illustrating three different monkey actors displaying (1) a face of aggressive threat displayed by a dominant animal, (2) a coo face often displayed in association with food, and (3) a scream face shown by a subordinate animal who has been attacked revealed that the coo face of one monkey evoked more activity in a neuronal cluster than that monkey's scream face. However, the scream face evoked more activity in the same neurons when the monkey actor was a different animal (Kuraoka & Nakamura, 2006). This result suggests that the amygdalar neurons respond to a perceptual whole that combines the separate features of eyes and mouth with the entire facial display, as the gestalt psychologists would have expected. The amygdala does not respond only to a configuration of eyes and mouth independent of the animal or human face displaying it. Onishi and Baillargeon (2005) concluded, on the basis of only one laboratory procedure, that 15-month-old infants were "born with an abstract computational system that guides their interpretation of others' behavior" (p. 257). Had they tested the infants in several procedures, they would have recognized that the supposed competence was not displayed in all of them.

Scientists who favor the broad generality of a competence or quality, despite the absence of the expected reaction in many appropriate contexts, usually begin their empirical work with an a priori concept they are convinced has a referent, rather than try to discover the conditions that produce a reliable observation. The decision to look for observable signs of an a priori concept reflects a commitment to abstract processes rather than to combinations of a process and the contexts in which it occurs. The sentence "Dogs can bark" implies that barking is an ability all dogs possess on all occasions. The English language might have included a different predicate for the sounds dogs make in varied settings, one word for barking to strangers and a different term for barking when their owner enters the house. A very small number of English verbs are restricted to a limited class of objects. *Murder, flatter, impeach,* and *hire* apply only to humans; no one would use the word "murder" to refer to a mosquito that was the victim of a swat on the arm. Unfortunately, most English verbs are far less restrictive.

Investigators who begin their work with images and thoughts that refer to a phenomenon—observed or imagined—rather than with semantic concepts appreciate that most psychological qualities and abilities vary with context. That is why biologists, chemists, and physicists, whose experiments are usually designed to explore the conditions that produce a reliable event, are acutely aware of the contextual constraints on all functions. The powerful theoretical structure of quantum mechanics was invented because an earlier cohort tried to understand the unique spectral lines each atom emitted. These scientists focused on a robust observation to be explained, rather than try to prove an a priori view of atoms. There is a serious validity gap between constructs derived from a priori conceptions and those inferred from observations. The 19th-century concept of the ether, which later evidence proved invalid, was an a priori idea; Darwin's concept of natural selection, which remains valid, originated in evidence. The most useful biological constructs originate in reliable observations; too many psychological concepts, which are free of contextual constraint, originate in a priori theory.

Psychologists who come to the laboratory with a prior commitment to a competence that transcends the species, gender, and age of the agent, as well as the local context, search for any condition that will affirm the a priori notion. If they discover just one experimental arrangement that confirms their assumption, they are prepared to conclude that their original conception was correct. If a presumed competence occurs in a limited number of settings, however, it is likely that a unique feature of those settings is a component of the ability. Because brain processes and the psychological states they permit are dynamic phenomena influenced by the context in which the measurement occurs, it is reasonable to doubt that agents possess broadly generalizable cognitive and emotional functions, such as the ability to think critically or to be empathetic, that are available for display across settings and stages of development.

Richard Shweder offered a lovely example of the importance of context in a talk he gave at Harvard University several years ago. Shweder and his wife, who were living in the temple town of Orissa in India where Shweder was doing fieldwork, were entertaining three guests for dinner. Because the guests had different statuses in the community, Shweder had to guarantee that the food served was acceptable to all of them. He went to the local temple to acquire food others had placed there earlier in the day because anyone is allowed to eat food once a god has removed its essence. Some rice remained after the guests had departed and Shweder's wife added some chicken to the rice and served it to her husband. Surprisingly, Shweder reported a feeling of disgust and an inability to eat the food. The moral standard of the temple town had become part of his own code, as long as he was in Orissa. Shweder would have had no problem eating diced chicken in a bowl of rice had he been with his wife in their dining room in Chicago. Many popular psychological concepts proposed to explain behavior, belief, and emotion that ignore context are too pretty to be true. They remain appealing because they satisfy a deep desire for simple explanations that place most of the causal force behind a phenomenon in the agent.

THE INFLUENCE OF LANGUAGE

The attraction to broad psychological processes, free of contextual limitations, is aided by the fact that the names for many of these processes are predicates that can be used with different classes of agents acting in varied settings. The predicate "running," for example, can apply to a boy fleeing a bear, a girl racing toward a friend, or a stream of water flowing down a hill. The absence of a large number of English verbs to convey a similar meaning tempts listeners to attribute the same core meaning to the word "running," even though its sense meaning is altered when a different agent or situation is the referent. There is always more ambiguity surrounding the meaning of a predicate than the meaning of a noun. Hence, "The cat ran" and "The water ran" have different meanings. Psychological states and competences, such as "anxious," "rewarding," "stressed," "attached," "depressed," and "aggressive," occur in sentences in which varied species behave in distinct settings; hence, the meanings of these words depend on the agent and setting. It is time to replace the telegraphic utterances characteristic of psychology with full sentences that specify an agent, a predicate, and an object. The attraction to abstract competences that transcend settings is inconsistent with the empirical evidence.

A second problem that continually trails semantic concepts, especially nouns naming categories of agents, is that the salience of the features defining the categories depends on the implied contrasting category. That is, the salience of an individual quality is a function of the semantic context selected. This fact influences the traits presumed to be the foundation of human personality. A class of persons can be contrasted with (1) an animal species, (2) another class of persons living in the same culture or time, or (3) a class of persons from a different culture or time. Each contrast automatically evokes a distinct hierarchy of salient traits. If, for example, contemporary Americans are contrasted with the Athenians of 400 B.C.E., loyalty to the community becomes salient. If the contrast is with the New England Puritans of 1650, piety assumes prominence. Variation in both traits is missing from modern personality theory. Because contemporary Americans and Europeans emphasize the imperative of personal accomplishment and the status and wealth it brings, the traits that contribute to, or block, attainment of this goal dominate current assessments. That is why extraversion, agreeableness, openness to the ideas of others, conscientiousness, and neuroticism (anxiety and guilt) are the Big Five traits. This list could only be popular in a cultural context in which sociability, a work ethic, flexibility, and an ability to take risks in order to attain enhanced status, fame, power, or wealth were primary goals. If these imperatives, which create a spiritually vacuous ambience when carried to an extreme, are rejected by future generations, a new trait that we might call "degree of moral certainty" might emerge.

Indeed, brash as it sounds, one can argue that the fundamental biological premise that all animals and, therefore, humans are first and foremost motivated to maximize their inclusive fitness, and the economic premise that all humans are motivated to maximize their self-interest, are not uncontested laws of nature but ethical assumptions that could only become dogma in historical contexts in which the individual, rather than the individual within a local group, was the primary category. The abstract concept of inclusive fitness, which is impossible to quantify in most natural situations, is invoked to explain the duration of survival of a species or a pedigree within a species. It is not obvious, however, that prolonged survival of an individual and his/her genetic relatives is a more fundamental fact of nature than the observation that changing ecologies lead to the extinction of some forms and the proliferation of others. The claim that change, not preservation, is a central characteristic of the natural world, as Heraclitus observed, is as reasonable as the premise that survival for the longest time is nature's favored desiderata. Dinosaurs, snow leopards, and polio viruses were perfectly adapted to their settings and met the criteria for fitness until ecological changes—natural catastrophe in the former case and human intervention in the latter two—compromised the fitness of all three forms. Now that large numbers of Americans, Europeans, and Japanese do not require the economic or psychological help of their offspring, and the cost of rearing and educating children has risen, many couples are restricting their fecundity and, therefore, compromising their fitness. Ecological changes affect the fitness of animals; historical changes have a similar effect on humans.

As for the economic premise, a majority of our species, since its appearance more than 150,000 years ago, has been more strongly motivated to adhere to the ethical mores of the community in order to avoid criticism and to assure itself of its virtue than to maximize its wealth, status, and sensory pleasure. "Lop off the tall poppies," a popular Australian motto, conveys this imperative. Both evolutionary biologists and economists have chosen to award greater influence to the intrinsic qualities and desires of an individual than to the relations between each agent's biologically based motives and the changing contexts in which his or her life is conducted. The extinction of the African hunter–gatherer groups who practiced cooperation and punished excessive self-aggrandizement should motivate reflection on this one-sided perspective.

All this evidence invites applause for Walter Mischel's recognition of the significance of context in personality theory. The archaeologist Loren Eiseley, in his 1971 memoir *The Night Country,* wrote that there are big bone hunters and little bone hunters, and there was probably a tear on Eiseley's cheek when he added, "I am a little bone hunter." Walter Mischel is a big bone hunter.

ACKNOWLEDGMENT

Preparation of this chapter was supported, in part, by the Bial Foundation and the Metanexus Institute.

REFERENCES

Andreasen, N. C. (2005). *The creating brain.* New York: Dana Press.

Balaban, E., Alper, J. S., & Kasamon, Y. L. (1996). Mean genes and the biology of aggression. *Journal of Neurogenetics, 11,* 1–43.

Beauregard, M., Levesque, J., & Bourgouin, P. (2001). Neural correlates of conscious self-regulation of emotion. *Journal of Neuroscience, 21,* 165–166.

Calandreau, L., Desmedt, A., Decorte, L., & Jaffard, R. (2005). A different recruitment of the lateral and basolateral amygdale promotes contextual or elemental conditioned association in Pavlovian fear conditioning. *Learning and Memory, 12,* 383–388.

Cimpian, A., & Markman, E. M. (2005). The absence of a shape bias in children's word learning. *Developmental Psychology, 41,* 1003–1019.

Diamond, A., Lee, E. Y., & Hayden, M. (2003). Early success in using the relation between stimulus and rewards to deduce an abstract rule. *Developmental Psychology, 39,* 825–847.

Eiseley, L. (1971). *The night country.* New York: Scribner.

Ferguson, S. M., Norton, C. S., Watson, S. J., Akil, H., & Robinson, T. E. (2003). Amphetamine-evoked c-fos mRNA expression in the caudate–putamen. *Journal of Neurochemistry, 86,* 33–44.

Fiorillo, C. D., Tobler, P. N., & Schultz, W. (2003). Discrete coding of reward probability and uncertainty by dopamine neurons. *Science, 203,* 1898–2005.

Fischer, K. (1980). A theory of cognitive development. *Psychological Review, 87,* 477–531.

Ganea, P. A. (2005). Contextual factors affect absent referent comprehension in 14-month-olds. *Child Development, 76,* 989–998.

Hagemann, D., Hewig, J., Seifert, J., Naumann, E., & Bartussek, D. (2005). The latent state–trait structure of resting EEG asymmetry. *Psychophysiology, 42,* 740–752.

Hill, R. A., & Barton, R. A. (2005). Red enhances human performance in contests. *Nature, 435,* 293.

Kagan, J. (1994). *Galen's prophecy.* New York: Basic Books.

Kagan, J., & Moss, H. A. (1962). *Birth to Maturity.* New York: Wiley.

Kagan, J., & Snidman, N. (2004). *The long shadow of temperament.* Cambridge, MA: Harvard University Press.

Kagan, J., Snidman, N., Kahn, V., & Towsley, S. (in press). The preservation of two temperaments into adolescence. *Monographs of the Society for Research in Child Development.*

Kauders, A. D. (2005). The mind of a rationalist. *History of Psychology, 8,* 255–270.

Kuraoka, K., & Nakamura, K. (2006). Impacts of facial identity and type of emotion on responses of amygdalar neurons. *NeuroReport, 17,* 9–12.

LaBar, K., & Phelps, E. A. (2005). Reinstatement of conditioned fear in humans is context dependent and impaired in amnesia. *Behavioral Neuroscience, 119,* 677–686.

Lahti, J., Raikkonen, K., Ekelund, J., Peltonen, L., Raitakari, O. T., & Keltikangas-Jarvinen, L. (2006). Socio-demographic characteristics moderate the association between DRD4 and novelty seeking. *Personality and Individual Differences, 40,* 533–543.

LeDoux, J. E. (1996). *The emotional brain.* New York: Simon & Schuster.

Manuck, S. B., Flory, J. D., Ferrell, R. E., & Muldoon, M. F. (2004). Socioeconomic status covaries with central nervous system serotonergic responsivity as a function of allelic variation in the serotonin transporter gene-linked polymorphic region. *Psychoneuroendocrinology, 29,* 651–668.

Mischel, W. (1973). Toward a cognitive social learning reconceptualization of personality. *Psychological Review, 80,* 252–283.

Naatanen, R., Fyssoeva, D., & Takegata, R. (2004). Automatic time perception in the human brain for intervals ranging from milliseconds to seconds. *Psychophysiology, 41,* 660–663.

Ohman, A., & Mineka, S. (2001). Fears, phobias, and preparedness. *Psychological Review, 108,* 483–522.

Onishi, K. H., & Baillargeon, R. (2005). Do 15-month-old infants understand false beliefs? *Science, 308,* 255–258.

Petrovic, P., Carlsson, K., Petersson, K. M., Hansson, P., & Ingvar, M. (2004). Context-dependent deactivation of the amygdala during pain. *Journal of Cognitive Neuroscience, 16,* 1289–1301.

Sapolsky, R. M. (2005). The influence of social hierarchy on primate health. *Science, 308,* 648–652.

Schwartz, C., Wright, C. I., Shin, L. M., Kagan, J., & Rauch, S. L. (2003). Inhibited and uninhibited infants grown up: Adult amygdalar response to novelty. *Science, 300,* 1952–1953.

Slotow, R., Vandyk, G., Poule, J., Page, B., & Klacke, A. (2000). Older bull elephants control young males. *Nature, 408,* 425–436.

Striano, T.. & Bushnell, E. W. (2005). Haptic perception of material properties by 3-month-old infants. *Infant Behavior and Development, 28,* 266–289.

Vervaecke, H., De Vries, H., & Van Elsacker, L. (1999). An experimental evaluation of the consistency of competitive ability and agnostic dominance in different social contexts in captive bonobos. *Behavior Genetics, 136,* 423–442.

Wittgenstein, L. (1984). *Culture and value* (G. H. Von Wright, Ed.; P. Winch, Trans.). Chicago: University of Chicago Press.

4

Eastern and Western Ways
of Perceiving the World

RICHARD E. NISBETT

For the last 10 years or so my colleagues and I have been conducting a kind of individual differences research, but the individual differences that we have been studying are all tied to culture. People who live in some cultures perceive and think about the world in ways that are very different from those of people who live in other cultures. I hope that the work we have done has something of the rigor that Walter Mischel has introduced into the study of individual differences within a culture. Certainly, his work—and the understanding of individual differences he has given us—are never far from my mind when I think about individual differences that happen to be linked with culture. A particularly close connection between Walter's work and our research is the suggestion that the layperson's exaggerated perception of stability and breadth of traits that Mischel's early work revealed may be largely limited to Westerners.

A study of intellectual history indicates that, for the past 2,500 years at least, people of Asian cultures and people of European cultures have had very different ways of understanding—and seeing—the world around them (Nisbett, 2003; Nisbett, Peng, Choi, & Norenzayan, 2001). Western perception and cognition from the ancient Greeks forward has been analytic. The focus is on some central object (which could be a person) with respect to which the individual has some goal. The attributes of the object are attended to with the intention of categorizing

62

it so that rules that allow for prediction and control can be applied. Eastern perception has been "holistic." The object or person is seen in a broad context or field, and behavior is understood in terms of relationships and similarities rather than generalized categories and rules.

Philosophy and science in ancient Greece versus in ancient China illustrate the dramatic differences in thought and perception (Cromer, 1993; Fung, 1983; Lloyd, 1990, 1991a, 1991b; Munro, 1969; Nakamura, 1985). Aristotle's physics focused almost exclusively on the object. A stone placed in water sinks because it has the property of gravity; a piece of wood floats because it has the property of levity. In contrast, Chinese conceptions of action took into account the interaction between the object and the surrounding field. The concept of action at a distance was understood by the Chinese almost 2,500 years before it was understood in the West. For example, the Chinese had substantial knowledge of magnetism and acoustics and understood the true reason for the tides (which escaped even Galileo).

Objects were conceived by the Greeks as being composed of particles or atoms, whereas the Chinese saw matter as substances in wave form. Because the Greeks believed in rules governing categories of objects, they had a sense of control over the world. In contrast, the Chinese did not have an elaborate set of rules to explain the behavior of objects and did not experience the world as being as controllable as the Greeks did. I believe these radical differences had to do with the nature of Chinese versus Greek societies.

Chinese society was based on agriculture and required substantial cooperation at the family and village levels. Substantial interdependence or collectivism was the result. Confucian philosophy both codified and encouraged the following of elaborate rules governing social existence, which was hierarchically arranged. Greek society was based on occupations such as herding, fishing, and trade that allowed for more independence or individualism. These social differences prompted different views of the world in the following way: the Chinese social system encouraged regarding the world as complex and highly dependent on relationships, whereas the Greek social system allowed for focus on objects (including social objects) with respect to which the individual had goals. The Chinese and Greeks attended to different aspects of the social world, which might have prompted different cognitions about it— holistic in the case of the Chinese and analytic in the case of the Greeks. The different understandings of the social world resulted in different understandings of the physical world because if the individual regards himself as being highly linked with other people, other objects and events will also be seen as highly related, whereas if the individual regards himself as an isolated unit, other objects and events will also be seen as unique and unrelated to other objects and events (Markus & Kitayama, 1991b).

People in Eastern cultures remain much more interdependent in their social lives than are Americans and other Westerners (Fiske, Kitayama, Markus, & Nisbett, 1998; Hsu, 1953, 1981; Markus & Kitayama, 1991a, 1991b; Triandis, 1989, 1995). Anthropologist Edward T. Hall (Hall, 1976) used the concept of "low-context" versus "high-context" societies to describe differences in social relations. Westerners regard themselves as possessing traits, abilities, and preferences that are unchanging across social contexts, but East Asians view themselves as being so connected to others that who they are literally depends on context. East Asians understand themselves in terms of the family, the corporation, and the society (Munro, 1985; Shih, 1919). If an important person is removed from the individual's social network, that individual literally becomes a different person.

Different types of self-perception are captured by descriptions that people from different cultures give of themselves. When Americans and Canadians are asked to describe themselves, they mention their personality traits and attitudes more than do Japanese, who are more inclined to mention relationships (Cousins, 1989; Kanagawa, Cross, & Markus, 2001). North Americans tend to overestimate their distinctiveness and to prefer uniqueness in themselves and in their possessions (Markus & Kitayama, 1991b). In one clever study, Koreans and Americans were given a choice among different colors of pens to have as a gift. Americans chose the rarest color, whereas Koreans chose the most common color (Kim & Markus, 1999).

Different cultures socialize infants in ways that shape them early for the independent or interdependent roles that they are expected to play. Western babies often sleep in a different bed or room from their parents, but this is rare for Asian babies. Adults from several generations often surround the Chinese baby, and the Japanese baby is almost always with its mother. When American mothers play with their children, they tend to focus their attention on objects and their attributes ("See the truck; it has nice wheels"), whereas Japanese mothers emphasize feelings and relationships ("When you throw your truck, the wall says, 'ouch' ") (Fernald & Morikawa, 1993). The different socializations show up in adulthood. Koreans are better able to judge an employer's true feelings about an employee from his or her ratings of the employee than are Americans (Sanchez-Burks et al., 2003). And when Masuda and I (2001) showed study participants videos of fish, they found that Japanese were more likely to see emotions in the fish than were Americans.

The Chinese American psychologist L.-H. Chiu (1972) described these differences this way:

Chinese are situation-centered. They are obliged to be sensitive to their environment. Americans are individual-centered. They expect their environment to be sensitive to them. Thus, Chinese tend to assume a passive attitude while Americans tend to possess an active and conquering attitude in dealing with their environment (p. 236).

[The American] orientation may inhibit the development of a tendency to perceive objects in the environmental context in terms of relationships or interdependence. On the other hand, the Chinese child learns very early to view the world as based on a network of relationships; he is *socio-oriented,* or *situation-centered.* (p. 241)

Contemporary Asian and Western societies differ in their emphasis on relationships versus independent action, so it might be expected that Asians and Westerners differ in their cognitive and perceptual habits along the lines of the holistic versus analytic stance characteristic of ancient Chinese versus ancient Greek science and philosophy. (By "Asia," I mean those East Asian countries in the Confucian tradition that originated in China, including China, Japan, and Korea. By "the West," I mean Europe and many of the present and former members of the British Commonwealth, including the United States, Canada, Australia, and New Zealand.) For the past several years, my colleagues and I have been examining the possibility of cultural differences in a number of cognitive and perceptual domains.

DIFFERENCES IN HABITS OF THOUGHT

East Asians and Westerners differ in the way they make causal attributions and predictions, in categorization based on rules versus family resemblance, and in ways of organization that are based either on taxonomic labels or on relationships.

Attributing Causes to Persons versus to Contexts

Westerners, like ancient Greek scientists, are inclined to explain events by reference to properties of the object of focus, and East Asians are inclined to explain the same events with reference to interactions between the object and the field (for reviews, see Choi, Nisbett, & Norenzayan, 1999; Norenzayan, Choi, & Nisbett, 1999; and Norenzayan & Nisbett, 2000). Morris and Peng (1994) and Lee, Hallahan, and Herzog (1996) have shown that Americans are inclined to explain murders and sports events by invoking presumed traits, abilities, or other characteristics of individuals, whereas mainland Chinese and citizens of

Hong Kong are more likely to explain the same events with reference to contextual factors, including historical ones. Cha and Nam (1985) and Choi and I (1998) found that East Asians used more contextual information than did Americans in making causal attributions. The same is true for predictions.

Easterners and Westerners give different types of explanations even for events involving animals or inanimate objects. Cartoon displays of an individual fish moving in various ways in relation to a group of fish were shown to Chinese and Americans by Morris and Peng (1994). Chinese participants were more likely to see the behavior of the individual fish as being produced by external factors (namely, the other fish) than were Americans, who were more inclined to see the behavior as being produced by factors internal to the individual fish. Peng and I (2002) and Peng and Knowles (in press) showed that for ambiguous physical events involving phenomena that appeared to be hydrodynamic, aerodynamic, or magnetic, Asian Americans were more likely to refer to the field when giving explanations (e.g., "the ball is more buoyant than the water") than were European Americans.

Categorization

People from Asian cultures have been found to classify objects and events on the basis of relationships and family resemblance, whereas Americans classify on the basis of rule-based category membership. Liang-Hwang Chiu (1972) showed triplets of objects like those in Figure 4.1 to Chinese and American children and asked them to indicate which of the two objects went together. American children put the chicken and the cow together and justified this by pointing out that "both are animals." Chinese children put the cow and the grass together and justified this by saying, "the cow eats the grass." Our research group has found the same sort of differential tendency in college students given word triplets to read (Ji, Zhang, & Nisbett, 2004). For example, Chinese and American participants were asked to indicate which two of these three go together: notebook, magazine, pen. Americans tended to put the notebook and the magazine together because both have pages. Chinese tended to put the pen and the notebook together because the pen writes in the notebook. Norenzayan, Smith, Kim, and I (2002) asked participants to report whether a target object like that at the bottom of Figure 4.2 was more similar to the group of objects on the left or the group on the right. The target object bears a strong family resemblance to the group of objects on the left, but there is a rule that allows placing the object in the group on the right, namely, "has a straight stem." Figure 4.3 shows that East Asians were inclined to think that the object was

FIGURE 4.1. "Which two go together?" items similar to those in Chiu (1972) test.

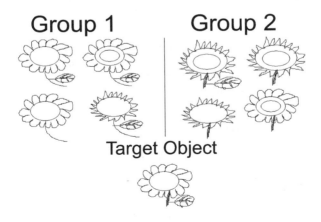

FIGURE 4.2. "Which group does the target object belong to?"

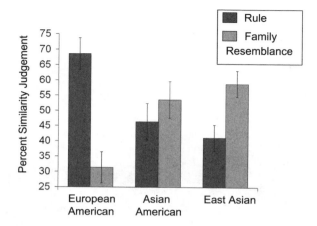

FIGURE 4.3. Percentage of participants basing similarity judgments on family resemblance versus rule.

more similar to the group with which it shared a family resemblance, whereas European Americans were more likely to regard the object as similar to the group to which it could be assigned by application of the rule. Asian Americans, though closer to East Asians, showed no overall preference. (We have included Asian Americans in several of our studies. They were always intermediate in their responses and most typically closer to the European Americans than to the East Asians.)

DIFFERENCES IN HABITS OF ATTENTION AND PERCEPTION

East Asians and Westerners differ not only with respect to cognition, but also in many mental operations that are attentional and perceptual in nature. Asians appear to attend more to the field and Westerners to attend more to salient objects.

Covariation Detection

Because East Asians pay more attention to the field, we would expect them to be better at detecting relationships among events. Ji, Peng, and I (2000) presented arbitrary objects like those in Figure 4.4 to Chinese and American participants. One of the objects on the left appeared on the left side of a split computer screen followed rapidly by one of the objects on the right appearing on the right side of the screen. The partici-

FIGURE 4.4. Sample of arbitrary objects shown in covariation detection task.

pant's task was to judge the strength of relationship between objects. The actual strength ranged from 0—that is, the probability of a particular object on the right appearing was independent of which object appeared on the left—to a relationship equal in strength to a correlation of .60. The Chinese participants saw more covariation than did American participants, they were more confident about their judgments, and their confidence was better correlated with the actual degree of covariation. When some control over the setup was given to participants by allowing them a choice as to which object to present on the left and how long an interval to have before presentation of the object on the right, however, American performance was entirely similar to Chinese performance.

Field Dependence: Difficulty in Separating an Object from Its Surroundings

If it is the case that East Asians are inclined to focus their attention simultaneously on the object and the field, then we might expect them to find it more difficult to make a separation between an object and the field in which it appears. Such a tendency is called "field dependence" (Witkin et al., 1954). One of the ways of examining it is the rod and frame test shown in Figure 4.5. The participant looks down a long box, at the end of which is a rod whose orientation can be changed and a frame around the rod that can be moved independently of the rod. The participant's task is to judge when the rod is vertical. Participants are

FIGURE 4.5. Rod and frame test apparatus.

deemed "field dependent" to the extent that their judgments of verticality of the rod are influenced by the orientation of the frame. Ji and colleagues (2000) found that Chinese participants were more influenced by the position of the frame than were American participants. Although Chinese and American participants were equally confident of their judgments in this setup, when participants were given control over the position of the rod, the Americans became more confident than the Chinese (and the actual performance of American males improved).

Attention to Object versus Context

Masuda and I (2001) presented 20-second animated vignettes of underwater scenes to Japanese and American participants. A still from one of the videos is presented in Figure 4.6. After seeing each video twice, participants were asked to report what they had seen. The first sentence was coded as to whether a participant initially mentioned one of the salient objects (with "salience" defined as being larger, faster moving, and more brightly colored than the other objects) or the field (e.g., color of the water, floor of the scene, inert objects). American participants started their statements by mentioning salient objects far more frequently than Japanese participants did. In contrast, Japanese participants began by mentioning information about the field almost twice as often as Americans did. Overall, Japanese made 65% more observations about the field than did Americans and mentioned almost twice as many relations between objects and the field as did American participants.

Participants were shown eight vignettes, after which they were presented with still photos of 48 objects that they had seen before and 48 that they had not. The previously seen objects were shown either against the original background or a novel background, as in Figure 4.7. The prediction was that, because they attend to objects in relation to the field, Japanese participants would be more thrown off by presentation of the object against the novel field than would Americans, and this was, in fact, the case. Whereas American performance was unaffected by the background manipulation, Japanese made substantially more errors when the object was seen against a novel background than when it was seen against the original background. In the parlance of perceptual psychologists, the Japanese "bound" the object to the field in perception and subsequent memory (Chalfonte & Johnson, 1996).

FIGURE 4.6. Still from animated underwater vignette.

FIGURE 4.7. Focal fish previously seen viewed against previously seen background (left) or novel background (right).

Change Blindness

A phenomenon called "change blindness" (Simons & Levin, 1997) has been much studied by perceptual psychologists of late. When a picture of a scene and a somewhat altered version of it are presented sequentially, with just a brief pause in between, people can find it very difficult to detect changes that are completely obvious when the two versions are shown side by side. This difficulty seems to be produced by an automatic tendency of the nervous system to render two highly similar scenes into a single consistent picture, something that the visual system constantly does in order to maintain a coherent view of the world. If it is the case that East Asians attend to the field more than do Westerners, then changes in the field, including changes in relationships between objects, should be easier for them to detect. If Westerners focus more on objects and their attributes, then it should be easier for them to detect changes in salient objects. Masuda and I (2006) presented Japanese and American participants with scenes like those in Figures 4.8 and 4.9, which are stills from 20-second animated vignettes. The scene in Figure 4.8 was intended to mimic the object salience of a Western city and that in Figure 4.9 to mimic the field salience, complexity, and interpenetration characteristic of East Asian cities. Other vignettes included an object-salient American farm scene and a field-salient Japanese farm scene. Finally, two scenes intended to be neutral with respect to culture—a construction scene and an airport scene were included.

We measured sensitivity to change by asking participants, after they had seen two versions of the same scene with changes both in salient foreground objects and in relationships between objects and less salient background objects, to tell us which aspects of the scene had changed from the first version of the vignette to the second. An example of an

FIGURE 4.8. Still from animated "American" city vignette in change blindness study.

FIGURE 4.9. Still from animated "Japanese" city vignette in change blindness study.

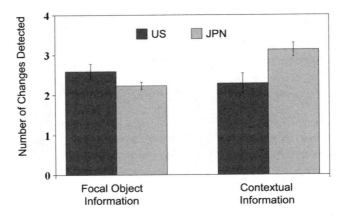

FIGURE 4.10. Focal object and contextual changes detected by Americans (US) and Japanese (JPN).

object change in Figure 4.8 is a change in the front car's hubcaps. An example of a relationship change is relocation of the buildings in the background. An example of a background object change is a change in the type of houses in the background. Figure 4.10 shows the differences in changes perceived by Americans and Japanese. American participants were more likely to detect changes in salient objects than were Japanese participants, who were more likely to detect relationship and environment (context) changes than were Americans.

Environmental "Affordances"

The different environments themselves had an effect on the perception of both Americans and Japanese. As may be seen in Figure 4.11, when the scenes were intended to resemble American environments, both Americans and Japanese found it easier to detect object changes than field changes. When the scenes were intended to resemble Japanese environments, both Americans and Japanese found it easier to detect field changes than object changes. These findings indicate that environmental factors—that is, the "affordances" to perception—may contribute to people's habitual patterns of attention and perception. When the environment affords mostly salient, distinctive objects, it may be that people attend to them more closely than to the field. When objects are more numerous, more complex, and more interpenetrated, the distinction between object and field may become blurred and relationships and background elements relatively salient.

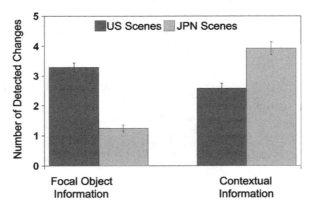

FIGURE 4.11. Focal object and contextual changes detected in "American" (US) and "Japanese" (JPN) environments. Figure combines American and Japanese participants.

The preceding generalizations would be valid only if the scenes that we composed actually capture real differences in Eastern and Western environments. In order to examine this question, Yuri Miyamoto, Taka Masuda, and I (Miyamoto, Nisbett, & Masuda, 2006) took photographs in front of, on each side of, and behind three kinds of buildings—post offices, schools, and hotels—in towns of three different sizes in Japan and America. Total populations were defined for each type of building in pairs of towns that were comparable in many respects across the two nations (New York and Tokyo; the towns of Ann Arbor, Michigan, and its "sister city," Hikone, Japan; and the villages of Chelsea, Michigan, and Torahime, Japan). Buildings were selected at random from the populations of each type. American and East Asian college students were questioned about the photographs, and both groups reported finding Japanese scenes to have more objects and more ambiguous boundaries for objects. Each picture was schematized and assessed for number of objects using the National Institutes of Health Image Program for Macintosh. An example of a schematized picture is shown in Figure 4.12. The number of objects in each picture was assessed based on the number of edges—the more edges, the more objects. The average number of objects defined in this way was 32% greater for Japanese scenes than for American scenes. The differences between Japanese and American scenes were marked at each city size but were especially great for the smaller towns.

To show that the affordance differences of the environment were the reason for the differences in perception of object versus field found

FIGURE 4.12. Schematized rendering of a Japanese street scene for the purpose of assessing number of objects.

by Masuda and I (2006), we (Miyamoto et al., 2006) presented Japanese and American participants with pictures taken either in Japan or in the United States and asked them to report on the changes they saw in the neutral construction site and airport vignettes drawn from the same study. They found, as expected, that participants who were primed with Japanese scenes were relatively more likely to be able to report changes in the field, and participants who were primed with American scenes were more likely to be able to report changes in salient objects. This was true both for Japanese and American participants.

Eye Movements

If Asians and Westerners are seeing different things, maybe they are looking at the world differently. In order to determine whether this was the case, Chua, Boland, and I (2005) showed participants pictures of salient objects in naturalistic scenes (e.g., a cow in a pasture, a jet flying above a landscape). Participants wore a 120-Hertz head-mounted eye-tracker (ISCAN, Burlington, Massachusetts). We were able to record where participants were looking at every moment of the 3-second presentation of stimuli. Americans fixated more quickly and longer on the salient object, whereas Chinese participants fixated more on the background and made many more eye movements between the salient object and the background. The latter finding may account for why the Asians in the Masuda and Nisbett (2001) study tended to bind the object to the field: The object is perceptually embedded in the field more for Asians than for Westerners.

Perception of Everyday-Life Events

The research reported to this point used materials that, to one degree or another, departed from everyday-life objects and events. Chua, Leu, and I (Chua, Nisbett, & Leu, 2005) examined perception and memory of more naturalistic materials. We asked American and Taiwanese college students to describe some personal events (e.g., their first day of the current term), to read and then summarize some narratives (e.g., about a day in the life of a woman in which everything seemed to prevent her from getting to work), and to watch and summarize videos of silent comedies. Taiwanese were randomly selected to write either in Mandarin or in English. The anticipations were that the Americans would make more mentions of the central character than would the Taiwanese and would make more "intentional" statements—that is, statements indicating that the central character had control over a situation or had a desire to achieve control. Taiwanese were expected to make more comments about the emotional states of various characters, reflecting a greater concern with interpersonal relations. The differences between Americans and Taiwanese turned out to be the same sort, regardless of whether personal stories, summarized narratives, or descriptions of the videos were examined. Thus, we added all three of these together for purposes of analysis. It may be seen in Figures 4.13–4.15 that all of the predictions were borne out and that the results were the same whether the Taiwanese answered in Mandarin or in English. This latter finding is consistent with the results of several other studies showing that language used and facility of Asians in English when the testing language is English are not generally predictive of results (Norenzayan et al., 2002).

DISCUSSION

There are substantial differences in the cognitive processes of East Asians and Westerners, including in categorization, causal attribution, and reliance on rules. In my view, these cognitive differences derive in good part from perceptual differences, particularly differences in what is

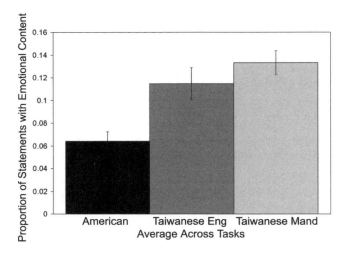

FIGURE 4.13. Number of statements referring to central figures minus number of statements referring to others by American and Taiwanese tested either in English or Mandarin.

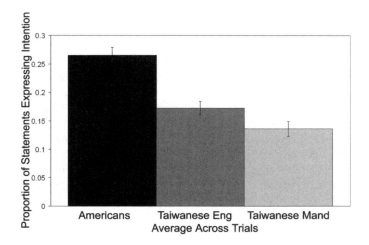

FIGURE 4.14. Proportion of statements with intentional content by Americans and Taiwanese tested either in English or in Mandarin.

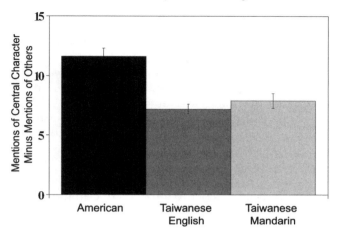

FIGURE 4.15. Proportion of statements with emotional content by Americans and Taiwanese tested either in English or in Mandarin.

attended to. Westerners pay more attention to focal objects, and East Asians pay more attention to the field. Attention to the object encourages categorization of it, application of rules to it, and causal attribution in terms of it. Attention to the field encourages noticing relationships and similarities and prompts causal attribution to take into account context and distal forces. In addition, attention to the field could be expected to make it difficult to segregate a particular object from its field.

In my view, the differences in attention, perception, and cognition are driven by differences in social structure and social practices that prompt Asians to look to the environment and allow Westerners the luxury of attending to a focal object and their goals with respect to it. Sometimes these differences may be caused or enhanced by economic factors. I endorse the speculation by others that East Asians emphasize role relations and social harmony in part because, since ancient times and until quite recently, they have been primarily farmers, and farmers need to get along with one another (Nakamura, 1985; Needham, 1954). In addition, irrigated agriculture, characteristic of much of East Asia throughout its history, requires effective hierarchies, adding vertical constraints to the horizontal constraints within the family and village. Such an emphasis on social concerns might have sustained itself in part out of sheer inertia.

Ancient Greece's economy was quite different from that of ancient East Asia. Consisting substantially of mountains descending to the sea, Greece did not lend itself to large-scale agriculture. Common occupations such as hunting, fishing, trading, and keeping kitchen gardens did not require extensive social collaboration. In the absence of substantial social constraints, attention to a focal object and one's goals in relation to it were luxuries that the Greeks could afford. Many aspects of Western industrial and postindustrial economies in the last 200 years are also characterized by relatively few social constraints, at least for those in middle-class and professional occupations.

I believe that there is a causal chain running from economy and social structure to social practice to attention to cognition. In support of this view, Knight, Varnum, and I (2005) examined categorization by Eastern Europeans and Western Europeans, asking them to group items on the basis of taxonomic category or relationships. Eastern Europeans are in general more interdependent and collectivist than Western Europeans (Triandis, 1995), and we might expect that they would categorize more like East Asians than would Western Europeans. This is what was found. Similarly, we compared the categorization of southern Italians and northern Italians. Southern Italians are more interdependent and collectivist than northern Italians (Gramsci, 1957; Putnam, 1993), and we would expect them to categorize in a fashion more nearly resembling that of East Asians than of northern Italians; again, this is what was found. Finally, working-class people are more interdependent and collectivist than middle-class people (Kohn & Schooler, 1969; Triandis, McCusker, & Hui, 1990), and we would therefore expect them to categorize in a fashion more like that of East Asians than of middle-class people. This theory was tested with the Italian sample and was found to be true for southern Italians but not for northern Italians.

I suspect that the psychology of the future will continue to focus as much on cultural differences as on individual differences within cultures. The rigorous methodology and the rich ideas of Walter Mischel will surely influence cultural psychology in much the same way that they have shaped individual difference psychology.

ACKNOWLEDGMENTS

This material is based on work supported by the National Science Foundation under Grant Nos. SBR 9729103 and BCS 0132074, Grant No. AG15047 from the National Institute of Aging, and support from the Russell Sage Foundation and a John Simon Guggenheim Fellowship. An earlier version of this chapter appeared in the *Proceedings of the National Academy of Sciences of the United States of America*.

REFERENCES

Cha, J.-H., & Nam, K. D. (1985). A test of Kelley's cube theory of attribution: A cross-cultural replication of McArthur's study. *Korean Social Science Journal, 12,* 151–180.

Chalfonte, B. L., & Johnson, M. K. (1996). Feature memory and binding in young and older adults. *Memory and Cognition, 24,* 403–416.

Chiu, L.-H. (1972). A cross-cultural comparison of cognitive styles in Chinese and American children. *International Journal of Psychology, 7,* 235–242.

Choi, I., & Nisbett, R. E. (1998). Situational salience and cultural differences in the correspondence bias and in the actor–observer bias. *Personality and Social Psychology Bulletin, 24,* 949–960.

Choi, I., Nisbett, R. E., & Norenzayan, A. (1999). Causal attribution across cultures: Variation and universality. *Psychological Bulletin, 125,* 47–63.

Chua, H. F., Boland, J. E., & Nisbett, R. E. (2005). Cultural variation in eye movements during scene perception. *Proceedings of the National Academy of Sciences of the United States of America, 102,* 12629–12633.

Chua, H. F., Nisbett, R. E., & Leu, J. (2005). Culture and diverging views of social events. *Personality and Social Psychology Bulletin, 31,* 925–934.

Cousins, S. D. (1989). Culture and self-perception in Japan and the United States. *Journal of Personality and Social Psychology, 56,* 124–131.

Cromer, A. (1993). *Uncommon sense: The heretical nature of science.* New York: Oxford University Press.

Fernald, A., & Morikawa, H. (1993). Common themes and cultural variations in Japanese and American mothers' speech to infants. *Child Development, 64,* 637–656.

Fiske, A. P., Kitayama, S., Markus, H. R., & Nisbett, R. E. (1998). The cultural matrix of social psychology. In D. T. Gilbert, S. T. Fiske, & G. Lindzey (Eds.), *Handbook of social psychology* (4th ed., pp. 915–981). Boston: McGraw-Hill.

Fung, Y. (1983). *A history of Chinese philosophy* (Vols. 1–2; D. Bodde, Trans.). Princeton, NJ: Princeton University Press.

Gramsci, A. (1957). *La questione meridionale.* Rome: Editori Riuniti.

Hall, E. T. (1976). *Beyond culture.* New York: Anchor Books.

Hsu, F. L. K. (1953). *Americans and Chinese: Two ways of life.* New York: Schuman.

Hsu, F. L. K. (1981). *Americans and Chinese: Passage to differences.* Honolulu: University of Hawaii Press.

Ji, L.-J., Peng, K., & Nisbett, R. E. (2000). Culture, control, and perception of relationships in the environment. *Journal of Personality and Social Psychology, 78,* 943–955.

Ji, L.-J., Zhang, Z., & Nisbett, R. E. (2004). Is it culture or is it language? Examination of language effects in cross-cultural research on categorization. *Journal of Personality and Social Psychology, 87,* 57–65.

Kanagawa, C., Cross, S. E., & Markus, H. R. (2001). "Who am I?": The cultural psychology of the concept of self. *Personality and Social Psychology Bulletin, 27,* 90–103.

Kim, H., & Markus, H. R. (1999). Deviance or uniqueness, harmony or conformity?: A cultural analysis. *Journal of Personality and Social Psychology, 77*, 785–800.

Knight, N., Varnum, M. E. W., & Nisbett, R. E. (2005). *Culture and class effects on categorization*. Ann Arbor: University of Michigan.

Kohn, M. L., & Schooler, C. (1969). Class, occupation, and orientation. *American Sociological Review, 34*, 657–678.

Lee, F., Hallahan, M., & Herzog, T. (1996). Explaining real life events: How culture and domain shape attributions. *Personality and Social Psychology Bulletin, 22*, 732–741.

Lloyd, G. E. R. (1990). *Demystifying mentalities*. New York: Cambridge University Press.

Lloyd, G. E. R. (1991b). *Methods and problems in Greek science*. Cambridge, UK: Cambridge University Press.

Markus, H. R., & Kitayama, S. (1991a). Cultural variation in the self-concept. In J. Strauss & G. R. Goethals (Eds.), *The self: Interdisciplinary approaches*. New York: Springer-Verlag.

Markus, H. R., & Kitayama, S. (1991b). Culture and the self: Implications for cognition, emotion, and motivation. *Psychological Review, 98*, 224–253.

Masuda, T., & Nisbett, R. E. (2001). Attending holistically vs. analytically: Comparing the context sensitivity of Japanese and Americans. *Journal of Personality and Social Psychology, 81*, 922–934.

Masuda, T., & Nisbett, R. E. (2006). Culture and change blindness. *Cognitive Science, 30*, 381–399.

Miyamoto, Y., Nisbett, R. E., & Masuda, T. (2006). Culture and physical environment: Holistic versus analytic perceptual affordances. *Psychological Science, 17*, 113–119.

Morris, M. W., & Peng, K. (1994). Culture and cause: American and Chinese attributions for social and physical events. *Journal of Personality and Social Psychology, 67*, 949–971.

Munro, D. J. (1969). *The concept of man in early China*. Stanford, CA: Stanford University Press.

Munro, D. J. (1985). Introduction. In D. Munro (Ed.), *Individualism and holism: Studies in Confucian and Taoist Values* (pp. 1–34). Ann Arbor: Center for Chinese Studies, University of Michigan.

Nakamura, H. (1985). *Ways of thinking of eastern peoples*. Honolulu: University of Hawaii Press. (Original work published 1964).

Needham, J. (1954). *Science and civilisation in China* (Vol. 1). Cambridge, UK: Cambridge University Press.

Nisbett, R. E. (2003). *The geography of thought: How Asians and Westerners think differently . . . and why*. New York: The Free Press.

Nisbett, R. E., Peng, K., Choi, I., & Norenzayan, A. (2001). Culture and systems of thought: Holistic vs. analytic cognition. *Psychological Review, 108*, 291–310.

Norenzayan, A., Choi, I., & Nisbett, R. E. (1999). Eastern and Western perceptions of causality for social behavior: Lay theories about personalities and social situations. In D. Prentice & D. Miller (Eds.), *Cultural divides: Understanding and overcoming group conflict* (pp. 239–272). New York: Sage.

Norenzayan, A., & Nisbett, R. E. (2000). Culture and causal cognition. *Current Directions in Psychological Science, 9,* 132–135.

Norenzayan, A., Smith, E. E., Kim, B. J., & Nisbett, R. E. (2002). Cultural preferences for formal versus intuitive reasoning. *Cognitive Science, 26,* 653–684.

Peng, K., & Knowles, E. (in press). Culture, ethnicity, and the attribution of physical causality. *Personality and Social Psychology Bulletin.*

Peng, K., & Nisbett, R. E. (2002). *Culture and perception of physical causality.* Unpublished manuscript, University of California, Berkeley.

Putnam, R. D. (1993). *Making democracy work: Civic traditions in modern Italy.* Princeton, NJ: Princeton University Press.

Sanchez-Burks, J., Lee, F., Choi, I., Nisbett, R. E., Zhao, S., & Jasook, K. (2003). Conversing across cultural ideologies: East–West communication styles in work and non-work contexts. *Journal of Personality and Social Psychology, 85,* 363–372.

Shih, H. (1919). *Chung-kuo che-hsueh shi ta-kang* [An outline of the history of Chinese philosophy]. Shanghai: Commercial Press.

Simons, D. J., & Levin, D. T. (1997). Change blindness. *Trends in Cognitive Sciences, 1,* 261–267.

Triandis, H. C. (1989). The self and social behavior in differing cultural contexts. *Psychological Review, 96,* 269–289.

Triandis, H. C. (1995). *Individualism and collectivism.* Boulder, CO: Westview Press.

Triandis, H. C., McCusker, C., & Hui, C. H. (1990). Multimethod probes of individualism and collectivism: Cross-cultural perspectives on self-in group relationships. *Journal of Personality and Social Psychology, 59,* 1006–1020.

Witkin, H. A., Lewis, H. B., Hertzman, M., Machover, K., Meissner, P. B., & Karp, S. A. (1954). *Personality through perception.* New York: Harper.

5

From Persons and Situations to Preferences and Constraints

RICHARD A. SHWEDER

For those who have a taste for the conceptual foundations of personality theory, 1968 and 1973 were vintage years. All the fun began, especially for those who imbibe explanatory theories of individual differences in behavior, when Walter Mischel published his monumental book-length critique of trait psychology, *Personality and Assessment* (1968), and then followed it up with a now classic *Psychological Review* article (1973) in which he aimed to "reconceptualize personality." In this brief chapter, I want to say a few words about what I see as the preeminent take-home message of Mischel's 1973 reconceptualization.

Mischel's main message, as I interpret it, is this: Explanatory (and predictive) success in personality psychology and social psychology requires that both disciplines revise their most basic (and shared) explanatory model, the "person–situation" model. That explanatory model is based on the assumption that all human behavior is a joint function of two mutually exclusive (separable, independent) and exhaustive causal factors, namely, inside-the-person vectors (such as global personality traits) × outside-the-person situational demands. As an alternative, both disciplines should seriously consider adopting a "preference–constraint" model of explanation, which is based on the assumption that all variations in human behavior (including individual differences) are a joint function of variations in individual preferences (ends or goals) × variations in constraints (means of various sorts) as mediated by human understanding and human agency. Special attention should be given to purposeful strategic actions motivated by our capacity for instrumental or means–ends reasoning and other aspects of human rationality.

Before I develop the story of Walter Mischel's invitation to substitute a "preference–constraint" model of explanation for a "person–situation" model, permit me to make a comment about one aspect of his famous book. To do so even minimally requires that I initially hazard a definition of the concept of an abstract mental state because the abstract mental states of personality trait psychology are the central object of Mischel's critical concerns.

MISCHEL'S CRITIQUE OF ABSTRACT MENTAL STATE CONCEPTS

By a mental state concept (such as "the feeling of anxiety" or "the desire to be dependent" or "valuing honesty"), in contrast to a physical state concept (such as "mass," "weight," or "gravity") or a mathematical state concept (such as "zero"), I mean a concept that refers to or is about something a person knows, wants, thinks, feels, or values as good or bad (e.g., that she feels afraid or that she wants others to support and take care of her rather than to do things for or by herself). By an *abstract* mental state concept, I mean a mental state concept that refers to something a person might know, want, think, feel, or value (e.g., feeling afraid) apart from any particular or concrete instance of it (e.g., feeling afraid to take financial risks on the stock market or feeling afraid of frogs).

In *Personality and Assessment*, Mischel challenged his readers to explain why, when ecologically valid behavior–observational evidence is available for examination, particular or concrete instances or manifestations of the same abstract mental state concept do not typically co-occur to even a moderate degree across individual differences in mental functioning and behavior. He brought to everyone's attention a provocative pattern of empirical findings that might be illustrated as follows: The person who is more likely than others to get angry when contradicted in an argument is not typically the person who is more likely than others to get angry when cut in front of in line. The person who feels more anxious than others while sitting in a dentist's chair is not typically the person who is more likely than others to feel anxious when standing in a crowded elevator. The child who is more likely than others to seek help from his or her teacher is not typically the child who is more likely than others to seek help from his or her peers. The financial risk taker is not typically a social risk taker; the intellectual risk taker is not typically a physical risk taker and vice versa.

Personality theory, when viewed as a theory of individual differences, is concerned with describing and explaining those mental states or processes that are both relatively stable in, and distinctive of, an individual person. By design, Mischel's provocative book invited us to have doubts about the role and value of abstract mental state concepts (e.g., the need for affiliation) in predicting and accounting for variations in behavioral outcomes (e.g., the likelihood that someone will seek or take advantage of this or that particular opportunity for social contact). In effect, one finished the book pondering the following question: If abstract mental states do not organize and motivate individual behavior, then precisely what types of mental states do?

SOME CRITICAL RESPONSES TO THE CRITIQUE

Mischel's critique of abstract mental states and global personality trait theory provoked many responses, including objections and calls for clarification. In this chapter, I plan to focus entirely on what I take to be the major point of his *Psychological Review* clarification (1973) and will not address those objections, some of which I consider sound, logical, and legitimate. For example, I agree that Mischel's doubts about the role and value of abstract mental state concepts as explanatory concepts do not necessarily follow from the empirical finding that particular case-based and context-embedded instances of an abstract mental state (taking financial risks in poker, taking intellectual risks in a debate, taking social risks in dating, taking physical risks on a ski slope) do not typically correlate in an impressively positive direction or hang together as a behavioral package deal across individual differences in risk-taking behavior.

The philosopher William Alston (1975) surely has a point when he writes with regard to mental state concepts such as needs, desires, expectations, interests, values, attitudes, and abilities that

> an ability is typically manifest in its exercise, a need in efforts to satisfy it, a favorable attitude in actions directed to promoting or benefiting its object. Nevertheless it is not part of what we *mean* in attributing (even a strong degree) of some ability, need, or attitude that such manifestations will frequently occur. A person may have abilities he rarely exercises. Thus a man may be a crack pistol shot, but because he doesn't have a pistol or because of lack of interest, rarely exercises his ability. A person may have a strong need for close relationships, but because of fear of rejection rarely or never seeks to satisfy it. (p. 22)

Taking this type of critical response one step further, consider a personality descriptive sentence of the form "So and so is disposed to act [name here a dispositional quality associated with an abstract mental state concept: for example, aggressively] in social situations." One agrees with Alston that an accurate translation of that sentence might state that the person is more likely than not to do something or other that is aggressive, and that the sentence does not imply that he or she will not be selective in the type of way that he or she aggresses.

Alston's particulars seem especially apt to me, in part because they exemplify some potential explanatory features of a preference–constraint model of precisely the sort that Mischel endorses (or so I argue below). In general, a preference–constraint model of explanation allows that variations in behavior might be caused either by variations in constraints (holding preferences constant), variations in preferences (holding constraints constant), or both. It is noteworthy that the field of microeconomics is defined in part by a specialized version of a preference–constraint model of explanation according to which one tries ones best to explain all variations in behavior as instrumental (rational means–ends) responses to variations in constraints (e.g., available material and symbolic resources, social capital, personal skills, causal beliefs). This mode of explanation is based on the assumption that (at some very high order of abstraction) the ordering of preferences (the desired ends or goals) for members of a population can be viewed as shared and stable and that any supposed end can always be re-interpreted as a means (to some other end), ad infinitum (thereby making it possible for all behavior to be explained in instrumental terms).

Perhaps it is debatable whether that specialized economic application of a preference–constraint model is always justified, based as it is on the assumption that all differences in behavior are adaptive responses to differences in constraints and should thus be interpreted as byproducts of the application of instrumental reasoning in the fulfillment of fixed preferences or ends. Mischel appears to embrace the preference–constraint model of explanation in its more general or inclusive sense, whereby changes in either preferences or constraints might be invoked to explain changes in behavior. Nevertheless, it is worth noting that at least one powerful way to explain interindividual and intraindividual variations in behavior is by reference to instrumental means–ends thinking and by focusing theoretical attention on variations in constraints (the means that are or are not available for attaining a given end). Alston's examples—the marksman who lacks the physical resource (the pistol) to make manifest his skill or the person whose need for close relationships is rarely exhibited in behavior because he or she subscribes to the substantive causal belief (which is itself a "constraint" on that person's behavior) that social initiative results in rejection—focus our attention in precisely that way.

DISPOSITIONAL AND NONDISPOSITIONAL REPRESENTATIONS OF THE "PERSON"

Alston raises many other points with regard to Mischel's critique of personality trait theory. For example, he is uncertain whether the critique is merely an objection to the generality or breadth of the proposed abstract mental state concepts in the personality literature ("risk taker" rather than "financial risk taker in a game of poker"; "extroverted" rather than "likes to talk before groups of wealthy patrons") or whether it is also an objection to the tendency to characterize individual differences (whether general or specific, broad or narrow) exclusively in dispositional terms. Alston notes that to say that a person has a certain "disposition" (e.g., conscientiousness) is to assert that if he or she is in a certain type of situation, he or she will emit a certain type of response (plus the minimal assumption of all personality theory that there must be some mental state or other that is either recurrent or relatively stable in that person's constitution, causing the emission of that type of response). Quite significantly, Alston notes that a "personality" can be conceptualized in either dispositional or nondispositional terms.

In clarifying the distinction between dispositional and nondispositional representations, Alston uses the example of the fragility of a physical object. Thus, he states, the quality of

> fragility is construed dispositionally when we think of x's being fragile simply as the truth of the hypothetical proposition, "If x is struck sharply x will break." But if we can discover what micro-structure of x is responsible for the truth of that hypothetical proposition, we can think of the same attribute in non-dispositional terms.

Applying that distinction to theories of personality, one might suggest that a "person" can, in theory, always be represented dispositionally: as a structured list of response tendencies to behave in certain ways in certain types of situations. Alternatively, a "person" can, in theory, always be represented nondispositionally: as an "agent" with a latent preference–constraint cognitive microstructure, a mental being motivated by his or her desires/goals, beliefs, feelings, values, skills, and other resources whose behavior is the outcome of choices made in the pursuit of valued ends in the face of some limited set of means for or constraints on the reaching of those ends.

Construed in those terms, one way to formulate my view of the main take-home message of Mischel's reconceptualization of personality theory is as follows: namely, that once we are able to produce a valid nondispositional representation of the latent cognitive microstructure of human behavior (for example, in terms of goals, causal beliefs, or expectations of success), it will become obvious why dispositional representations of individual differences in observable behavior in particular situations cannot rely on abstract mental state concepts (such as an abstract ability to resist temptation or exercise self-control) if they are to be useful from a predictive point of view. Why that should be obvious will become clearer once I am more explicit about Mischel's reconceptualization of personality theory, but it has something to do with the explanatory importance of what Clifford Geertz (1973) (following Gilbert Ryle) has called "thick description." The more detailed the representation of a person's preferences and constraints, the more apparent it becomes why (for example) different occasions to take risks either did or did not result in the same level of risk-taking behavior.

A FINAL PRELIMINARY REMARK: THE SYSTEMATIC DISTORTION HYPOTHESIS

One final preliminary remark is in order. My original interest in Walter Mischel's critique of global personality trait theory arose in the context of language and thought studies in anthropology, where Roy D'Andrade had pointed to personality trait theory as an example of the confusion of propositions about language with propositions about the world. I do not plan to extensively address what came to be called the systematic distortion hypothesis or discuss in any detail its connection to debates about the evidence (or lack of it) supporting a global trait theory of individual differences.

Roy D'Andrade first proposed the systematic distortion hypothesis in 1965, and both he and I were working on the topic between 1968 and 1973 when Mischel's critique of global personality trait theory burst forth on the academic scene (e.g., D'Andrade 1965, 1974; Shweder 1975, 1981; Shweder & D'Andrade, 1980, 1987). In effect, this hypothesis complemented Mischel's critique by providing a "method effect" explanation for much of the existing evidence in the personality psychology literature that purports to support global personality trait theories.

In the personality psychology literature, the interitem covariance clusters, factors, syndromes, dimensions, or traits (for example "extroversion": active, outgoing, assertive, gives parties a lot, likes speaking before groups) discovered by correlation analyses of subject response patterns on recall-based personality-rating tasks are typically interpreted as evidence of broad or global personality dispositions in the organization and motivation of individual behavior. The systematic distortion hypothesis proposes an alternative interpretation: (1) error in judgment, inference, and memory on personality-rating tasks is not only sufficiently frequent to influence the structure of interitem covariations, but also systematically biased in the direction of preexisting highly schematic and oversimplified understandings about how language and reality are organized (e.g., the folk understanding that "friendliness" and "aggression" do not go together, while "domination" and "aggression" do); and (2) those schematic understandings (many of which are derived from lay notions about the components of meanings of words such as "friendly," "aggressive," and "dominating") are not very good maps of actual interitem covariations across individual differences in human mental states and behavior (for example, friendliness and aggressiveness are often positively correlated in actual behavior, and dominance hierarchies may actually reduce the frequency of aggressive behavior).

The following claim is common to both the systematic distortion hypothesis and Mischel's critique of personality trait theory in his 1968 book: the closer one gets to ecologically valid on-line evidence of mental functioning and behavior, the less it looks *broadly* trait-like in its organization. Mischel's critique brought to our attention the rather low or insignificant intercorrelations in actual behavior among different instances of the same abstract mental state, while the systematic distortion hypothesis treated as dubious and problematic ("halo effect"-like) the rather high positive intercorrelations among specific abstract mental state indicators on memory-based personality-rating forms.

"THIS IS IT": FROM PERSONS AND SITUATIONS TO PREFERENCES AND CONSTRAINTS

I have recently located an old and very marked up personal copy of Mischel's 1973 classic article. Some decades ago, I had scribbled the phrase "This is it" at several places in the margins. In identifying the central message of Mischel's reconceptualization of personality theory, I am going to focus on a few of those places.

This Is It: A Dubious Distinction, Person–Situation

Mischel (1973) wrote:

> Is information about individuals more important than information about situations? The author has persistently refrained from posing this question because phrased that way it is unanswerable and can only serve to stimulate futile polemics. Moreover, in current debates on this topic, "situations" are often erroneously invoked as entities that supposedly exert either major or only minor control over behavior, without specifying what, psychologically, they are or how they function. (p. 255)

I have already previewed his main reconceptualization message, which is not primarily that abstract mental states are weak causal factors in the explanation of individual differences in behavior. His message is much more profound because it calls for a shift in metatheoretical assumptions about the nature of the person in both personality and social psychology (see Shweder & Sullivan, 1990). His message is that there are good reasons for moving from a model of explanation in which behavior is assumed to be the by-product of person variables and situational variables to a model of explanation in which behavior is assumed to be a by-product of preferences and constraints. The first explanatory model (behavior is a function of person × situation) conceptualizes the person as a vessel for autonomous mental states or response dispositions. The second explanatory model (behavior is a function of preferences × constraints) conceptualizes the person as a purposeful agent whose behavior in any context can best be explained by reference to aspects of human rationality, including instrumental means–ends thinking.

In the above quotation, Mischel expresses some forebodings about the person–situation distinction. Not only does he avoid trying to answer an unanswerable question (about the relative importance of person versus situation in the control and regulation of behavior), but he also suggests why the question is unanswerable. The distinction between person and situation (which presupposes that all relevant causal forces are either person forces or situational forces but not both) makes it impossible coherently to pose the key question, which he tries to formulate by asking how situations function psychologically.

Posing the question that way means that the fabric of contrast between a person and a situation begins to unravel; the situation is now at least partly a mentally mediated fact inside the person, and the person (including the meaning of things to that person) is not fully separable from one's description of the situation. The situation must now be represented or described in person-centered mental terms and no longer can be said to be external. In asking how situations function psychologically,

Mischel reveals that he is reaching for new units for causal analysis that circumvent the person–situation divide. Those units of analysis, describing the nondispositional cognitive microstructure of personality are indeed different and paradigm shattering because they derive from a preference–constraint perspective on the explanation of behavior. The irony is that, within the terms of the person–situation metalanguage, the call to study how situations function psychologically may appear to require the dissolution of the very definitional boundary between person and situation that is presupposed by that model of explanation. That irony suggests the need for a new metalanguage.

This Is It: Preferences and Constraints, Thick Description, and the Native Point of View

Here are three more quotations from Mischel's (1973) reconceptualization of personality essay:

> Rather than argue about the existence of "consistency," it would be more constructive to analyze and study the cognitive and social learning conditions that seem to foster—and to undermine—its occurrence. (p. 259)

> When the probable reinforcing consequences to the person for cheating, waiting, or working differ widely across situations depending on the particular task or circumstances, the behavior of others, the likelihood of detection, the probable consequences of being caught, the frustration induced, the value of success, etc., impressive generality will not be found. Conversely, when similar behaviors are expected and supported in numerous situations, consistency will be obtained. Because most social behaviors produce positive consequences in some situations but negative ones in other contexts, the relatively low associations found among an individual's response patterns even in seemingly similar situations should not be surprising. (p. 259)

> One type of expectancy concerns *behavior-outcome expectancies* under particular conditions. These behavior-outcome expectancies (hypotheses, contingency rules) represent the "if___; then ___" relations between behavioral alternatives and probable outcomes anticipated with regard to particular behavioral possibilities in particular situations. In any given situation, the person will generate the response pattern which he expects is most likely to lead to the most subjectively valuable outcomes. (p. 270)

Let me add one other quotation, from a Mischel and Mischel essay on morality and self-regulation (1976):

Even the noblest altruism still depends on expected consequences, although the consequences are often temporally distant, are not in the immediate external environment, and are not easily identified, and reside in the actor himself rather than in social agents.

I can now conclude this chapter by explicating the obvious. Mischel's reconceptualization of personality, is based on a preference–constraint metalanguage and model of explanation. He moves away from the received approach in personality and social psychology that tries to predict and explain behaviors from a combination of external situational forces and internal personality traits. He opts instead for a preference–constraint metatheory of human motivation and tries to predict and explain behavior from a combination of ends or goals of the agent and available cognized means and resources. All personality traits, dispositions, or response mode summaries, whether broad or narrow (from a cross-situational or cross–response–mode point of view) become grist for a nondispositional exegesis. You don't describe a person as "clumsy"; instead, you give an account of his or her preferences (What if the goal was to look like a clown?) and constraints (for example, the skills he or she lacks or possesses to navigate smoothly). Observed behavior is rendered intelligible through an interpretative analysis that makes reference to what the person thinks, feels, wants, and values (as good or bad) as a meaning maker, the "semiotic subject" of personality theory (Shweder & Sullivan, 1990). Once the agent of behavior (and subject of personality theory) is conceptualized in terms of his or her preferences and constraints, the instrumental rationality and the means–ends thinking of both the agent and the personality theorist come to play a central role in explanations of behavior. As a personality theorist, one is encouraged to construct an accurate nondispositional representation of the microstructure of human personality, which is very likely to be a "thick description" of preferences and constraints (including "behavior-outcome expectancies," available skills, causal beliefs, etc.) from a "native point of view." Speaking as a cultural anthropologist and cultural psychologist who regularly attends the economists' "rational choice" workshop at the University of Chicago, it seems to me that all this makes very good sense.

REFERENCES

Alston, W. P. (1975). Traits, consistency and conceptual alternatives for personality theory. *Journal for a Theory of Social Behavior, 5,* 17–48.

D'Andrade, R. G. (1965). Trait psychology and componential analysis. *American Anthropologist, 67,* 215–228.

D'Andrade, R. G. (1974). Memory and the assessment of behavior. In T. Blalock (Ed.), *Social measurement* (pp. 159–186). Chicago: Aldine-Atherton.

Geertz, C. (1973). Thick description: Toward an interpretive theory of culture. In C. Geertz, *The interpretation of cultures* (pp. 3–32). New York: Basic Books.

Mischel, W. (1968). *Personality and assessment.* New York: Wiley.

Mischel, W. (1973). Toward a cognitive social learning theory reconceptualization of personality. *Psychological Review, 80,* 252–283.

Mischel, W., & Mischel, H. N. (1976). A cognitive social learning approach to morality and self-regulation. In T. Lickona (Ed.), *Moral development and behavior* (pp. 84–107). New York: Holt, Rinehart & Winston.

Shweder, R. A. (1975). How relevant is an individual difference theory of personality? *Journal of Personality, 43,* 455–484.

Shweder, R. A. (1981). Fact and artifact in trait perception: The systematic distortion distortion hypothesis. In B. Maher (Ed.), *Progress in experimental personality research* (Vol. 11, pp. 65–106). New York: Wiley.

Shweder, R. A., & D'Andrade, R. G. (1980). The systematic distortion hypothesis. In R. A. Shweder (Ed.), *Fallible judgment in behavioral research. Special issue of New Directions for Methodology of Social and Behavior Sciences,* No. 4. San Francisco: Jossey-Bass.

Shweder, R. A., & D'Andrade, R. G. (1987). *The systematic distortion hypothesis: A clarification and update.* Unpublished Manuscript.

Shweder, R. A., & Sullivan, M. (1990). The semiotic subject of cultural psychology. In L. Pervin (Ed.), *Handbook of personality: theory and research* (pp. 399–416). New York: Guilford Press.

SELF-REGULATION
From Willpower to a System

6

Delay of Gratification in Children

Contributions to Social–Personality Psychology

OZLEM AYDUK

W alter Mischel's impact on person–situation interactionism in personality psychology is well known. A lesser-known area of his research but with no less importance is his experimental and longitudinal studies of young children's ability to delay gratification. It is this latter topic that I collaborated on with him over the past 10 years and that I focus on in this chapter, first briefly describing the research paradigm and summarizing its main findings, then discussing the major themes that emerged from it and their importance in a historical context. Finally, I provide a summary of where the longitudinal research program on delay currently is and the new directions in which it is being expanded.

THE PRESCHOOL DELAY OF GRATIFICATION PARADIGM AND ITS BASIC FINDINGS

In this paradigm, preschoolers are given a choice between an immediately available but smaller reward and a delayed but larger reward (Mischel, 1974). Children who choose the delayed reward are then presented with a contingency. They are told that the experimenter will leave the room for a while and that, to get the larger reward, they will have to wait for the experimenter to come back on his or her own. They can call back the experimenter at any time by ringing a bell, but then they only get the small reward. After it is made sure that children understand this contingency, they are left alone and the number of seconds they can wait is measured. Note that children do not know how long the wait is going to be (it varies between 15 and 20 minutes depending on the child's age) and that they have continuous free choice to reverse their initial preference, ring the bell, and settle for the smaller reward.

In longitudinal studies, individual differences in delay ability, measured by seconds children were able to wait, predict positive outcomes years later, including greater socioemotional competence and higher SAT scores (Mischel, Shoda, & Peake, 1988; Shoda, Mischel, & Peake, 1990). Given the links early delay ability has to consequential life outcomes longitudinally, the question of what processes underlie this ability becomes all the more important.

Between 1968 and 1972 a series of experiments was conducted with children attending Stanford University's Bing Nursery School to examine the processes that facilitated or hindered the ability to delay gratification (Mischel, Shoda, & Rodriguez, 1989; see Mischel & Ayduk, 2004, for review). This program of research identified two relevant classes of strategies, one where attention is focused on and the other where it is diverted from the rewards or their appetitive features. These studies showed that if a child focuses attention on the consummatory, emotion-eliciting, "hot" features of the rewards he or she is waiting for (thinking, for example, about how yummy and chewy marshmallows are), temptation increases, making waiting difficult and leading most children to terminate the delay period. In contrast, if the focus is on the cognitive, informational, and "cool" features of the rewards (thinking about the marshmallows as white, puffy clouds), the tempting features of the situation are less salient, making delay easier and increasing waiting times (e.g., Mischel & Baker, 1975). Similarly, if children move attention away from the reward altogether through self-distraction (for example, thinking about happy memories, such as the last time they were pushed on a swing), there is less of a dilemma between wanting to wait and wanting to have the reward; under such minimal temptation, delay times again increase (Mischel, Ebbesen, & Zeiss, 1972).

The same processes have been documented to underlie individual differences in delay ability. In a study examining delay behavior among adolescent boys with behavioral problems, Rodriguez, Mischel, and Shoda (1989) observed and coded for children's spontaneous attention deployment strategies during the delay task. They found that children were able to delay gratification to the extent that they deployed their attention away from the rewards via self-distraction. Children who spent most of their time looking at the rewards or the bell to summon the experimenter could not wait more than a few minutes.

The long-term associations observed between ability to delay gratification and positive life outcomes make it evident how this research has
significantly contributed to our understanding of the mechanisms and
the developmental course of self-regulatory competencies. In addition,
there are several themes that emerge from this work that underscore
Walter Mischel's theoretical contributions to social and personality psychology at large.

EMERGING THEMES
AND THEIR CONTRIBUTIONS

A Social-Cognitive Framework

By 1972, most of the experimental work on delay of gratification had been
completed. This was before the social-cognitive revolution (e.g., Higgins
& Bargh, 1987) had taken complete root and before basic principles about
knowledge activation and the concepts of availability and accessibility
were clearly articulated and commonly used in the literature, but Mischel's
experiments were using these concepts and illustrating their operation. In
different experiments, children were instructed, or, in social-cognitive
terms, were "primed" with particular strategies. Typically, the experimenter would deliver the experimental manipulation by a subtle suggestion as to what the child might want to think about while waiting. These
priming manipulations had profound effects on the amount of time children were able to wait. For example, when children were asked to bring to
mind fun thoughts during the waiting period (e.g., "If you want to, while
you wait), you can think of the last time your mommy pushed you on the
swing"), they were able to delay almost up to the criterion period of 15
minutes, whereas children who were not primed with self-distraction
could not sustain delay beyond the first few minutes (Mischel et al., 1972).
That children in a particular experimental group waited more or less time
for the reward indicates that knowledge structures about these strategies
were *available* to most children and were made *temporarily accessible* by
the experimenter's subtle ideation suggestions.

There were also clear individual differences in the *chronic accessibility* of these strategies. When experimenters did not prime any particular way of thinking about the rewards, different children used different
strategies to be able to wait—some used more hot than cool, others
more cool than hot strategies, and these individual differences were
meaningfully related to life outcomes even years later (Shoda et al.,
1990; Mischel et al., 1988).

In summary, Mischel's work on delay of gratification was ahead of
its time in that it examined the processes underlying the ability to self-

regulate both as a state and as stable individual differences, representing one of, if not the first, social-cognitive-oriented research programs in social–personality psychology.

The Power of the Situation: Malleability of Self-Regulatory Behavior

The delay-of-gratification studies also illustrate the power of the situation with regard to self-regulatory behavior. Most of the children at Bing participated in multiple studies, and their delay behavior varied greatly depending on the experimental situation. A child who was able to wait for only a few seconds in a study where rewards were exposed was able to wait up to the criterion time of 15 minutes in another in which the rewards were hidden or when he or she was primed to think abstractly about the rewards.

The pessimistic interpretation of these findings is that self-regulatory behavior is under the control of the situation, that there is no will to overcome the push and pull of external constraints. A more optimistic view of these findings is that self-regulatory behavior is malleable, that simple changes in the environment can modify our behavior in more adaptive ways, and that people can potentially be taught more effective self-regulatory skills. It is this latter interpretation that reflects Walter Mischel's long-lasting interest in humans' capacity for change and positive growth.

The Power of Mental Representations

Although some delay studies show how children's self-regulatory behavior can easily be modulated by subtle situational cues, the message of others is that it is how those cues are mentally represented in the mind that will be the final determinant of behavior.

Initial delay studies (Mischel & Ebbesen, 1970) showed that when rewards (whether delayed or not) were available for attention (i.e., exposed to the children), children had a particularly difficult time delaying gratification because the physical presence of the rewards increased temptation and frustration, leading children often to sabotage their good intentions to wait for the larger rewards. When the rewards were covered (e.g., put underneath a cloth), the situation became much more bearable because children's attention was distracted from temptation.

But is the objective situation (e.g., presence versus absence of rewards for attention) or how the situation is subjectively construed by the children a stronger determinant of delay behavior? To examine this question, Mischel and his colleagues ran a number of studies. In one study (Moore, Mischel, & Zeiss, 1976), experimenters suggested to the children who had the rewards in front of them to put a frame around the rewards in their head, like in a picture. In another condition, children had life-size pictures of the rewards, but experimenters suggested that they make believe the real rewards (not the pictures) were there in front of them. Children who thought about the actual rewards as pictures were able to delay for almost 18 minutes; among those who pretended the rewards were real, even though they were just pictures, the average delay time was less than 6 minutes.

In another study, Mischel and Baker (1975) cued children looking at the real rewards iin one of two ways: either to think of the rewards in terms of their hot, consummatory features (e.g., "If you want to, when you want to, you can think about how sweet and chewy the marshmallows taste") or their cool, cognitive features (e.g., "If you want to, when you want to, you can think about how the marshmallows look like white puffy clouds"). Whereas children primed with cool thoughts were able to wait for an average of 13 minutes, most of those primed with hot thoughts could not wait longer than 5 minutes.

These findings make a strong case that it is not the objective situation but the nature of mental representations of the situation that predicts self-regulatory behavior. Effective self-regulation can be attained by self-generated cool ideation about an emotionally arousing stimulus—in the case of the marshmallows, by mentally turning them into a picture that cannot be eaten and poses little or no temptation—but the findings have far-reaching implications for emotional regulation beyond delay of gratification. In fact, they are some of the first experimental demonstrations of "cognitive reappraisal." That the meaning of emotion-arousing stimuli can be mentally transformed in such a way that they no longer elicit excessive affect is an effective emotional regulation strategy has received much attention in recent work (e.g., Gross, 1998, 2001), the theoretical heritage of which can easily be traced back both to the delay-of-gratification studies and the early appraisal theories of emotion (e.g., Averill, 1973; Lazarus, 1993).

The Importance of Diagnostic Situations

Another theme running through Mischel's delay-of-gratification studies is the notion of "diagnostic situations"—that the meaning of behavior is context specific and the diagnostic utility of any behavior for predicting outcomes depends on this contextualized meaning.

As part of an ongoing longitudinal study of the children who took part in the original delay experiments between 1968 and 1972, Mischel and colleagues assessed their social and cognitive competencies and obtained their SAT scores when the participants were around 18 years old (Shoda et al., 1990). Recall that many different versions of the delay experiments were run. Shoda and colleagues (1990) showed that SAT scores were meaningfully related to the number of seconds children were able to wait at age 4 only if the delay behavior was assessed when rewards were exposed for children's attention and experimenters did not provide any ideation instructions for the child. Note that this is the situation that taxes the child's self-regulatory competencies the most—the rewards are exposed, creating a highly tempting situation, and children are left to their own cognitive devices in how they deploy their attention, construe the meaning of the rewards, and deal with the challenge of sustaining delay behavior. It is specifically in this situation that longer delay times reflect chronic individual differences in how children deal with temptations and frustrations and are consequently more diagnostic of how children fare in the long term.

Another study demonstrating the importance of diagnostic conditions examined links between early mother–child interactions when toddlers were 18 months old and their effect on children's delay ability when they were 4½ years old (Rodriguez et al., 2005). Maternal responsivity at age 18 months was assessed in a modified Strange Situation that typically presents the toddler with episodes of varying distress. For example, free play is a low-stress situation, whereas separation in which the mother briefly leaves the toddler alone in an unfamiliar environment and the reunion that follows are high-stress episodes. This study revealed that maternal unresponsivity was related to the child's spontaneous use of ineffective, hot strategies in the delay-of-gratification task in preschool when unresponsiveness occurred in highly stressful situations for the child but not when it occurred in relatively less stressful situations. At the level of more specific mother–child interactions, maternal unresponsiveness that followed the child's expressions of distress regardless of the whether negative affect occurred in low- or high-stress episodes of the Strange Situation, was also detrimental to effective delay behavior in preschool. In contrast, maternal behavior that appeared on the surface to be unresponsive but did not occur in the context of a distressed child had no effect on the child's ability to self-regulate in the delay situation.

At a general level, these findings stress the importance of going beyond the surface features of behavior to take into account the context within which it occurs to understand its underlying meaning. At a more specific level, they show that maternal unresponsiveness is particularly relevant to self-regulatory behavior when it occurs in emotionally stressful situations that are difficult to cope with for the child. In situations that are normatively stressful for young children or when the child is or has been upset, behaviors such as turning away from the child or ignoring the child's bids for attention reflect maternal unresponsiveness, which has detrimental effects on the child's ability to self-regulate effectively years later. When these same maternal behaviors occur in relatively low-stress situations or when the child is not or has not been particularly distressed, they do not necessarily reflect unresponsiveness on the part of the mother and consequently do not negatively affect the development of the child's capacity for effective self-regulation.

The Importance of Flexibility and Discrimination in Adaptive Behavior

Is it always better to engage in behaviors that reduce affect for effective self-regulation? In other words, should we always be cool, or are there situations in which focusing our attention on features that elicit affect and motivation can actually bring about more effective self-regulation?

The idea that socially intelligent behavior requires being flexible in accordance with the demands as well as with the opportunities different situations present for the individual (Chiu, Hong, Mischel, & Shoda, 1995; Mendoza-Denton, Ayduk, Mischel, Shoda, & Testa, 2001) is a common theme that appears in many different aspects of Walter Mischel's research. Here, I focus on two of his studies on delay of gratification that aptly illustrate this theme.

The classic delay paradigm presents children with a passive waiting task, but in real life we rarely simply have to wait for bigger, better, more desirable outcomes; rather, we have to work actively toward achieving those outcomes. Peake, Hebl, and Mischel (2002) examined whether the same cognitive and attention deployment processes underlie children's ability to delay gratification when achieving those delayed rewards is contingent on completing instrumental work. In one condition, children had to complete an inherently engaging, fun task (feeding a toy bird marbles). In another condition, children had to complete a relatively boring task to attain delayed rewards (sorting marbles according to color). In both conditions, the rewards were exposed for children to view while working, and Peake and colleagues conducted second-by-second analyses of attention deployment strategies children used as they worked and tried to sustain delay of gratification.

They found that the fun task functioned as a highly effective distracter because it easily engrossed children's attention. Similarly to passive waiting experiments, children were able to delay longer to the extent that they were distracted from the rewards. Children who focused their attention on the rewards instead of paying attention to the fun task quickly gave up. These findings thus largely replicated what we knew from passive waiting situations about the processes underlying delay ability.

A somewhat different pattern emerged for children who were asked to complete a boring task. In this condition, children who intermittently shifted their attention *toward* the rewards without fixating on them more than a few seconds were the best delayers. Because the task was boring, these children were giving themselves quick reminders of the ultimate goal they were working toward to motivate themselves but then quickly shifting their attention away from the rewards to prevent arousal and temptation from becoming excessive and disruptive. Overall, these findings emphasize that it is flexible attention deployment rather than the use of cooling strategies across the board that underlies effective self-regulation.

A consistent picture emerges from another study examining the way toddlers deal with stressful interactions with their mothers as an early precursor of delay-of-gratification ability (Sethi, Mischel, Aber, Shoda, & Rodriguez, 2000). Children's behavior in interacting with their mothers during a lab session was assessed when they were 18 months old and then again in the delay-of-gratification task when they were 4 or 5 years old. Mothers' parenting style, whether they were overcontrolling or not, was also assessed, to tap into the aversiveness of mother–child interactions at 18 months—a time in children's development during which they are particularly concerned with establishing autonomy and are likely to perceive maternal overcontrol as particularly aversive.

The results showed that toddlers of highly overcontrolling mothers used more effective delay strategies at age 4 (e.g., self-distraction) to the extent that they physically moved away from their mothers to explore the toys at a distance when mothers made bids to engage the child in play. In direct contrast, toddlers of mothers who were not overcontrolling used more effective attentional strategies and delayed gratification longer to the extent that they did *not* physically distance themselves from their mothers and instead approached them when the mothers made bids for play.

Thus overall, delay ability seems to be related to being flexible in responding to situations in accordance with their particular and specific demands: When mothers are overcontrolling and frustrating, being able to move way from them seems to be the precursor to preschool delay ability, but when mothers are not overcontrolling and present opportunities for pleasant interactions, then actively approaching rather than avoiding them is a precursor to children's ability to delay gratification at age 4.

CURRENT RESEARCH AND FUTURE DIRECTIONS

The bulk of the experimental work on delay of gratification was completed by 1972, but the longitudinal component of the research program, probing the implications of early delay ability for lifelong development, is ongoing and is being expanded in new and exciting ways. It is these efforts on which I have collaborated with Walter Mischel.

In the last two decades, the focus has been on following up on the children who took part in the original delay experiments, assessing the longitudinal inks between the number of seconds they were able to delay at age 4 to consequential life outcomes (Ayduk et al., 2000; Ayduk, Zayas et al., 2006; Ayduk, Shoda, & Mischel, 2006; Mischel et al., 1988; Shoda et al., 1990). As mentioned, preschool delay times in certain diagnostic conditions predicted social and cognitive competencies including SAT scores when participants were 18 years old (Mischel et al., 1988; Shoda et al., 1990). Approximately 10 years later, higher delay times continued to be associated with better social and interpersonal functioning (Ayduk et al., 2000, Study 1). In our most recent follow-up, conducted when the participants were on average age 38 years old, preschool delay times continued to predict important life outcomes such as lower rates of marital divorce or separation, minor violations of the law, and Body Mass Index, an important predictor of obesity and related health problems (Ayduk, Shoda, & Mischel, 2006).

The follow-up data also indicate that the ability to delay gratification in childhood serves as a protective buffer against the negative consequences of chronic personal vulnerabilities in adulthood, such as being sensitive to rejection. People who are high in rejection sensitivity (RS; Downey & Feldman, 1996) anxiously expect interpersonal rejection, are hypervigilant for rejection cues, and subsequently show a readiness to perceive intentional hurt in significant others' ambiguous or even innocuous behavior (see Levy, Ayduk, & Downey, 2001, for review). Perceptions of rejection elicit hostility and sometimes even violence that often compromise the longevity of high-RS people's relationships and lead ultimately to depression and low self-esteem (Ayduk, Downey, Testa, Yen, & Shoda, 1999; Downey, Feldman, & Ayduk, 2000; Ayduk, Downey, & Kim, 2001; Downey, Freitas, Michaelis, & Khouri, 1998).

In our follow-up study, we found that preschool delay ability predicted resiliency against the potentially destructive effects of being high RS. At age 28, high-RS individuals reported lower self-esteem, self-worth, coping ability, and even educational levels than low-RS individuals to the extent that they were unable to delay gratification at age 4.

Similarly, high-RS people with difficulties in delaying gratification reported higher use of cocaine/crack in the past year, but high-RS people
with greater delay ability were not different from people low in RS in
their substance use (Ayduk et al., 2000, Study 1). These findings were
consistent with a second study with middle school children from a different cohort and from a very different socioeconomic and ethnic inner-city
population (Ayduk et al., 2000, Study 2).

In more recent work (Ayduk et al., in press), we have examined the
implications of early delay ability for the development of borderline personality (BP). BP disorder is a complex and common mental disorder
that is most commonly diagnosed in women (DSM-IV-TR). It is characterized by marked instability in self-concept, affect, and behavior, with
shifts in these aspects of the individual linked closely with significant
relationship events. In prior research, BP disorder has been associated with heightened sensitivity to rejection (see Agrawal, Gunderson,
Holmes, & Lyons-Ruth, 2004, for review). Our study shows that the
link between fears and expectations of rejection and BP features at age
38 is attenuated for individuals who were able to delay gratification longer at age 4 (Ayduk et al., in press). It is thus the combination of high RS
and low self-regulatory competency that generates the constellation of
symptoms that make up BPD.

In this ongoing follow-up study, we are extending this work in new
directions. Most of the participants are now in middle adulthood
(around 38 years old), and many of them have children of their own
who are of approximately the age when the participants became subjects
in the original delay-of-gratification studies. A follow-up at this time is a
rare window of opportunity not only to link preschool delay ability to
other age-appropriate outcomes, and to try to understand the psychological mechanisms that explain these links, but also to probe into the
intergenerational transmission of this ability from the original Bing participants to their children. Thus second-generation participants are being
tested in the preschool delay task as well as on age-appropriate versions
of various cognitive control tasks that their parents also complete to
examine potential associations between parents' and children's performance on these tasks.

With recent advances in genotyping, we will also be able to examine
genetic factors that may contribute to intergenerational continuity in
self-regulatory competencies. Of particular interest are a dopamine
transporter gene, DAT1, and a dopamine receptor gene, DRD4, which
have shown associations with disorders in attention, cognitive control,
and hyperactivity in human gene association studies (e.g., Cook et al.,
1995; Swanson et al., 1998, 2000).

REFERENCES

Agrawal, H. R., Gunderson, J., Holmes, B. M., & Lyons-Ruth, K. (2004). Attachment studies with borderline patients: A review. *Harvard Review of Psychiatry, 12,* 94–104.

Averill, J. R. (1973). Personal control over aversive stimuli and its relationship to stress. *Psychological Bulletin, 80,* 286–315.

Ayduk, O., Downey, G., & Kim, M. (2001). Rejection sensitivity and depression in women. *Personality and Social Psychology Bulletin, 7,* 868–877.

Ayduk, O., Downey, G., Testa, A., Yen, Y., & Shoda, Y. (1999). Does rejection sensitivity elicit hostility in rejection sensitive women? *Social Cognition, 17,* 245–271.

Ayduk, O., Mendoza-Denton, R., Mischel, W., Downey, G., Peake, P., & Rodriguez, M. L. (2000). Regulating the interpersonal self: Strategic self-regulation for coping with rejection sensitivity. *Journal of Personality and Social Psychology, 79,* 776–792.

Ayduk, O., Shoda, Y., & Mischel, W. (2006). *Longitudinal links between preschool ability to delay gratification and adult life outcomes.* Unpublished data, Columbia University.

Ayduk, O., Zayas, V., Downey, G., Cole, A. B., Shoda, Y., & Mischel, W. (in press). Rejection sensitivity and executive control: Joint predictors of borderline personality features. *Journal of Research in Personality.*

Chiu, C., Hong, Y., Mischel, W., & Shoda, Y. (1995). Discriminative facility in social competence: Conditional versus dispositional encoding and monitoring-blunting of information. *Social Cognition, 13,* 49–70.

Cook, E. H., Jr., Stein, M. A., Krasowski, M. D., Cox, N. J., Olkon, D. M., Kieffer, J. E., et al. (1995). Association of attention-deficit disorder and the dopamine transporter gene. *Am J Hum Genet, 56*(4), 993–998.

Downey, G., & Feldman, S. (1996). Implications of rejection sensitivity for intimate relationships. *Journal of Personality and Social Psychology, 70,* 1327–1343.

Downey, G., Feldman, S., & Ayduk, O. (2000). Rejection sensitivity and male violence in romantic relationships. *Personal Relationships, 7,* 45–61.

Downey, G., Freitas, A., Michaelis, B., & Khouri, H. (1998). The self-fulfilling prophecy in close relationships: Do rejection sensitive women get rejected by romantic partners? *Journal of Personality and Social Psychology, 75,* 545–560.

Gross, J. (1998). Antecedent- and response-focused emotion regulation: Divergent consequences for experience, expression, and physiology. *Journal of Personality and Social Psychology, 74,* 224–237.

Gross, J. (2001). Emotion regulation in adulthood: Timing is everything. *Current Directions in Psychological Science, 10,* 214–219.

Higgins, E. T., & Bargh, J. A. (1987). Social cognition and social perception. *Annual Review of Psychology, 38,* 369–425.

Lazarus, R. S. (1993). From psychological stress to the emotions: A history of changing outlooks. *Annual Review of Psychology, 44,* 1–21.

Levy, S. R., Ayduk, O., & Downey, G. (2001). Rejection sensitivity: Implications for interpersonal and inter-group processes. In Mark Leary (Ed.), *Interpersonal rejection* (pp. 251–289). New York: Oxford University Press.

Mendoza-Denton, R., Ayduk, O., Mischel, W., Shoda, Y., & Testa, A. (2001). Person situation interactionism in self-encoding (I am . . . when . . .): Implications for affect regulation and social information processing. *Journal of Personality and Social Psychology, 80,* 533–544.

Mischel, W. (1974). Processes in delay of gratification. In L. Berkowitz (Ed.), *Advances in experimental social psychology* (Vol. 7, pp. 249–292). New York: Academic Press.

Mischel, W., & Ayduk, O. (2004). Willpower in a cognitive-affective processing system: The dynamics of delay of gratification. In R. Baumeister & K. Vohs (Eds.), *Handbook of self-regulation: Research, theory, and applications* (pp. 99–129). New York: Guilford Press.

Mischel, W., & Baker, N. (1975). Cognitive appraisals and transformations in delay behavior. *Journal of Personality and Social Psychology, 31,* 254–261.

Mischel, W., & Ebbesen, E. B. (1970). Attention in delay of gratification. *Journal of Personality and Social Psychology, 16,* 239–337.

Mischel, W., Ebbesen, E. B., & Zeiss, A. R. (1972). Cognitive and attentional mechanisms in delay of gratification. *Journal of Personality and Social Psychology, 21,* 204–218.

Mischel, W., Shoda, Y., & Peake, P. (1988). The nature of adolescent competencies predicted by preschool delay of gratification. *Journal of Personality and Social Psychology, 54,* 687–696.

Mischel, W., Shoda, Y., & Rodriguez, M. L. (1989). Delay of gratification in children. *Science, 244,* 933–938.

Moore, B., Mischel, W., & Zeiss, A. (1976). Comparative effects of the reward stimulus and its cognitive representation in voluntary delay. *Journal of Personality and Social Psychology, 34,* 419–424.

Peake, P., Hebl, M., & Mischel, W. (2002). Strategic attention deployment in waiting and working situations. *Developmental Psychology, 38,* 313–326.

Rodriguez, M., Ayduk, O., Aber, L. J., Mischel, W., Sethi, A., & Shoda, Y. (2005). Maternal unresponsivity and toddler negative affect: Precursors to ineffective self-regulatory strategies in preschool children. *Social Development, 14,* 136–157.

Rodriguez, M. L., Mischel, W., & Shoda, Y. (1989). Cognitive person variables in the delay of gratification of older children at risk. *Journal of Personality and Social Psychology, 57,* 358–367.

Sethi, A., Mischel, W., Aber, L. J., Shoda, Y., & Rodriguez, M. L. (2000). The role of strategic attention deployment in development of self-regulation: Predicting preschoolers' delay of gratification from mother–toddler interactions. *Developmental Psychology, 36,* 767–777.

Shoda, Y., Mischel, W., & Peake, P. (1990). Predicting adolescent cognitive and self-regulatory competencies from preschool delay of gratification: Identifying diagnostic conditions. *Developmental Psychology, 26,* 978–986.

Swanson, J. M., Sunohara, G. A., Kennedy, J. L., Regino, R., Fineberg, E.,

Wigal, T., et al. (1998). Association of the dopamine receptor D4 (DRD4) gene with a refined phenotype of attention-deficit/hyperactivity disorder (ADHD): A family-based approach. *Molecular Psychiatry, 3*(1), 38–41.

Swanson, J., Oosterlaan, J., Murias, M., Schuck, S., Flodman, P., Spence, M. A., et al. (2000). Attention-deficit/hyperactivity disorder children with a 7-repeat allele of the dopamine receptor D4 gene have extreme behavior but normal performance on critical neuropsychological tests of attention. *Proceedings of the National Academy of Sciences—USA, 97*(9), 4754–4759.

7

In Search
of Generative Mechanisms
The Case of Value from Engagement Strength

E. TORY HIGGINS

When I think of Walter Mischel, I think of two other intellectual giants of the 20th century—Sigmund Freud and Noam Chomsky. There are intriguing similarities for both sets of men. Let me begin with Freud and Mischel. Freud moved to Vienna in 1859 as a 3-year-old, and, about three quarters of a century later, Mischel was born in Vienna. Is the Viennese connection just a coincidence? I don't think so, but that is another story. In any case, there are more similarities between Freud and Mischel than their Viennese connection.

As personality psychologists, Freud and Mischel are similar in understanding that a person is more than a set of traits that produce cross-situational consistency in trait-related behaviors. According to the classic trait perspective, consistency across situations in the level of some behavior is produced by a corresponding level of dispositional force, such as a high level of behavioral dominance from a high level of the trait disposition to be dominant or a high level of behavioral submission from a high level of the trait disposition to be submissive. In contrast, the conceptualization of personality types inspired by the Freudian psychodynamic perspective does not postulate any direct correspondence between behavioral level and dispositional level. Instead, it recognizes that the behavior needed to satisfy some underlying need can vary across situations. The need remains stable over time, but the behaviors vary because the behaviors required to satisfy the need are different in different situations. High authoritarians, for example, have a need for a fixed social order that provides predictability and control regarding authority relationships (Adorno, Frenkel-Brunswick, Levinson, & Sanford, 1950). In order to satisfy this need, they are dominant to those who are lower in status than them and submissive to those who are higher in status than them. There is no cross-situational consistency in level of behavior—sometimes they are dominant, and sometimes they are submissive. There is, instead, a stable behavioral pattern—dominant with a lower-status other and submissive with a higher-status other. The stability derives from an underlying need for predictability and control regarding authority relationships.

The work of Mischel and his colleagues (e.g., Mischel, 1973; Mischel & Shoda, 1995) captures the Freudian psychodynamic insight that a person is defined not by cross-situational behavioral consistency produced by dispositional traits but by stable behavioral patterns produced by underlying motives. But there is a distinct historical contribution of the Mischelian viewpoint that goes beyond the Freudian one. The Freudian-inspired viewpoint on personality types postulates a content match or relevance between behavioral dimension and underlying need. For example, the authoritarian personality type concerns a pattern of authority behaviors, and the high-achiever type concerns a pattern of achievement behaviors (strong achievement response to challenging tasks and weak achievement response to easy tasks; see Atkinson & Feather, 1966; McClelland, Atkinson, Clark, & Lowell, 1953).

Thus, although there is no trait-like equating of level of behavior to corresponding level of disposition, there is an equating of type of manifest behavioral dimension (e.g., authority behaviors) to type of underlying need (e.g., need for predictable authority relationships). The Mischelian viewpoint, in contrast, makes no content-matching assumptions, neither level nor type. For example, a pattern of generous tipping behavior in mom-and-pop restaurants and stingy tipping behavior in elite restaurants is not assumed to relate to a personality type dimension associated with generosity motives. Rather, the pattern could reflect a strategic or tactical manner of responding that is consistent with a political attitude (e.g., blue-collar socialism). This is a novel perspective on personality that separates surface behavioral manifestations from underlying mechanisms even more fundamentally than psychodynamic theory—which brings me to my next comparison.

Walter Mischel and Noam Chomsky were born within 2 years of each other (Mischel is younger), and they received the American Psychological Association's Award for Distinguished Scientific Contributions within 2 years of each other (Mischel sooner). As with Freud, there is more similarity between Chomsky and Mischel than their "life mile-stones" connection. As psychologists, Chomsky and Mischel are similar in understanding that the mechanisms that generate manifest behavior patterns need have little resemblance to the behaviors themselves. Chomsky's breakthrough contribution to the psychology of language was to recognize that the mechanisms that generated word strings were very different from their surface manifestations. To understand how people create linguistic outputs, it was not sufficient to classify those outputs into different forms or types as classic descriptive linguists had done. It was also necessary to reject the widely held belief among language scholars that the order of words corresponds to the order of thoughts. Trait psychologists proceeded much like classic descriptive linguists in classifying different behavior outputs into behavior types and then postulating corresponding dispositional traits as the mechanisms underlying them.

Chomsky proposed that the mechanism that generated language behavior was an underlying system of transformational rules. The concept of rules is also critical to the Mischelian perspective on personality: it is situationally grounded *"if . . . then . . ."* contingency rules (i.e., "If situation A, then behave X"; "If situation B, then behave Y"; "If situation C, . . .") that generate the stable behavioral profiles that are the signature of each person. These rules are based on a person's goals, strategies, expectancies, feelings, and so on, whose variation across persons can create a wide variety of different personality profiles. As Chomsky's idea of transformational rules provided a richer account of language behavior, Mischel's idea of *if . . . then . . .* contingency rules of how to behave in a given situation provided a richer account of personality.

My own work has also been concerned with looking beyond manifest outcomes and the psychological processes directly associated with such outcomes. In both regulatory focus theory (Higgins, 1997) and regulatory fit theory (Higgins, 2000), I have considered how people's motivation to pursue goals in a particular manner influences their behavior independent of the outcomes. In this research, it is not possible to explain the goal pursuit behaviors in terms of the anticipated goal pursuit outcomes. More generally, my concern is with underlying mechanisms that generate behaviors or experiences where there is little obvious correspondence between the mechanisms and the behaviors or experiences.

In this chapter, I focus on people's attraction to or repulsion from something—their value responses. Traditionally, a rather direct correspondence between value responses and underlying mechanism has been assumed. Specifically, people's attraction to or repulsion from something has been explained in terms of their anticipated or experienced pleasures or pains associated with that thing—the classic hedonic principle. Even when Freud (1950) talked of the ego becoming controlled by the reality principle, and in this sense developing "beyond the pleasure principle" (Freud, 1950), he made it clear that the reality principle "at bottom also seeks pleasure—although a delayed and diminished pleasure" (p. 365). Environmental demands simply modify the pleasure principle such that avoiding pain becomes almost equal in importance to gaining pleasure. In recent papers (Higgins, 2006, 2007), I have proposed that there are mechanisms underlying value responses that go beyond the hedonic principle. I provide an overview of this proposal here.

In brief, I agree with those who believe that value is best understood as a psychological experience. It is not simply a belief, inference, or judgment. Inferences, judgments, and beliefs contribute to value, but they do so through their impact on experience. Consider the classic refrain that people often do not appreciate or value something until they do not have it. A related notion is that people take for granted (i.e., do not value), things that are objectively important, if not critical, to their well-being or even survival. A classic example is being in good physical health, especially for younger people. Young people know that being healthy is a good thing, but that knowledge alone is not enough to give health the value it objectively deserves—"Youth is wasted on the young." The general point of such refrains is that, because the need is generally being satisfied or the desired end-state maintained, without the need to pay much attention to it or make it a priority, the *experience* of attraction to the value target is weak. When suddenly the need is not being satisfied or the desired end-state is not being maintained, *then* people experience their attraction to it. Only *then* do they value it highly. This is true not only for health but also for resources such as electricity, water, and so on that are normally readily available, at least in wealthier nations. Something that satisfies a need, maintains a desired end-state, or meets a standard is not valuable for that reason alone. It can still be taken for granted and not appreciated. Experiencing the attraction to it is essential.

What exactly is the nature of this value experience? Inspired by Lewin's (1951) discussion of valence, I have proposed in a recent paper (Higgins, 2006) that value is a *motivational* experience. For Lewin, value related to force, which has direction and strength. For Lewin, the forces on a person's life space were analogous to natural physical forces on objects rather than something that a person experiences. Nonetheless, following his lead, I believe that value is a *force experience* that has direction and strength. Experiencing something as having positive value corresponds to experiencing attraction toward it (e.g., trying to move toward it), and experiencing something as having negative value corresponds to experiencing repulsion from it (e.g., trying to move away from it). Value experiences vary in strength. The experience of attraction toward something can be relatively weak or strong (low or high positive value), as can the experience of repulsion from something (low or high negative value).

As I noted earlier, people's attraction to or repulsion from something has been traditionally explained in terms of the pleasure or pain associated with that thing—the classic hedonic principle. I agree that, to understand the psychology of value, one must begin with the classic hedonic experiences of getting pleasure or pain from something (cf. Kahneman, Diener, & Schwarz, 1999). This experience is critical to the resultant force experience because it provides *direction*. Many sources of value described in the literature can be understood as contributing to hedonic experience, including need satisfaction, goal attainment, or meeting standards (see Higgins, 2007). One can distinguish between different contents of value experience, such as economic value (e.g., material resources), moral value (e.g., ethical character), political value (e.g., individual power), social value (e.g., social support networks), and so on, but they can all be understood as contributing to hedonic experience—making one's life more pleasurable. It is also notable that "cognitive" sources of value described in the literature can influence the experience of hedonic direction (for a discussion of such cognitive sources, see Higgins, 2007). For example, shared beliefs about what is desirable and what is undesirable—both social values (e.g., Rokeach, 1973) and personal ideals and oughts (Higgins, 1987)—directly concern what has positive value and what has negative value. The evidence used to make evaluative inferences also provides information about the positive or negative value of something.

In a recent paper (Higgins, 2006), I proposed that the value experience of the force of attraction or repulsion has two sources. One source is the hedonic pleasure/pain experience of the target that I have just discussed, but as shown in Figure 7.1, I proposed that there is a second source of the value experience that involves the experience of the motivational force to make something happen (experienced as a force of attraction) or not (experienced as a force of repulsion).

Although these two force experiences—hedonic and motivational force—often are experienced holistically, they are distinct from one another. Some activity that provides little hedonic pleasure, for example, may have a strong motivational force because it is the proper thing to do or matches shared beliefs about appropriate procedures of goal pursuit—I don't "enjoy" doing this, but I feel "compelled" to do it. What is critical here is the notion that value is not just an experience of pleasure or pain. Instead, value is essentially a directional force experi-

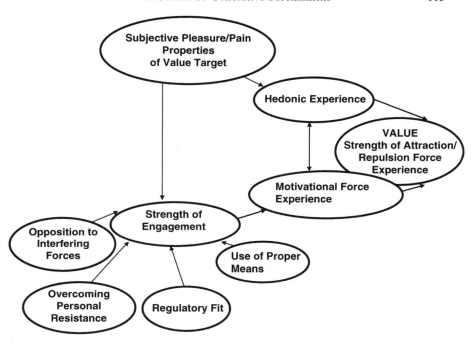

FIGURE 7.1. Illustration of proposed relational influences among variables contributing to the value force experience.

ence. Because value is an experience of directional force and not just an experience of pleasure or pain, there can be contributions to value that are independent of hedonic experience.

WHAT ARE THE SOURCES OF THE MOTIVATIONAL FORCE EXPERIENCE?

As shown in Figure 7.1, the pleasure/pain hedonic experience is a critical determinant of the motivational force experience, but it is not the only determinant. I have proposed (Higgins, 2006) that there is also a *nondirectional* source of motivational force experience—"strength of engagement." The state of being engaged with some object or activity is to be involved, occupied, interested, and attentive to it. Strong engagement is to be absorbed by or engrossed with it. Independent of their experience of a target's properties, for example, individuals can experience their opposition to interfering forces or experience overcoming their own resistance in relation to that target, and these experiences can increase the strength of engagement with that target.

In contrast to experienced properties of the value target, strength of engagement has strength but not valence direction in itself. Strength of engagement concerns how much people are absorbed in what they are doing regardless of the strength of the pleasure/pain experience. In keeping with the theme of this book, "persons in context," strength of engagement concerns not just the properties of the value target but the context surrounding a person's goal pursuit or decision making. For example, strength of engagement can increase by someone having to remove an obstacle to a goal. Although the situation can be unpleasant and the effort costly, the increased engagement strength from opposing the interfering force can increase the attractiveness of the target. The sources of engagement strength involve the situational conditions surrounding a person's goal pursuit and decision making. Thus, to the extent that engagement strength is an important mechanism underlying the generation of value, a person's situational conditions during goal pursuit and decision making need to be taken into account when constructing a science of value.

Historically, strength of engagement relates to the notion that people can be interested in something independent of its hedonic valence and that this has value implications. Perry (1926), for example, said that an object is valuable when interest is taken in it. Ziff (1960) said that "good" means answering to certain interests. Mandler (1984) noted that what makes us attend to things also invests them with value, and events that are interesting may or may not be positively valued. Berlyne (1973) also distinguished "interesting" from pleasing or pleasant. Strength of engagement alone does not make something attractive or repulsive; it does not have direction. Instead, strength of engagement contributes to the experience of motivational force, to the strength of the experienced force of attraction or repulsion. Strength of engagement contributes to *how* positively or negatively something is experienced.

The present model distinguishes explicitly between the impact of engagement strength on one's experience of what one is doing versus its impact on the value of some focal target (see the later discussion of "flow" in this chapter). The critical property of engagement for value creation is the strength of engagement rather than whether the activity itself happens to be pleasant or unpleasant. It is possible, for example, to be engaged strongly in the pursuit of some value target despite its being unpleasant as an activity or to disengage from the goal pursuit despite its being pleasant as an activity. What matters for value creation is the strength of the engagement, which contributes to the intensity of the motivational force experience of the value target. For instance, individuals could experience as unpleasant their opposition to forces interfering with their pursuit of a positive value target (e.g., the effort needed to remove an obstacle), but this condition of opposition, by increasing engagement strength, could intensify their attraction to the positive target. Conversely, individuals could feel positive about pursuing a goal in the right way, but this condition of regulatory fit, by increasing engagement strength, could intensify their repulsion from a negative value target.

An everyday example of these kinds of effects occurs when academics review papers for potential publication. The reviewing process itself could be experienced as pleasant or unpleasant, but in either case the reviewers could be highly engaged in what they are doing. According to the present model, reviewers' attraction to a paper they like and repulsion from a paper they dislike will be more intense under conditions that make them more strongly engaged in the review process, and this will be true both when the reviewing process itself is pleasant and when it is unpleasant.

There are various kinds of evidence that hedonic experience and motivational force from strength of engagement can independently contribute to value. I now briefly discuss three sources of engagement strength that are independent of hedonic experience (for fuller discussions, see Higgins, 2006, 2007): opposition to interfering forces, overcoming personal resistance, and regulatory fit.

OPPOSITION TO INTERFERING FORCES

An important way of interacting with the environment occurs when people oppose forces that would make something happen that they don't want to happen. Woodworth (1940), for example, stated that a central characteristic of people and other animals is that they exert considerable opposition or resistance to environmental forces on them in order to maintain a degree of independence. They have an active give-and-take relation with the environment, and value "springs from the individual's ability to deal effectively with some phase of the environment" (p. 396). When individuals oppose interfering forces, they oppose something that would hinder, impede, or obstruct a preferred state or course of action. They oppose a choice situation that would force them to select from an impoverished set of alternatives. This opposition can create value. Lewin (1935) considered value creation from opposition to interfering forces to be a realm of fundamental psychological significance.

Value creation from opposition to interfering forces or pressure is illustrated in social psychological research on reactance theory (Brehm,

1966; Brehm & Brehm, 1981; Wicklund, 1974). Reactance theory concerns people's belief that they can significantly control their own destiny, and that they are free to act, believe, or feel as they see fit. It states that when a subjectively important freedom is threatened with elimination or is actually eliminated, people will react so as to protect or restore that freedom. In a study by Brehm, Stires, Sensenig, and Shaban (1966), participants listened to taped selections from four different records for which they then provided a preference ranking. They were told that they would receive a complimentary record when the actual records arrived the next day, either randomly selected (for half the participants) or selected by themselves (for the other half). When they later arrived to pick up the complimentary record, half of the participants learned that their third-ranked record was not included in the shipment and was thus eliminated from the choice set (the Choice-Elimination condition). The participants were then asked to rate again the attractiveness of all the records. The attractiveness of the third-ranked record increased in the Choice-Elimination condition only.

According to reactance theory, the underlying mechanism for value creation in this study and similar ones is a motivation to reassert or restore a freedom that has been eliminated or threatened with elimination. The situation might also create value in another way. The elimination of a choice alternative and the resultant pressure to make a selection from an impoverished option set interferes with participants' preferred course of action, and they oppose this interfering force. This opposition should increase strength of engagement in what they are doing. To the extent that receiving the to-be-eliminated record as a gift was a positive outcome to the participants at the beginning of the study (i.e., their initial responses to that record were positive), the increase in strength of engagement from opposing an interfering force should increase that record's positive value.

One variable that can be conceptualized as an interfering force is "difficulty." Lewin (1935, 1951) described a force that impedes or obstructs locomotion or progress to a goal as a "barrier" or "difficulty." The difficulty can be an actual physical object blocking progress, such as a bench blocking a child's path to a toy (e.g., Lewin, 1935), or it can be an authority figure's prohibition of some act, the complexity of a task, and so on. Lewin (1935) points out that, psychologically, such a difficulty, whether physical or social, constitutes a barrier or interfering force.

Opposition to interfering forces naturally occurs when goal-oriented activity is blocked. An especially interesting form of such opposition is the Zeigarnik effect, in which a task is interrupted before completion (Lewin, 1935; Zeigarnik, 1938). Consistent with the notion that opposition to goal blockage as an interfering force would increase strength of engagement and enhance the value of achieving the goal, such interruption has been found to increase the attractiveness of the interrupted task (Cartwright, 1942). Mischel and Masters (1966) provide another early illustration of how opposition to interruption as an interfering force may intensify a positive value target. In their study, an entertaining movie was interrupted by projector failure at an exciting point. A confederate posing as an electrician provided different information about whether the interruption was temporary. When participants believed that the movie was unlikely to resume (i.e., their goal was blocked), they valued the movie more.

OVERCOMING PERSONAL RESISTANCE

Opposition to interfering forces occurs when individuals want to do something but experience external interference when trying to do it. There are also times when individuals initially resist doing something because it is aversive in some way and must overcome their resistance in order to proceed with the activity. They do something despite *not* wanting to do it. This overcoming of one's resistance also increases strength of engagement. In social-psychological research, value creation from overcoming personal resistance is illustrated by studies testing cognitive dissonance theory (Brehm & Cohen, 1962; Festinger, 1957; Wicklund & Brehm, 1976).

According to Festinger (1957), two cognitive elements, X and Y, are in a dissonant relation to one another if not-X would follow from Y. According to this definition, the situational conditions in which people overcome personal resistance produce a state of dissonance because the belief that doing something is aversive (Y predicts the decision *not* to do it (not-X), but instead people overcome their resistance. Instead of Y and not-X occurring together, which would make sense and should happen, Y and X occur together. Dissonance theory concerns people's motivation to reduce such states of dissonance in order to achieve cognitive consistency (i.e., make sense of the world), and it considers the different ways that such dissonance reduction can occur.

There are conditions under which inducing dissonance changes the value of something, as illustrated in a classic study by Festinger and Carlsmith (1959). Participants first worked on a rather repetitive, monotonous task, then agreed to tell another participant that the task was very interesting and enjoyable. Because participants say something that contradicts, or at least exaggerates, what they actually believe, this behavior is dissonant. The participants were promised either $1 or $20 to tell others that they had found the task very interesting. The experimenter informed all participants afterwards that most previous participants had found the task quite interesting. Finally, the participants themselves evaluated the task. Participants who were promised $1 evaluated the task more positively than those who were promised $20.

In this and similar studies, the proposed dissonance mechanism underlying value creation involves participants' reducing their dissonance by changing their attitude about the task so as to make it more consistent with their misleading statement. Because a promise of $20 provides more justification for having made the misleading statement than a promise of $1, the pressure to reduce dissonance through attitude change is greater in the $1 than the $20 condition. The situational conditions associated with such studies might create value in another way as well. To exaggerate the interest of the task to another is likely to be aversive for most of the participants. Thus, participants should be resistant to making the exaggerated statement. Whereas being promised $20 to make the statement is likely to reduce participants' resistance greatly, being promised only $1 is unlikely to reduce their resistance substantially. In the $1 condition, then, participants must overcome their own resistance in order to agree to make the misleading statement. By overcoming their resistance in the $1 condition, the participants' engagement would increase in strength, which would enhance the value of being favorable toward the task.

Difficulty is a variable that, as discussed, may be conceptualized as an interfering force or barrier that contributes to strength of engagement through the opposition it creates. Difficulty is also an aversive property of a situation. As an aversive condition, difficulty can also contribute to strength of engagement through creating personal resistance to doing something that is then overcome. When goal pursuit is difficult, there are high costs associated with it. Doing something despite the high costs imposed by difficulty (i.e., high effort requirements) involves overcoming resistance to doing something aversive. William James, Sigmund Freud, Kurt Lewin, Jean Piaget, and other great figures in psychology recognized that overcoming one's own resistance is a special kind of agentic experience that relates to psychological commitment and "will."

There are times when people knowingly face adverse or difficult circumstances to engage in some activity and continue with the activity despite those circumstances. This agentic experience of overcoming one's resistance can increase the value of that activity. Lewis (1965) reports a study, for example, in which rats were required to pull either a heavy weight (high effort) or a light weight (low effort) over several training trials in order to obtain a small amount of a distinctive food reward. The weight that a rat pulled during the training phase was constant across trials. Then, during the test phase, all the rats were placed in a straight maze and were allowed to run freely to the goal area (i.e., no weight to pull), where they were rewarded each time. During this test phase, the high-effort rats displayed a stronger preference for the food reward than did the low-effort rats, as indicated by their running faster to the food, consuming the food faster, and consuming more of the food in a free-feeding situation when they were already satiated.

Lawrence and Festinger (1962), inspired by dissonance theory, conducted an especially intriguing set of studies on value creation in animals. The rats in their studies needed to run up an inclined runway in order to get a food reward. There was 100% reinforcement. The incline was either 25 degrees (low-effort) or 50 degrees (high-effort). The value to the rats of getting a particular food reward was measured by trials to extinction after the reward was removed. During the extinction trials, the incline remained the same as during the training, and all the rats went from 100% reward to 0% reward. Lawrence and Festinger (1962) found that the trials to extinction were *greater* for the higher incline. Moreover, despite the higher incline being more difficult during extinction, average running time during the extinction trials was *faster* for the higher incline.

In addition to Lawrence and Festinger's (1962) dissonance explanation for their findings (i.e., the rats added positivity to the food in order to justify their decision to perform an aversive activity), the conditions of this and other "effort justification" studies (e.g., Aronson & Mills, 1959; Axsom & Cooper, 1985; Zimbardo, 1965) suggest that strength of engagement might contribute to the effect. For example, consider the situational conditions of the Lawrence and Festinger (1962) study. Strength of engagement could have been increased in two possible ways. One possibility is that opposition to interfering forces is involved; when rats actually ran up the high-effort incline, it functioned as an interfering force that needed to be opposed to get to the food. The other possibility is that overcoming personal resistance is involved; at the beginning of each trial, the high-effort incline functioned as an aversive cost producing personal resistance that had to be overcome to initiate the goal pursuit. The increase in strength of engagement from these two possible sources would intensify the positive response to the food. Brickman (1987) also suggested that the effort involved in the dissonance studies created value for the activity by increasing commitment to it.

Creating value from overcoming difficulty might also explain why infant animals become attached to an object, even an inanimate one when they receive pain from that object (Cairns, 1967). Resistance to the pain involved in remaking contact with the object had to be overcome in order to be close to the object. A history of overcoming this resistance made the object valuable, as reflected in the animal's becoming attached to it. This only happens, of course, if the infant persists in making contact with the object despite the pain received. This example raises a general point that applies equally to the previous examples of value creation from overcoming personal resistance: difficulty will not increase value if it makes someone give up. Resistance to difficulty must be overcome in order to increase value. An especially interesting example of increased attachment value when an animal does not give up in the face of increased difficulty has been described by Hess (1959) in his "law of effort." Ducklings had to climb over hurdles or up an incline in order to follow an imprinting object. Hess (1959) found that strength of imprinting was positively correlated with the effort exerted by the ducklings in following the imprinting object. When animals were given meprobamate, a muscle relaxant, the strength of imprinting no longer related to effort required. This result is consistent with the notion that experience of engagement strength is important.

REGULATORY FIT

When people pursue a goal, they begin with some motivational orientation, some concerns or interests that direct the pursuit. According to regulatory fit theory (Higgins, 2000), people experience regulatory fit when their goal orientation is sustained by the manner in which they pursue the goal, and they experience non-fit when their orientation is disrupted by the manner of their goal pursuit. Individuals may pursue the same goal with different orientations and in different ways. Consider, for example, students in the same course who are working to achieve an A. Some students have a promotion focus orientation toward an A as something they hope to attain (an ideal). Others have a prevention focus orientation toward an A as something they believe they must attain (an ought). With regard to *how* they pursue the goal, some students read material beyond the assigned readings as an "eager" way to attain an A, whereas others are careful to fulfill all course requirements as a "vigilant" way to attain an A.

An eager strategy sustains a promotion focus (fit), but disrupts a prevention focus (non-fit). A vigilant strategy sustains a prevention focus (fit), but disrupts a promotion focus (non-fit). Given these differences in what creates fit and non-fit, one would expect that people with a promotion focus would prefer to use eager (rather than vigilant) strategies to pursue their goals, and people with a prevention focus would prefer to use vigilant (rather than eager) strategies. This is indeed the case (see Higgins, 1997, 2000). Regulatory fit theory proposes that an actor's current orientation is sustained under conditions of regulatory fit and is disrupted under conditions of non-fit. One would then expect that actors' strength of engagement in a task activity would be greater under conditions of fit than under conditions of non-fit. The results of several studies support this prediction.

One set of studies by Förster, Higgins, and Idson (1998), for example, examined both chronic and situational instantiations of regulatory focus orientation in the context of anagram performance. Regulatory focus was situationally manipulated by telling participants either that by finding 90% or more of the words they would earn an extra dollar and by failing to do so they would not get the extra dollar (promotion gain/ nongain framing) or that by not missing more than 10% of the words they would avoid losing a dollar and by failing to do so they would lose the dollar (prevention nonloss/loss framing). Chronic regulatory focus was measured by participants' reaction times to providing their hope or aspiration goals (chronic accessibility of promotion ideals) and to providing duty or obligation goals (chronic accessibility of prevention oughts). Performing the task in an eager versus vigilant manner was manipulated by using an arm pressure technique (Cacioppo, Priester, & Berntson, 1993). While performing the anagram task, participants either pressed downward on the plate of a supposed skin conductance machine that was attached to the top of the table (a vigilance/avoidance-related movement of pushing away from oneself) or pressed upward on the plate attached to the bottom of the table (an eagerness/approach-related movement of pulling toward oneself).

Participants' arm pressure while pressing downward or upward on the plate was recorded and served as the measure of engagement strength. Förster and colleagues (1998) found that the strength of engagement was stronger when there was regulatory fit (i.e., promotion– eager movement; prevention–vigilant movement) than when there was non-fit (i.e., promotion–vigilant movement; prevention–eager movement). As one might expect from fit yielding greater strength of engagement in the task activity, participants in the fit conditions solved more anagrams than did participants in the non-fit conditions. Several other studies have also found higher performance under conditions of fit than non-fit (e.g., Bianco, Higgins, & Klem, 2003; Freitas, Liberman, & Higgins, 2002; Shah, Higgins, & Friedman, 1998; Spiegel, Grant-Pillow, & Higgins, 2004). Finally, a separate study by Förster and colleagues (1998) used persistence in the task as a different measure of engagement strength and found that persistence was greater when there was fit than when there was non-fit.

According to the model illustrated in Figure 7.1, regulatory fit should increase strength of engagement in what one is doing (Higgins,

2000), and strength of engagement should create value through its contribution to motivational force independently of hedonic experience. The most direct evidence supporting this proposed independence comes from some recent regulatory fit studies by Idson, Liberman, and Higgins (2004), who modified a well-known example from Thaler (1980). All participants were instructed to imagine that they were in a bookstore buying a book for a class. The orientation toward the buying decision was framed in two different ways—a promotion "gain/nongain" framing and a prevention "nonloss/loss" framing—while keeping the desirable choice outcome (paying $60 for the book) and the undesirable choice outcome (paying $65 for the book) the same in both framing conditions.

In both the promotion and prevention framing conditions, the participants were asked to imagine either how it would feel to make the desirable choice or how it would feel to make the undesirable choice on a scale ranging from "very bad" to "very good." As one would expect, the participants felt good when they imagined making the desirable choice and felt bad when they imagined making the undesirable choice. This is the classic outcome-valence effect. There were also significant effects within the desirable choice condition and within the undesirable choice condition. The participants imagined feeling better in the desirable choice condition when they were in the promotion focus condition (high eager fit) than in the prevention focus condition (low vigilant non-fit) and imagined feeling worse in the undesirable choice condition when they were in the prevention focus condition (high vigilant fit) than in the promotion focus condition (low eager non-fit). These same findings were obtained in another study by Idson and colleagues (2004) that experimentally primed either a promotion focus (ideal priming) or a prevention focus (ought priming).

The studies by Idson and colleagues (2004) also examined whether pleasure/pain hedonic experience and strength of motivational force make independent contributions to the value experience of attraction or repulsion. In addition to measuring how good or bad participants felt about the imagined decision outcome, separate measures of pleasure/pain intensity and strength of motivational force were taken. The framing study and the priming study used slightly different measures to provide convergent validity. The priming study, for example, measured pleasure/pain intensity by asking the participants how pleasant the positive outcome would be or how painful the negative outcome would be and measured strength of motivational force by asking them how motivated they would be to make the positive outcome happen (in the positive outcome condition) or to make the negative outcome not happen (in the negative outcome condition). Both studies found that pleasure/pain intensity and strength of motivational force each made significant independent contributions to the perceived value of the imagined outcome (i.e., its goodness/badness).

A final example of how regulatory fit can create value independent of hedonic outcomes is provided by a set of studies that examined whether regulatory fit can influence the monetary value of a chosen object (Higgins, Idson, Freitas, Spiegel, & Molden, 2003). Prior to the experimental session, Higgins and colleagues (2003) measured participants' chronic or habitual orientations (promotion or prevention) to pursuing goals using the same measure discussed above. When the participants arrived for the experiment they were told that, over and above the usual payment for participating, they could choose between a coffee mug and a pen as a gift. (Pretesting indicated that the mug was clearly preferred.) The manner of making the decision was manipulated by telling half the participants to think about what they would gain by choosing the mug and what they would gain by choosing the pen (an eager strategy), and telling the other half to think about what they would lose by not choosing the mug and what they would lose by not choosing the pen (a vigilant strategy). It should be noted that both the eager and vigilant choice strategies direct participants' attention to the positive qualities of each alternative. As expected, almost all participants chose the coffee mug. These participants were then asked either to assess the price of the chosen mug or to offer a price to buy it with their own money.

Participants in the fit conditions (promotion–eager; prevention–vigilant) gave a much (40–60%) higher price for the mug than did participants in the non-fit conditions. This fit effect on the money offered to buy the mug was independent of the participants' reports of their pleasure/pain feelings after making their decision. Indeed, the manipulation of fit did not affect participants' reports of their postdecision pleasure/pain feelings (see Camacho, Higgins, & Luger, 2003, for additional evidence of a fit effect on value that is independent of pleasure/pain valence). There was also no effect of the fit manipulation on participants' perception of the efficiency (ease) or the effectiveness (instrumentality) of the means that they used to make their choice. The fit effect on monetary value remained significant when participants' perceptions of the efficiency and effectiveness of the way in which they made their choice were statistically controlled.

CONCLUDING REMARKS

I have proposed in this chapter that strength of engagement is a psychological mechanism that generates value beyond hedonic experience by increasing the intensity of attraction to or repulsion from a value target.

The sources of engagement strength include the situational conditions of opposition to an interfering force, overcoming personal resistance, and regulatory fit. Evidence supporting the contribution of these situational conditions to value reactions illustrates how a deeper understanding of the mechanisms generating behavior requires a consideration of persons in context.

ON A MORE PERSONAL NOTE

I began this chapter by comparing Walter Mischel with Sigmund Freud. On the Friday evening before the conference began, I also related Mischel to Freud. I would like to end this chapter by including some of what I said that evening:

> Walter is the closest person to the eminence and influence of Freud that we have in the world of social-personality today. So what *if* Freud were around today? *What would Freud say?*
>
> Walter's first burning issue was self-control. Why can some people resist temptation but others can't? Why can some people make clouds out of marshmallows while others can't? Why can some be cool when it's hot, but others not? *What would Freud say?* Why does Walter care so much about these issues? What are his marshmallows? Is his art collection the marshmallows or the clouds? Is he under-controlled or overcontrolled? What, exactly, is his art collection disguising? Simple sublimation or reaction formation?
>
> Walter's second burning issue was the person × situation interaction. *What would Freud say?* Why does Walter resist main effects? Why does he intellectualize what we all know—that people are people? Is this his Julian Rotter contingency training? Is this his Kellyian personal construct mediation? Is this his Rogerian situated becoming? *What would Freud say?* Is it all a Vienna fixation during Walter's anal period?
>
> I first met Walter over 25 years ago. He was a star even then. Now he is more like a constellation. Tomorrow we will hear ballads sung about this constellation that I need not foreshadow here. More significant to me tonight is Walter the mere mortal.
>
> *Walter is the best kid to join in the sandbox.* Whatever toys he has—whether it is the theory he is working on or the latest addition to his art collection—he shares it with enthusiasm. Not only that, but if you have a new toy to share, such as a new idea, he is equally enthusiastic. It is this quality that is the secret to his famous charm. *He loves to share enthusiasms.* If there is a single behavior that reflects this unique element to his charm, it is his "instant replay" when he enjoys someone's comment. You say something he likes—he laughs, then

instantly repeats what you said, then laughs again. He lets you enjoy what you said in a way that together you share the moment. Now that's a kid worth joining in the sandbox.

REFERENCES

Adorno, T. W., Frenkel-Brunswick, E., Levinson, D. J., & Sanford, R. N. (1950). *The authoritarian personality.* New York: Harper.

Aronson, E., & Mills, J. (1959). The effect of severity of initiation on liking for a group. *Journal of Abnormal and Social Psychology, 59,* 177–181.

Atkinson, J. W., & Feather, N. T. (Eds.). (1966). *A theory of achievement motivation.* New York: Wiley.

Axsom, D., & Cooper, J. (1985). Cognitive dissonance and psychotherapy: The role of effort justification in inducing weight loss. *Journal of Experimental Social Psychology, 21,* 149–160.

Berlyne, D. E. (1973). The vicissitudes of aplopathematic and thelematoscopic pneumatology (or the hydrography of hedonism). In D. E. Berlyne & K. B. Madsen (Eds.), *Pleasure, reward, preference.* New York: Academic Press.

Bianco, A. T., Higgins, E. T., & Klem, A. (2003). How "fun/importance" fit impacts performance: Relating implicit theories to instructions. *Personality and Social Psychology Bulletin, 29,* 1091–1103.

Brehm, J. W. (1966). *A theory of psychological reactance.* New York: Academic Press.

Brehm, J. W., & Cohen, A. R. (1962). *Explorations in cognitive dissonance.* New York: Wiley.

Brehm, J. W., Stires, L. K., Sensenig, J., & Shaban, J. (1966). The attractiveness of an eliminated choice alternative. *Journal of Experimental Social Psychology, 2,* 301–313.

Brehm, S. S., & Brehm, J. W. (1981). *Psychological reactance: A theory of freedom and control.* New York: Academic Press.

Brickman, P. (1987). *Commitment, conflict, and caring.* Englewood Cliffs, NJ: Prentice Hall.

Cacioppo, J. T., Priester, J. R., & Berntson, G. G. (1993). Rudimentary determinants of attitudes II: Arm flexion and extension have differential effects on attitudes. *Journal of Personality and Social Psychology, 65,* 5–17.

Cairns, R. B. (1967). The attachment behavior of animals. *Psychological Review, 73,* 409–426.

Camacho, C. J., Higgins, E. T., & Luger, L. (2003). Moral value transfer from regulatory fit: "What feels right *is* right" and "What feels wrong *is* wrong." *Journal of Personality and Social Pschology, 84,* 498–510.

Cartwright, D. (1942). The effect of interruption, completion and failure upon the attractiveness of activity. *Journal of Experimental Psychology, 31,* 1–16.

Festinger, L. (1957). *A theory of cognitive dissonance.* Evanston, IL: Row, Peterson.

Festinger, L., & Carlsmith, J. M. (1959). Cognitive consequences of forced compliance. *Journal of Abnormal and Social Psychology, 58,* 203–211.

Forster, J., Higgins, E. T., & Idson, C. L. (1998). Approach and avoidance strength as a function of regulatory focus: Revisiting the "goal looms larger" effect. *Journal of Personality and Social Psychology, 75,* 1115–1131.

Freitas, A. L., Liberman, N., & Higgins, E. T. (2002). Regulatory fit and resisting temptation during goal pursuit. *Journal of Experimental Social Psychology, 38,* 291–298.

Freud, S. (1950). *Beyond the pleasure principle.* New York: Liveright. (Original work published 1920)

Hess, E. H. (1959). Imprinting. *Science, 130,* 130–141.

Higgins, E. T. (1987). Self-discrepancy: A theory relating self and affect. *Psychological Review, 94,* 319–340.

Higgins, E. T. (1997). Beyond pleasure and pain. *American Psychologist, 52,* 1280–1300.

Higgins, E. T. (2000). Making a good decision: Value from fit. *American Psychologist, 55,* 1217–1230.

Higgins, E. T. (2006). Value from hedonic experience *and* engagement. *Psychological Review, 113,* 439–460.

Higgins, E. T. (2007). Value. In A. W. Kruglanski & E. T. Higgins (Eds.), *Social psychology: Handbook of basic principles* (2nd ed., pp. 454–472). New York: Guilford Press.

Higgins, E. T., Idson, L. C., Freitas, A. L., Spiegel, S., & Molden, D. C. (2003). Transfer of value from fit. *Journal of Personality and Social Psychology, 84,* 1140–1153.

Idson, L. C., Liberman, N., & Higgins, E. T. (2004). Imagining how you'd feel: The role of motivational experiences from regulatory fit. *Personality and Social Psychology Bulletin, 30,* 926–937.

Kahneman, D., Diener, E., & Schwarz, N. (1999). *Well-being: The foundations of hedonic psychology.* New York: Russell Sage.

Lawrence, D. H., & Festinger, L. (1962). *Deterrents and reinforcement.* Stanford, CA: Stanford University Press.

Lewin, K. (1935). *A dynamic theory of personality.* New York: McGraw-Hill.

Lewin, K. (1951). *Field theory in social science.* New York: Harper.

Lewis, M. (1965). Psychological effect of effort. *Psychological Bulletin, 64,* 183–190.

Mandler, G. (1984). *Mind and body: The psychology of emotion and stress.* New York: Norton.

McClelland, D. C., Atkinson, J. W., Clark, R. A., & Lowell, E. L. (1953). *The achievement motive.* New York: Appleton-Century-Crofts.

Mischel, W. (1973). Toward a cognitive social learning reconceptualization of personality. *Psychological Review, 80,* 252–283.

Mischel, W., & Masters, J. C. (1966). Effects of probability of reward attainment on responses to frustration. *Journal of Personality and Social Psychology, 3,* 390–396.

Mischel, W., & Shoda, Y. (1995). A cognitive-affective system theory of personality: Reconceptualizing situations, dispositions, dynamics, and invariance in personality structure. *Psychological Review, 102,* 246–268.

Perry, R. B. (1926). *General theory of value: Its meaning and basic principles construed in terms of interest.* Cambridge, MA: Harvard University Press.

Rokeach, M. (1973). *The nature of human values.* New York: Free Press.

Shah, J., Higgins, E. T., & Friedman, R. (1998). Performance incentives and means: How regulatory focus influences goal attainment. *Journal of Personality and Social Psychology, 74,* 285–293.

Spiegel, S., Grant-Pillow, H., & Higgins, E. T. (2004). How regulatory fit enhances motivational strength during goal pursuit. *European Journal of Social Psychology, 34,* 39–54.

Thaler, R. H. (1980). Toward a positive theory of consumer choice. *Journal of Economic Behavior and Organization, 1,* 39–60.

Wicklund, R. A. (1974). *Freedom and reactance.* New York: John Wiley.

Wicklund, R. A., & Brehm, J. W. (1976). *Perspectives on cognitive dissonance.* Hillsdale, NJ: Erlbaum.

Woodworth, R. S. (1940). *Psychology* (4th Ed.). New York: Henry Holt & Company.

Zeigarnik, B. (1938). On finished and unfinished tasks. In W. D. Ellis (Ed.), *A source book of gestalt psychology* (pp. 300–314). New York: Harcourt, Brace, & World.

Ziff, P. (1960). *Semantic analysis.* Ithaca, NY: Cornell University Press.

Zimbardo, P. G. (1965). The effect of effort and improvisation on self-persuasion produced by role-playing. *Journal of Experimental Social Psychology, 1,* 103–120.

Positive Affect, Cognitive Flexibility, and Self-Control

ALICE M. ISEN

The main focus of this chapter is the influence of positive affect on self-control, including attention control, a topic that my colleagues, students, and I are working on in the context of a broader program of research on the influence of positive affect on cognition and behavior. Before turning to that topic, however, it is appropriate to say a few words about Walter Mischel's work, which will also provide some interesting context for discussion of this work on affect and self-control.

Walter Mischel's contributions to personality and social psychology are extensive and deep, widely regarded as revolutionary and generative. His innovative thought, pointing out the weakness of traditional models or approaches to personality as static, and his offering of an innovative alternative, are nearly universally acknowledged as constituting a great advance for the field. So, too, is his work on delay of gratification, especially its illumination of the importance of a person's focus of attention and construals of the situations he or she confronts, as determinants of the ability to delay gratification or show self-control. Less often discussed are Mischel's methodological contributions, and I want to draw attention to some of his methods of investigation and methodological rigor because I think they may be among the most important contributions that Mischel has made, and is continuing to make, during a brilliant and illustrious career. While he has not written as widely on these methodological points and principles as on the content areas for which he is so well known, these principles underlie all of his work and constitute a major contribution in themselves.

Before turning to these methodological contributions, it would be appropriate to say a bit about Mischel's substantive contributions. As noted above, he was innovative in pointing out that traditional models that regarded personality as static said little about the origin, maintenance, or possibilities for change in what theorists, as well as the public, viewed as stable, unchanging personality characteristics and/or types that people merely display. Not only did Mischel point out in his influential 1968 book that behavior was not as consistent across situations as was typically assumed by most personality theorists, but he also argued convincingly that there would be greater utility in searching for the factors that influenced behavior than in just describing or assessing the degree to which a person "had" various static qualities. He argued for a more scientific approach to understanding personality than just measurement and description.

I often try to illustrate this point to my students, as did my teachers, by taking the conversation into the realm of the physical sciences, where there are many examples of early scientific approaches to understanding the world around us in terms of measurement and description of the objects of interest, approaches that gave way to more process-oriented views as the sciences advanced. One example contrasts a scientific understanding of the weight of an object in terms of the laws of gravity with a more everyday understanding of weight in terms of perceived or measured "heaviness" of the object. Another example might be the scientific understanding of the color of an object—in terms of the refraction of light hitting an object and reflecting to the eye—with a more everyday understanding of color as a property of the object. Such measures of the qualities or traits of objects may represent a starting point, but, as Mischel would point out regarding personality, one will not get very far scientifically without an understanding of the processes involved. As someone whose career has been devoted to the study of emotion, I noted the similar frustration that was expressed by William James (1892/1963) in the section on emotion in his text *Psychology*, regarding the purely descriptive approach to emotion that was taken by most emotion scholars of his day:

> I should as lief read verbal descriptions of the shapes of the rocks on a New Hampshire farm as I would toil through them again. . . . They distinguish and refine and specify *in infinitum* without ever getting on to another logical level. Whereas the beauty of all truly scientific work is to get to even deeper levels. (p. 332)

Besides their descriptive nature, what seems to characterize these examples of early ways of trying to understand various physical phenomena—which eventually gave way to more process understandings—is that they conceptualized the crucial determinant of the phenomena they sought to understand as residing within the object of study—weight as a characteristic of an object rather than as a product of the effect of gravity on objects; color as a characteristic of an object rather than as the result of the interaction of light, the object, the background, and the eye and retina (and, some might add, the beholding mind). Another example would be the Aristotelian view of fire as an element residing within objects to greater or lesser degree.

In contrast, Mischel argued that the key to understanding personality in a scientifically useful way lay in understanding the processes at work to produce and maintain (and, therefore, potentially to change) what appears to be a "personality" or even a personality characteristic. This approach to thinking about personality was novel and broke the mold of existing personality psychology. It was so revolutionary that it caused some people to conclude that Mischel did not believe in "personality." Because he was not satisfied with mere descriptions or measurement of presumed static traits, traditional personality theorists concluded that he rejected the concept of personality. Mischel, on the other hand, thought that he was working on understanding personality, and he was shocked to learn how people interpreted his argument. He often mentions, with amazement still, the time that one of his students informed him that his name was the answer to a test question asking which theorist did not believe in personality.

Mischel's work on delay of gratification has also been path-breaking. Taking the approach that ability to control oneself (as evidenced by the ability to delay gratification) depends on aspects of the situation and the skills, strategies, and cognitive processes that are facilitated by that situation, he and his students began investigating the processes that might promote that ability. They quickly focused on the way a person construes the situation, or the stimulus itself, as important determinants of successful self-control (e.g., Mischel, 1973, 1974; Mischel, Shoda, & Rodriguez, 1989).

In my view there are two important principles in the approach that Mischel and his coworkers have taken: (1) that situations play a role in the kinds of things that people do, think, expect, and learn; and (2) that what people take from situations depends not only on the situation itself but also on how they construe and understand the situation and its affordances. This approach, then, is not just a simplistic statement that people's behavior is determined by "both personality and situation" or the simple "interaction of personality and situation," as some theorists characterize the "person–situation interaction." Rather, it represents an understanding of the subtle interplay between how a person thinks about a situation, about his or her options in the situation, possible goals and pathways in situations, and what the person decides to do in that situation. It construes personality and the determinants of behavior as involving active processes that are influenced by a person's understanding, expectations, and goals, rather than as more static qualities or automatic responses that are simply displayed or constrained in different situations.

This approach allows for development of habits or characteristics through learning or practice that are potentially amenable to change through similar processes of learning, changing expectations and understandings, and the like. Thus the approach developed by Mischel and his colleagues allows for the development of what look like characteristics, while at the same time it promotes understanding that there are processes that maintain and control those characteristics. Several papers show that the ability to delay gratification in early childhood (e.g., age 4) has been associated with positive life outcomes, and superior coping and interpersonal interaction skills, and ability to deal with frustration and stress, more than 10 years later (e.g., reviewed in Mischel, Shoda, & Rodriguez, 1989). What I find especially exciting about this approach—besides its very important identification of a powerful process-factor (cognitive control or ability to delay gratification) that can account for important distal outcomes related to self-control—is that it offers a link between a quality that may appear to be stable over time (self-control) and processes that allow understanding of factors that actually enable or facilitate that process, maintain and support it, determine the breadth of its impact and the situation in which it occurs, and upon which interventions to effect change could possibly be based.

Over the years, Mischel's work has integrated these two approaches into an understanding that ability to delay gratification, as enabled by cognitive control and interpretation of situations, may be a factor underlying other skills and abilities related to self-control. This connection is an impressive illustration of how his original insight regarding the importance of process can be utilized in understanding personality. Of course, his students all along the way, especially those with whom he worked closely, have also contributed to developing and extending his original ideas.

I turn now to the methodological contributions Mischel has made. I choose to point out the methods he used and taught his students because these methods are not only a key to the clever and creative work he has done throughout his career, but they are also key to understanding how his work is so accurate, insightful, and timeless.

First, Mischel emphasizes the importance for researchers of avoiding assuming what unseen processes or thoughts in people's minds are the causes of a person's behavior or some outcome, if they do not have sufficient observable evidence of those processes. Some researchers, with only the scantest hint of evidence suggestive of or indirectly compatible with their proposed underlying unseen process, will claim sufficient evidence of the hypothesized process (or even series of processes) and conclude that that process is operating and is the determinant of the behavior in question. In such situations, Mischel would urge finding observable evidence not only of the process, but also of the causal connection between the process and the behavior in question. He would say, "Let's not be crawling around inside people's heads." I still use this phrase with my students, most of whom find it a very graphic and convincing illustration of the need to obtain observable evidence of any process being postulated. As empirical scientists, we perhaps should not need to be reminded of this principle, but one often sees such assumptions of processes and causality in our literature.

It is not that what is going on inside people's heads is not important in Mischel's approach—a person's cognitions are crucial, actually. Expectations, construals of stimuli or events, and other cognitions (including what might be called cognitive–emotional configurations) are important determinants of outcomes. Rather, the issue is to find a way to render those unobservable thoughts and feelings observable. This is where Mischel's methodological contributions have been at their most impressive and delightful.

In tandem with this principle of making the unobservable observable is that of having the methods of assessment or experimentation be as realistic as possible. By that I mean that they should be as close as possible to the situation in which they occur naturally in people's lives. As context makes a great difference, it is appropriate to present as much of the real context in which the behavior will occur as possible.

Mischel emphasized coming up with inventive, realistic ways of observing behavior reflective of the underlying conceptualization, but he also pointed out that one observable way of assessing unobservable processes is not sufficient. Building on understandings established over 100 years of work in the testing and assessment literature, Mischel urged applying to experimentation the important principles underlying construct validation (triangulation, converging operations and discriminant validation), or that one should use multiple converging and discriminating measures that together establish that the underlying construct of interest is being measured (e.g., Cronbach, 1960; Cronbach & Meehl, 1955).

Relatedly, Mischel has always cautioned against reliance on self-reports of current states or likely future behavior, in part because the methods of assessment used to obtain such self-reports are usually questionnaires of unknown or weak reliability and/or validity. Sometimes researchers mistakenly believe that if they ask someone how he or she is feeling—how happy or sad, for example—then the answer that they receive reflects the person's affective state. What I have discovered over the years is that such statements of feelings do not always correspond to the person's actual affective state as indicated by other measures. Mischel's point about not using self-report scales to measure unseen mental states is that responses on scales are just that and no more—responses. As such, they are subject to all of the influences that affect any responses, factors such as response style, response bias, the way the person uses any scale regardless of its content, the way the person uses a scale that is presented in a particular format, the way the person understands the questions and their implications, and factors such as self-presentational concerns in the situation, experimenter effects in the setting, and so forth.

Self-report is problematic, then, not because people's thoughts or estimates are not important, but because the methods used to measure those thoughts and feelings are of unknown validity, subject to situational or response influences, and may not correspond to actual feelings or thoughts, or to those alone. In addition, behavior depends so much on context, and goals in a given context, but the context that will be operative is not always clear from the questions posed. Thus, the person does not have enough context to answer informatively. Beyond that, the context that is present when the self-reports are obtained may not reflect the context in which the feelings or behaviors of interest will be played out in situations of interest. Given that behavior is multidetermined by the confluence of many different motives and expected contexts' resulting in differing goals, expectations, and strategies exerting influence simultaneously, people cannot always provide the kinds of responses that experimenters are seeking, in part because they do not know from the questions what the context will be and what they will be trying to do in that situation (see, e.g., Isen & Erez, 2007, for fuller discussion). Furthermore, they may have goals when responding to the researcher's inquiry, no matter what format that inquiry takes, that are different from what their goals will be in other situations. Consequently, Mischel proposed finding behavioral measures to represent the concepts of interest.

Finally, it should be clear that Mischel emphasized a conceptualization of the person as an active, purposive agent, construing situations, having goals, and devising and trying out ways of accomplishing those goals, given the opportunities and constraints of the situation. The person is not seen as the passive recipient of external stimuli or internal impulses beyond his or her control, but as an active agent trying to manage and accomplish ends—sometimes through a maze of alternative motives, opportunities, stimuli impinging on him or her; sometimes through a thicket of obstacles; and sometimes down a clear roadway—but always an active agent.

POSITIVE AFFECT AND SELF-CONTROL

Now I turn to the influence of mild positive affect on cognition and behavior, in particular self-control.

Background

For a number of years, I have studied the influence of mild positive affect, of the kind that people can experience every day, on cognitive processes and social behavior. My work has focused on everyday affective experiences, in keeping with the principle that the operations used in experiments to manipulate or measure the factors of interest should be as similar as possible to the ways in which those factors occur naturally. By studying these realistically induced kinds of affective states, my colleagues and I have demonstrated that the effects we have observed occur in natural settings and are applicable to common life situations. These affect inductions in our experiments have included finding a small amount of money (such as a coin in the coin-return of a public telephone), receiving a free sample in a shopping mall or from a door-to-door representative, receiving a report of success on a task (in a school setting), or seeing a few minutes of a nonsexual, nonaggressive comedy film, to name a few.

In the present context, the question arises as to why we would expect that mild positive affect of the sort induced in our experiments—or, indeed, any affect or emotion—would foster or enable self-control. Why would we propose that positive affect leads to thinking or carefulness rather than impulsiveness? Most treatments of affect or emotion conceptualize it as triggering impulsive, nonreflective, uncontrolled, "hot" responding rather than thoughtful, careful, or controlled responding (e.g., Abelson, 1963). That view of positive affect, however, is not in keeping with a large body of findings in the research literature that has begun to accumulate. Let me begin by briefly reviewing some of our findings that are relevant to this topic and that form a background for our work on positive affect and self-control.

First, experiments on mild positive affect show, repeatedly and in many different contexts, that the influence of positive affect depends on other factors in the situation, including the actual characteristics of the stimuli and factors interacting with a person's goals in the situation. Thus, although people with positive affect sometimes do evaluate some stimuli more favorably, positive affect is not like "rose-colored glasses," simply coloring everything in a person's line of vision. Rather, a person's interpretation of the situation and his or her expectations in the situation make an important difference in the evaluations, behavior, and choices that result from the feelings he or she experiences. For example, positive affect has been found to have an influence on perception of neutral stimuli but not on perception of clearly positive or negative stimuli. For another example, in an organizational context, research has shown that positive affect improves satisfaction with, and evaluation of, an enriched job but not a dull, routine job (Kraiger, Billings, & Isen, 1989). This flexibility and responsiveness to the context suggests a process involving thinking and weighing of multiple aspects of the target stimulus and the context, rather than a simple lowering of standards for evaluation, or impulsive, "hot" responding.

Second, there is the content of what has been found to result from positive affect: Over the years, experiments have shown that positive affect induced in the everyday ways described above fosters social responsibility, helpfulness, and improved social interaction and functioning, and also facilitates effective cognitive processes, some of those apparently mediating the improved social interaction and coping processes observed. It is important to note that the increased social responsibility and improved social interaction that result from positive affect occur not through simple compliance or giving in to others' wishes or demands but through flexible thinking and adopting a problem-solving approach to addressing the conflicting needs of people with differing concerns, resolving differences of opinion, or settling disputes. These effects include helping others and donating to charity, all else equal, but not where the helping task would cause discomfort to a third party or threaten the helper's affective state (and the other's need is not pressing) and not where the cause to be helped would benefit a disliked group (much of this work is summarized in, e.g., Isen, 1987, 2000). The work also shows that positive affect can facilitate improved negotiation processes and outcomes, through flexible thinking and adopting a problem-solving approach (e.g., Carnevale & Isen, 1986). Thus it can be seen that positive affect fosters social responsibility, cooperativeness, and effective cognitive processes in a way that is appropriately responsive to the current situation. These are not effects that would typically be considered impulsive, "hot" responding.

This work shows, then, that flexible cognitive processes and thought are central to determining the influence that positive affect will have on behavior, so we have also focused more directly on the cognitive processes fostered by positive affect. In the early years of this research program, we found that positive affect at the time of recall facilitates recall of positive material in memory while not impairing memory for other kinds of material, a finding also reported by other researchers (e.g., Isen, Shalker, Clark, & Karp, 1978; Teasdale & Fogarty, 1979). Given that positive material is a large and well-interconnected set of otherwise diverse ideas (e.g., Cramer, 1968), this finding suggested that positive affect would lead to a complex, rich cognitive context for other cognitive processes, a hypothesis that was borne out in subsequent experimental work showing that positive affect leads a person to have more unusual and diverse word associations to neutral stimuli and more flexible ways of categorizing neutral material (e.g., Isen & Daubman, 1984; Isen, Johnson, Mertz, & Robinson, 1985; Kahn & Isen, 1993). Additional work confirmed that positive affect gives rise to flexible thinking, flexible cognitive organization, and creativity, including creative problem solving (e.g., Amabile, Barsade, Mueller, & Staw, 2005; Greene & Noice, 1988; Isen, 1987; Isen, Daubman, & Gorgoglione, 1987; Isen, Daubman, & Nowicki, 1987; Staw & Barsade, 1993).

It is important to distinguish between creativity, or flexible thinking, and impulsiveness because people sometimes assume that creativity involves risk taking or acting without thinking. This assumption is based on a stereotype about creativity, especially when speaking of creative problem solving. In fact, successful innovation or inventive problem solution requires not only divergent thinking, to come up with possible solutions or material or ideas that could contribute to a solution, but also inhibition of that process, and thoughtful convergent pulling together of those diverse thoughts, to address the specific problem under investigation. For this reason, it is important to note here that the problem-solving tasks that positive affect has been shown to facilitate include the Duncker (1945) Candle Task and items from the Mednicks' (1964) Remote Associates Test, both of which are thought to require creative innovation, and both of which require a specific answer to a difficult problem that only 11–16% of people in the neutral-affect and nontreatment conditions can solve (compared with about 58–75% in the positive-affect conditions). Compatible findings in a cognitive-social domain have shown that positive affect enables taking the other person's perspective and achieving the optimal outcome in a negotiation situation where, in the neutral condition, participants typically break off negotiation and fail to reach any agreement (Carnevale & Isen, 1986). This kind of improved performance, then, is compatible with self-control, not impulsive responding.

Another line of work compatible with the proposition that mild positive affect fosters self-control, rather than carelessness or impulsivity, is research on positive affect and risk taking. What this work shows is that although positive affect appears to foster risk taking in a hypothetical situation or where there is no meaningful risk to the decision-maker, if a person in a positive state is faced with a risk decision that involves a potential real loss that is meaningful to the person (for example, if the person is risking his or her credit for participating in the experimental session), then people in the positive affect condition are significantly more cautious and less likely to take the risk—more risk averse—than controls. This effect has been shown using amount to be bet (Isen & Patrick, 1983), lowest acceptable probability of winning (Isen & Geva, 1987), and choices among gambles (e.g., Isen, Nygren, & Ashby, 1988; Nygren, Isen, Taylor, & Dulin, 1996), to name a few. It has also been shown that people in positive affect prefer variety, among safe, enjoyable snack products, but not if the products are of dubious taste quality (Kahn & Isen, 1993).

Other lines of investigation also support the view that positive affect does not belong in the class of factors that promote impulsive, uncontrolled responding, but rather enhances constructive, problem-focused coping (see papers by Aspinwall, especially Aspinwall, 1998, and Aspinwall & MacNamara, 2005) and open-minded deliberation (e.g., Estrada, Isen, & Young, 1997). It helps people build resources (e.g., Fredrickson, 2001) and undo negative effects of stressful events (e.g., Fredrickson, Mancuso, Branigan, & Tugade, 2000) and leads them to be able to process information more finely (Johnson & Fredrickson, 2005).

Finally, another line of reasoning contributing to the suggestion that positive affect might promote self-control rather than impulsivity comes from the current work being done on neuropsychological approaches to increasing the field's understanding of the role of affect on cognition. In particular, it has recently been proposed that positive affect is accompanied by release of dopamine in the brain, and that this increased brain dopamine may underlie many of the cognitive (and behavioral) effects of positive affect that have been described (Ashby, Isen, & Turken, 1999). Further, this dopamine hypothesis is compatible with the suggestion that positive affect may promote self-control. This is because the regions of the brain that are rich in dopamine receptors include the frontal areas, governing complex thinking and working memory, including the anterior cingulate region, thought to be essential to conflict resolution and to maintaining multiple ideas in mind and the ability to switch among them purposively, as needed. Thus, the dopamine hypothesis suggests that positive affect should foster improved cognitive processing, especially where multiple options need to be considered or weighed against one another. Activation of frontal regions should facilitate working memory, inhibition of one process while concentrating on another; and activation of the anterior cingulate region in particular should facilitate resolution of conflicting material or maintaining multiple concepts in mind and switching attention among them. These capabilities seem similar to those that would enable self-control as that construct has been represented in the research literature, because self-control would seem to require considering multiple factors at once, weighing their implications and future or long-term effects, and gating of multiple impulses or inclinations.

The purpose of briefly reviewing this research work in the present context has been to gather some of the evidence showing that mild positive affect of the kind that people may experience in their everyday lives facilitates thinking and a "cool," or thoughtful, problem-focused (in contrast to a "hot," or impulsive) approach to a wide range of choices and behavior. This includes even difficult problem solving, dispute resolution, and choices in threatening or gambling situations. As such, this work offers a picture of affect (or at least of one type of affect) that differs from the view typically held among both lay people and researchers. Usually, people assume that affect interferes with thinking or competes with cognition for brain resources. While this assumption may be true of some kinds of affect, in some situations, the evidence suggests that it may not be true of all kinds of affect, in particular mild, everyday, positive affect.

In addition, because the research shows that positive affect enables flexible thinking and multiple ways of construing situations and stimuli, it makes sense in terms of the literature on self-control that positive affect should promote controlled behavior. According to the principles established by Mischel and his colleagues, being able to construe stimuli in multiple ways should facilitate, for example, ability to delay gratification in the face of temptation. Thus the findings that positive affect facilitates flexible thinking and multiple construals of stimuli and situations suggest that mild positive affect should be a factor that helps enable self-control.

Positive Affect Facilitates Self-Control

I now describe a program of research that my colleagues and I have begun, investigating the influence of positive affect on self-control. Results of these experiments are indicating that positive affect does promote self-control, especially where the task is difficult and self-regulation is needed. To triangulate on the construct of self-control or self-regulation, we have used different paradigms to assess self-control, different methods of affect induction, and multiple measures of self-regulation.

First, using a paradigm compatible with the work on intrinsic motivation and autonomy (e.g., Deci & Ryan, 1985), we investigated the influence of positive affect on choice between activities that reflect either intrinsic or extrinsic motivation. In two studies using this choice paradigm, results showed that positive affect gives rise to both intrinsic motivation and responsible work behavior (Isen & Reeve, 2005). Specifically, although positive affect does promote intrinsic motivation—increased choice of the more interesting task and greater enjoyment of that task— it also fosters performance of an unpleasant task if that task needs to be done.

In the first of these experiments, people were given a choice between performing an interesting puzzle task or performing a tedious task on which it would be possible to earn $2 if the entire task were completed in the allotted time. Those in whom positive affect had been induced by the technique of receipt of a small bag of candies (10 wrapped hard candies in a fold-top sandwich bag tied with a piece of red yarn—to be taken home, not consumed at the session), spent more time than controls on the puzzle task, and they reported enjoying the puzzle task more than controls. People in the positive-affect condition did, however, try out the tedious task and worked on it for about 10 of the 20 minutes they were given to try the tasks, long enough to provide feedback to the experimenter about the task, which was the cover story for asking participants to choose tasks to work on during the session. The task was designed so that one could see, from working on it, that it would not be possible to complete the task and earn the $2, in the 20 minutes allotted (and, indeed, no one—not even people in the control condition who spent the entire 20 minutes working on the dull task—was able to complete it and earn the $2).

It should be noted that in these studies, compatibly with results of earlier experiments that found differential effects of positive affect on different types of stimuli, while positive affect improved liking of the enjoyable task, it did not lead to greater liking of the tedious task. As noted earlier in this chapter, this indicates that positive affect does not simply function as a biasing lens and does not influence all stimuli or evaluations in the same way.

In the second experiment of this set of studies, there was no monetary incentive, but in one set of conditions people were told that there was work that needed to be done (two pages of the tedious work task), although they were free to choose how to spend their time during the session. In the other conditions, no mention was made of any work needing to be done. Where there was no mention of work that needed to be done, people in the positive-affect condition spent more time on the puzzle task, and enjoyed it more, than controls. Where participants were told that there was work that needed to be done, however, people in positive affect reduced their time on the enjoyable task and completed the work task, while still reporting greater enjoyment of the puzzle task (but not of the work task) than controls. These results show that positive affect does foster intrinsic motivation, enjoyment and performance of enjoyable tasks, but not at the cost of responsible work behavior on an uninteresting task that needs to be done (Isen & Reeve, 2005).

Another series of experiments has used the "depletion" paradigm developed by Baumeister, Vohs, and colleagues (e.g., Baumeister, Bratslavsky, Muraven, & Tice, 1998) to investigate the influence of positive affect on self-regulation. That paradigm involves having participants perform a difficult task, which is thought to require self-control or self-regulation, and then observing participants' performance on a subsequent difficult task involving self-regulation. It is typically found that people who engaged in the taxing first task are less able to resist a subsequent temptation, or spend less time on a difficult second task that requires self-regulation (e.g., Baumeister, et al., 1998); Baumeister and colleagues assume that expenditure of regulatory effort on the first task "depletes" people of self-regulatory capacity. In our studies investigating the influence of positive affect on self-control using this paradigm, thus far, it has been found that positive affect induced by the technique of a small gift at the experimental session leads people to be able to persist longer at a difficult task following a previous difficult or self-control task (Wan, Isen, & Sternthal, 2006).

We are also studying the influence of positive affect on delay behavior of the kind studied by Mischel and colleagues, including examination of the role of construal level and construal of stimuli. At its simplest, the reasoning is that if positive affect fosters flexible thinking, which includes the ability to think about material or situations in multiple ways, then positive affect may also be expected to enhance a person's ability to construe the tempting stimulus in multiple, or alternative, ways, and thus enhance the ability to delay.

The hypotheses advanced here deal not only with self-control behavior of continuing in a relatively unpleasant task or delaying gratification, but—compatibly with the ideas of Mischel and colleagues—they also propose that the effects occur through cognitive processes, such as construal, multiple and seemingly simultaneous considerations of ideas, and so forth. This, then, implicates cognitive control in the process of self-control. For example, the ability to construe a tempting stimulus as something else, which has been shown by Mischel and colleagues to improve ability to delay gratification, requires cognitive control. Consequently, it seems appropriate to report on the results of several studies in our lab investigating whether positive affect enables cognitive control as well as self-control in the more usual sense.

In three experiments so far, it has been found that positive affect fosters incidental learning and divided attention without loss of performance on a primary task (Isen & Shmidt, 2007). In the first study, people were given a surprise recall test asking about items that had appeared (with no warning) in the margins of the pages while they worked on a tedious letter-cross-out task. The pictures were of neutral items such as a round door handle, a box of tissue, or a roll of twine. In the second study, participants were told ahead of time that pictures of items would appear in the margins of the pages and that they would be asked about those pictures at the end of the task. Results of both studies revealed that people in the positive-affect condition performed better on the memory task (incidental-learning task or divided-attention task), while not performing any worse than controls on the main task, and even showing superior performance on the main task.

The format of the third study was a bit different, but the experiment still investigated the ability of people to perform a task requiring concentration in the presence of potentially distracting stimuli, so as to gauge their relative distractibility. In this task, participants performed a complex letter-cross-out task as before; however, in this task, after 3 minutes looking for horizontal pairs of letters, the task was changed to looking for vertical pairs of letters. Thus, participants had to perform the second task (finding vertical pairs of letters) in the presence of potentially interfering stimuli (the presence of horizontal pairs of letters) that were items that previously had been correct. Results again showed that people in the positive-affect condition performed better than controls, making fewer errors and doing more pages of letters correctly, while average reaction time was not affected. These studies indicate that positive affect enables people to stay focused on the problem they must complete, while at the same time noticing a broader range of stimuli present in the situation, whether they are warned about the presence of those items (study 2) or not (study 1), and can resist being distracted by them, even if they were previously correct answers to the problem that is their focus (study 3) or are completely novel.

In summary, all four of these lines of investigation, which involve self-control paradigms and cognitive-control paradigms, indicate that positive affect and the processes thought to underlie its influence on cognition, promote self-control and cognitive control. Typically, it is assumed that emotion is "hot" and fosters impulsive, thoughtless behavior, while cognition is "cool" and gives rise to careful, prudent deliberation. The point that I have raised for consideration, however, is that although some emotions may lead to thoughtless action, mild positive affect engages frontal areas of the brain and facilitates thinking (and caution if the situation is dangerous). In particular, mild positive affect seems to exert a "cooling" influence that helps people be thoughtful and careful in their choices and behavior, and thus facilitates self-control through some of the same processes identified by Mischel and colleagues. The further integration of these lines of investigation seems an exciting topic for continued investigation.

Finally, Mischel and colleagues have related their findings regarding the effects of thinking and construal processes on self-control to a personal characteristic of individuals and have shown that ability to delay gratification at age 4 predicts achievement behavior more than a decade later (e.g., Mischel, et al., 1989). However, that program of research also found that randomly assigned cognitive manipulation fosters children's ability to delay gratification. Thus direct intervention in the cognitive processes being used by the child has also been shown to facilitate his or her ability to wait for rewards. Similarly, in the work I have presented regarding mild positive affect as a facilitator of self-control, the affect was induced in randomly assigned groups, but other studies have also reported that relatively stable positive affect is associated with some of the effects we have found with induced positive affect, such as increased creative problem-solving ability (e.g., Staw & Barsade, 1993). Thus it may also be possible, as I suggested in an earlier paper (Isen, 1990), that experiences with positive affect over the course of time could lead to cognitive changes and habits that could result in a positive-affect style that could then contribute to the kinds of long-term outcomes that were observed by Mischel and colleagues. For positive affect as an influence on self-control, this possibility remains to be investigated. But together these lines of investigation suggest, for example, that cognitive interventions may lead to apparently stable differences or abilities, and that apparently stable differences may nonetheless remain amenable to change through intervention. The interplay of stability and change in people's approach to achieving their goals in various situations remains an intriguing area for continued investigation.

REFERENCES

Abelson, R. P. (1963). Computer simulations of "hot cognitions." In S. Tompkins & S. Messick (Eds.), *Computer simulations of personality* (pp. 277–298). New York: Wiley.

Amabile, T. M., Barsade, S. G., Mueller, J. S., & Staw, B. M. (2005). Affect and creativity at work. *Administrative Science Quarterly, 50,* 367–403.

Ashby, F. G., Isen, A. M., & Turken, A. U. (1999). A neuropsychological theory of positive affect and its influence on cognition. *Psychological Review, 106,* 529–550.

Aspinwall, L. G. (1998). Rethinking the role of positive affect in self-regulation. *Motivation and Emotion, 22,* 1–32.

Aspinwall, L. G., & MacNamara, A. (2005). Taking positive changes seriously: Toward a positive psychology of cancer survivorship and resilience. *Cancer, 104*(11 Suppl), 2549–2556.

Baumeister, R. F., Bratslavsky, E., Muraven, M., & Tice, D. M. (1998). Ego Depletion: Is the Active Self a Limited Resource? *Journal of Personality and Social Psychology, 74,* 1252–1265.

Carnevale, P. J. D., & Isen, A. M. (1986). The influence of positive affect and visual access on the discovery of integrative solutions in bilateral negotiation. *Organizational Behavior and Human Decision Processes, 37,* 1–13.

Cramer, P. (1968). *Word association.* New York: Academic Press.

Cronbach, L. J. (1960). *Essentials of psychological testing* (2nd ed.). New York: Harper.

Cronbach, L. J., & Meehl, P. E. (1955). Construct validity in psychological tests. *Psychological Bulletin, 52,* 281–302.

Deci, E. L., & Ryan, R. M. (1985). *Intrinsic motivation and self-determination in human behavior.* New York: Plenum Press.

Duncker, K. (1945). On problem-solving. *Psychological Monographs, 58* (Whole No. 5).

Estrada, C. A., Isen, A. M., & Young, M. J. (1997). Positive affect facilitates integration of information and decreases anchoring among physicians. *Organizational Behavior and Human Decision Processes 72,* 117–135.

Fredrickson, B. L. (2001). The role of positive emotions in positive psychology: The broaden-and-build theory of positive emotions. *American Psychologist, 56,* 218–226.

Fredrickson, B. L., Mancuso, R. A., Branigan, C., & Tugade, M. M. (2000). The undoing effect of positive emotions. *Motivation and Emotion, 24,* 237–258.

Greene, T. R., & Noice, H. (1988). Influence of positive affect upon creative thinking and problem solving in children. *Psychological Reports, 63,* 895–898.

Isen, A. M. (1987). Positive affect, cognitive processes, and social behavior. In L. Berkowitz (Ed.), *Advances in experimental social psychology* (pp. 203–253). New York: Academic Press.

Isen, A. M. (1990). The influence of positive and negative affect on cognitive organization: Some implications for development. In N. Stein, B. Leventhal, & T. Trabasso (Eds.), *Psychological and biological approaches to emotion* (pp. 75–94). Hillsdale, NJ: Erlbaum.

Isen, A. M. (2000). Positive affect and decision making. In M. Lewis & J. M. Haviland-Jones (Eds.), *Handbook of emotions* (2nd ed., pp. 417–435). New York: Guilford Press.

Isen, A. M., & Daubman, K. A. (1984). The influence of affect on categorization. *Journal of Personality and Social Psychology, 47,* 1206–1217.

Isen, A. M., Daubman, K. A., & Gorgoglione, J. M. (1987). The influence of positive affect on cognitive organization: Implications for education. In R. E. Snow & J. M. Farr (Eds.), *Aptitude, learning, and instruction* (pp. 143–164). Hillsdale, NJ: Erlbaum.

Isen, A. M., Daubman, K. A., & Nowicki, G. P. (1987). Positive affect facilitates creative problem solving. *Journal of Personality and Social Psychology, 52,* 1122–1131.

Isen, A. M., & Erez, A. (2007). Some measurement issues in the study of affect. In A. D. Ong & M. H. M. van Dulmen (Eds.), *Oxford handbook of methods in positive psychology* (pp. 250–265). New York: Oxford University Press.

Isen, A. M., & Geva, N. (1987). The influence of positive affect on acceptable level of risk: The person with a large canoe has a large worry. *Organizational Behavior and Human Decision Processes, 39,* 145–154.

Isen, A. M., Johnson, M. M. S., Mertz, E., & Robinson, G. F. (1985). The influence of positive affect on the unusualness of word associations. *Journal of Personality and Social Psychology, 48,* 1413–1426.

Isen, A. M., Nygren, T. E., & Ashby, F. G. (1988). The influence of positive affect on the perceived utility of gains and losses. *Journal of Personality and Social Psychology, 55,* 710–717.

Isen, A. M., & Patrick, R. (1983). The influence of positive feelings on risk taking: When the chips are down. *Organizational Behavior and Human Performance, 31,* 194–202.

Isen, A. M., & Reeve, J. (2005). The influence of positive affect on intrinsic and extrinsic motivation: Facilitating enjoyment of play, responsible work behavior, and self-control. *Motivation and Emotion, 29,* 297–325.

Isen, A. M., Shalker, T., Clark, M., & Karp, L. (1978). Affect, accessibility of material in memory, and behavior: A cognitive loop? *Journal of Personality and Social Psychology, 36,* 1–12.

Isen, A. M., & Shmidt, E. (2007). *Positive affect facilitates incidental learning and divided attention while not impairing performance on a focal task.* Unpublished manuscript, Cornell University, Ithaca, NY.

James, W. (1963). *Psychology, briefer course.* New York: Fawcett World Library. (Original work published 1892)

Johnson, K. J., & Fredrickson, B. L. (2005) "We all look the same to me": Positive emotions eliminate the own-race bias in face recognition. *Psychological Science, 16,* 875–881.

Kahn, B. E., & Isen, A. M. (1993). The influence of positive affect on variety-seeking among safe, enjoyable products, *Journal of Consumer Research, 20,* 257–270.

Kraiger, K., Billings, R. S., & Isen, A. M. (1989). The influence of positive affective states on task perceptions and satisfaction. *Organizational Behavior and Human Decision Processes, 44,* 12–25.

Mednick, M. T., Mednick, S. A., & Mednick, E. V. (1964). Incubation of creative performance and specific associative priming. *Journal of Abnormal and Social Psychology, 69,* 84–88.

Mischel, W. (1968). *Personality and assessment.* New York: Wiley.

Mischel, W. (1973). Toward a cognitive social learning reconceptualization of personality. *Psychological Review, 80,* 252–283.

Mischel, W. (1974). Processes in delay of gratification. In L. Berkowitz (Ed.), *Advances in experimental social psychology* (Vol. 7, pp. 249–292). San Diego, CA: Academic Press.

Mischel, W., Shoda, Y., & Rodriguez, M. L. (1989). Delay of gratification in children. *Science, 244,* 933–938.

Nygren, T. E., Isen, A. M., Taylor, P. J., & Dulin, J. (1996). The influence of positive affect on the decision rule in risk situations: Focus on outcome rather than probability. *Organizational Behavior and Human Decision Processes, 66,* 59–72.

Staw, B. M., & Barsade, S. G. (1993). Affect and managerial performance: A test of sadder-but-wiser versus happier-and-smarter hypotheses. *Administrative Science Quarterly, 38,* 304–331.

Teasdale, J., & Fogarty, S. J. (1979). Differential effects of induced mood on retrieval of pleasant and unpleasant events from episodic memory. *Journal of Abnormal Psychology, 88,* 248–257.

Wan, W., Isen, A. M., & Sternthal, B. (2006, September). *The influence of positive affect on regulatory depletion.* Paper presented at the annual meeting of the Association for Consumer Research, Orlando, FL.

9

Expectancy and the Perception of Aversive Events

EDWARD E. SMITH

In his groundbreaking 1973 *Psychological Review* paper, "Toward A Cognitive Social Learning Reconceptualization of Personality", Mischel argued that theories of personality would do well to consider concepts that were then being adopted (or readopted) in the unfolding cognitive revolution. Chief among them was the concept of expectancy. Mischel proposed that "effectiveness of [events] rests on their ability to modify expectancies" (p. 270) (as opposed to responses). In essence, Mischel was suggesting that the world we perceive is rarely based on just the input, but rather is modulated by what we expect that input to be. His emphasis on expectancy has proved prescient.

COMBINATION VERSUS BIAS

Since the earliest psychological discussions of expectancy, a critical question has been whether expectancy affects our perceptual experience or biases our reporting of that experience. The contrast between these extremes was already evident in the 1950s and early 1960s and can be illustrated by considering proposals by two prominent players in the cognitive revolution: Jerry Bruner (1957) and the team that developed the theory of signal detectability (TSD)—Swets, Tanner, and Birdsall (1961). Bruner was concerned with the problem of how we perceive objects and argued that the perception of an object frequently involves categorization of that object (e.g., "It's a cat"). One of Bruner's concerns was the role of expectancy in this categorization process. There were already demonstrations that increasing the perceiver's expectancy that the input would belong to a certain category increased the chances that the perceiver would assign the input to that category (e.g., Bruner, Postman, & Rodrigues, 1951), but what cognitive mechanisms were involved? Bruner proposed that expecting a particular category increases the accessibility of that category, meaning less input information is needed to activate the category. Critically, the role played by expectancy is comparable to the role played by stimulus information—they both activate the same underlying representation. Expectancy and input can combine because they contain the same kind of information.

The view from TSD was very different. According to Swets and colleagues (1961), the expectancy of a particular class of events does not combine with the input but *biases* our criterion for reporting the event. TSD distinguishes between an observer's sensitivity and his or her placement of a response criterion and views sensitivity as governed by factors having to do with stimulus discriminability and criterion placement as affected by factors such as payoffs and expectancy. Thus, according to TSD, stimulus information and expectancy play different roles—they do not directly combine.

PLACEBO EFFECTS

In the 40 years since these proposals were offered, a great deal of behavioral work has been done documenting that each proposal works in certain domains (see e.g., Higgins, 1996, for an update on expectancy effects in categorization, and Swets, 1995, for extensions of TSD to new domains). But there are many domains in which it is by no means clear whether stimulus and expectancy combine. One such broad domain is the perception of aversive events, such as pain perception.

There has been much interest in expectancy in this domain of pain perception, not just in psychology, but also in clinical medicine, where there is a direct connection between the expectancy issue and the question of placebo effects. A placebo is typically defined as an inert substance, and a placebo effect occurs when the placebo alone ameliorates the symptoms of some disease or disorder. It has long been thought that many placebo effects are mediated by an expectation of symptom release (see Harrington, 1999, for a review), so it is again important to ask whether expectancy combines with stimulus information or biases it. This issue is particularly important in clinical treatment of pain.

Although there are literally hundreds of published reports showing that placebos can ameliorate aversive conditions, a relatively recently published meta-analysis argued that the placebo effect is largely a myth (Hrobjartsson & Gotzsche, 2001, 2004). Most studies that compared a medical treatment and placebo conditions failed to include a "natural history" control (i.e., a condition in which the patient receives no treatment and no expectation), and it is quite possible that the symptomatology of interest (e.g., sad mood in the case of depression) would abate in the natural course of events. An exception to this sweeping criticism is the clinical domain of pain. Here, there have been numerous studies that included a natural history control as well as treatment and placebo conditions, and collectively they indicate that placebos lead to a greater decline in reported pain than does a natural history control. Critically, Hrobjartsson & Gotzsche dismiss these studies on the grounds that reports of pain may reflect patients' attempts to comply with the experimenters' goals or some other kind of bias. Essentially, they argue that subjective reports in this case offer no real evidence that the expectancy engendered by placebo combined with the experience of pain, clearly taking a TSD approach.

The literature on placebo effects is not limited to clinical studies; there are also experimental studies of the effects of placebo-induced expectancy on the perception of pain. Many experimental studies investigated whether a placebo pill or cream reduces the experience of pain in healthy participants in a controlled experiment (i.e., unlike in the clinical studies, the experimenter determines who gets the placebo and who gets the control). These studies generally show that a placebo reduces the amount of pain that participants report (see Kirsch, 1985, for a partial review), but again the measures are subjective reports and are open to the interpretation that the expectancies engendered by the placebo may have affected only the participants' biases. There is no convincing evidence that expectancy and stimulus combine.

THE ROLE OF NEUROIMAGING EVIDENCE

What is needed is some kind of measure that is closer to perceptual experience than verbal reports. Autonomic measures, such as skin conductance or heart rate, are clear possibilities, and studies have provided evidence that a placebo-based expectancy of less pain leads to a reduction in a measure of autonomic activity (e.g., Pallo et al., 2003). The problem with autonomic measures is that they are not very specific. In a pain situation, many factors other than a decrease in perceived pain can cause reductions in autonomic activity (for example, a reduction in anxiety). We need measures that are more directly linked to pain perception.

One measure that seems to fit the bill is that of neural activity in regions of the brain known to mediate the perception of pain. Such activity can now be measured by functional magnetic resonance imaging (fMRI). Indeed, there are numerous published neuroimaging studies of pain, and they typically show that the perception of pain is accompanied by increased neural activity in a network of neural regions that involves cortical areas including somatosensory cortex and anterior cingulate cortex, as well as subcortical areas includiing the thalamus and anterior insula (e.g., Craig, Chen, Bandy, & Reiman, 2000). Tracking activation changes in this pain matrix or in other neural regions known to be associated with aversive experience is the approach my colleagues and I have taken in studying the effects of expectancy on the perception of aversive events. In the next two sections, I review two neuroimaging experiments that varied participants' expectancies about how aversive an upcoming stimulus would be and showed that these expectancies altered neural activity in areas associated with perceptual experience. These findings evidence that expectancy and stimulus (pain) information can combine.[1]

IMAGING EXPECTANCY EFFECTS

Expectancy-Based Placebo Effects

My colleagues' and my first experiments focused on placebo effects in the experience of pain, which was induced either by electric shock or thermal heat (Wager et al., 2004). Our primary concern was the effects of expectancy. Our first question was: Does the expectancy of reduced pain result in decreased neural activity in the pain matrix when a painful stimulus is actually administered? A positive answer to this question would provide a new source of evidence for the proposal that expectancy can directly combine with perceptual experience. Our second concern focused on the neural bases of expectancy per se: Does the expectancy of reduced pain lead to increased neural activity in selective regions before the pain is actually administered (i.e., during the anticipation period)? The selective regions of interest were most likely to be in the prefrontal cortex, because this area has already been implicated in maintaining expectancies (e.g., MacDonald, Cohen, Stenger, & Carter, 2000; Miller & Cohen, 2001).

It is sufficient here to focus on the results obtained with thermal heat pain (electric shock pain produced similar results). Participants rated the pain level of heat pain administered to their right forearm while being imaged by fMRI. In all trials the experimenter applied a cream to the critical forearm region. For the placebo blocks, participants were told that the cream was an analgesic (Lidocaine) that would effectively reduce their pain; for the *control* blocks participants were told that the cream was "just a control." In fact, the same cream was always used, with different dyes employed to give it different colors for the placebo and control blocks. This placebo versus control manipulation was a variation in expectancy.

A schematic of a trial is presented in Figure 9.1A. The trial started with a cue (to alert participants), followed by an anticipation period that lasted between 1 and 16 seconds. Presumably, what exactly was anticipated would differ in the placebo and control conditions, and these cognitive differences would be reflected in neural differences in frontal cortex. The next critical event was the administration of the heat pain, via a thermode, which lasted for 20 seconds. According to the combination hypothesis, it is during this period that expectancy might combine with thermal sensation to form the overall experience of pain. The pain stim-

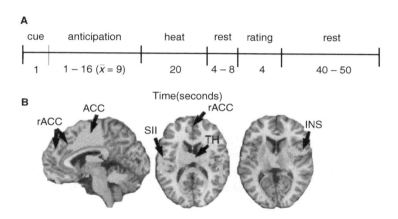

FIGURE 9.1.(A) Trial structure in the Wager and colleagues (2004) experiment. Each trial began with a 1-second warning cue, followed by a blank anticipation period that lasted between 1 and 16 seconds. Then a painful thermal stimulus was applied for 20 seconds (1.5-second ramp up, 17-second peak, 1.5-second ramp down). The thermal stimuli were applied to one of two patches of skin on the left forearm, where one patch had been treated with a placebo cream and the other with a control cream (the two creams were, in fact, identical except for color). The thermal stimulus was followed by a rest period of 4–8 seconds, which in turn was followed by a 4-second rating period during which participants rated their pain on a 10-point scale (1 = "just painful," 10 = "unbearable pain"). The trial ended with a 40- to 50-second rest period. (B) Average pain-responsive regions for the participants. These regions were determined by varying the level of pain presented (in a phase of the experiment prior to the test phase). Adapted from Wager et al. (2004). Copyright 2004 by the American Association for the Advancement of Science. Adapted by permission.

ulus was followed by a brief rest interval, and then by a period during which participants rated the severity of their pain on a scale from 1 to 10, where 1 was labeled "just painful" and 10 was labeled "unbearable pain." According to the bias hypothesis, it is during this rating period that expectancy might have its effect. The trial ended with a 40- to 50-second rest period, allowing neural activity in all regions to return to base level before the next trial began.[2]

Consider first the behavioral results, those involving reports of perceptual experience. These reports showed a very substantial placebo-based expectancy effect, as 22 out of 24 participants rated the heat pain as less severe on placebo than on control trials.[3]

The results of greatest interest are two sets of fMRI findings. First, during the pain period, there was a decrease in neural activity in the placebo compared to the control condition in a number of regions in the pain matrix. (The pain matrix for our participants was determined by independent means, and the contributing areas are shown in Figure 9.1B.) The pain areas that showed reduced activation under placebo included the anterior insular, the anterior cingulate cortex, and the thalamus. These reductions in activation are neural placebo effects, and presumably they are the consequences of expectations set up during the anticipation period. These neural placebo effects provide striking evidence that expectation and input can combine (the same regions can be activated by pain in the absence of any specific expectancy and can be modulated by expectancy). The second set of fMRI findings pertains to the anticipation period. There was an *increase* in neural activity in the placebo compared to the control condition in a number of regions in the frontal cortex, including the dorsolateral prefrontal cortex (dorsolateral PFC). These effects presumably reflect expectation processes.

It is worth unpacking both of these major findings. We begin with the neural placebo effects (or neural expectancy effects) obtained during the pain period. Figure 9.2 shows images of some critical regions of the pain matrix that showed reduced activity when participants had a placebo-based expectancy of reduced pain. The results for the rostral anterior cingulate cortex (rACC), the anterior insula (INS), and the thalamus (TH) are in panels A, B, and C, respectively. With regard to the rACC, although the overall reduction of activity in this area with placebo did not reach statistical significance, there was a significant correlation across participants between the magnitude of the neural placebo effect in this region and the magnitude of the behavioral placebo effect. Brain–behavior correlations such as this one (and others reported in Wager et al., 2004) provide a needed convergence of neural and behavioral evidence, and increase our confidence in the validity of subjective reports of pain.

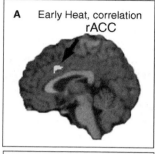

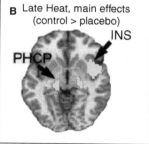

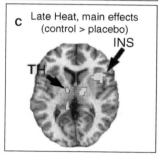

FIGURE 9.2. Pain regions of the brain that show correlations between behavioral placebo effects and neural placebo effects: (A) Rostral anterior cingulate (rACC). (B) Right-hemisphere insula (INS) and parahippocampal cortex (PHCP). The latter activations extended into the basal forebrain and are contiguous with thalamic activations; however, only thalamic activations are in pain-sensitive regions. (C) Right-hemisphere INS and bilateral thalamus (TH). Adapted from Wager et al. (2004). Copyright 2004 by the American Association of the Advancement of Science. Adapted by permission.

Recall that the pain interval was 20 seconds, and that the trial continued for another 50 seconds or so. Such a long trial makes it possible to chart the time course of our neural placebo effects, and such time courses are presented in Figure 9.3, which plots the fMRI response for the placebo and control conditions in two regions—the right-hemisphere insula (A) and the thalamus (B)—and in each region the difference between the control and placebo functions gives the neural placebo effect. It is apparent that the effect arises in the later stage of the pain response—expectancy takes awhile to show its influence. This delay suggests that placebo-induced expectancy has its effect on an interpretive process in pain perception, as opposed to affecting initial sensory registration. (I return to the implications of this point later.)

Consider now the placebo effect obtained during the anticipation period, which is manifested as greater activation for placebo than control conditions in frontal regions. There was increased activation in two critical areas: the dorsolateral PFC, known to be involved in the media-

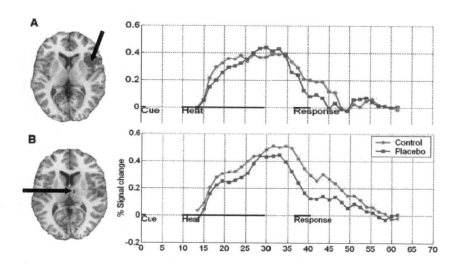

FIGURE 9.3. Time courses of neural activity in two regions showing neural placebo effects. (A) Neural activity during pain for placebo and control in the right-hemisphere INS (the arrow indicates the exact region in the slice at left). Horizontal black bars show average timing of trial events, although timing varied from trial to trial. (B) Neural activity during pain for placebo and control in the right-hemisphere thalamus, as in (A). Adapted from Wager et al. (2004). Copyright 2004 by the American Association of the Advancement of Science. Adapted by permission.

tion of expectancy, and a region in the midbrain that is known to send outputs to the pain matrix (see Wager, 2005). These activation effects are pure expectancy effects; there is no stimulus present and no response required during this time period. While behavioral measures are silent, the brain measures show the reality of expectancy.

Pure Expectancy Effects

I contend that the effects obtained in the prior study are due *solely* to expectancy (i.e., the only role played by the placebo cream is to increase the participants' belief that their pain will be lessened). If this claim is correct, then we should be able to find comparable neuroimaging results, particularly the decreases in neural activity during aversive events, even when there is *no* placebo manipulation. Toward this end, my colleagues and I recently studied the effects of expectancy on the judgments of aversive tastes (Nitschke et al., 2005).

We imaged participants by fMRI while they were experiencing an aversive taste, varying whether the participants expected a mildly bitter taste or a very bitter one. In half of the critical trials participants tasted a highly aversive liquid, in a quarter of the trials the liquid they tasted was only mildly aversive, and in the remaining quarter of the trials the liquid had a neutral taste. A highly aversive taste could be preceded by a "valid" cue indicating that the taste would be highly aversive, or it could be preceded by a "deceptive" cue that the taste would be only mildly aversive; this was the expectancy manipulation. Because we know from previous work that the neural regions that mediate taste perception comprise the primary taste cortex, including the insula and the operculum (e.g., Ogawa, 1994; Rolls, 1999), the combination hypothesis (but not the bias hypothesis) predicts that an expectancy that a taste will be less aversive should lead to a decrease in neural activity in the primary taste cortex.

The sequence of trial events is schematically presented in Figure 9.4. Again the trial started with a cue, but in this study the cue set up the expectation by signaling whether the liquid that was about to be tasted would be neutral (water), mildly aversive, or aversive. The neutral and aversive cues were always valid in that they were always followed by the predicted taste, whereas the mildly aversive cue was sometimes followed by a mildly aversive taste but other times followed by a highly aversive taste. Because cues were valid most of the time, expectations should have been relatively strong. The participants then tasted the liquid. After swallowing the liquid, participants rated their gustatory experience on a 9-point scale (see Figure 9.4).

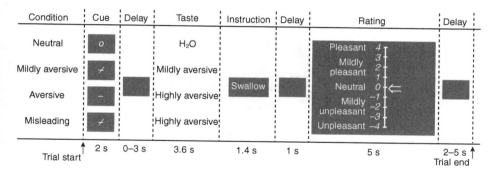

FIGURE 9.4. Trial structure for four conditions of interest in the Nitschke and colleagues (2005) experiment. For the neutral condition shown at the top, a circle cue invariably preceded a neutral taste (distilled water). Aversive taste solutions were delivered in three conditions: for the mildly aversive condition, a minus sign with a slash preceded a mildly aversive taste (0.25 mM quinine); for the aversive condition, a minus sign preceded a highly aversive taste (1.0 mM quinine); and for the misleading condition, the minus sign with a slash preceded the highly aversive taste (1.0 mM quinine). The only other difference among the four conditions was the taste delivered, as indicated for each condition. Adapted from Nitschke et al. (2005). Copyright 2005 by Nature Publishing Group. Adapted by permission.

As usual, there was a substantial expectancy effect on the behavioral ratings, as participants rated the highly aversive taste as less unpleasant when it was preceded by a mildly aversive cue than an aversive cue. This is a kind of placebo effect without a placebo, which fits with our assumption that many placebo effects are entirely due to altered expectations. (Unexpected highly aversive tastes were still rated more aversive than mildly aversive tastes, which shows that expectancy has its limits.)

Again the results of greater interest are the fMRI findings. During the period when participants were experiencing the taste, the expectation of a less aversive taste led to a decrease in neural activity in posterior insula in both the left and right hemispheres. Figure 9.5 presents images of two broad regions—the insula and operculum—that were activated in the various conditions. A correlational analysis across participants showed that the greater the reduction in right-hemisphere insula activity, the greater the expectation effect on the behavioral ratings (i.e., the greater the rating difference between a highly aversive taste that is expected to be such and one that is expected to be only mildly aversive). Once more the results support the combination hypothesis and show a convergence between neural effects and behavioral ratings.

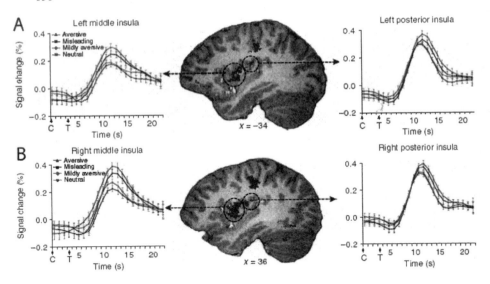

FIGURE 9.5. The circled clusters indicate areas that were more strongly activated by the highly aversive taste than by the neutral taste. These clusters include the middle INS and frontal operculum, and posterior insula and parietal operculum. Panels A and B show the results for the left and right hemispheres, respectively. Most important, the left- and right-hemisphere INS and operculum clusters were more strongly activated by the highly aversive taste following the aversive cue than by the same taste following the misleading cue. This expectancy effect is shown in the time course data, presented on the left and right of the brain images. Each time course illustrates the change in neural activity across all time points of the trial in each of the four conditions. Note that the time course for the misleading cue lies below that for the aversive cue (this is the neural expectancy effect). Adapted from Nitschke et al. (2005). Copyright 2005 by Nature Publishing Group. Adapted by permission.

Constraints on Combination

The notion of combining stimulus and expectancy information seems too simple in light of the imaging evidence. For one thing, in the pain experiment, neural placebo effects occurred in later stages of the pain experience, which suggests that expectancy is not affecting the initial registration of sensory experience. For another, in both studies described, some of the brain regions implicated (e.g., the anterior insula) are thought to be involved in the interpretation of affective experience, rather than in initial sensory registration. Thus we need to distinguish at least three levels of perceptual experience at which expectancy might enter the picture: sensory registration, interpretation of the sensory information, and subsequent biases in reporting the experience. This tripart division is reflected in Figure 9.6, which is adapted from Wager's (2005) recent review of the neural bases of placebo effects of pain.

Figure 9.6A shows three different routes by which expectancy can influence the perceptual experience of pain. The top route, labeled "Demand characteristic," is essentially the same as our bias hypothesis. The bottom route, "Gate control," posits that expectancy can affect the sensory registration of pain. Gate control is the name of the well-known theory that posits that the brain can block pain early in processing by

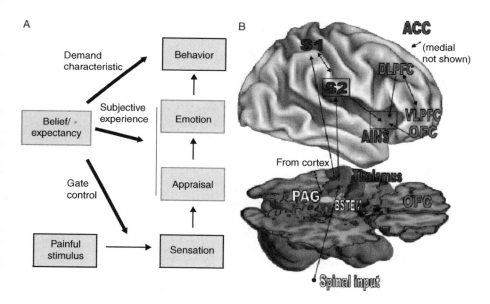

FIGURE 9.6. (A) Routes by which expectancy may lead to changes in the perceptual experience of pain and (B) some important brain regions in the pain pathway. Pain begins when sensory signals from the spinal cord reach the brain via the TH and are sent to the primary (S1) and secondary somatosensory cortex (S2). These areas may be most important for the sensory aspects of pain. From there, signals are sent to the anterior insula (AINS) and ACC, which are involved in the subjective experience and emotional quality of pain. These signals undergo an appraisal (interpretive) process, in which potential harm is assessed and corresponding emotions are generated. Appraisals are generated through interactions among the orbitofrontal cortex (OFC), AINS, ACC, and other regions, and they may be maintained in the dorsolateral PFC (DLPFC). Expectancies may inhibit spinal input (bottom route in panel A), alter the experience of pain directly (middle route), or affect behaviors and pain reporting (top route). Adapted from Wager (2005). Copyright 2005 by Blackwell Publishing. Adapted by permission.

engaging opioid neurons in a midbrain region, which in turn inhibits pain in the spinal cord (Melzack & Wall, 1965). Placebo effects based on this route should occur relatively early in the time course of pain, which was not the case in the study we described. The middle route labeled "Subjective experience," involves an interpretation of the sensory input and presumably gives rise to the felt experience. This middle route is the one that was most likely operative in the studies we discussed. Figure 9.6B displays some of the important brain regions in the pain matrix (see caption for further explanation).

RELATION TO EMOTIONAL EXPERIENCE

Expectancy and Emotion Regulation

In setting up the contrast between the combination and bias hypotheses, I mentioned studies by Bruner (1957) and others on object recognition and psychophysical studies by Swets et al. (1961). Although these two domains of studies may be useful for highlighting the distinction of interest, they differ in a fundamental way. The process of object recognition is a matter of activating the appropriate representations of external objects, and expectancy has its influence via these representations. Perceptual experience of pain or taste is not about representations of external objects. Experiencing heat pain on your arm need not involve a representation of any object in the external world. It is therefore useful to consider expectancy effects in a domain that is closer to perceptual experience, a domain that also has a strong nonrepresentational component. An obvious candidate is emotional experience.

In the domain of emotional experience there are numerous studies of a phenomenon that seems closely related to expectancy effects on perceptual experience, namely, the regulation of emotion. Since the seminal work of Lazarus (e.g., 1966), researchers have been interested in our ability to reinterpret, or reappraise, an emotional stimulus so as to alter its level of arousal, its valence, or both. Instead of an aversive experience such as pain induced by heat, we are now dealing with an aversive feeling like disgust induced by looking at victims of horrific accidents; and instead of a prior expectancy influencing the interpretation of a subsequently presented stimulus, we are now dealing with interpretive processes that ensue once the emotion-inducing stimulus has been presented. These apparent differences may not be that great. Meta-analyses of the brain regions involved in negative emotions reveal some of the same areas as those implicated in studies of pain perception, such as the anterior insular (Phan, Wager, Taylor, & Liberzon, 2002; Wager, Phan, Liberzon, & Taylor, 2003). There is also direct evidence that physical pain and psychological pain have overlapping neural bases (Eisenberger, Lieberman, & Williams, 2003). It is plausible, then, that the cognitive processes involved in expectancy may be of the same sort as those involved in the regulation of emotion (particularly because expectancy-based processes may have some of their effects only after the stimulus has been presented).

It is worth considering some neuroimaging experiments of the regulation of emotion. In a representative study (Ochsner, Bunge, Gross, & Gabrieli, 2002), participants viewed a photograph that elicited either a negative emotional response or a neutral one (as determined by previous norms). On some trials, participants received an instruction that told them just to attend to the photo (essentially giving their emotions free reign); on other trials, participants were instructed to reappraise the photo or to reinterpret it so that it no longer elicited a negative feeling (participants had been pretrained on reappraisal strategies). Then all participants rated the strength of their negative affect.

Consider first the behavioral findings. In line with many other studies in the literature (see Gross, 2002, for a recent review), reappraisal led to a decrease in the rated emotionality of the photo. (Reappraised negative pictures were still rated more negatively than neutral ones—reappraisal, like expectancy, has its limits).

The fMRI results confirmed that whatever cognitive processes were operative in reappraisal succeeded in reducing the intensity of the negative experience. Some of the target brain regions for negative emotional experience include the amygdala and the orbitofrontal cortex, and both of these regions showed a decrease in activation in the reappraisal compared to the attend condition. This is similar to the decreases in activation seen in the insula in the expectancy studies, as all of these areas are involved in the mediation of affective experience. Also, Ochsner and colleagues (2002) found greater activation in left-hemisphere dorsolateral PFC and other lateral areas of PFC in the reappraisal than in the attend condition. This is similar to the increases in activation in dorosolateral PFC seen in the placebo study, the only difference being that now the increase is occurring concurrent with stimulus processing rather than prior to it. Last, Ochsner and colleagues found brain–behavior correlations like those obtained in the placebo experiment. In the reappraisal condition, increased activity in the anterior cingulate is accompanied by an increase in the behavioral appraisal effect.

The general pattern of results for reappraisal is, therefore, similar to that obtained in expectancy studies—increased activity in prefrontal areas that correlates with decreased activity in areas associated with affect and emotion. The same pattern also obtains with a different kind of emotion, sexual arousal. In a representative study, Beauregard, Levesque, and Bourgouin (2001) imaged the brains of male participants while they watched erotic or neutral films and instructed the participants either to respond normally to the films (control) or to "distance themselves," and "become a detached observer" (reappraisal). Compared to the control condition, the reappraisal condition showed (1) a decrease in an emotional area of the brain—in this case, the hypothalamus, which has long been known to be involved in sexual feelings and behavior—and (2) an increase in a frontal area—in this case, the right-hemisphere PFC. These results fit the general pattern of prefrontal areas down-regulating emotional areas.

Given these parallels between emotion regulation and expectancy studies, can we use the reappraisal research to learn something about the nature of expectancy processes? The reason the reappraisal research might be revealing is that participants in these studies are given explicit instructions about how to process each stimulus, whereas participants in expectancy studies are typically left to their own devices. Assuming that participants in reappraisal experiments are indeed following instructions, we can ask what core cognitive processes are recruited by these instructions.

In the Beauregard and colleagues (2001) study, participants were instructed to distance or detach themselves from the erotic stimulus. Similar instructions have been used in other reappraisal experiments. Interestingly, the notions of distancing and detachment also play a role in recent work by Kross, Ayduk, and Mischel (2005), who applied these notions in what might be considered a reappraisal study. To engender an emotional reaction, the participants were asked to think about an interpersonal experience in which they felt anger and hostility. Then they were taught different strategies for reprocessing the emotional experience. One strategy required the participants to focus on the specific feelings they were experiencing during the angry episode (these are the "what" instructions). Another strategy asked the participants to adopt a self-distanced perspective and to focus on the reasons underlying their feelings (these are the "why" instructions, which provide a kind of reappraisal). Compared to the "what" condition, the "why" condition led to a decrease in emotion in a number of behavioral measures, including ones that should not be susceptible to bias.

The upshot is that reappraisal may depend on psychological distancing, which then becomes a candidate explanation for how expectancy affects the perceptual experience of aversive events. For example, participants in a study described earlier who expected a decrease in heat pain may have somehow distanced themselves from the pain.

The Nature of Psychological Distance

The problem with the preceding analysis is that the notions of distancing and detachment are closer to metaphors than they are to basic cognitive processes, and it is the latter that are of concern, not only because they offer a more fundamental explanation but also because they are more likely to be localized in the brain. So the question becomes: What cognitive–affective processes are involved in distancing? A couple of tentative hypotheses follow.

One possibility is that when we increase our psychological distance from an object or situation, we affect the perceptual aspects of our representation of that object or situation. This is more likely when there is no physical stimulus present and people instead are retrieving a memory (as in the Kross et al., 2005, study), which may be at least partly in the form of a visual image. In such a case, an instruction to distance oneself may result in a reduction of the size of the visual image of that object or situation. Furthermore, the smaller the size of an imaged object or situation, the less intense may be one's emotional reaction to it. At this point, there is no direct evidence for the claims that distancing instructions in emotion regulation studies lead to smaller visual images or that smaller images lead to less intense emotional reactions.

Another possibility is that: (1) increasing psychological distance leads one to represent objects and situations in more abstract terms, and (2) emotional reactions are usually less intense to more abstract representations. This hypothesis, particularly the first part of it, has been systematically investigated by Trope and colleagues (e.g., Trope & Liberman, 2003), who have convincingly shown that objects or situations that are more distant in time are indeed represented more abstractly than those closer in time. How would this abstractness hypothesis apply to the reappraisal experiments discussed earlier? In the Ochsner and colleagues (2002) study, a negative photograph, say of a gun, might be represented as a "murderer's gun" under control instructions, but as a "modern weapon" under reappraisal instructions. In the Kross and colleagues (2005) experiment, a memory of a heated argument might be represented as an "unfair fight" under "what" instructions, but as a "breakdown in communication" under "why" instructions. In both examples, the more abstract interpretation intuitively seems less emotionally arousing.

Image size and abstractness may both play a role in reappraisal processes in some situations, but neither hypothesis seems to deal with what may be the heart of reappraisal: a change in perspective so that what was initially interpreted from a first-person vantage point comes to be interpreted from a third-person perspective (as described in Kross et al., 2005). For example, the expectancy of relief in a pain situation may reduce one's physical pain by allowing one to experience it from the perspective of an outside observer, and similarly for the experience of negative emotion induced by an arousing picture or the feeling of anger induced by recall of an argument. What is needed is a way of describing this perspective shift in terms of component processes of the sort used to study other cognitive and affective phenomena.

SUMMARY

A long-standing question about the role of expectancy is whether it has its effect on perceptual experience by directly combining with the input or by biasing report of the experience. To address this question, I focused on neuroimaging studies that used neural changes in target brain areas as proxies for perceptual experience. I discussed in detail an experiment concerned with pain perception, which showed that placebo-based expectancy reduced neural activity in the pain matrix (Wager et al., 2004). This result supports the combination hypothesis. I next discussed an experiment concerned with aversive tastes, which showed that expectancy reduced neural activity in brain regions known to mediate taste perception (Nitschke et al., 2005). Again the results supported the combination hypothesis. I noted, however, that analyses of the time courses of these neuroimaging findings suggested that expectancy had its effects not on initial sensory registration, but rather on subsequent interpretative processes.

The last section of the chapter examined parallels between expectancy effects on perceptual experience and cognitive regulation of emotional experience, particularly as shown in neuroimaging studies of reappraisal. The two classes of experiments reveal a common general pattern—increased neural activity in prefrontal areas that is correlated with decreased activity in areas associated with affect and emotion. A further understanding of reappraisal processes, then, may benefit our understanding of expectancy processes.

ACKNOWLEDGMENT

The research reported in this chapter was supported by the Mind, Brain, Body, and Health (MBBH) Foundation.

NOTES

1. In cognitive neuroscience, neuroimaging is often used to determine if two related psychological tasks involve different mechanisms (a dissociation) or whether two seemingly different tasks in fact involve common mechanisms (an association). In the current case, we are concerned neither with dissociations or associations but use neuroimaging for localizing purposes—previous

imaging research has isolated a set of regions that register aversive experience, and we use variations in these regions as a proxy for perceptual experience.

2. Prior to the experiment proper, pain levels for the different heats used were calibrated for each participant. Participants differed extensively in how painful they found a particular temperature to be, so we first had to map the different temperatures onto pain ratings for each individual. The temperature that a participant rated as level 5 was used in both the placebo and control conditions.

3. This behavioral placebo effect is greater than that usually obtained because we imaged only participants who had shown a placebo effect in a previous session. Even in the earlier session with unselected participants, however, there was a significant behavioral placebo effect, with more than 70% of the participants showing such an effect.

REFERENCES

Beauregard, M., Levesque, J., & Bourgouin, P. (2001). Neural correlates of conscious self-regulation of emotion. *Journal of Neuroscience, 21,* RC165.

Bruner, J. S. (1957). On perceptual readiness. *Psychological Review, 64,* 123–152.

Bruner, J. S., Postman, L., & Rodrigues, J. (1951). Expectation and the perception of color. *American Journal of Psychology, 64,* 216–227.

Craig, A. D., Chen, K., Bandy, D., & Reiman, E. M. (2000). Thermosensory activation of insular cortex. *Nature Neuroscience, 3,* 184–190.

Eisenberger, N. I., Lieberman, M. D., & Williams, K. D. (2003). Does rejection hurt? An fMRI study of social exclusion. *Science, 302,* 290–292.

Gross, J. J. (2002). Emotion regulation: Affective, cognitive, and social consequences. *Psychophysiology, 39,* 281–291.

Harrington, A. (Ed.). (1999). *The placebo effect.* Cambridge, MA: Harvard University Press.

Higgins, E. T. (1996). Knowledge activation: Accessibility, applicability, and salience. In E. T. Higgins & A. W. Kruglanski (Eds.), *Social psychology: Handbook of basic principles* (pp. 133–168). New York: Guilford Press.

Hrobjartsson, A., & Gotzsche, P. C. (2001). Is the placebo powerless? —An analysis of clinical trials comparing placebo with no treatment. *New England Journal of Medicine, 344,* 1594–1602.

Hrobjartsson, A., & Gotzsche, P. C. (2004). Is the placebo powerless? Update of a systemic review with 52 new randomized trials comparing placebo with no treatment. *Journal of Internal Medicine, 256,* 91–100.

Kirsch, I. (1985). Response expectancy as a determinant of experience and behavior. *American Psychologist, 40,* 1189–1202.

Kross, E., Ayduk, O., & Mischel, W. (2005). When asking "why" does not hurt: Distinguishing rumination from reflective processing of negative emotions. *Psychological Science, 16,* 709–715.

Lazarus, R. S. (1966). *Psychological stress and the coping process.* New York: McGraw Hill.

Lazarus, R. S. (1991). Cognition and motivation in emotion. *American Psychologist, 46,* 352–367.

MacDonald, A. W. III, Cohen. J. D., Stenger, V. A., & Carter, C. S. (2000). Dissociating the role of the dorsolateral prefrontal and anterior cingulated cortex in cognitive control. *Science, 288,* 1835–1838.

Melzack, R., & Wall, P. D. (1965). Pain mechanisms: A new theory. *Science, 150,* 971–979.

Miller, E. K., & Cohen, J. D. (2001). An integrative theory of prefrontal cortex function. *Annual Review of Neuroscience, 24,* 167–202.

Mischel, W. (1973). Toward a cognitive social learning reconceptualization of personality. *Psychological Review, 80,* 252–283.

Nitschke, J. B., Dixon, G. E., Sarinopoulos, I., Short, S. J., Cohen, J. D., Smith, E. E., et al. (2005). Altering expectancy dampens neural response to aversive taste in primary taste cortex. *Nature Neuroscience, 9,* 435–442.

Ochsner, K. N., Bunge, S. A., Gross, J. J., & Gabrieli, J. D. E. (2002). Rethinking feelings: An fMRI study of the cognitive regulation of emotion. *Journal of Cognitive Neuroscience, 14,* 1215–1229.

Ogawa, H. (1994). Gustatory cortex of primates: Anatomy and physiology. *Neuroscience Research, 20,* 1–13.

Phan, K. L., Wager, T. D., Taylor, S. F., & Liberzon, I. (2002). Functional neuroanatomy of emotion: A meta-analysis of emotion activation studies in PET and fMRI. *Neuroimage, 16,* 331–348.

Pollo, A., Vighetti, S., Rainero, I., & Benedetti, F. (2003). Placebo analgesic and the heart. *Pain, 102,* 125–133.

Rolls, E. T. (1999). *The brain and emotion.* Oxford, UK: Oxford University Press.

Swets, J. A. (1998). Separating discrimination and decision in detection, recognition, and matters of life and death. In D. Scarborough & S. Sternberg (Eds.), *Invitation to cognitive science* (Vol. 4, pp. 635–702). Cambridge, MA: MIT Press.

Swets, J. A., Tanner, W. P., Jr., & Birdsall, T. G. (1961). Decision processes in perception. *Psychological Review, 68,* 301–340.

Trope, Y., & Liberman, N. (2003). Temporal construal. *Psychological Review, 110,* 403–421.

Wager, T. D. (2005). The neural bases of placebo effects in pain. *Current Directions in Psychological Science, 14,* 175–179.

Wager, T. D., Phan, K. L., Liberzon, I., & Taylor, S. F. (2003). Valence, gender, and lateralization of functional brain anatomy in emotion: A meta-analysis of findings from neuroimaging. *Neuroimage, 19,* 513–531.

Wager, T. D., Rilling, J. K., Smith, E. E., Sokolik, A., Casey, K. L., Davidson, R. J., et al. (2004). Placebo-induced changes in fMRI in the anticipation and experience of pain. *Science, 303,* 1162–1167.

INCORPORATING SITUATIONS INTO A SCIENCE OF THE INDIVIDUAL

10

Character in Context
The Relational Self and Transference

SUSAN M. ANDERSEN
JENNIFER S. THORPE
CHRISTINA S. KOOIJ

As controversial as it was, early research on behavioral variability in individual personality traits and how these traits are expressed across varying situations (Mischel, 1968) became field-transforming, theoretically and empirically. Even at the time, this work specified the importance of context and emphasized the discriminative facility people exercise in navigating situations and the role of cognition in this process (Mischel, 1973). The research showed that person variables (e.g., Mischel, 1973) are triggered by contextual cues that result in the experience of a psychological situation and, thus, relevant behavior. Extending traditional behaviorism and learning theory, this research demonstrated the primary importance of contextual variability to personality. While trait theory acknowledged person–situation interactions early on in understanding personality (e.g., Allport, 1937; Murray, Barrett, & Homburger, 1938), this trend was largely absent from the scientific enterprise.

In the late 1960s, this program of empirical research issued a profound challenge in empirical terms and provoked heated controversy. There was intense criticism from researchers focused on the study of personality, and perhaps no small amount of consternation and desire for this misguided approach to fall by the wayside. But without this essential insight about context, one misses what has become increasingly navigable about the terrain of personality. In all its nuance and perhaps unwieldiness, an individual's behavior varies with context, presumably because the internal states and the mental representations underlying behavior vary in this manner as well (Mischel, 1973, 1977). This variation is revealing about individual personality. Global traits may be ascribed to a person, but they often ignore the contextual complexity of individual lives and possible encounters. Sophisticated in situ research has by now demonstrated this even more fully and clearly (e.g., Mischel & Shoda, 1995). This research is of value for the field of personality and for researchers in other areas wishing to conceptualize and examine personality. Conceptualizing variance in cognitive, affective, and behavioral phenomena across situations is as important as, and perhaps more important than, studying what is invariant or constant (if any response in fact is).

On the basis of this breakthrough, implicit assumptions about human nature and behavioral predictability have begun to change. Fluctuation across contexts is considered the norm rather than the exception and of significance in understanding the person. Variation should not be treated as error variance. Instead, it reflects the "personality signature" of an individual (Mischel & Shoda, 1995). This concept is the basis of the cognitive–affective model of personality, and while contextual variation has long been examined in social cognition (and in social psychology) it is now more broadly assumed in studies of personality and human nature.

One could argue that it took the eye of a cartographer (which Mischel has) to chart the topography of personality after grasping that a map across contexts was needed. Capturing personal meaning via construal of context, this work focuses on the psychological situation, which is what enables effective prediction. Generalized characterizations of a person in terms of personality traits or dispositions are often compelling (as a trait profile is) and are even longitudinally consistent in self-reports (Epstein, 1979; see also Block, 1971, 1977; Block & Block, 1980; Block, Buss, Block, & Gjerde, 1981; Funder, 1991), but they miss the texture (and composition) of personality across situations (its choreography). An individual's personality signature of variability across situations is also stable over time and has the advantage of better predicting behavior across situations.

The cognitive–affective system theory of personality (e.g., Mischel & Shoda, 1995) is an *if . . . then . . .* theory in which the *if* is a context and the *then* a response. Geographically, the context is a physical situation. Cognitively, it is the meaning the individual assigns to the situation (i.e., to the stimulus cues in the geographic situation, which may encompass affect). The *then*s are the psychological experiences, cognitive and affective, that guide the actions that result; the *then*s are also the actual actions. Even if some predilections that people have are general and chronic, the specific *if . . . then . . .* expectancies that arise in pertinent situations offer a refined understanding of the meanings that an individual makes in situations. Variability in behavior is a function of contextual cues and interpersonal meanings that tend to be ascribed to such cues. Hence, if individual differences are assessed, they are best examined in conjunction with situations and interpretations of these situations. This approach offers a wide and deep grasp of the person that goes beyond labels presumed to reflect entities within the person and is precisely honed and sensitive to an individual's unfolding life experience over situations.

Early tensions sparked by this approach have mostly subsided, giving way to acknowledgment that variability exists and matters. This quiet but steady shift embraces global dispositions and contexts. A rapprochement has perhaps been reached (see Funder, 2001, 2006; Kenrick & Funder, 1988) in which the interaction between person and context is assumed to reflect the meanings activated and ascribed to stimuli. This description reflects mental representations and contexts activated within the cognitive–affective model of personality and other models.

In this chapter, we speak to these developments through emphasis on a model and a line of work that fits easily within this overall perspective. That is, we present our research and theory on the social-cognitive process of transference. This research has examined mental representations in memory that have a special longevity for the person and are activated by contexts. Specifically, it focuses on mental representations of significant others, which are highly laden with affect and motivation and, by definition, linked to the self. The model and the evidence point to what is interpersonal about the self and about personality and demonstrate how variability provoked by context is central.

THE RELATIONAL SELF

Our model concerns the relational self (Andersen & Chen, 2002; see also Andersen, Reznik, & Chen, 1997; Chen & Andersen, 1999) and is grounded in research on how contextual cues activate mental representations of significant others and of the self, setting in motion shifts in interpersonal perception and responses to newly met people in a process we have termed "transference" (Andersen & Cole, 1990; Andersen & Baum, 1994). We define transference as the process by which a significant-other representation is activated by interpersonal cues encountered (in a new person or in a situation) and is then applied to a new person. We assume that the activation of a significant-other representation and its application to a new person can be measured through inferences and memory about the new person as they are or are not colored by the representation. That is, the individual should come to perceive features of the significant other as having been learned earlier about this new person even though they were not. The individual should also evaluate the new person positively (liking or love) when a representation of a positive significant other is activated and applied to the new person. These ways of filling in the blanks about a new person are thought to define the transference process as people experience it in their day-to-day lives (e.g., Andersen & Cole, 1990; Andersen & Baum, 1994; Andersen, Glassman, Chen, & Cole, 1995; Chen, Andersen, & Hinkley, 1999).

Extending this work, our model of the relational self emphasizes the importance of the relationship the individual has with each significant other and how these relationships are linked to the self (Andersen & Chen, 2002). It moves beyond the focus on discrete representations of significant others to examine the link between each significant other and the self. Whether a family member, friend, or other person who is or was influential in the individual's life), this significant other should be linked to the self in memory. This is a person whom the individual knows well and cares or cared deeply about and one who has emotional and motivational significance (Andersen, Glassman, & Gold, 1998; Hinkley & Andersen, 1996; Higgins, 1989b). The individual thus forms and experiences a particular version of the self with this person—a way of seeing, feeling, hoping, planning, dreading—constituting the nature of the self in that relationship.

It is in this sense that a part of the self is entangled with each significant other in the individual's life. As a result, the individual comes to see him- or herself in transference as he or she did while with the significant other, in spite of being with someone else now. Aspects of the self that are linked with the significant other in memory should be indirectly activated when the significant-other representation is activated. This process should lead to shifts in private experience—that is, in how the individual thinks about the self when the significant other is not present—and should be manifested in relevant overt behavior as well.

In part, what we mean in saying that the self is entangled with significant others is that the physical presence of the significant other is not required for the expression and experience of this version of the self in the right context or circumstance. If cues in a context (i.e., interpersonal cues) are relevant enough to evoke the mental representation of that significant other, this will activate the self-with-other, which will then be experienced. This process (and related phenomena) is what occurs in the social-cognitive process of transference.

Even in the presence of an entirely new person, it may seem that one has known this new person for years. More to the point, whether or not it consciously seems this way, one's perceptions of the new person may become infused with prior knowledge of the relevant significant other, leading one in effect to perceive the person as that significant other is perceived and to "become" the kind of person one typically is with that significant other (i.e., the self-with-other). In this manner, the relational self arises based on context.

Our model of the relational self and personality (Andersen & Chen, 2002) specifies links in memory between the self and the significant other. The links with any significant other are unique to that relationship, reflecting idiosyncratic qualities, and include any generic relational roles that define the relationship (e.g., a kind of authority figure–novice relation). In the latter sense, our conception resembles the idea of "relational schemas" linking the self and other in memory through generalized patterns (Baldwin, 1992). It differs, however, in emphasizing what is unique about each significant other and each relationship, rather than focusing on generalized patterns of interaction across such relationships. We assume that it is precisely the mix of the specific and the general in these representations that best captures the personal meaning they bestow.

Representations of significant others and the aspects of the self experienced with each should be triggered by relevant contextual cues and without awareness. In short, the process is not intentional and does not appear to require effort or to be the result of control exercised over responses (see Andersen, Reznik, & Glassman, 2005). Hence, the set of significant others and relationships one has in memory should constitute a repertoire of possible selves that circumscribe what one is likely to become and express. When these significant-other representations are activated and used automatically in social perception and interpersonal relations, this is the basic process of transference, defined in terms of social cognition, which constitutes a basis for shifts in the self and personality as a function of context in accord with the relational self.

Whether or not there is a core to the person and to personality is a fair question in light of this model, but it is a question beyond the scope of this paper and perhaps the model. What is clear is that prior experience with significant others and the mental representations formed on the basis of such experience, as combined with variability in context, determine the psychological situation in which the individual finds him- or herself, and what happens next. Contextual variability in the psychological situation matters and tells us something important about the self and personality.

The cues one encounters as one navigates social life predict which of one's significant-other representations will become active, determining in turn which relational self will appear. The distinction among various significant-other representations for an individual is important because it suggests that the specific relationship one has with each significant other may not be reducible to generalized significant-other knowledge (Pierce & Lydon, 1998; see also Baldwin, Keelan, Fehr, Enns, & Koh-Rangarajoo, 1996). It also helps explain how unique links with each significant other can arise and be individually influential as a function of context (with the context being another individual in another situation). Not only do you have mental links between your sense of self and your mental representation of your mother, for example, but you also have such links with the mental representation of your father, your sister, and your brother, and these respective links should not be identical. These links deliver the "baggage" one brings to new encounters. It is as if the prior other were in the room and the old relationship reenacted.

Our concept of transference is grounded in experimental measurement using the methods of social cognition with emphasis on the operation of social constructs in memory (Bargh, Bond, Lombardi, & Tota, 1986; Higgins, 1996a; Higgins & King, 1981; see also Kelly, 1955). Social constructs (including significant-other representations) are known to be triggered by transient sources of accessibility (i.e., from contextual cues such as those used in priming). They are also subject to being frequently used and thus to becoming chronically accessible. How applicable a construct is to a stimulus matters to whether or not it is used.

In transference, the transient source of accessibility is a new person who is similar in some minimal way to a significant other. The chronic source of accessibility is the significant other him- or herself, whom one has frequently thought about and engaged with, and who is designated by a mental representation. The applicability of the representation to the new person (i.e., to the stimulus), indicated by even minimal cues, triggers the representation in our paradigm, which we use to study the transference process experimentally. Whether consciously detected or not, these cues and their apparent similarity to something about the significant other provoke the representation and a variety of relevant effects.

The relational self model thus quite clearly assumes the pattern of inter- and intrapersonal responding laid out in the broader *if . . . then . . .* model of personality (Mischel & Shoda, 1995). We assume such *if . . . then . . .* responding in the interpersonal domain with the interpersonal self and suggest that transference (defined in terms of the activation and use of significant-other representations) is an underlying source of variability in the experience and expression of the relational self. Significant-other representations are relatively stable over time, but contextual shifts, such as the presence of a person similar to a significant other, can differentially activate specific significant-other representations and, therefore, specific relational selves. People bring their prior experiences with each of their significant others (and each of the relevant selves-with-others) to new situations. It is the context that spells out what will be evoked. A particular significant-other representation will be triggered based on the overlap between stimuli in the environment and the significant-other representation in memory, and this will in turn activate aspects of the self-with-other. The interpersonal cues in the environment are the *ifs* that activate the mental representation of a significant other and the relevant relational self. The *thens* are the activated mental representations, the relevant psychological experience the person has, and his or her interpersonal responses. Such findings trace both transference and the relational self across contexts. Although relational selves are each bound up with a significant other and are unlikely to make up the entire self, such representations in total are integral to how the self is defined and experienced. The relevance of significant others to the self is assumed to be reflected both in how the self develops and in how relevant aspects of the self are evoked in immediate contexts.

In sum, we assume that the relational self is an aspect of the self that is linked with significant others in memory. It relies on prior knowledge of these significant others and is evoked by varying contexts that activate a significant-other representation in the process of transference. Because this process results in shifts in the self, a variety of motivational and affective consequences arise, some of which we summarize once we present the basic evidence. First, however, we offer a bit more scholarly backdrop on the context of transference and describe how traditional concepts (such as those in psychoanalysis) have worked and can be reconceptualized in cognitive–social terms, while highlighting the relevance of both learning theory and attachment.

SCHOLARLY CONTEXT

Cognitive and Cognitive-Behavioral Theories of Personality

In 1955 George Kelly proposed the idea of "personal constructs," or specific and personal adjective concepts that people use to understand the world, particularly significant others. This assumption has a happy home in the cognitive–social learning reconceptualization of personality (Mischel, 1973), to which personal constructs are integral, with some exceptions. Both Kelly and Mischel assume that personal constructs are crucial cognitive mediators and that these constructs are individualized or idiosyncratic for each person. From our perspective, it is important that Kelly assumed that significant others are central to personal constructs and to how these constructs function. He assumed that they capture how significant others are different from each other and from the self, as well as how they're similar. Kelly did not, however, claim that constructs are learned, nor did he address the question of how they are acquired. His model was silent on the basic principles of learning, which were the focus of behavioral learning theorists of the day (Rotter, 1966). In this vein, the cognitive–social personality model has the advantage because it is grounded in basic principles of learning. The assumptions of social learning theory (Bandura, 1965, 1977) and their evidential basis are well understood, and these principles are compatible with the cognitive–social learning model (Mischel, 1973).

The relational self and transference are anchored both in personal construct theory (Kelly, 1955) and in the cognitive–social learning reconceptualization of personality (Mischel, 1968, 1973). In the latter, contextual stimuli evoke personal constructs, expectancies, and encoding strategies as well as self-regulatory systems and plans for each person. These mental representations and processes are then used to interpret stimuli, defining how the stimuli are encoded and determining the meaning ascribed to them. The notion that contextual stimuli evoke personal constructs and encoding strategies that subsequently influence interpretation is basic.

Personality Prototypes as Mental Representations

Another empirical and theoretical advance that offered an opening for research on the social-cognitive process of transference was seen in work on personality prototypes in the late 1970s (Cantor & Mischel, 1977, 1979). The research employed a recognition-memory paradigm to show that personality prototypes can be used to go beyond the information given about a new person. Personality prototypes were shown to influence social perception in ways that speak to the nature of personality. By treating traits as cognitive concepts, the research suggested that they are concepts in the eye of the beholder rather than entities in the individual being perceived (see also Kenrick & Stringfield, 1980).

With this idea in mind, it seemed to one of us that this kind of method could be utilized to reconceptualize and examine how trait concepts are represented in memory (Andersen & Klatzky, 1987) and the efficiency with which they are used (Andersen, Klatzky, & Murray, 1990). By targeting mental representations designated by an adjective term (i.e., a trait label) rather than by a noun label (i.e., a stereotype), this research showed greater richness, distinctiveness, and efficiency of stereotypes. These special properties of noun categories that label people made possible the relatively small step of asking if "proper nouns," such as the name of a personally significant person, may have the same kinds of special properties as stereotypes. If some of these methods could be adapted, the first experimental demonstration of transference seemed possible, and it was (Andersen & Cole, 1990).

More recently, the *if . . . then . . .* model of personality—which focuses on numerous constructs and expectancies activated in parallel as a cognitive–affective processing system (or CAPS; Mischel & Shoda, 1995)—helped provoke the extensions of our work on transference into the realm of the relational self. The model's emphasis on how the self and personality vary by context provided the basis for this extension (Andersen & Chen, 2002). In the *if . . . then . . .* personality model, an individual's "personality signature" represents his or her variability across situations and reflects the patterning of the individual's responses while also being stable over time. The relational self reflects one such personality signature in showing how a person can vary across different interpersonal situations in behavior, feelings, and sense of self in a manner traceable to varying significant others. This combination of variability and consistency is precisely what makes up a person's repertoire of relational selves.

In order to understand transference and the relational self, one must more thoroughly consider how knowledge is represented in memory and subsequently utilized, which research on the transient and chronic activation of social constructs addresses (Higgins, 1996a; Higgins & King, 1981). Transient cues contribute to the activation and application of stored constructs, including *n*-of-1 exemplars, as when priming a construct leads to the assimilation of a newly encountered person into that construct. In addition, chronic accessibility is relevant even without other transient sources of activation from a prime or from cues in a new person (e.g., Higgins, 1989a, 1990, 1996b; Higgins & Brendl, 1995; Higgins & King, 1981; Higgins, King, & Mavin, 1982). Social constructs that are *n*-of-1 exemplars, designating one particular person, can still be used like other constructs (e.g., Andersen & Glassman, 1996; Linville & Fischer, 1993; Judd & Park, 1988; Park & Hastie, 1987; Smith & Zarate, 1990, 1992). Interpersonal cues activate the significant-other exemplar, contributing activation beyond any chronic accessibility (and these representations are chronically accessible), leading to application in the form of assimilation (Chen & Andersen, 1999). Social-cognitive theory has thus greatly informed our model of how transference occurs based on a perceived match to the significant other (see Tversky, 1977). In addition, theory and research on the automatic activation and use of motives and goals have been important in laying the groundwork for our assumption that activating significant-other representations should also activate the motives and goals associated with that significant other (Bargh, 1990).

The Notion of a Trait Disposition in Classic Trait Theory

A conceptual innovation in traditional trait theory can be found in the work of Allport (1937), the first to propose that understanding the person requires understanding what is unique to the person. That is, he assumed that what is idiographic is important, not only what is shared with similar others—which is what the classic individual differences approach to personality measurement emphasizes. In this way of thinking, people have both idiographic (unique) traits and nomothetic (general or global) traits. While this distinction has seldom been assessed or examined in personality research (for exceptions, see Lamiell, 1981; Pelham, 1993), the distinction is compelling and of value. We argue that it applies to distinguishing the relatively unique content of significant-other representations from the processes by which those mental representations are used (Andersen & Chen, 2002).

In terms of the cognitive–social learning view of personality (Mischel, 1973), individuals exercise a discriminative facility as they navigate differing situations in their lives. Minimally, they learn to associate through basic learning processes various discriminative stimuli with particular responses. What is learned is thus unique. Even though research on the cognitive–social learning model of personality (Mischel, 1973) and the cognitive–affective model of personality (Mischel & Shoda, 1995) has tended to assess nomothetic person variables and nomothetic underlying processes, the theory and the idiographic nature of the person's psychological situation is clear. Moreover, in recent research, the idiographic personality signature of the person has been assessed (Mischel & Shoda, 1995). In our research, we specifically assess the content of mental representations of significant others and the self idiographically. We also define relevant contexts idiographically so that the match is idiographic as well. In addition, we focus on and assess the nomothetic underlying processes of transference. We thus adopt a combined idiographic–nomothetic approach.

Psychoanalytic and Interpersonal Psychodynamic Theories

In classical Freudian theory (Freud, 1958), transference is the process in which a patient undergoing psychoanalysis imposes his or her childhood conflicts and sexual fantasies about his or her parents on the analyst

(Freud, 1963; see also Andersen & Glassman, 1996). Despite Freud's assumption that people hold "imagoes" of significant others in memory, these imagoes carried little causal weight in his drive-structure model (Greenberg & Mitchell, 1983). The tripartite structure of mind—id, ego, superego—that was assumed to be fueled by psychosexual, libidinal drive is central to the theory. Hence, Freud considered unconscious psychosexual drive to be at the heart of transference, in terms of what material should be the focus of analysis. Freud assumed that transference occurs both in psychoanalysis and in everyday life (Freud, 1958; Luborsky & Crits-Christoph, 1990; Schimek, 1983), an assumption we adopt as well.

Sullivan's notion of parataxic distortion—his term for transference—is based on his interpersonal psychodynamic model focusing on relations between the self and other. The model does not rely on notions of infantile sexuality, sexual urges, or drive states and abandons the drive-structure model. Our theory thus bears some resemblance to this early theory, particularly because it proposes that early interpersonal relationships (e.g., with a caretaker) result in "personifications" of the self and significant other that are linked in memory via "dynamisms," or the relational patterns typically exhibited in that relationship (Sullivan, 1953). Although personifications and dynamisms are not precisely mental representations (Sullivan was not sanguine about assuming psychic structures), they are not vastly dissimilar. New personifications and dynamisms are formed as new relationships with significant others are formed. Dynamisms link the self to significant-other personifications, which are ultimately reexperienced in parataxic distortion. The same relational pattern experienced with the significant other is reexperienced and exhibited with the new person through this process.

Sullivan assumed basic motivations that are not reducible to the psychosexual. That is, he assumed people have a basic need for satisfaction, which derives from expressing their developing competencies and feelings. He also assumed a basic need for safety and security that involves protecting the self while experiencing tenderness and connection with loved ones. Needs of this kind, especially needs for connection and security, are also central to our model (Andersen et al., 1997). While Sullivan was a psychodynamic theorist, he did not distance himself from the processes of learning. Basic motivations arise in important relationships and are intimately intertwined with what is learned in relation to significant others.

The clinical concept of transference has long been considered an essential component of psychoanalysis and psychotherapy, although its precise definition has varied with the theorist (e.g., Ehrenreich, 1989; Greenson, 1965). Because the focus has been on theory and therapy, transference has generally not been examined empirically (although there are exceptions, e.g., Luborsky & Crits-Christoph, 1990; Horowitz, 1989, 1991). The definition of transference that is most widely adopted seems to be "the experiencing of feelings, drives, attitudes, fantasies, and defenses toward a person in the present which are inappropriate to the person and are a repetition, a displacement of reaction originating in regard to significant persons of early childhood" (Greenson, 1965, p. 156). Our data and our version of transference fit this definition quite well (for related theoretical work, see Singer, 1988; Westen, 1988).

Our own social-cognitive model of transference rejects Freud's drive-structure model and assumes that significant-other representations are stored in memory and linked with the self. We focus centrally on transference as a "normal" process that occurs in everyday life and do not assume that it is limited to clinical patients.

Attachment Theory as an Integrative Model

Another model that adopts some of these psychodynamic tenets is attachment theory. Attachment theory emphasizes the dynamic interactions between infants or young children and their caretakers and how they come to be represented in the child's internal working models. Though much attachment research has focused on the influence of early caretakers (e.g., Ainsworth, Blehar, Waters, & Wall, 1978; Bombar & Littig, 1996; Bowlby, 1969, 1973, 1980; Bretherton, 1985; Thompson, 1998), adult attachment and attachment styles have also been extensively researched (e.g., Hazan & Shaver, 1994). In recent years, these internal working models that arise from attachment processes have also been examined empirically (e.g., Baldwin, Fehr, Keedian, Seidel, & Thompson, 1993; Baldwin et al., 1996; Mikulincer, 1998; Mikulincer & Horesh, 1999; Shaver & Mikulincer, 2002; Pierce & Lydon, 2001). Furthermore, attachment theory is inherently integrative—across behavioral, ethological, and psychodynamic perspectives. We assume that transference acts as a mechanism for evoking attachment processes by activating a significant-other representation and the associated self-representation (i.e., the working model). In our research on transference, therefore, we integrate attachment theory with relevant concepts in social cognition in a way that interfaces with the cognitive–social learning model.

Having characterized our model of the relational self and transference and its theoretical basis, we turn to a brief review of the evidence that has experimentally demonstrated the process of transference and the relational self.

EVIDENCE CONCERNING
THE SOCIAL-COGNITIVE PROCESS OF TRANSFERENCE

Procedural Preliminaries

Research on transference employs a two-session paradigm in which the significant other is described by an equal number of positive and negative sentences that participants list and then rank for their descriptiveness. Participants also identify irrelevant descriptors (adjectives) from a list. In a supposedly unrelated second session, participants are told they will meet with a new person and are presented with features supposedly describing this new person. In actuality, for those in the transference condition, some of the presented features are derived from those listed by the participant in the first session. In the yoked control condition, the features do not resemble those of their own significant other, but those of another participant's significant other. Such yoking is used to control for any possible effects of the features themselves. The features presented are equally positive and negative across subjects and are interspersed with irrelevant filler items. After encountering this manipulation, participants report their inferences about and memory of the new person, in terms of features that are relevant (or not) to the significant other. They also report their evaluation of the new person, motives toward him or her, expectancies, emotions, definitions of self at the moment, or interpersonal behavior. Transference elicits effects in all of these measures.

Inference and Memory

The initial research on transference assessed the activation of a significant-other representation in terms of the participant's memory of and inferences about a new person. Findings showed that we fill in the blanks about new people using prior knowledge of a significant other when the new person resembled the significant other at the outset. In particular, people who were exposed to some features of their significant other when learning about the new person later inferred that features of their significant other that had *not* been presented were learned about the new person. In a recognition-memory paradigm (adapted from Cantor & Mischel, 1977), individuals in the significant-other resemblance condition reported more confidence that they had been exposed to non-presented significant-other features in relation to the new person than individuals in control conditions (e.g., Andersen et al., 1995; Andersen & Cole, 1990). This effect is observed even when stimuli are presented subliminally (Glassman & Andersen, 1999a) for 85 milliseconds in parafoveal vision using a pattern mask and a similar inference measure.

Hence, the inference and memory effect does not require intention, awareness, consciousness, or effort—it occurs relatively automatically (see Andersen, Moskowitz, Blair, & Nosek, 2007). The effect also lasts over time, at least for 1 week (Glassman & Andersen, 1999b).

These data show that significant others are readily cued by some interpersonal similarity between a new person and a significant other. They are also readily cued by an incidental prime encountered before learning about a new person (Andersen et al., 1995). On the other hand, this effect occurs at a low level (Andersen et al., 1995). That is, these representations are chronically accessible and are thus readily used (Andersen et al., 1995; Chen et al., 1999). Contextual cueing increases this effect by combining additively with chronicity in influencing what will be used to interpret situational stimuli, irrespective of whether priming or applicability to a new person triggered the transference effect. Other work in the interpersonal literature focused on priming has likewise demonstrated an additive effect of chronic accessibility and transient cues (e.g., Baldwin et al., 1996).

It is also worth noting that experimental artifacts have been ruled out of these transference effects in a variety of ways, including the possible influence of self-generation effects (Greenwald & Banaji, 1989). Enhanced memory can result when stimulus words are initially self-generated, which aids in the memory of these words later. Such an effect could perhaps account for participants' memory of having learned significant-other features about the new person that were not actually presented, as participants had generated both learned and unlearned features earlier to describe their significant other. To control for self-generation effects, a series of studies compared participants' significant-other representations with other types of self-generated representations—those of nonsignificant others, public figures, and social categories (e.g., a stereotype). Inference and memory effects were strongest when the features were those of a significant other, suggesting that the effect is not due to self-generation or stereotype activation alone (e.g., Andersen et al., 1995; Glassman & Andersen, 1999a).

This inference and memory effect occurs for both positive and negative significant others (e.g., Andersen & Baum, 1994; Andersen, Reznik, & Manzella, 1996; Hinkley & Andersen, 1996). It arises independently of individual difference variables such as having differing self-discrepancies from a parent's standpoint (Reznik & Andersen, 2005a), being physically abused by a parent (versus not) (Berenson & Andersen, 2006), or being depressed (versus not) for 2 or more weeks (Andersen & Miranda, 2006). The effect appears to be quite robust and is thus used as a standard index of transference in our research.

Evaluation and Facial Affect

Often when we encounter a new person, it may be surprising even to us how quickly we form an impression of him or her. Research in social cognition has demonstrated that when a mental representation is activated in the context of an interpersonal encounter and applied to a new person, the same evaluation (positive or negative) associated with the mental representation is experienced in relation to the new person. This result is in accordance with schema-triggered affect (Fiske & Pavelchak, 1986). When people encounter someone who reminds them of a positively regarded significant other, they come to view the new person more positively than do participants in the control condition (Baum & Andersen, 1999) and also more positively than do participants reminded of a negative significant other (Andersen et al., 1996; Andersen & Baum, 1994; Berk & Andersen, 2000). Even if the positive significant other is a parent associated with a self-discrepancy, participants' responses toward the new person are still more positive than in a control condition (Reznik & Andersen, 2007). On the other hand, participants in the negative significant-other-resemblance condition come to view the new person less positively than do participants in the negative yoked-control condition (Andersen & Baum, 1994; see also Andersen et al., 1996; Berk & Andersen, 2000).

Affective responses have also been assessed nonverbally in this work. One's immediate, automatic reaction toward any significant other should reflect one's overall regard for that person. When a positive significant-other representation is activated in transference, it should be reflected in an immediate, positive emotional response (as shown in facial expressions; Andersen et al., 1996). Evidence shows just this. When people learn about a new person who shares features with a significant other, they exhibit subtle facial expressions revealing the same overall affect experienced toward the significant other, as reexperienced in the moment while reading the new person's features. Participants expressed more positive facial affect when the new person resembled a positive versus a negative significant other, a pattern that did not occur in the no-resemblance control condition. Since these affective expressions, coded by trained judges, were emitted relatively immediately, they likely contained no forethought, reflecting automatic evaluation (Bargh, Chaiken, Raymond, & Hymes, 1996) consistent with the evaluation of the significant other.

Such effects occur even when the relevant significant other is an abusive parent (Berenson & Andersen, in press). Regardless of what their parents may or may not have done to them, participants tend to report loving their parents. Hence, adult children of abusive parents nonetheless show positive facial expressions when exposed to features of their abusive parent while learning about a new person, just as non-abused people do (Berenson & Andersen, 2006).

Expectancies

For each significant other in our lives, we have a sense of whether he or she is generally accepting or rejecting of us. In our research, we assume that love and acceptance (or its opposite) from a significant other will translate into expectancies about how a new person will respond (i.e., to the expectation that he or she will be accepting or rejecting). The evidence tends to support this assumption. When individuals encounter a person who is similar to a positive significant other, they report that they expect this new person to accept more than they do when encountering a person who is similar to a negative significant other, a difference not arising in the control condition (Andersen et al., 1996; Berk & Andersen, 2000). These expectancies arise despite some individual differences, such as in the type of self-discrepancy one might have from a parent's point of view (Reznik & Andersen, 2005a), and yet can also be reversed in transference involving a parent, even if the parent is "loved," if the parent was abusive while the individual was growing up (Berenson & Andersen, 2006).

More generalized expectancies of rejection also exist, which can and often do carry profound consequences (Downey & Feldman, 1996). Such expectations may be linked to relationships and stored with relational knowledge in memory, as research on relational schemas has shown (Baldwin & Sinclair, 1996). Activated relational expectancies about how one will be evaluated in a significant relationship can also, as priming research has shown, have an impact on subsequent self-evaluation (e.g., Baldwin, Carrell, & Lopez, 1990).

In summary, the process of going beyond the information given in transference involves not only making inferences about a new person (and misremembering him or her) and immediately evaluating him or her as one evaluates the significant other, but also expecting this new person to have the kinds of feelings toward one that one believes the significant other has. The latter is among the advantages that a dyadic, interpersonal theory of personality offers.

Interpersonal Behavior

One's mental representation of a significant other evokes not only inferences about and feelings toward a new person, but also ways of behaving that are characteristic of the relationship with the significant other. In relevant research, participants experiencing transference (or not) had an unstructured phone conversation with an entirely naïve participant (the target of transference) that was tape recorded (Berk & Andersen, 2000). This behavioral confirmation paradigm (Snyder, Tanke, & Berscheid, 1977) allows examination of participants' conversations with the new person in a way that focuses on the new person's actual reciprocal response in the interaction. In brief, the audiotape of the naïve target's portion of the conversation was assessed by independent judges blind to condition without listening to the main participant's part of the conversation. In transference, the target's behavior exhibited affect more consistent with the overall affect associated with the significant other. In fact, targets of positive transference (i.e., the naïve participants said to resemble a positive significant other) came to exhibit more positive affect in the conversation than did targets of a negative transference, an effect that was absent in the control condition (Berk & Andersen, 2000). Such evidence demonstrates that behavioral confirmation occurs in transference. As with any behavioral confirmation phenomenon, participants did not consciously attempt to elicit this behavior from the target (e.g., Chen & Bargh, 1997).

The Self in Relation to the Other

In transference, it is not simply the target whose behavior changes, but also the reported description of self by the participant whose significant-other representation is activated. One's mental representation of a significant other is tightly linked to aspects of the self typically experienced with that other. These aspects of self, or self-with-other, are also experienced when the significant-other representation is activated in transference. That is, the way a person conceives of him- or herself becomes more congruent with the self-with-other or relational self associated with that significant other.

When transference occurs, the self that tends to be experienced in the presence of the relevant significant other arises, controlling for participants' baseline self-definition (elicited at pretest; Hinkley & Andersen, 1996). Both neutral and valenced aspects of the relational self are reexperienced, regardless of whether the significant other is positively or negatively regarded. Self-evaluation changes in transference. In a positive transference, there is an influx of positively valenced self-features into the self-concept, and in a negative transference there is an influx of negative features (Hinkley & Andersen, 1996).

Moreover, it is entirely possible to experience a negative self with a positive significant other and, thus, show negative changes in the relational self based on activating a positive significant other in transference (Reznik & Andersen, 2005b). That is, when the representation of a positive significant other with whom one experiences a dreaded self is activated in transference, participants experience a markedly negative shift in self-evaluation (from baseline pretest to test). The negative features associated with the dreaded self also became more accessible, as evidenced through decreased response latencies in making lexical decisions about relevant words, which did not occur in the control condition or for those whose significant-other representation was activated but associated with a desired self.

These relational selves depend on the context and capture the variability in the *if . . . then . . .* model (Mischel & Shoda, 1995). The chronic accessibility of significant-other representations and relational selves creates stability in the kinds of selves typically activated, but which one is activated at any given moment will be based on contextual cues in the environment (i.e., people encountered or primes presented). Putting this in *if . . . then . . .* terms, the *if* is the context or the triggering cue in a new person, and the *then* is the activated mental representation of the significant other and the other cognitive, affective, and interpersonal responses, including the emergence of the relevant relational self that follows (Andersen & Chen, 2002). Such shifts in the self that occur as a function of transference are consistent with the kinds of shifts that occur in other *if . . . then . . .* models (e.g., Crocker & Wolfe, 2001; Downey & Feldman, 1996).

Closeness Motivation

In transference involving a positive significant other, people also become more motivated to approach the new person by being emotionally open with him or her and less motivated to avoid him or her (Andersen et al., 1996; Berk & Andersen, 2000). Indeed, people not only want to be closer to a new person who resembles their positive significant other, but they actually also feel closer to him or her (Andersen & Strasser, 2000). This effect for closeness motivation also holds even when a positive significant-other representation designates a parent with whom one has a self-discrepancy from the parent's perspective (Reznik & Andersen, 2005a). Hence, some relational difficulties do not promote the motive to distance oneself from the other. When a loved significant other has chronically rejected one's bids for love and acceptance, however, transference involving that significant other evokes less self-reported closeness motivation than does the control condition (Berk & Andersen, 2004).

Recent work has begun to address auto-motives in interpersonal situations, showing that priming a significant-other representation can activate other kinds of goals as well, including goals to compete, achieve, or help (Fitzsimons & Bargh, 2003; Shah, 2003a, 2003b), which lead to goal-directed behavior. The work on motivation, which is presumably activated automatically (see also Andersen et al., 2007), builds on prior research showing more generally that goals can be activated automatically (Bargh & Barndollar, 1996; Bargh & Chartrand, 1999; Bargh, Gollwitzer, Lee-Chai, Barndollar, & Trötschel, 2001; see also Aarts & Dijksterhuis, 2000).

Self-Regulation

Protecting the Self

Self-regulation is also affected by transference. In one form of self-regulation, the influx of negative self-features provokes compensatory self-enhancement. Considerable research shows that when the self is threatened, people often engage in self-inflating thought processes to protect the self (e.g., Greenberg & Pyszczynski, 1985; Steele, 1988; Taylor & Brown, 1988). Likewise, in transference, when the activation of a significant-other representation somehow poses a threat to the self, compensatory processes should occur. Indeed, when negative self-with-other features stream into the working self-concept, there is an influx of positive self-features into the self-concept as well that are opposite to the valence of and irrelevant to the self-with-other. The person thereby boosts overall self-regard, protecting him- or herself from the negative self-qualities brought to mind.

The same effect can occur when activation of a positive significant other threatens the self, as when the significant other is associated with experiencing a dreaded self (Reznik & Andersen, 2005b). When such a significant-other representation is activated, the dreaded self-with-other features flow into the self as described, which evokes an opposing reaction of self-protective self-regulation that appears to counteract the threat to the self posed by the significant other with whom one associates a dreaded self.

Protecting the Other

As with self-protective self-regulation, when significant others with whom one experiences interdependence are somehow threatened, other-protective self-regulation occurs. It may be beneficial for people to believe that the significant others on whom they rely are basically good and loving, despite their flaws. People go so far as to transform the flaws of significant others into virtues, seeing them as quirks or desirable (e.g.,

Murray & Holmes, 1993). An irresponsible boyfriend may thus be viewed as fun-loving. This transformation should be so well practiced in the course of relationship maintenance that it should occur relatively automatically and may thus occur in transference.

As noted earlier, automatic facial affect in transference tends to reflect the overall affect associated with the significant other. Interestingly, in a positive transference, participants' immediate facial expressions were more positive while reading negative significant-other features about a new person than when reading positive features, and no such pattern was seen in the control condition (Andersen et al., 1996). This result verifies that the emotion evoked is associated with the overall representation, instead of with feature valence, and that self-regulation occurs in response to threatening information about the other that challenges one's overall positive view of him or her.

This protection of the other also occurs in transference based on other negative cues about the new person in the setting (e.g., suggesting that he or she is becoming increasingly irritable). When the positive significant other was a parent, this negative cue evoked far more positive facial expressions in transference than in the control condition, even when the parent had been abusive (Berenson & Andersen, 2006). This other-protective self-regulation can be very dangerous in abusive relationships, as it is exactly such negative contextual cues that signal the onslaught of abusive behavior. An overly positive response to a new person resembling an abusive other could be potentially dangerous, leaving the victim in the position to experience abuse again with a similar new person.

Affect in Positive Transference: Why Isn't It Always Good?

The influence of positive significant others on our lives can clearly be powerful. As indicated, these relationships and significant-other representations, when activated, lead to positive evaluation, expectancy, motivation, and behavior; a more positive sense of self; and other-protective self-regulation under the right circumstances. They also influence positive affect in facial expressions. The results on free-floating mood states, however, are more mixed. While participants in transference involving a positive significant other sometimes report feeling less depressive mood than those in transference with a negative significant other (Andersen & Baum, 1994), a pattern not seen in a control condition, the effect size is small, and the effect has failed to replicate (Andersen et al., 1996). Perhaps mood is influenced by other contextual factors, such as the relational self-with-other (e.g., a dreaded, versus desired, self), self-discrepancies with the other, or differences in attachment style (on the latter, see Pietromonaco & Feldman Barrett, 1997).

The question of when positive mood states do not occur in a positive transference is important because it implies that evaluative and affective responses in a positive transference are not necessarily unitary or monolithic: Evaluative and self-reported mood states may diverge. The answer may come down to the nature of the stored significant-other relationship.

An Incongruent Interpersonal Role

The interpersonal role with a significant other includes expectations for how to behave and how the other will behave, defining the norms in the relationship. Expectations that are part of the role should thus be activated when the significant-other representation is activated, which should in turn activate the role. If a new person is in an opposing interpersonal role, this role violation suggests that expectancies will go unfulfilled, provoking negative mood. This does indeed play out in transference. When the new person in transference acts in a way that implies that he or she will not adopt the interpersonal role of the significant other, positive affect is attenuated and reversed (Baum & Andersen, 1999); this reaction extends the expectancy and role violation literatures (e.g., Fiske, 1992; Mills & Clark, 1994; see also Bugental, 2000; Kenrick, Li, & Butner, 2003) into the realm of transference by showing role activation when the significant-other representation is activated in transference.

An Unsatisfied Goal in the Significant-Other Relationship

Another reason for the attenuation of positive affect in a positive transference may be that basic needs and goals in the relationship have gone unmet (Berk & Andersen, 2004). Hence, when a significant-other representation is activated, these goals and how that other responded to them (by satisfying them or not) should be activated in transference as well, leading to disappointment despite an overall positive view of the other. In fact, when representations of positive significant others of this kind (involving unsatisfied versus satisfied goals) are activated, they clearly evoke negative affect, specifically hostility. That is, when a loved significant other is perceived as thwarting the individual's goal to feel loved or accepted by him or her, evoking the representation of this significant other in transference provokes hostility and resentment. Interestingly, when the significant other was in one's family, these increases in hostility were also positively correlated with increases in performing behaviors designed to solicit positive responses (e.g., liking and acceptance) from the new person. In this case, negative hostile affect in a positive transference is associated with proactive action to gain acceptance from the new person (the very thing that was not provided by the significant other) (Berk & Andersen, 2004).

The Dreaded Self

Research has shown that it is entirely possible to like or love a significant other and yet repeatedly find oneself enacting a dreaded version of the self with this other (Reznik & Andersen, 2005b), becoming a version of oneself (e.g., through one's behavior) of which one does not approve. When a positive significant-other representation is activated in transference, and the significant other is one associated with a dreaded self, this relational self should be activated, resulting in increases in negative mood and decreases in positive mood. This is exactly what occurs, and it does not occur in the absence of transference.

Self-Discrepancies and Discrete Negative Affects

Theory and research on self-discrepancy and self-regulatory focus offer another possible means of conceptualizing the processes by which a representation of a positive significant other may be associated with and evoke negative affect. Self-discrepancies are known to be associated with specific emotional response patterns. When a person's actual self is discrepant from "ideal" standards (or hopes), it evokes dejection-related affect, whereas when the actual self is discrepant from "ought" standards (or duties), it evokes agitation-related affect. One may have a self-discrepancy from one's own perspective or from the perspective of a parent (e.g., Higgins, 1987, 1996b); hence, a parental representation should be linked to self-standards and self-discrepancies. Activation of a parental representation should thus activate a self-discrepancy from the parent's perspective as well as the emotions associated with the discrepancy. Indeed, when the parental representation was activated, people with an ideal self-discrepancy from this parent's perspective came to experience more depressed mood as compared with a control condition; this did not occur among ought-discrepant individuals (Reznik & Andersen, 2005a). Likewise, ought-discrepant individuals showed more agitation-related affect (see also Strauman & Higgins, 1988) in transference than in a control condition, an effect not observed among ideal-discrepant people. Therefore, individual differences in how one believes one is viewed by a parent predict specific negative affect in a positive transference. These data concern not only affect, but also self-regulation, and dovetail nicely with the notion that self-regulatory strategies are person variables contributing to the personality system (Mischel, 1973; Mischel & Shoda, 1995; Metcalfe & Mischel, 1999).

Attachment Styles

Another source of discrete emotions in transference should be the attachment style that an individual has with the relevant significant other. There is evidence that people have different attachment styles with different individuals in their lives (Pierce & Lydon, 2001) and that these differing styles can be triggered by contextual cues (Mikulincer, Gillath, & Shaver, 2002).

Recent research has shown that, depending on the attachment style with a parent, activation of that parental representation in transference evokes different affective states (Andersen, Bartz, Berenson, & Keczemethy, 2006). Specifically, when one has a secure attachment to the parent, the transference leads to increased positive affect (relative to the control condition), which does not occur for individuals with dismissive, preoccupied, or fearful attachment styles with the parent. In addition, those with a preoccupied attachment style experienced increased anxiety in transference (relative to the control condition), which did not occur for participants with secure, dismissive, or fearful styles with this parent. Finally, for those with a dismissive attachment to the parent, what is observed is diminished negative affect (compared to the control condition) and an apparent suppression of hostile affect, which was quite pronounced in the control condition, an effect not seen among the other participants. A lack of emotional expression is typical of a dismissive attachment style and this pattern is thus revealed in the context of transference.

Hence, internal working models and the attachment system appear to be activated in the context of transference; we thus argue that transference, which relies on representations of significant others, may be a mechanism by which attachment processes are evoked in adult life.

CONCLUDING COMMENTS

The Relational Self:
An *If . . . Then . . .* Model of the Self and Personality

In summary, research on the relational self demonstrates that varying relational selves can be activated through the mechanism of transference, even in a culture such as that of the United States that prioritizes individuality. Relational selves can be readily activated in both men and women, an effect that is not dependent on preselection for relational-interdependent self-construal. These effects occur automatically, without conscious awareness or effort (Andersen et al., 2005; Chen, Fitzsimons, & Andersen, 2007; Andersen et al., in press). Inferences, evaluation, and expectancies about the new person all are elicited automatically. This aspect is further proof of the power of situational variability, which evokes not only the relevant significant-other representation, but also the relational self linked to that significant other entirely outside of awareness. The relational self accounts for shifts in the self across varying contexts in *if . . . then . . .* terms—*if* you are with someone who reminds you of a given significant other, *then* you will become the self that is typically experienced with that significant other, and all the aforementioned implications apply.

The *if . . . then . . .* model of personality (Mischel & Shoda, 1995) is central to the field of personality, as well as to social cognition and self-regulation, and research on the relational self can be situated in these terms. Each of these subfields takes advantage of the rich complexity of human behavior to explain behavior as it varies across contexts, rather than setting that complexity aside as mere error variance. We assume that significant-other representations are chronically accessible and linked to the self in memory, thus accounting for some of the stability experienced over time in these relational patterns. These representations and relationships are contextually cued, provoking shifts in the relational self across varying situations in a way that involves particular interpersonal patterns heavily colored by affect. The emphasis on motivation and self-regulatory strategies among the person variables in the classic *if . . . then . . .* theory (Mischel, 1973; Mischel & Shoda, 1995) shows their pertinence, and we have focused in part on these variables. Overall, our work demonstrates how contextual and interpersonal variability influences the self—in particular, the relational self that comes to the fore and guides experience at that moment. Our model of the relational self adds to the *if . . . then . . .* model by honing in on what is interpersonal about the self and directly binding the work not only to social cognition and personality, but also to psychodynamic thought. In these ways, the work inspired by Mischel's groundbreaking theorizing has tied together diverse areas in psychology and helped paint a picture of human personality that represents how a person's history, relationships, and situation come together to create an individual.

REFERENCES

Aarts, H., & Dijksterhuis, A. (2000). Habits as knowledge structures: Automaticity in goal-directed behavior. *Journal of Personality and Social Psychology, 78,* 53–63.

Ainsworth, M. D. S., Blehar, M. C., Walters, E., & Wall, S. (1978). *Patterns of attachment: A psychological study of the strange situation.* Hillsdale, NJ: Erlbaum.

Allport, G. (1937). *Personality: A psychology interpretation.* New York: Holt, Rinehart & Winston.

Andersen, S. M., Bartz, J., Berenson, K., & Keczemethy, C. (2006). *Triggering the attachment system in transference: Evoking specific emotions through implicit activation of a parental representation.* Unpublished manuscript, New York University.

Andersen, S. M., & Baum, A. (1994). Transference in interpersonal relations: Inferences and affect based on significant-other representations. *Journal of Personality, 62,* 459–498.

Andersen, S. M., & Chen, S. (2002). The relational self: An interpersonal social-cognitive theory. *Psychological Review, 109,* 619–645.

Andersen, S. M., & Cole, S. W. (1990). "Do I know you?": The role of significant others in general social perception. *Journal of Personality and Social Psychology, 59,* 383–399.

Andersen, S. M., & Glassman, N. S. (1996). Responding to significant others when they are not there: Effects on interpersonal inference, motivation, and affect. In R. M. Sorrentino & E. T. Higgins (Eds.), *Handbook of motivation and cognition: Vol. 3. The interpersonal context* (pp. 262–321). New York: Guilford Press.

Andersen, S. M., Glassman, N. S., Chen, S., & Cole, S. W. (1995). Transference in social perception: The role of chronic accessibility in significant-other representations. *Journal of Personality and Social Psychology, 69,* 41–57.

Andersen, S. M., Glassman, N. S., & Gold, D. (1998). Mental representations of the self, significant others, and nonsignificant other: Structure and processing of private and public aspects. *Journal of Personality and Social Psychology, 75,* 845–861.

Andersen, S. M., & Klatzky, R. L. (1987). Traits and social stereotypes: Levels of categorization in person perception. *Journal of Personality and Social Psychology, 53,* 235–246.

Andersen, S. M., Klatzky, R. L., & Murray, J. (1990). Traits and social stereotypes: Efficiency differences in social information processing. *Journal of Personality and Social Psychology, 59,* 192–201.

Andersen, S. M., & Miranda, R. (2006). Through the lens of the relational self: Triggering psychopathology and emotional suffering in the social-cognitive process of transference. In R. Kreuger & J. Tackett (Eds.), *Personality and psychopathology* (pp. 292–334). New York: Guilford Press.

Andersen, S. M., Moskowitz, G. M., Blair, I. B., & Nosek, B. (2007). Automatic thought. In A. W. Kruglanski & E. T. Higgins (Eds.), *Social psychology: Handbook of basic principles* (2nd ed., pp. 138–175). New York: Guilford Press.

Andersen, S. M., Reznik, I., & Chen, S. (1997). The self in relation to others: Motivational and cognitive underpinnings. In J. G. Snodgrass & R. L. Thompson (Eds.), *The self across psychology: Self-recognition, self awareness, and the self-concept* (pp. 233–275). New York: New York Academy of Science.

Andersen, S. M., Reznik, I., & Glassman, N. S. (2005). The unconscious relational self. In R. Hassin, J. S. Uleman, & J. A. Bargh (Eds.), *The new unconscious*. New York: Oxford University Press.

Andersen, S. M., Reznik, I., & Manzella, L. M. (1996). Eliciting facial affect, motivation, and expectancies in transference: Significant-other representations in social relations. *Journal of Personality and Social Psychology, 71,* 1108–1129.

Andersen, S. M., & Strasser, T. (2000). *Self-maintenance processes in transference: Dis-identifying with aspects of self to remain close to another and to regulate affect.* Unpublished manuscript, New York University.

Baldwin, M. W. (1992). Relational schemas and the processing of information. *Psychological Bulletin, 112,* 461–484.

Baldwin, M. W., Carrell, S. E., & Lopez, D. F. (1990). Priming relationship schemas: My advisor and the Pope are watching me from the back of my mind. *Journal of Experimental Social Psychology, 26,* 435–454.

Baldwin, M. W., Fehr, B., Keedian, E., Seidel, M., & Thompson, D. W. (1993). An exploration of the relational schemata underlying attachment styles: Self-report and lexical decision approaches. *Personality and Social Psychology Bulletin, 19,* 746–754.

Baldwin, M. W., Keelan, J. P. R., Fehr, B., Enns, V., & Koh-Rangarajoo, E. (1996). Social-cognitive conceptualization of attachment working models: Availability and accessibility effects. *Journal of Personality and Social Psychology, 71,* 94–109.

Baldwin, M. W., & Sinclair, L. (1996). Self-esteem and "if . . . then . . ." contingencies of interpersonal acceptance. *Journal of Personality and Social Psychology, 71,* 1130–1141.

Bandura, A. (1965). Influence of models' reinforcement contingencies on the acquisition of imitative responses. *Journal of Personality and Social Psychology, 1*(6), 589–595.

Bandura, A. (1977). *Social learning theory.* Oxford, UK: Prentice Hall.

Bargh, J. A. (1990). Auto-motives: Preconscious determinants of social interaction. In E. T. Higgins & R. M. Sorrentino (Eds.), *Handbook of motivation and cognition: Foundations of social behavior* (Vol. 2, pp. 93–130). New York: Guilford Press.

Bargh, J. A., & Barndollar, K. (1996). Automaticity in action: The unconscious as repository of chronic goals and motives. In P. M. Gollwitzer & J. A. Bargh (Eds.), *The psychology of action: Linking cognition and motivation to behavior* (pp. 457–481). New York: Guilford Press.

Bargh, J. A., Bond, R. N., Lombardi, W. L., & Tota, M. E. (1986). The additive nature of chronic and temporary sources of construct accessibility. *Journal of Personality and Social Psychology, 50,* 869–878.

Bargh, J. A., Chaiken, S., Raymond, P., & Hymes, C. (1996). The automatic evaluation effect: Unconditionally automatic attitude activation with a pronunciation task. *Journal of Experimental Social Psychology, 32,* 185–210.

Bargh, J. A., & Chartrand, T. (1999). The unbearable automaticity of being. *American Psychologist, 54,* 462–479.

Bargh, J. A., Gollwitzer, P. M., Lee-Chai, A., Barndollar, K., & Trötschel, R.

(2001). The automated will: Nonconscious activation and pursuit of behavioral goals. *Journal of Personality and Social Psychology, 81,* 1014–1027.

Baum, A., & Andersen, S. M. (1999). Interpersonal roles in transference: Transient mood states under the condition of significant-other activation. *Social Cognition, 17,* 161–185.

Berenson, K. R., & Andersen, S. M. (2006). Childhood physical and emotional abuse by a parent: Transference effects in adult interpersonal relationships. *Personality and Social Psychology Bulletin, 32,* 1509–1522.

Berk, M. S., & Andersen, S. M. (2000). The impact of past relationships on interpersonal behavior: Behavioral confirmation in the social-cognitive process of transference. *Journal of Personality and Social Psychology, 79,* 546–562.

Berk, M. S., & Andersen, S. M. (2004). *Chronically unsatisfied goals with significant others: Triggering unfulfilled needs for love and acceptance in transference.* Unpublished manuscript, New York University.

Block, J. (1971). *Lives through time.* Berkeley, CA: Bancroft.

Block, J. (1977). Advancing the psychology of personality: Paradigmatic shift or improving the quality of research. In D. Magnusson & N. S. Endler (Eds.), *Personality at the crossroads: Current issues in interactional psychology* (pp. 37–63). Hillsdale, NJ: Erlbaum.

Block, J., & Block, J. H. (1980). The role of ego-control and ego resiliency in the organization of behavior. In W. A. Collins (Ed.), *The Minnesota symposium on child psychology* (Vol. 13, pp. 39–101). Hillsdale, NJ: Erlbaum.

Block, J., Buss, D. M., Block, J. H., & Gjerde, P. F. (1981). The cognitive style of breadth of categorization: Longitudinal consistency of personality correlates. *Journal of Personality and Social Psychology, 40*(4), 770–779.

Bombar, M. L., & Littig, L. W., Jr. (1996). Babytalk as a communication of intimate attachment: An initial study in adult romances and friendships. *Personal Relationships, 3*(2), 137–158.

Bowlby, J. (1969). *Attachment and loss: Vol. 1. Attachment.* New York: Basic Books.

Bowlby, J. (1973). *Attachment and loss: Vol. 2. Separation: Anxiety and anger.* New York: Basic Books.

Bowlby, J. (1980). *Attachment and loss: Vol. 3. Loss: Sadness and depression.* New York: Basic Books.

Bretherton, I. (1985). Attachment theory: Retrospect and prospect. *Monographs for the Society for Research in Child Development, 50,* 3–35.

Bugental, D. B. (2000). Acquisition of algorithms of social life: A domain-based approach. *Psychological Bulletin, 126,* 187–219.

Cantor, N., & Mischel, W. (1977). Traits as prototypes: Effects on recognition memory. *Journal of Personality and Social Psychology, 35*(1), 38–48.

Cantor, N., & Mischel, W. (1979). Prototypes in person perception. In L. Berkowitz (Ed.), *Advances in experimental social psychology* (Vol. 12, pp. 3–52). New York: Academic Press.

Chen, M., & Bargh, J. A. (1997). Nonconscious behavioral confirmation processes: The self-fulfilling consequences of automatic stereotype activation. *Journal of Experimental Social Psychology, 33,* 541–560.

Chen, S., & Andersen, S. M. (1999). Relationships from the past in the present: Significant-other representations and transference in interpersonal life. In M. P. Zanna (Ed.), *Advances in experimental social psychology* (Vol. 31, pp. 123–190). San Diego, CA: Academic Press.

Chen, S., Andersen, S. M., & Hinkley, K. (1999). Triggering transference: Examining the role of applicability and use of significant-other representations in social perception. *Social Cognition, 17,* 332–365.

Chen, S., Fitzsimons, G. M., & Andersen, S. M. (2007). Automaticity in close relationships. In J. A. Bargh (Ed.), *Automatic processes in social thinking and behavior* (pp. 133–172). New York: Psychology Press.

Crocker, J., & Wolfe, C. T. (2001). Contingencies of worth. *Psychological Review, 108,* 593–623.

Downey, G., & Feldman, S. I. (1996). Implications of rejection sensitivity for intimate relationships. *Journal of Personality and Social Psychology, 70,* 1327–1343.

Ehrenreich, J. H. (1989). Transference: One concept or many? *The Psychoanalytic Review, 76,* 37–65.

Epstein, S. (1979). The stability of behavior: I. On predicting most of the people much of the time. *Journal of Personality and Social Psychology, 37*(7), 1097–1126.

Fiske, A. P. (1992). The four elementary forms of sociality: Framework for a unified theory of social relations. *Psychological Review, 99,* 689–723.

Fiske, S. T., & Pavelchak, M. (1986). Category-based versus piecemeal-based affective responses: Developments in schema-triggered affect. In R. M. Sorrentino & E. T. Higgins (Eds.), *Handbook of motivation and cognition* (pp. 167–203). New York: Guilford Press.

Fitzsimons, G. M., & Bargh, J. A. (2003). Thinking of you: Nonconscious pursuit of interpersonal goals associated with relationship partners. *Journal of Personality and Social Psychology, 84,* 148–164.

Freud, S. (1958). The dynamics of transference. In J. Strachey (Ed. & Trans.), *The standard edition of the complete psychological works of Sigmund Freud* (Vol. 12, pp. 97–108). London: Hogarth. (Original work published 1912)

Funder, D. C. (1991). Global traits: A neo-Allportian approach to personality. *Psychological Science,2*(1), 31–39.

Funder, D. C. (2001). Personality. *Annual Review of Psychology, 52,* 197–221.

Funder, D. C. (2006). Towards a resolution of the personality triad: Persons, situations, and behaviors. *Journal of Research in Personality, 40*(1), 21–34.

Glassman, N. S., & Andersen, S. M. (1999a). Activating transference without consciousness: Using significant-other representations to go beyond what is subliminally given *Journal of Personality and Social Psychology, 77,* 1146–1162.

Glassman, N. S., & Andersen, S. M. (1999b). Transference in social cognition: Persistence and exacerbation of significant-other based inferences over time. *Cognitive Therapy and Research, 23,* 75–91.

Greenberg, J. R., & Mitchell, S. A. (1983). *Object relations in psychoanalytic theory.* Cambridge, MA: Harvard University Press.

Greenberg, J., & Pyszczynski, T. (1985). Compensatory self-inflation: A response to the threat to self-regard of public failure. *Journal of Personality and Social Psychology, 49,* 273–280.

Greenson, R. R. (1965). The working alliance and the transference neurosis. *Psychoanalytic Quarterly, 34*(2), 155–179.

Greenwald, A. G., & Banaji, M. R. (1989). The self as a memory system: Powerful, but ordinary. *Journal of Personality and Social Psychology, 57,* 41–54.

Hazan, C., & Shaver, P. (1994). Attachment as an organizational framework for research on close relationships. *Psychological Inquiry, 5,* 1–22.

Higgins, E. T. (1987). Self discrepancy: A theory relating self and affect. *Psychological Review, 94,* 319–340.

Higgins, E. T. (1989a). Knowledge accessibility and activation: Subjectivity and suffering from unconscious sources. In J. S. Uleman & J. A. Bargh (Eds.), *Unintended thought* (pp. 75–123). New York: Guilford Press.

Higgins, E. T. (1989b). Continuities and discontinuities in self-regulatory and self-evaluative processes: A developmental theory relating self and affect. *Journal of Personality* (Special Issue: Long-term stability and change in personality), *57*(2), 407–444.

Higgins, E. T. (1990). Personality, social psychology, and person–situation relations: Standards and knowledge activation as a common language. In L. A. Pervin (Ed.), *Handbook of personality* (pp. 301–338). New York: Guilford Press.

Higgins, E. T. (1996a). Knowledge: Accessibility, applicability, and salience. In E. T. Higgins & A. W. Kruglanski (Eds.), *Social psychology: Handbook of basic principles* (pp. 133–168). New York: Guilford Press.

Higgins, E. T. (1996b). Ideals, oughts, and regulatory focus: Affect and motivation from distinct pains and pleasures. In P. M. Gollwitzer & J. A. Bargh (Eds.), *The psychology of action* (pp. 91–114). New York: Guilford Press.

Higgins, E. T., & Brendl, C. M. (1995). Accessibility and applicability: Some "activation rules" influencing judgment. *Journal of Experimental Social Psychology, 31,* 218–243.

Higgins, E. T., & King, G. (1981). Accessibility of social constructs: Information processing consequences of individual and contextual variability. In N. Cantor & J. F. Kihlstrom (Eds.), *Personality, cognition, and social interaction* (pp. 69–121). Hillsdale, NJ: Erlbaum.

Higgins, E. T., King, G. A., & Mavin, G. H. (1982). Individual construct accessibility and subjective impressions and recall. *Journal of Personality and Social Psychology, 43*(1), 35–47.

Hinkley, K., & Andersen, S. M. (1996). The working self-concept in transference: Significant-other activation and self change. *Journal of Personality and Social Psychology, 71,* 1279–1295.

Horowitz, M. J. (1989). Relationship schema formulation: Role-relationship models and intrapsychic conflict. *Psychiatry, 52,* 260–274.

Horowitz, M. J. (Ed.). (1991). *Person schemas and maladaptive interpersonal patterns.* Chicago: University of Chicago Press.

Judd, C. M., & Park, B. (1988). Outgroup homogeneity: Judgments of variability at the individual and group levels. *Journal of Personality and Social Psychology, 54*(5), 778–788.

Kelly, G. A. (1955). *The psychology of personal constructs*. New York: Norton.

Kenrick, D. T., & Funder, D. C. (1988). Profiting from controversy: Lessons from the person–situation debate. *American Psychologist, 43*, 23–34.

Kenrick, D. T., Li, N. P., & Butner, J. (2003). Dynamical evolutionary psychology: Individual decision rules and emergent social norms. *Psychological Review, 110*, 3–28.

Kenrick, D. T., & Stringfield, D. O. (1980). Personality traits and the eye of the beholder: Crossing some traditional philosophical boundaries in the search for consistency in all of the people. *Psychological Review, 87*(1), 88–104.

Lamiell, J. T. (1981). Toward an idiothetic psychology of personality. *American Psychologist, 36*, 276–289.

Linville, P. W., & Fischer, G. W. (1993). Exemplar and abstraction models of perceived group variability and stereotypicality. *Social Cognition, 11*, 92–125.

Luborsky, L., & Crits-Christoph, P. (1990). *Understanding transference: The CCRT method*. New York: Basic Books.

Metcalfe, J., & Mischel, W. (1999). A hot/cool-system analysis of delay of gratification: Dynamics of willpower. *Psychological Review, 106*, 3–19.

Mikulincer, M. (1998). Adult attachment style and affect regulation: Strategic variations in self-appraisals. *Journal of Personality and Social Psychology, 75*, 420–435.

Mikulincer, M., Gillath, O., & Shaver, P. R. (2002). Activation of the attachment system in adulthood: Threat-related primes increase the accessibility of mental representations of attachment figures. *Journal of Personality and Social Psychology, 83*(4), 881–895.

Mikulincer, M., & Horesh, N. (1999). Adult attachment style and the perception of others: The role of projective mechanisms. *Journal of Personality and Social Psychology, 76*, 1022–1034.

Mills, J., & Clark, M. S. (1994). Communal and exchange relationships: Controversies and research. In R. Erber & R. Gilmour (Eds.), *Theoretical frameworks for personal relationships* (pp. 29–42). Hillsdale, NJ: Erlbaum.

Mischel, W. (1968). *Personality and assessment*. Hoboken, NJ: Wiley.

Mischel, W. (1973). Toward a cognitive social learning reconceptualization of personality. *Psychological Review, 80*(4), 252–283.

Mischel, W. (1977). On the future of personality measurement. *American Psychologist, 32*(4), 246–254.

Mischel, W., & Shoda, Y. (1995). A cognitive–affective system theory of personality: Reconceptualizing situations, dispositions, dynamics, and invariance in personality structure. *Psychological Review, 102*, 246–268.

Murray, H. A., Barrett, W. G., & Homburger, E. (1938). *Explorations in personality*. New York: Oxford University Press.

Murray, S. L., & Holmes, J. G. (1993). Seeing virtues in faults: Negativity and the transformation of interpersonal narratives in close relationships. *Journal of Personality and Social Psychology, 65*, 707–722.

Park, B., & Hastie, R. (1987). Perception of variability in category development: Instance-versus abstraction-based stereotypes. *Journal of Personality and Social Psychology, 53*(4), 621–635.

Pelham, B. W. (1993). The idiographic nature of human personality: Examples of the idiographic self-concept. *Journal of Personality and Social Psychology, 64*(4), 665–677.

Pierce, T., & Lydon, J. (1998). Priming relational schemas: Effects of contextually activated and chronically accessible interpersonal expectations on responses to a stressful event. *Journal of Personality and Social Psychology, 75,* 1441–1448

Pierce, T., & Lydon, J. E. (2001). Global and specific relational models in the experience of social interactions. *Journal of Personality and Social Psychology, 80,* 613–631.

Pietromonaco, P. R., & Feldman Barrett, L. (1997). Working models of attachment and daily social interactions. *Journal of Personality and Social Psychology, 73*(6), 1409–1423.

Reznik, I., & Andersen, S. M. (2007). Agitation and despair in relation to parents: Activating emotional suffering in transference. *European Journal of Personality, 21,* 281–301.

Reznik, I., & Andersen, S. M. (2005b). *Becoming the dreaded self: Diminished self-worth with positive significant others in transference.* Unpublished manuscript, New York University.

Rotter, J. B. (1966). Generalized expectancies for internal versus external control of reinforcement. *Psychological Monographs: General and Applied, 80*(1), 1–28.

Schimek, J. (1983). The construction of the transference: The relativity of the "here and now" and the "there and then." *Psychoanalysis and Contemporary Thought, 6,* 435–456.

Shah, J. (2003a). Automatic for the people: How representations of significant others implicitly affect goal pursuit. *Journal of Personality and Social Psychology, 84,* 661–681.

Shah, J. (2003b). The motivational looking glass: How significant others implicitly affect goal appraisals. *Journal of Personality and Social Psychology, 85,* 424–439.

Shaver, P. R., & Mikulincer, M. (2002). Attachment-related psychodynamics. *Attachment and Human Development, 4,* 133–161.

Singer, J. L. (1988). Reinterpreting the transference. In D. C. Turk & P. Salovey (Eds.), *Reasoning, interference, and judgment in clinical psychology* (pp. 182–205). New York: Free Press.

Smith, E. R., & Zarate, M. A. (1990). Exemplar and prototype use in social categorization. *Social Cognition, 8,* 243–262.

Smith, E. R., & Zarate, M. A. (1992). Exemplar-based model of social judgment. *Psychological Review, 99,* 3–21.

Snyder, M., Tanke, E. D., & Berscheid, E. (1977). Social perception and interpersonal behavior: On the self-fulfilling nature of social stereotypes. *Journal of Personality and Social Psychology, 35,* 656–666.

Steele, C. M. (1988). The psychology of self-affirmation: Sustaining the integrity of the self. In L. Berkowitz (Ed.), *Advances in experimental social psychology* (Vol. 21, pp. 261–302). New York: Academic Press.

Strauman, T. J., & Higgins, E. T. (1988). Self-discrepancies as predictors of vulnerability to distinct syndromes of chronic emotional distress. *Journal of Personality, 56,* 685–707.

Sullivan, H. S. (1953). *The interpersonal theory of psychiatry.* New York: Norton.

Taylor, S. E., & Brown, J. D. (1988). Illusion and well-being: A social psychological perspective on mental health. *Psychological Bulletin, 103,* 193–210.

Thompson, R. A. (1998). Early sociopersonality development. In W. Damon (Series Ed.) & N. Eisenberg (Vol. Ed.), *Handbook of child psychology: Vol. 3. Social, emotional, and personality development* (5th ed., pp. 25–104). New York: Wiley.

Tversky, A. (1977). Features of similarity. *Psychological Review, 84*(4), 327–352.

Westen, D. (1988). Transference and information processing. *Clinical Psychology Review, 8,* 161–179.

11

Integrating Personality Traits and Processes
Framework, Method, Analysis, Results

NIALL BOLGER
RAINER ROMERO-CANYAS

Although personality psychology over the past several decades has been characterized by many and diverse programs of research (Hogan, Johnson, & Briggs, 1997; Pervin & John, 1999), two major categories of programs are those based on trait accounts and those based on process accounts. Trait approaches tend to emphasize the broad dimensions of differences between persons repeatedly found in natural language and self-reports. Process approaches, in contrast, emphasize regularities in within-person thoughts, feelings, and behavior, often in particular situational contexts. Examples of trait approaches are the personality models underlying the NEO Personality Inventory by Costa and McCrae and the Trait Descriptive Adjectives by Goldberg and colleagues (see John & Srivastava, 1999, for a review). Examples of process approaches are the Carver and Scheier self-regulation model (Carver & Scheier, 1999) and the Cognitive–Affective Processing System (CAPS) model of Mischel and Shoda (1995). It is the latter that was the point of departure for the work described below.

In this chapter, we describe an approach to personality that attempts to integrate trait and process approaches in studies of adjustment processes in daily life. We do not want to argue that ours is the first or only attempt to do so (see, e.g., Mischel & Shoda, 1999). What we hope is useful about our approach, however, is that it is a concrete demonstration of how this integration can be accomplished at the level of research design, data collection, and statistical modeling.

CAPTURING PERSONALITY PROCESSES

If the worth of a theory can only be gauged with appropriate research designs and methods, there is no doubt that the Wediko study of boys in a summer camp served as a crucial testing ground for Mischel and Shoda's CAPS model of personality. The Wediko data set, comprising behavioral observations of the children in diverse situations over several weeks, permitted the researchers to demonstrate that each child in the study had a distinctive pattern of *if . . . then . . .* behavioral signatures. Some children were highly reactive to peer teasing but not to adult punishment, whereas others showed the reverse pattern. These signatures showed sufficient stability over time to be regarded as within-person patterns of personality organization (e.g., Mischel & Shoda, 1995; Shoda, Mischel, & Wright, 1994).

For those wishing to follow in the footsteps of Mischel and Shoda, the prospect of collecting data as rich as those from Wediko and submitting them to fine-grained, intraindividual analyses must seem truly daunting. We argue in this chapter that advances in data collection and analysis make the investigation and understanding of personality processes a viable prospect for those who do not have the resources to mount another Wediko study. The key requirement is that investigators use intensive repeated-measures methods that permit them to follow persons as they move through a variety of situations. It is with a particular form of those methods, one based on self-reports in diaries, that we illustrate our argument.

Diary methods (also known as experience sampling and ecological momentary assessment) are based on intensive self-report designs that allow the collection of sufficient data to characterize individuals in terms of the situations they encounter and how they think, feel, and behave in those situations. For example, a diary study can have people keep a record of their daily lives over several weeks. They might provide reports one, two, or many times each day, depending on the research design. In addition to self-reports, observer reports and other personal and contextual measures can also be obtained (see Bolger, Davis, & Rafaeli, 2003, for a review of these methods). These types of data provide a basis for assessing the behavioral signatures identified by Shoda and colleagues (1994)—that is, unique patterns of *if . . . then . . .* links between situations and behavior that are the basis of a contextualized model of personality.

HOW CAN PERSONALITY TRAITS AND PROCESSES BE INTEGRATED?

If one has access to intensive repeated-measures data such as can be obtained using diary studies, how can these help integrate trait and process approaches to personality? Consider the repeated-measures data presented in Figure 11.1. Here we see a representation of a simple linear model for a single individual where degree of exposure to a particular type of situation is shown on the X-axis and degree of psychological or behavioral response is shown on the Y-axis. This could be a graph of the amount of social contact a person has each day (number of people the person interacted with) and his or her anxiety level that day. The essential insight to be gleaned from the figure—and it is common to all linear models—is that the mean of Y is perfectly predicted by the mean of X multiplied by the X-to-Y slope (the person's *if . . . then . . .* link) plus the Y-intercept (see Kutner, Nachtsheim, Neter, & Li, 2005, p. 24). Thus, a

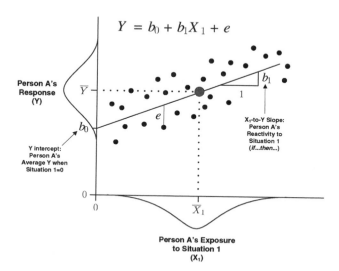

FIGURE 11.1. Relationship between average situation exposure, X_1, *if . . . then . . .* situation reactivity, b_1, and trait level of psychological or behavioral response, $\overline{Y}$, for Person A and Situation 1.

central feature of the CAPS model, the within-person *if* . . . *then* . . . link, can be used to predict a central feature of trait models, a person's typical level of some psychological variable.

Figure 11.2 expands the model further, to the case of multiple persons with multiple situations such that each person has a profile of multiple *if* . . . *then* . . . links. This figure shows that the *if* . . . *then* . . . profiles or behavioral signatures of each person predict the person's mean behavioral or psychological outcomes. What the figure also shows, and what has not been prominent in the CAPS model, is that one must take account of a second behavioral signature, that of situation exposure, in producing mean behavioral outcomes. In other words, it is the particular pattern of situation exposure combined with the pattern of situation–behavior *if* . . . *then* . . . links (together with an intercept term) that predicts the typical level of outcomes.

$$\overline{Y}_i = b_{0i} + \sum_{1}^{k} b_{ki} \overline{X}_{ki}$$

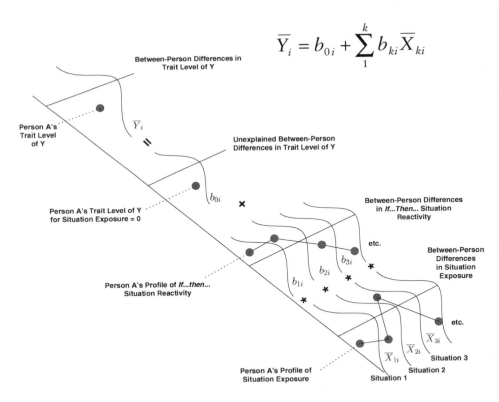

FIGURE 11.2. Relationship of between-person differencines in average situation exposure, $\overline{X}_{ki}$, *if* . . . *then* . . . situation reactivity, b_{ki}, and trait level of psychological or behavioral response, $\overline{Y}_i$, for many persons i and situation types k.

$$\overline{Y}_i = b_{0i} + \sum_1^k b_{ki} \overline{X}_{ki}$$

More formally, the idea is represented in the above multiple regression equation, which relates a person's score on Y to his or her exposure to each of k situations, X_1 to X_k. Specifically, each person i's average Y (that is, $\overline{Y}_i$) is perfectly predicted by his or her average exposure to each situation k (that is $\overline{X}_{ki}$) multiplied by his or her *if . . . then . . .* reactivity to that situation (b_{ki}), summed across all k situations, and added to his or her Y-intercept score (b_{0i}).

A critic could argue that traits are causes of psychological outcomes, whereas in the framework above they are regarded as the outcomes themselves. Our response is to say that self-report measures of traits often ask people to report their typical thoughts, feelings, and behaviors and that a summary measure of these in the form of a mean level is a valid assessment of a trait. Moreover, as we show in an empirical example, a trait measure is related to individual differences in the process measures in the expected way, given the model.

A FRAMEWORK FOR STUDYING PERSONALITY IN THE STRESS PROCESS

Statistical developments in the 1980s and 1990s enable us to model intensive repeated-measures data in ways that were previously difficult, if not impossible. First, the development of multilevel models has made it possible to deal with nonindependence due to nesting of observations within persons (Hox, 2002; Raudenbush & Bryk, 2002; Snijders & Bosker, 1999). Second, sophisticated multilevel models for longitudinal data are now readily available in standard software packages (Collins & Sayer, 2001; Fitzmaurice, Laird, & Ware, 2004; Moskowitz & Hershberger, 2002; Singer & Willett, 2003; Walls & Schafer, 2006). Most important for studying personality, these models allow the person to be studied idiographically. More specifically, multilevel models allow the researcher to ask what is common and what is unique about how people are exposed to and react to situations.

In prior work, Bolger and colleagues used the analytical framework presented in Figure 11.2 to show how within-person stress processes explained the link between personality traits and mean levels of emotional outcomes (Bolger & Schilling, 1991; Bolger & Zuckerman, 1995). This work involved the use of intensive daily diary data to explore how exposure to stressors and reactivity to those stressors predicted daily distress. Both exposure and reactivity were important predictors.

These studies also included a trait measure of neuroticism, which is usually regarded as the central personality determinant of negative affect. As might be expected, neuroticism strongly predicted average levels of daily distress. It also predicted average exposure and emotional reactivity to daily stressors, and these daily process variables helped explain the neuroticism–distress relationships.

Figure 11.3 shows data from Bolger and Schilling (1991) on the profile of exposure to daily stressors for high- and low-neuroticism persons. Overall, the figure shows greater exposure among the high-neuroticism group. Even if there were no differences in reactivity (*if . . . then . . .* links) between the two groups, exposure alone could help explain why the high-neuroticism group showed higher average daily distress.

Other research teams that have used diary methodologies to study stress have looked at exposure to stressors as a function of personality characteristics and other individual differences. Gunthert, Cohen, and Armeli (1999) used a 14-day diary to study neuroticism and coping with daily stressors. In their study, neuroticism was associated with exposure to more interpersonal stressors, as was the case in Bolger and Schilling's study (1991). Similar patterns emerged for Suls, Green, and

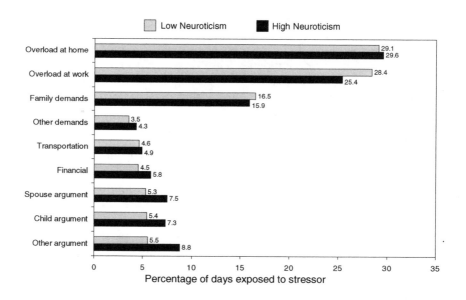

FIGURE 11.3. Daily stressor exposure profiles ($\overline{X}_{1,2,\ldots k}$'s) for low- and high-neuroticism groups.

Hillis (1998) in a study of neuroticism and exposure to everyday problems.

Bolger and Schilling's (1991) study examined *if . . . then . . .* emotional reactivity to specific stressors such as arguments with one's spouse, financial trouble, or work overload and compared the reactivity of those people low and high in neuroticism. As expected, the index of reactivity—the comparison of daily distress on stressor-free days with days when the stressor was present—was generally greater for participants high in neuroticism. These signatures are captured in Figure 11.4, which compares the reactivity of both groups and profiles each of them in a manner similar to that proposed by Mischel and Shoda (1995).

Similar patterns have emerged in the work of other researchers (Mroczek & Almeida, 2004; Suls & Martin, 2005), and some research teams have looked at the extent to which reactivity is predictive of longer-term outcomes. For instance, Felsten (2002) and Cohen, Gunthert, Butler, O'Neill, and Tolpin (2005) have shown that the affective reactivity of college students over the course of a diary study was predictive of the development of depressive symptoms.

More generally, the use of diary methods to examine personality processes has become more widespread. Studies have examined personality variables other than neuroticism as predictors of responses to

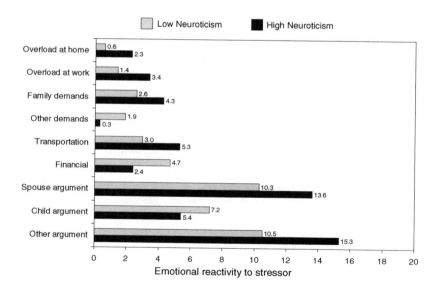

FIGURE 11.4. Daily stressor *if . . . then . . .* reactivity profiles ($b_{1,2,...k}$'s) for low- and high-neuroticism groups.

daily stress (e.g., DeLongis & Holtzman, 2005; Newth & DeLongis, 2004) or general changes in mood (Larsen & Cutler, 1996; Zelenski & Larsen, 1999). Evident in these studies are signatures for reactivity like those shown by Bolger and Schilling.

Individual differences other than personality dispositions can also be used to generate stressor exposure and *if . . . then . . .* emotional reactivity signatures. Birditt, Fingerman, and Almeida (2005) looked at age as a predictor of exposure to interpersonal tensions. In an 8-day diary study they found age differences in exposure to interpersonal tensions such that older adults reported less interpersonal tension than younger adults. The nature of the interpersonal tensions (with family, with children) also varied as a function of age. Other researchers have looked at between-person variables such as marital satisfaction as predictors of reactivity (Tolpin, Cohen, Gunthert, & Farrehi, 2006).

The studies we have cited thus far have focused on negative outcomes. Some researchers, however, have used the diary method to identify situations in which people with particular traits (e.g., neuroticism, agreeableness) are more likely to experience positive mood (Coté & Moskowitz, 1998; Moskowitz & Coté, 1995). Yet other researchers have explored positive daily events and people's responses to them. Zautra, Affleck, Tennen, Reich, and Davis (2005), for example, have identified two processes, engagement and responsiveness, that parallel the processes of exposure and reactivity for negative events and mood.

SUMMARY

Two key developments in personality psychology in recent decades have been the emergence of contextualized conceptions of personality and the rise in the availability of statistical models for intensive repeated-measurement designs. Drawing on these developments, we have described how essential features of personality can be captured by tracking the thoughts, feelings, and behaviors of individuals as they move through a stream of contexts in daily life. In particular, we have shown that data of this kind can be used to reconcile trait and process models of personality.

REFERENCES

Birditt, K. S., Fingerman, K. L., & Almeida, D. M. (2005). Age differences in exposure and reactions to interpersonal tensions: A daily diary study. *Psychology and Aging, 20,* 330–340.

Bolger, N., Davis, A., & Rafaeli, E. (2003). Diary methods: Capturing life as it is lived. *Annual Review of Psychology, 54*, 579–616.

Bolger, N., & Schilling, E. A. (1991). Personality and the problems of everyday life: The role of neuroticism in exposure and reactivity to daily stressors. *Journal of Personality, 59*, 355–386.

Bolger, N., & Zuckerman, A. (1995). A framework for studying personality in the stress process. *Journal of Personality and Social Psychology, 69*, 890–902.

Carver, C. S., & Scheier, M. F. (1999). Stress, coping, and self-regulatory processes. In L. A. Pervin & O. P. John (Eds.), *Handbook of personality: Theory and research* (2nd ed., pp. 553–575). New York: Guilford Press.

Cohen, L. H., Gunthert, K. C., Butler, A. C., O'Neill, S. C., & Tolpin, L. H. (2005). Daily affective reactivity as a prospective predictor of depressive symptoms. *Journal of Personality, 73*, 1687–1714.

Collins, L. M., & Sayer, A. G. (Eds.). (2001). *New methods for the analysis of change*. Washington, DC: American Psychological Association.

Coté, S., & Moskowitz, D. S. (1998). On the dynamic covariation between interpersonal behavior and affect: Prediction from neuroticism, extraversion, and agreeableness. *Journal of Personality and Social Psychology, 75*, 1032–1046.

DeLongis, A., & Holtzman, S. (2005). Coping in context: The role of stress, social support, and personality in coping. *Jounal of Personality, 73*, 1633–1656.

Felsten, G. (2002). Minor stressors and depressed mood: Reactivity is more strongly correlated than total stress. *Stress and Health, 18*, 75–81.

Fitzmaurice, G. M., Laird, N. M., & Ware, J. H. (2004). *Applied longitudinal analysis*. Hoboken, NJ: Wiley.

Gunthert, K. C., Cohen, L. H., & Armeli, S. (1999). The role of neuroticism in daily stress and coping. *Journal of Personality and Social Psychology, 77*, 1087–1100.

Hogan, R., Johnson, J., & Briggs, S. R. (1997). (Eds.). *Handbook of personality psychology*. San Diego, CA: Academic Press.

Hox, J. (2002). *Multilevel analysis: Techniques and applications*. Mahwah, NJ: Erlbaum.

John, O. P., & Srivastava, S. (1999). The Big Five trait taxonomy: History, measurement, and theoretical perspectives. In L. A. Pervin & O. P. John (Eds.), *Handbook of personality: Theory and research* (2nd ed., pp. 102–138). New York: Guilford Press.

Kutner, M. H., Nachtsheim, C. J., Neter, J., & Li, W. (2005). *Applied linear statistical models* (5th ed.). Boston: McGraw-Hill/Irwin.

Larsen, R. J., & Cutler, S. E. (1996). The complexity of individual emotional lives: A within-subject analysis of affect structure. *Journal of Social and Clinical Psychology, 15*, 206–230.

Mischel, W., & Shoda, Y. (1995). A cognitive–affective system theory of personality: Reconceptualizing situations, dispositions, dynamics, and invariance in personality structure. *Psychological Review, 102*, 246–268.

Mischel, W., & Shoda, Y. (1999). Integrating dispositions and processing dynamics within a unified theory of personality: The Cognitive–Affective Personality System. In L. A. Pervin & O. P. John (Eds.), *Handbook of personality: Theory and research* (2nd ed., pp. 197–218). New York: Guilford Press.

Moskowitz, D. S., & Coté, S. (1995). Do interpersonal traits predict affect? A comparison of three models. *Journal of Personality and Social Psychology, 69*, 915–924.

Moskowitz, D. S., & Hershberger, S. L. (Eds.). (2002). *Modeling intraindividual variability with repeated measures data: Methods and applications.* Mahwah, NJ: Erlbaum.

Mroczek, D. K., & Almeida, D. M. (2004). The effect of daily stress, personality, and age on daily negative affect. *Journal of Personality, 72*, 355–378.

Newth, S., & DeLongis, A. (2004). Individual differences, mood, and coping with chronic pain in rheumatoid arthritis: A daily process analysis. *Psychology and Health, 19*, 283–305.

Pervin, L. A., & John, O. P. (Eds.). (1999). *Handbook of personality: Theory and research* (2nd ed.). New York: Guilford Press.

Raudenbush, S. W., & Bryk, A. S. (2002). *Hierarchical linear models: Applications and data analysis methods* (2nd ed.). Thousand Oaks, CA: Sage.

Shoda, Y., Mischel, W., & Wright, J. C. (1994). Intra-individual stability in the organization and patterning of behavior: Incorporating psychological situations into the idiographic analysis of personality. *Journal of Personality and Social Psychology, 65*, 674–697.

Singer, J. D., & Willett, J. B. (2003). *Applied longitudinal data analysis: Modeling change and event occurrence.* New York: Oxford University Press.

Snijders, T. A. B., & Bosker, R. J. (1999). *Multilevel analysis: An introduction to basic and advanced multilevel modeling.* London: Sage.

Suls, J., Green, P., & Hillis, S. (1998). Emotional reactivity to everyday problems, affective inertia, and neuroticism. *Personality and Social Psychology Bulletin, 24*, 127–136.

Suls, J., & Martin, R. (2005). The daily life of the garden-variety neurotic: Reactivity, stressor exposure, mood spillover, and maladaptive coping. *Journal of Personality, 73*, 1485–1509.

Tolpin, L. H., Cohen, L. H., Gunthert, K. C., & Farrehi, A. (2006). Unique effects of depressive symptoms and relationship satisfaction on exposure and reactivity to daily romantic relationship stress. *Journal of Social and Clinical Psychology, 25*, 565–583.

Walls, T. A., & Schafer, J. L. (Eds.). (2006). *Models for intensive longitudinal data.* New York: Oxford University Press.

Zautra, A. J., Affleck, G. G., Tennen, H., Reich, J. W., & Davis, M. C. (2005). Dynamic approaches to emotions and stress in everyday life: Bolger and Zuckerman reloaded with positive as well as negative affects. *Journal of Personality, 73*, 1511–1538.

Zelenski, J. M., & Larsen, R. J. (1999). Susceptibility to affect: A comparison of three personality taxonomies. *Journal of Personality, 67*, 761–791.

12

Toward a Science
of the Social Perceiver

RODOLFO MENDOZA-DENTON
SANG HEE PARK
ALEXANDER O'CONNOR

As many of the chapters in this volume attest, Walter Mischel's contributions to personality science are widely recognized. Less well known are Mischel's contributions to the science of person perception, which is concerned with the ways in which lay perceivers make sense of and infer the personalities of others. In the tradition of Allport (1937), albeit with different methodologies and perspective, Mischel's work on person perception has from the start been predicated on the notion that insights about the nature of personality can be gleaned by listening carefully to the ways that people talk about other people.

At the outset, it is important to place Mischel's contributions to person perception in historical and theoretical context. It can be argued that, for much of Mischel's career, the basic theoretical framework informing person perception research mirrored the traditional view in personality that person forces and situational forces are independent, separable entities. As Gilbert and Malone (1995) summarize:

> [Attribution theories] are grounded in a common metaphor that construes the human skin as a special boundary that separates one set of "causal forces" from another. . . . On the sunny side of the epidermis are the external or situational forces that press inward on the person, and on the meaty side are the internal or personal forces that exert pressure outward. . . . Is the basketball player a graceless shooter, or

did poor lighting cause him to miss the free throw? . . . Did the student appear sad because he is chronically drepressed, or had he just
received word of a failing grade? . . . Each of these is a question about
the relative contributions to behavior of situational and dispositional
factors, and this distinction is, perhaps, the defining feature of attribution theory. (pp. 21–22)

The theoretical view that distinguishes personal from situational
forces has remained, up until relatively recently, an unquestioned assumption in the field of person perception. From the perspective of traditional attribution theories, one of the goals of perceivers is to distinguish
between the external, transitory, situational forces on a target's behavior
on the one hand and the internal, stable, dispositional forces driving that
behavior on the other (Ross & Nisbett, 1991). The "intuitive scientist"
(Heider, 1958) was seen, quite naturally, as operating under the same
assumptions as traditional personality theorists of the time.

For almost as long as Mischel and colleagues have been demonstrating that person–situation interactions are a key component of personality coherence, they have been building a parallel body of research showing that perceivers pay attention to situation–behavior relationships
when given the opportunity to do so (Cantor, 1981; Cantor, Mischel, &
Schwartz, 1982; Shoda & Mischel, 1993; Shoda, Mischel, & Wright,
1993; Wright & Mischel, 1988). Rather than conceptualizing the intuitive scientist solely as a "global trait theorist," who might treat variations in behavior as error variance or as reflecting external pressures of
the situation upon behavior (and contrasted with dispositional forces
upon behavior), Mischel's body of work suggests that the intuitive scientist may also behave like a "cognitive social theorist," who expects, is
aware of, and actively utilizes information from the ways in which others' behavior varies stably across situations (Shoda & Mischel, 1993).
The personality and person perception lines of research go hand in hand:
if person–situation interactions are important expressions of the personality system, it stands to reason that perceivers should be attentive to
such interactions as well. For Mischel's intuitive scientist, changes in the
target's behavior as a function of the situation provide clues about personality dispositions, albeit not global behavior tendencies. Mischel's
intuitive scientist does not so much ask, "person or situation?" but
rather "why this behavior in this situation?" (cf. Reeder, Kumar, &
Hesson-McInnis, 2002; Reeder, Vonk, Ronk, Ham, & Lawrence, 2004;
Sabini, Siepman, & Stein, 2001). The perceiver becomes less of an intuitive statistician and more of an intuitive detective who attempts to piece
together a puzzle about the mental life of the target not by factoring the
situation out, but precisely by factoring it *in*.

Shoda and Mischel (1993) provide a vivid example: Suppose that the tipping behavior of Jim and Jack is observed. Although both Jim and Jack are equally generous at restaurants, Jack is observed leaving a large tip at a "mom and pop" restaurant and a meager tip at a French bistro. Jim, by contrast, leaves the meager tip at the mom and pop restaurants, but a large one at the French restaurant. Shoda and Mischel observe that while Jim and Jack's mean-level generosity does not differentiate the two men, attention to their tipping patterns in different contexts begins to reveal the deeper motivations that differentially drive them. Jack, for example, may believe in rewarding people of modest means and derive self-esteem from it, whereas Jim may be a socially self-conscious individual who feels proud of his high-society status. Thus a person's beliefs, feelings, and ways of construing the social world may be evident from his or her stable patterns of behavioral variability.

PERSON, SITUATION, AND PERSON-IN-SITUATION PROTOTYPES

Mischel's work with Nancy Cantor on person, situation, and person-in-situation prototypes (Cantor, 1981; Cantor & Mischel, 1977, 1979; Cantor et al., 1982) provided some of the first evidence that perceivers' representations of others can contain both person and situation components. In one image-formation task, Cantor and colleagues (1982) asked participants to formulate mental images of person (e.g., "criminal madman"), situation (e.g., "scene of a crime"), or person-in-situation (e.g., "criminal madman at the scene of a crime") categories and to indicate when they had fully formed an image by pressing a key that measured their reaction time. Participants then wrote down on a piece of paper the components of the image that they had formed. The results revealed that participants formulated person images substantially more slowly than either person-in-situation images or situation images, suggesting that participants may have had a more difficult time satisfactorily formulating person images when they were removed from context. The alternative explanation that participants spent longer formulating person images because they were richer and more complex was not supported by content analyses of participants' written protocols. Further analyses revealed that much of the content of the situation protocols actually described characteristics of the persons found in them, indicating that people's knowledge about situations is intimately intertwined with their knowledge about the types of people who inhabit those situations.

To examine more specifically whether perceivers have detailed expectations about the match between people and situations, Cantor and colleagues (1982) asked perceivers to rate the degree to which each of 12 "personality types" would feel comfortable or uncomfortable in each of 15 situations. The results supported the idea that perceivers expected high degrees of person–situation matches. The "responsible" target, for example, was expected to feel comfortable at a family dinner but uncomfortable at a bar. The "risk taker," by contrast, was expected to show the opposite pattern: comfortable at a bar but uncomfortable at a family dinner.

This study is consistent with the notion that perceivers may expect patterns of behavioral variability across situations for different personality prototypes. As Cantor (1981) concludes:

> The intuitive psychologist is a person-oriented theorist, one who focuses on persons and interprets behavior in dispositional and personal terms. The perceptions and interpretations of the lay psychologist, are, however, not really context-free. People shape their interpretations of the behavior of other people according to the situation in which they readily observe the others' behaviors. Their tendency to focus on their own or other people's dispositions in predicting the outcome of a social interaction is similarly affected by the nature of the interaction situation. Whereas the lay observer is primarily an observer of people and personality, he/she thinks in person–situation terms and is influenced (if only in an indirect way) by the situations in which a person is observed. (p. 243)

NOMINAL VERSUS PSYCHOLOGICAL SITUATIONS

In collaboration with Jack Wright and Yuichi Shoda, Mischel began his seminal work on behavioral variability across situations at Wediko Children's Services, which sponsored a residential summer camp for children. At this camp, the researchers had the opportunity to amass a unique social science archive that consisted of behavioral information as well as information about the situations in which behavior occurred. With this unusually extensive data archive, it was possible to assess the existence and stability of situation–behavior relationships that had been hypothesized but for which adequate data was lacking (see Shoda, Mischel, & Wright, 1994).

The symbiotic relationship between Mischel's research in personality and his research in person perception is clearly evident in the work emerging from Wediko. Fundamental insights about the nature of behavioral variability across situations were gleaned by listening to the ways in which the campers and the counselors spoke about the campers. In deciding how to keep track of the children's behavior across situations, a scheme to organize and classify the myriad possible situations at the camp was needed. At one level, it seemed possible to describe situations nominally; that is, according to their surface features (e.g., study hall, cabin meeting; see Whiting & Whiting, 1975). Unfortunately, nominal situations often contain a wide array of interpersonal psychological events for different people and different cultural groups. For example, study hall may represent an opportunity for growth or advancement for one camper, whereas it may represent confinement for another. At a deeper level, it is possible to group situations according to their potential psychological impact on, and meaning for, the population at the camp.

To identify the psychological features that were important to the children, Wright and Mischel (1988) asked the camp counselors, as well as the children's peers, to "tell me everything you know about (target) so I will know him as well as you do" (p. 457). This methodology allowed the researchers to parse those features that they agreed were important to the population. Much of the content of the descriptions consisted of trait terms, confirming their importance in natural language. The data also revealed that these trait descriptors tended to be spontaneously hedged—that is, described in terms of the *conditions* under which targets displayed particular qualities (e.g., "Johnny gets aggressive when he gets teased about his glasses"). The younger children tended to use modifiers such as "sometimes," "sort of," and "a little" when describing behavior, suggesting that even younger perceivers notice that behavior is not always consistent across time and situations. Older children and adults used different qualifiers such as "if," "when," and "after," suggesting a developmental sequence from frequency-type qualifiers to more sophisticated mental models encoding a relationship between behavior and situation.

Further, Shoda and colleagues (1994) showed that clustering the types of situational hedges in the children's descriptions revealed five psychological situations that seemed important to the kids at the camp: three negative situations ("peer teased, provoked, or threatened," "adult warned," and "adult punished") and two positive situations ("adult praised" and "peer approached prosocially"). This distinction between nominal and psychological situations, though subtle, proved critical in the discovery of the stability of *if . . . then . . .* behavioral profiles.

Do Perceivers' Impressions Incorporate *If . . . Then . . .* Profile Information?

Do perceivers use situation–behavior information in judging and predicting behavior? Shoda, Mischel, and Wright (1989) hypothesized that if perceivers are guided by an implicit global trait theory of personality and average the target's behavior across situations to arrive at a dispositional judgment, then varying the relationship between the behaviors and the contexts in which they occur should have no effect on dispositional judgments. In this model, the only thing that would have to remain constant in order for the targets to be judged similarly is their overall behavioral frequencies. If, on the other hand, perceivers are guided by something closer to an intuitive cognitive-social view of personality, then altering the natural relationships between behaviors and their naturally co-occurring contexts should result in differences in judgment.

The results supported the latter model. Experimentally manipulating the veridical situation–behavior contingencies (i.e., describing a target's behavior in situations in which it did not actually occur) led to perceptions that the targets were maladjusted, odd, and even implausible. Moreover, as the relationships between behaviors and their naturally co-occurring situations were altered, participants were less able to predict with accuracy actual differences in the behavior that the target had displayed over the summer. When no situational information was provided, overall target judgments were similar to those in the condition in which the situation–behavior relationships had not been altered; however, more specific predictions of actual target behavior still suffered.

Evidence that situation–behavior relationships are important to perceivers in forming coherent impressions also comes from a more recent series of elegant studies conducted by Plaks, Shafer, and Shoda (2003). They presented participants with information about the open-minded behavior of either fraternity A or fraternity B. Members of both fraternities displayed, on average, similar levels of open-mindedness. Whereas the open-mindedness of fraternity B did not systematically covary with any particular situation, members of fraternity A were consistently open-minded in situations related to physical fitness but not in situations unrelated to physical fitness. Participants reported that fraternity A made more sense and was better understood than fraternity B. Furthermore, when participants were asked to describe what the group was like in a sentence-completion format, participants made goal and value attributions more readily for fraternity A than fraternity B.

Additionally, there is evidence that people use *if . . . then . . .* situation–behavior information in their self-assessments of consistency. In a reanalysis of Mischel and Peake (1982), Mischel and Shoda (1995) tested whether students' self-perceptions of consistency were related to the stability of their situation–behavior profiles. This analysis revealed that cross-situational consistency with respect to conscientiousness did not differentiate students who perceived themselves as consistent from those who did not. Tellingly, however, for individuals who perceived themselves as consistent, the average situation–behavior profile stability coefficient was near .5, whereas it was trivial for those who viewed themselves as inconsistent. It is the stability in the situation–behavior profiles, therefore, and not the cross-situational consistency of behavior that seems related to the perception of consistency.

In summary, a wide range of data stemming from Mischel's lab shows that perceivers are not only sensitive to, but actively utilize information about the ways in which people's behavior varies across situations to form coherent impressions both of others and of the self. The finding that behavior that covaries with certain types of situations makes more sense to perceivers than average behavioral trends that do not covary across situations is consistent with research showing that perceivers spontaneously hedge their descriptions of others with qualifiers such as "when" and "if."

Why would perceivers be sensitive to this information? Answers to this question once again show the symbiosis between Mischel's research on personality and his research on person perception. Here, Mischel's reconceptualization of personality dynamics and coherence, in collaboration with Yuichi Shoda, paved the way for a newer generation of researchers to answer the question of why perceivers might be attentive to person–situation interactions in the behavior of others.

COGNITIVE–AFFECTIVE PROCESSING SYSTEM THEORY AND ITS RELATION TO PERSON PERCEPTION

Mischel and Shoda's (1995) Cognitive–Affective Processing System (CAPS) theory proposes that behavior is mediated by a set of "cognitive–affective units" (CAUs)—a person's goals, values, construals, beliefs, and self-regulatory abilities—organized within a stable network of interconnections. CAPS theory accounts for meaningfully patterned expression of behavior vis-à-vis situations by postulating that the psychological features of different situations activate different CAUs and their characteristic pathways. Within the field of personality science, CAPS theory (Mischel & Shoda, 1995, 1999) has proven to be a useful and widely applied model for understanding personality dynamics (Ayduk et al., 2000; Mischel & Morf; 2003; Mendoza-Denton, Downey, Purdie, Davis, & Pietrzak, 2002; Mendoza-Denton & Mischel, 2007; Borkenau, Riemann, & Angleitner, 2005).

CAPS theory has also provided person perception scholars with a framework within which to understand the ways perceivers interpret the *if . . . then . . .* profiles that they seem to readily perceive in others. A new wave of researchers interested in impression formation has begun to ask whether perceivers may have something akin to a lay version of CAPS theory, whereby perceivers care as much about overall behavior trends as they do about answering the questions "What does this particular person think like?" and "How does this person see the world?"

In a wonderful convergence of research literatures, a number of investigators were independently beginning to postulate CAU-type units as playing a fundamental role in person perception, variously referred to as belief–desire states (Wellman, 1991), mental states (Ames, 2004), intentions (Audi, 1993; Searle, 1983; Wellman, 1991), and reasons (Locke & Pennington, 1982; Malle, 1999). These models emphasize that perceivers do not so much try to separate person forces from situation forces (Fein, 2001), as try to figure out the motivations, drives, fears, and dreams of their targets on the basis of both situational and behavioral information.

RECONCILING TRAITS IN EVERYDAY LANGUAGE USE WITH PROFILES AND CAUs

A question that Mischel and his students began to grapple with was the relationship between trait terms and CAUs. It seems reasonable that the questions "What does this person think like?" and "What makes this person tick?" require a degree of involvement that perceivers may not be willing to accord all social targets. Chen-Idson and Mischel (2001) maintained that reasoning about the mental life of targets is probably reserved for people with whom we have more than just a casual acquaintance—certainly not the bank teller or the clerk at the checkout counter on the way home. Chen-Idson and Mischel reasoned, then, that we think about others in CAU terms when we have had the opportunity to observe them for a long time or when the relationship is important to us. In other instances, they figured, we might be more likely to use context-free, generalized trait terms to describe unfamiliar others. Thus, one way to reconcile trait terms with CAUs was by positing that whereas perceivers might describe others mostly in terms of traits, they might describe familiar and important others more in terms of CAUs.

The findings of the study were exactly as the researchers expected: CAU descriptions increased linearly, and trait descriptions decreased linearly, with the amount of time the perceivers had known someone. Also notably, the findings were moderated by importance, such that when a target was not important to the perceiver, the proportion of CAUs to traits did not vary as a function of the amount of time.

Other research, however, suggests an alternative relationship between traits and CAUs. Read and Miller (1993, 1998) have proposed a model of social perception in which traits act as higher-level "plot units" or "economical scripts," that integrate relationships between behaviors and situations in terms of a target's underlying goals. This view suggests that traits may not stand in opposition to CAUs. Support for this notion comes from Shoda and colleagues (1993). Using data from Wediko, they examined prototypical patterns of situation–behavior variability among kids whom the camp counselors had rated to be "friendly," "aggressive," or "withdrawn." The methodology used in the analysis of the counselors' intuitive judgments is worth noting. At the end of the summer session, the counselors were asked to fill out "Global Child Assessment" questionnaires for the campers, in which they were to indicate, on the whole, how aggressive, friendly, and withdrawn each of the children they rated was. Multiple counselors rated each of the children, reducing the likelihood that the results of the study reflected the idiosyncratic ratings of any one counselor. The researchers then used the counselors' ratings to select children who were prototypical exemplars (0.75 *SD* or more above the mean) of aggressive, friendly, and withdrawn children. They then analyzed the stable patterns of behavioral variability, or *if . . . then . . .* signatures (if *A,* then the camper does *X,* but if *B,* then the camper does *Y),* of these prototypical exemplars.

The results of the study clearly supported the idea that the counselors' end-of-summer assessments were influenced by the relationships between the campers' behavior and the situations in which the behavior had occurred. The aggressive exemplars, for example, were characterized by aggression when they were teased, provoked, or threatened. Interestingly, the withdrawn exemplars were also characterized by aggression; however, their aggression was displayed in response to prosocial behavior by peers. These results suggest that specific situation–behavior relations may constitute central and defining characteristics of perceivers' social categories, rather than overall behavior trends as suggested by the global labels. Shoda and Mischel (1993) note that

> to characterize a prototype, it was not enough to specify relevant behaviors. Rather, they must be contextualized in the appropriate context, suggesting that the intuitive representation of the prototype may be in terms of characteristic sets of *if . . . then . . .* situation relations, or specific patterns by which the behaviors (the *thens*) vary over particular situations (the *ifs*). (p. 581, emphasis in original)

Thus the authors echo the ideas proposed by Cantor (1981) a decade earlier.

In a more recent set of experiments, Kammrath, Mendoza-Denton, and Mischel (2005) presented participants with fictitious targets whose behavior displayed the same overall level of sociable behavior. The situation–behavior patterns, however, were different: One target was warm toward superiors but cold toward peers, while the other was warm toward peers but cold to superiors. Despite showing exactly the same overall level of sociability, the former target was rated low on agreeableness, whereas the latter target was seen as highly agreeable. Further, ratings of agreeableness (using a well-established trait measure) were mediated by the goal inferences participants made: The "agreeable" target was assumed to have egalitarian beliefs and a genuine concern for others, while the "unagreeable" target was assumed to have the goal of getting ahead at the expense of others. These findings, then, directly link CAU-type inferences to perceivers' beliefs about targets' *if . . . then . . .* profiles and are important because they show that a conceptualization of the perceiver as one who thinks about others in terms of goals, motives, and *if . . . then . . .* profiles is not incompatible with the fact that people routinely describe others using broad trait terms (see also John, 1990; Read, Jones, & Miller, 1990; Read & Miller, 1998).

In summary, although trait descriptors were originally seen as incompatible with a dynamic *if . . . then . . .*/CAU perspective (Chen-Idson & Mischel, 2001), a majority of research in this area suggests that traits may serve as summary labels for intuitive theories that incorporate behavior, situations, and CAUs.

AN EMERGING VIEW OF THE PERCEIVER

As we have seen, perceivers seem to readily take account of *if . . . then . . .* profiles and to be able to form relatively complex impressions about the goals, values, beliefs, and motives that may drive the behavior of others. Nevertheless, as noted earlier (Chen-Idson & Mischel, 2001), it seems that such inferences are both involving and time-consuming, requiring a type of interest, engagement, or motivation that the "cognitive miser" (Fiske & Taylor, 1984) may simply not have. As Chen-Idson and Mischel (2001) have suggested, inferences about the mental life of targets—questions about their motivational states—may be reserved only for a few individuals, while for most a relatively broad average may do.

Chen-Idson and Mischel's (2001) conclusions, however, are predicated on the assumption that when perceivers first meet a new person, they find a way to explain or make sense of the person's behavior absent preconceived notions. As decades of research on stereotyping tell us, this assumption may be the exception rather than the norm. We propose that, at least sometimes, perceivers may be able to think in CAU or profile terms even about relative strangers about whom perceivers have little or no information by matching targets to person prototypes (Cantor & Mischel, 1979) that already contain such information. To the degree that a single behavior-in-situation episode matches a particular point of an *if . . . then . . .* profile, perceivers may fill in the rest of the profile—and its mediating units—from very little other information. Such CAPS-like "prototypes," if available and accessible, may be used to provide a complex and dynamic picture of even a relatively unknown person with minimal effort.

For this to be true, perceivers' preconceptions about different types of people—their stereotypes—would need to contain profile as well as CAU information. Reminiscent of Cantor and Mischel's earlier research on prototypes, Mendoza-Denton, Park, Kammrath, and Peake (2005) asked whether stereotypes may contain both *if . . . then . . .* profile information and CAU-type information. Specifically, they examined perceivers' expectations about men's and women's assertiveness across meaningful situational domains. They anticipated stereotypical gender differences in CAUs such that perceivers would view the stereotypical man as valuing motives associated with power and achievement (e.g., seeking social status and power) and the stereotypical woman as valuing motives associated with affiliation and intimacy (e.g., valuing romantic love, intimacy, emotions). Such perceived gender differences in CAUs should cause expectations of assertiveness from men in domains that highlight power and achievement such as work and sport (e.g., in a conversation about what is happening on Wall Street). On the other hand, perceivers should expect more assertiveness from women in domains that highlight affiliation and intimacy (e.g., when planning their 4-year-old son's birthday party).

Indeed, they found that perceivers expected differing levels of assertiveness based on the above interaction between gender and situational domain. At the same time, perceivers expected the same targets to have CAUs stereotypical of their gender. These findings show that at least some stereotypes are qualified by context *and* that mentalistic attributes often accompany trait expectations. These stereotypical mentalistic attributes mediated the link between gender stereotypes and behavioral profiles, such that perceivers who expected larger gender differences in mentalistic attributes also expected more distinct *if . . . then . . .* profiles. The findings held true even under cognitive load, suggesting that such complex schemas need not take up a lot of effort or cognitive resources.

The findings suggest that even if a perceiver does not have a lot of information about another person, he or she may have at his or her disposal stereotypical "mental life" information that can be attributed to a target. As such, even with unimportant or not well-known others, perceivers may be able to make inferences about their CAUs and have expectations about their *if . . . then . . .* profiles.

CONCLUSIONS

The research inspired by Mischel and carried forward by his collaborators and students leaves us with a different model of how perceivers make sense of others' behaviors. As summarized, traditional attributional models conceptualize the intuitive scientist as engaging in a variety of strategies that enable him or her to distinguish situational influences on behavior from the target's "true score." From a Mischelian perspective, the perceiver remains an intuitive scientist but one with a different set of hypotheses. This "cognitive-social theorist" may entertain different theories about a target based on the target's pattern of behavior across situations. Impressions may change depending on new behavior-in-situation information that is acquired. A colleague who is extremely nice to the boss, for example, may be very sociable or very upstanding, but she might also be a kiss-up (or slime; see Vonk, 1998) depending on how she treats her peers.

As Plaks and colleagues (2003) note, typical person perception and attribution paradigms ask participants to observe and make judgments about a target's behavior in only one situation. These paradigms make sense under the assumption that behavioral variability across situations is not informative. To the degree that the questions we ask shape the kinds of responses our participants are able to provide us with, however, paradigms that allow observers to rate targets across multiple situations can yield surprising new insights about the way perceivers make sense of others. As we have tried to show here, Mischel has remained ahead of the curve by listening intently to the intuitive scientist.

REFERENCES

Allport, G. W. (1937). *Personality: A psychological interpretation.* New York: Holt, Rinehart & Winston.

Ames, D. R. (2004). Inside the mind reader's tool kit: Projection and stereotyping in mental state inference. *Journal of Personality and Social Psychology,* 87, 340–353.

Audi, R. (1993). Mental causation: Sustaining and dynamic. In J. Heil & A. R. Mele (Eds.), *Mental causation* (pp. 53–74). New York: Clarendon Press/ Oxford University Press.

Ayduk, O., Mendoza-Denton, R., Mischel, W., Downey, G., Peake, P. K., & Rodriguez, M. (2000). Regulating the interpersonal self: strategic self-regulation for coping with rejection sensitivity. *Journal of Personality and Social Psychology,* 79, 776–792.

Borkenau, P., Riemann, R., & Angleitner, A. (2005). *Genetic and environmental influences on person situation profiles.* Unpublished manuscript, Martin Luther University.

Cantor, N. (1981). Perceptions of situations: situation prototypes and person–situation prototypes. In D. Mangusson (Ed.), *Toward a psychology of situations: An interactional perspective* (pp. 229–244). Hillsdale, NJ: Erlbaum.

Cantor, N., & Mischel, W. (1977). Traits as prototypes: Effects on recognition memory. *Journal of Personality and Social Psychology,* 35, 38–48.

Cantor, N., & Mischel, W. (1979). Prototypes in person perception. In L. Berkowitz (Ed.), *Advances in experimental social psychology* (Vol. 12, pp. 3–52). New York: Academic Press.

Cantor, N., Mischel, W., & Schwartz, J. C. (1982). A prototype analysis of psychological situations. *Cognitive Psychology,* 14, 45–77.

Chen-Idson, L., & Mischel, W. (2001). The personality of familiar and significant people: The lay perceiver as social-cognitive theorist. *Journal of Personality and Social Psychology,* 80, 585–596.

Fein, S. (2001). Beyond the fundamental attribution era? *Psychological Inquiry,* 12, 16–40.

Fiske, S. T., & Taylor, S. E. (1984). *Social cognition.* Reading, MA: Addison-Wesley.

Gilbert, D. T., & Malone, P. S. (1995). The correspondence bias. *Psychological Bulletin,* 117, 21–38.

Heider, F. (1958). *The psychology of interpersonal relations.* New York: Wiley.

John, O. P. (1990). The "Big Five" factor taxonomy: Dimensions of personality in the natural language and in questionnaires. In L. Pervin (Ed.), *Handbook of personality: Theory and research* (pp. 66–100). New York: Guilford Press.

Kammrath, L., Mendoza-Denton, R., & Mischel, W. (2005). Incorporating *if . . . then* . . . signatures in person perception: Beyond the person–situation dichotomy. *Journal of Personality and Social Psychology,* 88, 605–613.

Locke, D., & Pennington, D. (1982). Reasons and other causes: Their role in attribution processes. *Journal of Personality and Social Psychology,* 42, 212–223.

Malle, B. F. (1999). How people explain behavior: A new theoretical framework. *Personality and Social Psychology Review,* 3, 23–48.

Mendoza-Denton, R., Downey, G., Purdie, V. J., Davis, A., & Pietrzak, J. (2002). Sensitivity to status-based rejection: Implications for African American students' college experience. *Journal of Personality and Social Psychology, 83,* 896–918.

Mendoza-Denton, R., & Mischel, W. (2007). Integrating system approaches to culture and personality: The Cultural Cognitive–Affective Processing System (C-CAPS). In S. Kitayama & D. Cohen (Eds.), *Handbook of cultural psychology.* New York: Guilford Press.

Mendoza-Denton, R., Park, S. H., Kammrath, L., & Peake, P. K. (2005, May). *Perceivers as cognitive-social theorists: The case of gender stereotypes.* Paper presentation, Psychology Department, University of Washington, Seattle, WA.

Mischel, W., & Morf, C. C. (2003). The self as a psycho-social dynamic processing system: A meta-perspective on a century of the self in psychology. In M. R. Leary & J. P. Tangney (Eds.), *Handbook of self and identity* (pp. 15–43). New York: Guilford Press.

Mischel, W., & Peake, P. K. (1982). Beyond déjà vu in the search for cross-situational consistency. *Psychological Review, 89,* 730–755.

Mischel, W., & Shoda, Y. (1995). A cognitive-affective system theory of personality: Reconceptualizing situations, dispositions, dynamics, and invariance in personality structure. *Psychological Review, 102,* 246–268.

Mischel, W., & Shoda, Y. (1999). Integrating dispositions and processing dynamics within a unified theory of personality: The cognitive–affective personality system. In L. A. Pervin & O. P. John (Eds.), *Handbook of personality: Theory and research* (2nd ed., pp. 197–218). New York: Guilford Press.

Plaks, J. E., Shafer, J. L, & Shoda, Y. (2003). Perceiving individuals and groups as coherent: How do perceivers make sense of variable behavior? *Social Cognition, 21,* 26–60.

Read, S. J., Jones, D. K., & Miller, L. C. (1990). Traits as goal-based categories: The importance of goals in the coherence of dispositional categories. *Journal of Personality and Social Psychology, 58,* 1048–1061.

Read, S. J., & Miller, L. C. (1993). Rapist or "regular guy": Explanatory coherence in the construction of mental models about others. *Personality and Social Psychology Bulletin, 19,* 526–541.

Read, S. J., & Miller, L. C. (1998). On the dynamic construction of meaning: An interactive activation and competition model of social perception. In S. J. Read & L. C. Miller (Eds.), *Connectionist models of social reasoning and social behavior* (pp. 27–68). Mahwah, NJ: Erlbaum.

Reeder, G. D., Kumar, S., & Hesson-McInnis, M. S. (2002). Inferences about the morality of an aggressor: The role of perceived motive. *Journal of Personality and Social Psychology, 83,* 789–803.

Reeder, G. D., Vonk, R., Ronk, M. J., Ham, J., & Lawrence, M. (2004). Dispositional attribution: Multiple inferences about motive-related traits. *Journal of Personality and Social Psychology, 86,* 530–544.

Ross, L., & Nisbett, R. E. (1991). *The person and the situation: Perspectives of social psychology.* New York: McGraw-Hill.

Sabini, J., Siepman, M., & Stein, J. (2001). The really fundamental attribution error in social psychological research. *Psychological Inquiry, 12,* 1–15.

Searle, J. R. (1983). *Intentionality: An essay in the philosophy of mind.* Cambridge, UK: Cambridge University Press.

Shoda, Y., & Mischel, W. (1993). Cognitive-social approach to dispositional inferences: What if the perceiver is a cognitive-social theorist? *Personality and Social Psychology Bulletin, 19,* 574–585.

Shoda, Y., Mischel, W., & Wright, J. C. (1989). Intuitive interactionism in person perception: Effects of situation–behavior relations on dispositional judgments. *Journal of Personality and Social Psychology, 65,* 1023–1035.

Shoda, Y., Mischel, W., & Wright, J. C. (1993). Links between personality judgments and contextualized behavior patterns: Situation–behavior profiles of personality prototypes. *Social Cognition, 4,* 399–429.

Shoda, Y., Mischel, W., & Wright, J. C. (1994). Intraindividual stability in the organization and patterning of behavior: Incorporating psychological situations into the idiographic analysis of personality. *Journal of Personality and Social Psychology, 67,* 674–687.

Vonk, R. (1998). The slime effect: Suspicion and dislike of likeable behavior toward superiors. *Journal of Personality and Social Psychology, 74,* 849–864.

Wellman, H. M. (1991). From desires to beliefs: Acquisition of a theory of mind. In A. Whiten (Ed.), *Natural theories of mind: Evolution, development, and simulation of everyday mindreading* (pp. 19–38). Cambridge, MA: Basil Blackwell.

Whiting, B. B., & Whiting, J. W. M. (1975). Children of six cultures: A psychocultural analysis. Cambridge, MA: Harvard University Press.

Wright, J. C., & Mischel, W. (1988). Conditional hedges and the intuitive psychology of traits. *Journal of Personality and Social Psychology, 55,* 454–469.

13

Toward a Science
of the Individual
A Molecular View of Personalized Medicine

PAUL S. MISCHEL

The most exciting scientific work in the 21st century will arise from interactions among, not within, traditional academic disciplines (Sung et al., 2003). This chapter is based on such an interdisciplinary interaction. Walter Mischel has given us powerful insights into the paradox of personality, and his scientific approach has provided a map for scientists from a diverse array of disciplines. As a cancer biologist trying to develop new molecularly targeted therapies, I draw inspiration from Walter's work. My problem shares important themes with Walter's work, including (1) a recognition of the richness and complexity of individuals, (2) a growing awareness of the inability of global trait theories to explain the observed behavior being studied, and (3) an emerging sense that uncovering key interactions will be critical. In this chapter, I proceed through a series of parallels that highlight the conceptual similarities and challenges we face and the ways in which the conceptual strategies so effectively used by Walter have begun to facilitate our detection of potential new treatments for brain cancer.

PARALLEL 1: THE INADEQUACY OF GLOBAL
TRAIT AND STATE EXPLANATIONS

Walter taught us that global trait and state models are inadequate to provide explanations that encompass the complexity and richness of human experience (Mischel, 1968, 1973, 2004). Despite their intuitive appeal and simplicity, these models do not reliably predict behavior. They provide only limited understanding of that behavior, and they do not yield specific points of intervention for changing it (Mischel, 2004). By incorporating context into the search for coherence, Mischel has shown us that stable behavioral signatures can be identified (Mischel, 2004; Mischel & Shoda, 1995, 1998; Wright & Mischel, 1988), thus opening up new avenues to identify predictive patterns, to understand behavior, and to develop approaches to help people learn and grow. Biologists must take this lesson seriously because we face a remarkably similar challenge as we try to understand how to diagnose and treat individual cancer patients.

Cancer diagnosis is based on a pathologist's interpretation of the appearance of diseased tissue. While this process takes great observational skill that requires years of highly specialized training to develop (I am a pathologist and can attest to the rigors and value of this training), we must acknowledge that this type of diagnosis is broad (i.e., a particular cancer type), subjective (there is considerable variability among pathologists' opinions), and does not address the underlying molecular networks that we have come to appreciate as the key determinants of malignant behavior (P. S. Mischel, Cloughesy, & Nelson, 2004). The parallels with global state and trait descriptions of personality are apparent, including the fact that diagnosing global traits and states takes great observational skills requiring years of specialized training. And, just as Walter has shown us that behavioral consistency is missing from these global trait and state descriptions, we pathologists have come to recognize that our broad diagnostic categories also fail to capture critical information. For example, while these pathological diagnoses are relatively accurate predictors of the survival or response to treatment of a large group of patients, they are not good at predicting response to therapy or time of survival for an individual (P. Mischel et al., 2004). Risk stratification is based on these morphological diagnoses, and the patient is typically first treated with relatively toxic, nonspecific therapies such as DNA-damaging agents and radiation. For most cancer patients, the results are not satisfactory.

Medicine is in the midst of a paradigm shift. Instead of relatively broad pathological diagnoses, population-based risk assessments, and nonspecific "one-size-fits-all" therapies, we are moving to an era of predictive individualized care based on molecular classification and targeted therapy. This shift has been specifically recognized and highlighted by the National Institutes of Health in their public fact sheet for 2006 (www.nih.gov/about/researchresultsforthepublic/ppps.pdf). The application of high-throughput approaches to study thousands of genes and proteins within diseased tissues has accelerated the pace of this discovery and opened up the possibility of developing a systems view of disease (P. Mischel et al., 2004).

The ability to perform high-throughput molecular analysis has led to the observation that disease states such as cancer are complex, and this complexity has begun to challenge the translation of knowledge from bench to bedside, as some have suggested that it is too great ever to be understood. The key to addressing it, however, may be in finding the simple rules that underlie it, just as Walter Mischel and his colleague Yuichi Shoda have begun to do for personality (Mischel, 2004; Mischel & Shoda, 1995, 1998).

By way of a metaphor, the opening sentence of *Anna Karenina* is illuminating: "All happy families are alike; each unhappy family is unhappy in its own way." In cancer, perhaps the ultimate "unhappy" state, genetic and postgenetic changes, as well as interactions between the individual and his or her environment, result in highly individualized disease states. Cancer develops and progresses through a series of changes in intracellular networks involving a process of gains and losses of function (Hood, Heath, Phelps, & Lin, 2004). New molecular diagnostics are being developed to track these changes and characterize individual's disease in terms of these specific molecular transitions. Tracking these changes will guide the development and matching of individual patients and therapies to target specifically the responsible genetic or postgenetic changes that drive the development and progression of cancer (Hood et al., 2004).

Drugs are being developed to target the genes that play a key role in promoting cancer, holding the promise of effective and nontoxic treatments, but, with the exception of a few remarkable success stories, most efforts to help cancer patients with these drugs have failed. It is important to consider a critical factor for this failure. Because patient inclusion in clinical trials is highly reliant on traditional broad diagnostic categories that provide only limited insight into the molecular diversity of disease at the level of an individual, potentially effective molecularly targeted treatments often fail to be recognized. This failure is largely responsible for the relative bottleneck in moving from potential molecular targets to effective drugs and has resulted in a tremendous loss of life, time, and resources.

We need to develop a personalized, systems approach to disease that integrates many diverse inputs, including molecular signatures, phenomenological and clinical information, and environmental information, and integrates them into a network using graphical models (Hood et al., 2004). As more inputs are integrated, the structure of the networks is refined, enabling generation of hypotheses about how the system works (or, in the case of disease, how it has gone awry by repro-gramming the integrated cell circuits and intercellular networks). As complete a picture of the system as possible is developed, and this knowledge can translate into new diagnostic and therapeutic tools (Hood et al., 2004). This approach implies that traditional "one-size-fits-all" approaches to disease diagnosis and treatment need to be recon-sidered. It indicates that refined biomarkers of disease states that identify specifically targetable networks and pathways need to be identified, and it suggests that this information needs to be considered to get the right drug to the right patient.

If cancer medicine, like personality psychology, faces the challenge of uncovering the simple rules that underlie seemingly hopelessly com-plex systems, can some of the approaches Walter Mischel and colleagues used to find these rules in personality help us? In the next two parts of this chapter, I specifically demonstrate how we have been inspired by Walter Mischel's approaches to reducing this complexity into meaning-ful and useful rules by (1) incorporating context into the search for coherence in massive and "thick" data sets (Mischel, 2004; Mischel & Shoda, 1995, 1998; Shweder, 1999) and (2) developing *if . . . then . . .* signatures that are the true locus of consistency (Mischel & Shoda, 1995, 1998).

PARALLEL 2: LOOKING FOR COHERENCE IN VARIABILITY, THE NEED FOR A MASSIVE DATA ARCHIVE, AND INCORPORATING CONTEXT INTO THE SEARCH FOR COHERENCE

Powerful new technologies have provided an unprecedented opportunity to study the expression of thousands of genes and proteins in clinical samples, but the interpretation of such massive amounts of data remains a critical challenge. This problem is not dissimilar from the one Mischel and colleagues faced when they embarked on the groundbreaking Wediko study (Wright & Mischel, 1988; Mischel & Shoda, 1995; Rodriguez, Mischel, & Shoda, 1989). The intent of that study, to the best of my understanding, was to address a key challenge raised in response to Mischel's (1968) monograph, *Personality and Assessment*. Namely, one potential explanation for the lack of cross-situational con-sistency was that the inconsistencies were due to noisy data and mea-surement error. If this were the case, the rational approach would be to aggregate the individual's behavior on a given dimension, thus restoring some degree of consistency. Any single measurement could be imprecise and noisy, but averaging many such inputs ought to obtain a reliable signature. This argument is certainly compelling; however, if there are "active ingredients" of the signature based on important interactions, and if these interactions are actually the locus of consistency, then new analytical strategies need to be developed because the aggregation procedure will eliminate our ability to detect these interactions. One would need instead to look for specific interactions within a "thick" data set (Shweder, 1999) that contains large amounts of retrievable contextualized information—hence, the Wediko study.

Somewhat startlingly, a parallel debate is occurring in the field of cancer genetics. The development of powerful high-throughput technologies for analyzing the entire expressed genome in clinical samples has put us in possession of the equivalent of "thick" datasets (Shweder, 1999) in which interaction signatures may be nested. Many biologists have suggested that the measurement of individual genes is noisy and imprecise and that an aggregation procedure will provide a more powerful classifier or predictor. This approach has become standard. To help manage and interpret the prodigious amounts of genomic data, cancer geneticists have developed aggregate types of analytical methods such as hierarchical clustering. These approaches have been highly successful at classifying previously unrecognized molecular subtypes of cancers or predicting those that differ in their aggressiveness or response to therapy. Aggregate global gene expression signatures can robustly identify different subsets of cancer patients whose tumors look alike under the microscope, but whose cancers clearly have different molecular signatures and who could be considered to have essentially different diseases. Such approaches are of value, and our group has contributed to this literature (P. Mischel et al., 2004; Freije et al., 2004; Shai et al., 2003).

Walter Mischel (2004), in his prefatory chapter of the *Annual Review of Psychology*, has argued that this type of strategy (which he refers to as eliminating context by aggregation) may treat important data outliers as noise and may thus miss some critical "active ingredients" of the behavioral signature. Is it possible that such aggregation approaches may be similarly eliminating context in gene expression data sets and, in so doing, missing key elements? Further, while these aggregation-based approaches are invaluable for differentiating disease types and biological states, the assignment of relative importance to individual genes and the subsequent identification of biologically significant therapeutic targets remain difficult. The standard approach to finding putative targets from aggregate lists of differentially expressed genes has required making hypotheses based on known or implied functional implications in particular phenotypes or diseases. Not only is this approach time-consuming and subjective, but it also often overlooks potentially novel important targets for which no previous disease associations have been made.

If we are aiming to (1) elucidate the underlying biology, (2) develop new drugs to target specific causative genes and pathways in cancer, and (3) facilitate the identification of individual patients who are most likely to benefit from these molecularly targeted agents, then we need to pay very close attention to the relationships that are eliminated by the aggregation strategy. By showing us how to look for *if . . . then . . .* signatures, Walter Mischel may have given us an important clue, and a number of parallel strategies are being developed.

One strategy focuses on using the power of bioinformatics to leverage the considerable amount of data present in the scientific literature about all possible genetic interactions. With an expanding number of experimental technologies that characterize large-scale molecular states and interactions becoming available, the interface of global gene expression data with other knowledge platforms may help maximize data effectiveness and unveil new therapeutically relevant discoveries. Studies combining gene expression signatures with other large-scale technologies, different genomic platforms and sample sets, or various databases are already recognizing genes previously unassociated with cancers as potential biomarkers or targets (Hood & Perlmutter, 2004). Knowledge-based computational pathway analysis bioinformatics tools that integrate global genomic data with a comprehensive global molecular interaction network based on individually modeled, known molecular pathway relationships may help reveal new disease pathways and highlight important targets from gene expression data (Calvano et al., 2005). These databases of biological networks, consisting of millions of individually modelled peer-reviewed pathway relationships can be used to try to find an interactional structure in complex global gene expression datasets.

A second, closely related approach involves analyzing gene expression data sets to look for statistical enrichment of sets of genes that are known to be involved in specific pathways or functions (Bild & Febbo, 2005; Bild et al., 2006; Subramanian et al., 2005). This process, called "gene set enrichment," aims to identify specific pathways or biological processes that may be differentially activated and therefore targeted in cancer. Gene set enrichment has also begun to transform the approach to analyzing cancer data sets.

A third strategy involves looking for empirical interactions in the data sets without a priori knowledge of interactions (i.e., the kinds of a priori knowledge required for the two approaches mentioned above) (Bild et al., 2006; Carlson et al., 2006; Zhang & Horvath, 2005). If the systems view of disease postulates a fundamental rewiring of biological circuits in diseases like cancer, then developing approaches to map that circuitry that are not dependent upon our preexisting knowledge of normal circuits may be important for developing circuit diagrams that accurately describe the wiring of cancer, particularly if these circuits are different from normal (Hood et al., 2004). Developing such circuit diagrams of cancer is likely to be crucial for pointing out vulnerable nodes to target, particular nodes upon which cancer cells, but not normal cells, are dependent. With this strategy in mind, our group has been applying graphic network methods to global gene expression data to identify empirical coexpression relationships, to find robust coexpression modules, and to identify new targets (Carlson et al., 2006; Zhang & Horvath et al., 2005). Note that coexpression does not necessarily imply causality. Therefore, such approaches mandate more classical biology experiments to study the dynamics of these newly identified circuits in cancer cells. This process, too, is parallel to Walter Mischel's studies of personality. Large-scale associational data sets are used to find potential key interactions, which can then be tested empirically in well-controlled dynamic experiments.

PARALLEL 3: THE DEVELOPMENT
OF THE *IF . . . THEN . . .* SIGNATURE

The future of cancer therapy lies in molecularly targeted therapies. Developing ways to find meaningful molecular signatures will be critical for identifying individual patients most likely to benefit. The concept of "pathway addiction" is central to this strategy. Key regulators of intracellular signaling are commonly overactive in cancer, resulting in persistent signals that promote tumor growth and invasion (P. Mischel & Cloughesy, 2006). Mounting evidence suggests that tumor cells become "addicted" to these persistent signals, making them potentially vulnerable to targeted attack by small molecular inhibitors (P. Mischel et al., 2004; P. Mischel & Cloughesy, 2003, 2006). Thus, the very signals that promote aggressive behavior may be the Achilles' heel of cancer. Identifying the vulnerable point of each individual's cancer may allow for effective, selective, and nontoxic therapy, and these points are likely to differ among individuals (P. Mischel et al., 2004; P. Mischel & Cloughesy, 2003). Note the profound difference between this approach and the current model, in which patients are given toxic therapies with the hope that cancer cells, by virtue of their increased growth rate, will sustain more of the damage.

Our group focuses on glioblastoma, the most common malignant primary brain tumor of adults and one of the most lethal of all cancers. Patients with this disease survive, on average, less than 15 months despite surgery, radiation, and traditional toxic chemotherapies (P. Mischel et al., 2004; P. Mischel & Cloughesy, 2003). Clearly, new approaches to the disease are needed. Many researchers have stayed away from this problem, considering it too difficult and depressing a challenge. We reasoned that patients with this tumor may be very well suited for molecularly targeted therapies because the disease possesses clear pathway targets that are thought to play a role in its development and progression and for which new drugs are available. We further reasoned that studying this disease would not only help identify new strategies for treating brain cancer, but also might help us begin to understand the wiring of cancer in general.

One potential molecular target in glioblastoma is the epidermal growth factor receptor (EGFR) tyrosine kinase. This protein, which is normally present at low levels in normal cells, is carefully regulated in health. Its activation state is controlled to tell cells when to proliferate under specific conditions and when to stop. In glioblastoma, it is commonly amplified and/or overexpressed, often in association with expression of a chronically activated mutant receptor (EGFRvIII) (P. Mischel & Cloughesy, 2003). This mutation promotes persistent activation of downstream signaling pathways, resulting in uncontrolled cellular proliferation and glioblastoma development and progression. Glioblastomas also commonly lose expression of the tumor suppressor protein PTEN, a negative regulator of one of these key signaling pathways, further potentiating dependence upon this pathway (P. Mischel & Cloughesy, 2003).

In early clinical trials, only a subset of patients (10–20%) appeared to benefit from the EGFR kinase inhibitors erlotinib and gefitinib. Which patients are most likely to benefit? Here, again, we asked if Walter Mischel's work had something to teach us. In the Wediko study, Walter Mischel and his colleagues Yuichi Shoda and Jack Wright demonstrated something remarkable. The long-sought-after personality consistency was not an illusion. How a person's behaviors increased or decreased in response to situations, far from disappearing with adequately reliable sampling and observation, was stable and distinctive for each person, revealing patterns of *if . . . then . . .* situation–behavior regularities, a sort of contextualized "behavioral signature of personality" (Shoda, Mischel, & Wright, 1994). This observation suggested that *if . . . then . . .* behavioral signatures might provide a window into the social-cognitive and affective mediating dynamic processes—the appraisals, goals/motives, beliefs, and affective reactions—that underlie them (Mischel, 2004). Could we find similar *if . . . then . . .* signatures that would give us a window into the underlying biology of cancer, provide an emerging understanding of mechanisms of sensitivity and resistance to molecularly targeted drugs, and help us figure out how to get them to glioblastoma patients that were most likely to benefit?

We hypothesized that the interaction between the EGFRvIII onco-gene and the PTEN tumor suppressor protein might constitute such an *if . . . then . . .* relationship. That is, we hypothesized that the EGFRvIII oncogene, by creating a pathway dependence, could act to sensitize tumors, while loss of the PTEN tumor suppressor protein, by dissociat-ing inhibition of the receptor from the critical downstream signaling apparatus, could create resistance (Mellinghoff et al., 2005). Thus, the *if . . . then . . .* rule would be: if a patient's tumor has the EGFRvIII oncogene and has not lost the PTEN tumor suppressor gene, then he or she is likely to respond. To conduct this analysis, we needed to develop new molecular tools for analyzing these key genes and their protein products in the tumor tissue of patients who would be treated with this drug (i.e., the status of these genes/proteins prior to initiation of ther-apy). We examined the tumor tissue from patients treated with molecu-larly targeted inhibitors that specifically block this EGFR receptor (Mellinghoff et al., 2005). The results were remarkable: for patients whose tumors coexpressed EGFRvIII/PTEN protein coexpression, the targeted drugs were 51 times more likely to shrink the tumor ($p < .001$; odds ratio = 51.0; 95% confidence interval = 3.9–669). These findings were validated in an independent data set of 33 patients treated at a dif-ferent institution ($p = .001$; odds ratio = 40; 95% confidence interval = 3.4–468 (Mellinghoff et al., 2005). To move from association to mecha-nism, we modeled the system by expressing each of the relevant proteins alone or in combination in an isogenic background (in a cell system in which the only genetic changes were those caused by the addition of the proteins). Just as in the clinical studies, the dynamic biological modeling experiments showed us that coexpression of these two proteins sensi-tized glioblastoma cells to the targeted therapy (Mellinghoff et al., 2005).

This study taught us three important things. First, patients with glioblastoma can benefit from molecularly targeted therapies (P. Mischel & Cloughesy, 2006; Mellinghoff et al., 2005). Second, molecular infor-mation can be used to direct drugs to the patients most likely to benefit (P. Mischel & Cloughesy, 2006; Mellinghoff et al., 2005). Third, person-alizing molecularly based treatment with genetic analysis is possible, and careful, hypothesis-driven analysis of complex datasets can help us uncover simple rules—our correlate of Walter Mischel's *if . . . then . . .*—on which we could base treatment decisions (P. Mischel & Cloughesy, 2006; Mellinghoff et al., 2005). In a way, the study also showed us something about interactionism. To assume that the presence of the molecular target is enough to predict response is probably naïve; we need to understand how multiple genetic modifiers (our *if . . . then . . .*) interact to regulate response (P. Mischel & Cloughesy, 2006; Mellinghoff et al., 2005).

The work also challenges us. It tells us that we need to assess the utility of this approach in a prospective fashion. It demonstrates that malignant glioblastoma patients can benefit from targeted kinase inhibitor therapy, and it suggests that molecular stratification might be used to identify patients most likely to respond to molecularly targeted therapy (Mellinghoff et al., 2005). It also identifies some important challenges. There may be few ways to respond to a drug and many ways to fail, but the failures teach us a great deal about where to go next. Can we begin to combine molecularly targeted drugs in a rational fashion to treat disease? Further, glioblastomas display striking intratumor molecular heterogeneity. Will treatment with these targeted drugs select for tumor cells lacking the relevant molecular targets or pathway addiction states? Understanding the molecular mechanisms underlying either of these phenomena will be critical in terms of designing effective combinations of therapy. Comprehending the mechanisms of acquired resistance can potentially enable the development of more effective combination therapies to induce long-term disease suppression or potentially even cure (P. Mischel & Cloughesy, 2006).

BUILDING BRIDGES

I started this chapter with a comment about the importance of cross-disciplinary interactions in science. The bridge here between Walter Mischel's work and our work is an example. He has spoken and written cogently and clearly about the excitement of constructing bridges to connect

> ongoing research projects that demand the joint study of different aspects of phenomena as they are being found in nature. Such bridges make it possible to share promising new methods and models, and build jointly on new discoveries that reveal natural interconnections. (Mischel, 2005, p. xxx)

This theme is near and dear to Walter Mischel and myself, as it was to the late Theodore Mischel (my father and Walter's brother). Theodore Mischel was a professor of philosophy and director of the Interdisciplinary Program in the History and Philosophy of the Social and Behavioral Sciences at the State University of New York at Binghamton. He led attempts by philosophers and psychologists jointly to explore the interrelations between conceptual and empirical issues and argued for the need for interdisciplinary collaboration and crossing artificial academic boundaries in the early 1970s, long before it was fashionable. This spirit lives on in my work and that of Walter Mischel, and our ability to share it has been a source of tremendous professional sustenance and personal comfort.

REFERENCES

Bild, A. H., Yao, G., Chang, J. T., Wang, Q., Potti, A., Chasse, D., et al. (2006). Oncogenic pathway signatures in human cancers as a guide to targeted therapies. *Nature, 439,* 353–357.

Bild, A., & Febbo, P. G. (2005). Application of a priori established gene sets to discover biologically important differential expression in microarray data. *Proceedings of the National Academy of Sciences USA, 102,* 15278–15279.

Calvano, S. E., Xiao, W., Richards, D. R., Felciano, R. M., Baker, H. V., Cho, R. J., et al. (2005). A network-based analysis of systemic inflammation in humans. *Nature, 437,* 1032–1037.

Carlson, M. R., Zhang, B., Fang, Z., Mischel, P. S., Horvath, S. & Nelson, S. F. (2006). Gene connectivity, function, and sequence conservation: Predictions from modular yeast co-expression networks. *BMC Genomics, 7,* 40.

Freije, W. A., Castro-Vargas, F. E., Fang, Z., Horvath, S., Cloughesy, T., Liau, L. M., et al. (2004). Gene expression profiling of gliomas strongly predicts survival. *Cancer Research, 64,* 6503–6510.

Hood, L., & Perlmutter, R. M. (2004). The impact of systems approaches on biological problems in drug discovery. *Nature Biotechnology, 22,* 1215–1217.

Hood, L., Heath, J. R., Phelps, M. E., & Lin, B. (2004). Systems biology and new technologies enable predictive and preventative medicine. *Science, 306,* 640–643.

Mellinghoff, I. K., Wang, M. Y., Vivanco, I., Haas-Kogan, D. A., Zhu, S., Dia, E. Q., et al. (2005). Molecular determinants of the response of glioblastomas to EGFR kinase inhibitors. *New England Journal of Medicine, 353,* 2012–2024.

Mischel, P. S., & Cloughesy, T. F. (2003). Targeted molecular therapy of GBM. *Brain Pathology, 13,* 52–61.

Mischel, P. S., & Cloughesy, T. F. (2006). Using molecular information to guide brain tumor therapy. *Nature Clinical Practice Neurology, 2,* 232–233.

Mischel, P. S., Cloughesy, T. F., & Nelson, S. F. (2004). DNA-microarray analysis of brain cancer: Molecular classification for therapy. *Nature Reviews Neuroscience, 5,* 782–792.

Mischel, W. (1968). *Personality and assessment.* New York: Wiley.

Mischel, W. (1973). Toward a cognitive social learning reconceptualization of personality. *Psychological Review, 80,* 252–283.

Mischel, W. (2004). Toward an integrative science of the person. *Annual Review of Psychology, 55,* 1–22.

Mischel, W. (2005). Alternative futures for our science. *APS Observer, 18*(3).

Mischel, W., & Shoda, Y. (1995). A cognitive–affective system of personality: Reconceptualizing situations, dispositions, dynamics, and invariance in personality structure. *Psychological Review, 102,* 246–268.

Mischel, W., & Shoda, Y. (1998). Reconciling processing dynamics and personality dispositions. *Annual Review of Psychology, 49,* 229–258.

Rodriguez, M. L., Mischel, W., & Shoda, Y. (1989). Cognitive person variables in the delay of gratification of older children at risk. *Journal of Personality and Social Psychology, 57,* 358–367.

Shai, R., Shi, T., Kremen, T. J., Horvath, S., Liau, L. M., Cloughesy, T. F., et al. (2003). Gene expression profiling identifies molecular subtype of gliomas. *Oncogene 22,* 4918–4923.

Shoda, Y., Mischel, W., & Wright, J. C. (1994). Intra-individual stability in the organization and patterning of behavior: Incorporating psychological situations for the idiographic analysis of personality. *Journal of Personality and Social Psychology, 67,* 674–687.

Shweder, R. A. (1999). Humans really are different. *Science, 283,* 798–799.

Subramanian, A., Tamayo, P., Mootha, V. K., Mukherjee, S., Ebert, B. L., Gillette, M. A., et al. (2005). Gene set enrichment analysis: A knowledge-based approach for interpreting genome-wide expression profiles. *Proceedings of the National Academy of Sciences USA, 102,* 15545–15550.

Sung, N. S., Gordon, J. I., Rose, G. D., Getzoff, E. D., Kron, S. J., Mumford, D., et al. (2003). Science education: Educating future scientists. *Science, 301,* 1485.

Wright, J. C., & Mischel, W. (1988) Conditional hedges and the intuitive psychology of traits. *Journal of Personality and Social Psychology, 55,* 454–469.

Zhang, B., & Horvath, S. (2005). A general framework for weighted gene co-expression network analysis. *Statistical Applications in Genetics and Molecular Biology, 4,* Article 17.

14

Intelligence as
a Person–Situation Interaction

ROBERT J. STERNBERG

Many researchers view personality as a trait (Cattell, 1973; Costa & McCrae, 1992a, 1992b, 1995; Goldberg & Saucier, 1995). In this view, people have personality traits that are largely stable and that apply across a wide variety of situations. As a student, I reveled in Hall and Lindzey's (1978) *Theories of Personality,* which sees the question not as *whether* personality comprises a set of traits, but *which* set of traits it comprises. The most widely accepted trait theory currently is probably Five-Factor theory (Costa & McCrae, 1995), according to which individual differences in personality can be understood in terms of differences among individuals on five stable and relatively permanent traits: agreeableness, conscientiousness, extraversion, neuroticism, and openness to experience. Someone who is agreeable with one person, in this view, is more or less agreeable with all people.

Does trait theory work? The answer generates lively debate. A few personality theorists (Bem & Allen, 1974; Bem & Funder, 1978; Mischel, 1968, 1969, 1973) view personality not as a trait but as a person–situation interaction. According to these theorists, people are not consistent in their behavior across situations. For example, someone might be generally honest but not pay money due into a coffee pool. You might find that you are very agreeable with your boss but not with your mother-in-law. Interactionists believe that people differ in their patterns of behavior across situations and may differ consistently even in the extent to which they are consistent versus inconsistent across situations.

Ever since taking a graduate personality course with Walter Mischel in the fall of 1972, I have been a strong interactionist. His writing was convincing, but I tended to rely on personal experience to verify my beliefs. I *know* I behave differently with my mother than with my daughter. I imagine my mother would rate me quite low on agreeableness, but my daughter would rate me quite high. My mother and my daughter elicit different behavior from me, and I respond differently in turn. Parents who have more than one child almost always know that multiple children elicit different behavior from them and that, as a result, they respond differently. Within-family influences are much stronger determinants of personality than between-family influences (Plomin, DeFries, McClearn, & Rutter, 1997), in part because children elicit different responses from adults.

When we come to intelligence, there is much greater consensus than there is with personality. The large majority of theorists of intelligence view intelligence as a relatively stable trait (Carroll, 1993; Gardner, 1983; Jensen, 1998; Spearman, 1927; Thurstone, 1938; see essays in Sternberg, 2000). Theorists may disagree as to what the abilities are that underlie intelligence, but they concur that it is relatively stable and largely cross-situational. To the extent that people vary in their intelligence cross-situationally, it is because different stable abilities may come into play in different situations, but the abilities themselves are stable, regardless of when they are called on in task performance. An alternative view is that of intelligence as a personality–situation interaction.

Underlying the notion of intelligence as a person–situation interaction is, for my colleagues and me, the theory of successful intelligence (Sternberg, 1997, 1999). The theory views intelligence not as a broad ability that applies in any situation, but as determined by how the person interacts with the situations in which he or she finds him- or herself.

THE THEORY OF SUCCESSFUL INTELLIGENCE

Successful intelligence is defined in terms of the ability to achieve success in life in terms of one's personal standards, within one's sociocultural context. Change the sociocultural context or one's standards within it, and one changes the intelligence. For example, someone who wants to be a rocket scientist will need very different abilities than someone who wants to be a literary scholar. A person who might be a very smart and adaptively effective rocket scientist might appear not very bright if he or she had decided to become a literary scholar, and vice versa.

The field of intelligence has at times tended to put the cart before the horse, defining the construct of intelligence conceptually on the basis of how it is measured. This practice has resulted in tests that stress the academic aspect of intelligence, as one might expect given the origins of modern intelligence testing in the work of Binet and Simon (1916) in designing an instrument that would distinguish children who would succeed from those who would fail in school. But the construct of intelligence needs to serve a broader purpose, accounting for the bases of success in all of one's life, not just in school.

The use of societal criteria of success (e.g., school grades, personal income) can obscure the fact that these measures often do not capture people's personal notions of success. Some people choose to concentrate on extracurricular activities such as athletics or music and pay less attention to grades; others may choose occupations that are personally meaningful to them but that will never yield the income they could gain doing work that is less personally meaningful. Although scientific analysis requires some kinds of agreed-upon criteria, the definition of success for an individual is individual.

In the theory of successful intelligence, the conceptualization of intelligence is always within a sociocultural context. Although the processes of intelligence may be common across such contexts, what constitutes success is not. Being a successful member of the clergy of a particular religion may be highly rewarded in one society and viewed as a worthless pursuit in another.

One's ability to be successfully intelligent depends on capitalizing on one's strengths and correcting or compensating for one's weaknesses. How well one is able to do this depends in part upon oneself and in part upon one's situations. Theories of intelligence typically specify some relatively fixed set of abilities, whether one general factor and a number of specific factors (Spearman, 1904), seven factors (Thurstone, 1938), or eight multiple intelligences (Gardner, 1999). Such a specification is useful in establishing a common set of skills to be tested, but people achieve success, even within a given occupation, in many different ways. For example, successful teachers and researchers achieve success through many different blendings of skills rather than through any single formula that works for all of them.

Because the academic situation dominated for Binet and his successors, and because academic abilities probably are more situationally general than are abilities outside of academe, intelligence has seemed more situation-independent than it is. But life pursuits can be astonishingly varied, and one's intelligence in the life pursuit one chooses depends in large part upon a choice that is a good match to one's skills. If one capitalizes on weaknesses rather than strengths, one may create a life in which one never allows oneself to be intelligent.

Successful intelligence is attained through a balance of analytical, creative, and practical abilities. Analytical abilities are the abilities primarily measured by traditional tests, but success in life requires one not only to analyze ideas but also to generate ideas and to persuade other people of their value, as in the world of work (when a subordinate tries to convince a superior of the value of his or her plan), in the world of personal relationships (when a child attempts to convince a parent to do what he or she wants or when a person tries to convince his or her spouse to do things in the person's preferred way), and in the world of the school (when a student writes an essay arguing a point of view).

Abilities are balanced to adapt to, shape, and select environments. Definitions of intelligence traditionally have emphasized the role of adaptation to the environment ("Intelligence and Its Measurement," 1921; Sternberg & Detterman, 1986), but intelligence also involves modifying the environment to suit oneself (shaping) or finding a new environment that is a better match to one's skills, values, or desires (selection). In other words, one tailors one's skills to the kinds of situations in which one finds oneself.

Not all people have equal opportunities to adapt to, shape, and select their environments. How well they can adapt, shape, or select depends in part upon the situation in which they find themselves. In general, people of higher socioeconomic standing tend to have more opportunities, and people of lower socioeconomic standing have fewer. The economy or political situation of the society also can be factors. Other variables that may affect such opportunities are education (especially literacy), political party, race, religion, and so forth. For example, someone with a college education typically has many more career options than does someone who dropped out of high school to support a family. How and how well an individual adapts to, shapes, and selects environments must always be viewed in terms of the opportunities he or she has.

On a recent trip to Slovakia (June 2005), I visited two prisons in Presov (in the eastern part of the country). I was struck by how different the demands are for adaptation in a prison from the outside world. One's skills outside the prison may be poorly predictive of one's skills inside. Indeed, many "intelligent" white-collar criminals request special protective custody to isolate themselves from the dangers they would face from other inmates, against whom their adaptive skills would be poor.

Testing the Theory of Successful Intelligence

Analytical Intelligence.

Research on the components of human intelligence has yielded some interesting results. For example, in a study of the development of figural analogical reasoning, Rifkin and I found that although children generally became quicker in information processing with age, not all components of it were executed more rapidly with age (Sternberg & Rifkin, 1979). The encoding component first showed a decrease in component time with age and then an increase. Apparently, older children realized that their best strategy was to spend more time in encoding the terms of a problem so that they later would be able to spend less time in operating on these encodings. A related finding was that better reasoners tend to spend relatively more time than do poorer reasoners in global, up-front higher-order planning, when they solve difficult reasoning problems. Poorer reasoners, on the other hand, tend to spend relatively more time in local planning (Sternberg, 1981). Presumably, the better reasoners recognize that it is better to invest more time up front so as to be able to process a problem more efficiently later. Nigro and I found, in a study of the development of verbal analogical reasoning, that, as children grew older, their strategies shifted so that they relied on word association less and abstract relations more (Sternberg & Nigro, 1980).

Some of my colleagues' and my studies concentrated on knowledge acquisition. For example, in one set of studies, we were interested in sources of individual differences in vocabulary (Sternberg & Powell, 1982; Sternberg, Powell, & Kaye, 1982; see also Sternberg, 1987). We were not content to view these as individual differences in declarative knowledge because we wanted to understand why some people acquired this declarative knowledge and others did not. What we found is that there were multiple sources of individual and developmental differences. The three main sources were in knowledge-acquisition components, use of context clues, and use of mediating variables. For example, in the sentence "The blen rises in the east and sets in the west," the knowledge-acquisition component of selective comparison is used to relate prior knowledge about a known concept, the sun, to the unknown word (neologism) in the sentence, *blen*. Several context cues appear in the sentence, such as the fact that a blen rises, the fact that it sets, and where it does so. A mediating variable is that the information can occur after the presentation of the unknown word.

Creative Intelligence

In work with convergent problems, we presented 80 individuals with novel kinds of reasoning problems that had a single best answer. For example, they might be told that some objects are green and others blue; other objects might be grue, meaning green until the year 2000 and blue thereafter, or bleen, meaning blue until the year 2000 and green thereafter. Or they might be told of four kinds of people on the planet Kyron: blens, who are born young and die young; kwefs, who are born old and die old; balts, who are born young and die old; and prosses, who are born old and die young (Sternberg, 1982; Tetewsky & Sternberg, 1986). Their task was to predict future states from past states, given incomplete information. In another set of studies, 60 people were given more conventional kinds of inductive reasoning problems, such as analogies, series completions, and classifications; the problems had premises preceding them that were either conventional (dancers wear shoes) or novel (dancers eat shoes). The participants had to solve the problems as though the counterfactuals were true (Sternberg & Gastel, 1989a, 1989b).

In these studies, we found that correlations of scores on these tests with scores on conventional kinds of tests depended on how novel or nonentrenched the conventional tests were. The more novel the items, the higher the correlations of our tests with scores on successively more novel conventional tests were. Thus, the components isolated for relatively novel items would tend to correlate more highly with more unusual tests of fluid abilities (e.g., that of Cattell & Cattell, 1973) than with tests of crystallized abilities. We also found that when response times on the relatively novel problems were componentially analyzed, some components better measured the creative aspect of intelligence. For example, in the "grue–bleen" task mentioned above, the information-processing component requiring people to switch from conventional green–blue thinking to grue–bleen thinking and then back to green–blue thinking was a particularly good measure of the ability to cope with novelty.

In work with divergent reasoning problems having no one best answer, we asked 63 people to create various kinds of products (Lubart & Sternberg, 1995; Sternberg & Lubart, 1991, 1995, 1996) where an infinite variety of responses was possible. Individuals were asked to create products in the realms of writing, art, advertising, and science. In writing, they would be asked to write very short stories for which we would give them a choice of titles, such as "Beyond the Edge" or "The Octopus's Sneakers." In art, they were asked to produce art compositions with titles such as *The Beginning of Time* or *Earth from an Insect's Point of View*. In advertising, they were asked to produce advertisements for products such as a brand of bow tie or doorknob. In science, they were asked to solve problems such as how we might detect extraterrestrial aliens among us who are seeking to escape detection. Participants created two products in each domain.

We found that creativity is relatively but not wholly domain-specific. Correlations of ratings of the creative quality of the products across domains were lower than correlations of ratings within domains and generally were at about .4. Thus, there was some degree of relation across domains but plenty of room for someone to be strong in one or more domains but not in others. More important, perhaps, we found, as we had for the convergent problems, a range of correlations with conventional tests of abilities. As was the case with convergent problems, correlations of scores on the two kinds of tests were higher to the extent that problems on the conventional tests were non-entrenched. For example, correlations were higher with fluid than with crystallized ability tests and higher the more novel the fluid test was. These results show that tests of creative intelligence overlap some with conventional tests (e.g., in requiring verbal skills or the ability to analyze one's own ideas; Sternberg & Lubart, 1995) but also tap skills beyond those measured even by relatively novel kinds of items on the conventional tests.

Practical Intelligence

Practical intelligence involves individuals applying their abilities to the kinds of problems that confront them in daily life, such as on the job or in the home, to (1) adapt to, (2) shape, and (3) select environments. People differ in their balance of adaptation, shaping, and selection and in the competence with which they balance.

Much of my colleagues' and my work on practical intelligence has centered on the concept of tacit knowledge. We have defined this construct, for our purposes, as what one needs to know in order to work effectively in an environment that is not explicitly taught and often not even verbalized (Hedlund et al., 1998; Sternberg et al., 2000; Sternberg & Wagner, 1993; Sternberg, Wagner, & Okagaki, 1993; Sternberg, Wagner, Williams, & Horvath, 1995; Wagner, 1987; Wagner & Sternberg, 1986). We represent tacit knowledge in the form of production systems, or sequences of *if . . . then . . .* statements that describe procedures one follows in various kinds of everyday situations.

We typically have measured tacit knowledge using problems one might encounter on the job. We have measured tacit knowledge for both children and adults and for people in more than two dozen occupations, such as management, sales, academia, secretarial work, and the military. In a typical tacit-knowledge problem, people are asked to read a story about a problem someone faces and to rate, for each statement in a set, how adequate a solution the statement represents. For example, in a paper-and-pencil measure of tacit knowledge for sales, one of the problems deals with sales of photocopy machines. A relatively inexpensive machine is not moving and has become overstocked. The examinee is asked to rate the quality of various solutions for moving the particular model. In a performance-based measure for salespeople, the test taker makes a phone call to a supposed customer, who is actually the examiner. The test taker tries to sell advertising space over the phone, while the examiner raises various objections. The test taker is evaluated for the quality, rapidity, and fluency of his or her responses.

In our studies, we found that practical intelligence as embodied in tacit knowledge increases with experience, but it is profiting from experience, rather than experience per se, that results in increases in scores. Some people can have been in a job for years and still have acquired relatively little tacit knowledge. We also have found that subscores on tests of tacit knowledge—such as for managing oneself, managing others, and managing tasks—correlate significantly with each other. Moreover, scores on various tests of tacit knowledge, such as for academics and managers, are also correlated fairly substantially (at about the .5 level) with each other. Thus, tests of tacit knowledge may yield a general factor; however, scores on tacit-knowledge tests do not correlate with scores on conventional tests of intelligence, whether the measures used are single-score measures or multiple-ability batteries. Thus, any general factor from the tacit-knowledge tests is not the same as any general factor from tests of academic abilities (suggesting that neither kind of g factor is truly general, but general only across a limited range of measuring instruments). Despite the lack of correlation of practical intelligence with conventional measures of intelligence, the scores on tacit-knowledge tests predict performance on the job as well as or better than do conventional psychometric intelligence tests. In one study done at the Center for Creative Leadership, we further found that scores on our tests of tacit knowledge for management were the best single predictor of performance on a managerial simulation. In a hierarchical regression, scores on conventional tests of intelligence, personality, styles, and interpersonal orientation were entered first and scores on the test of tacit knowledge were entered last. Scores on the test of tacit knowledge were not only the single best predictor of managerial simulation score, but they also contributed significantly to the prediction even after everything else was entered first into the equation. In work on military leadership (Hedlund et al., 1998), we found that scores of 562 participants on tests of tacit knowledge for military leadership predicted ratings of leadership effectiveness, whereas scores on a conventional test of intelligence and on our tacit-knowledge test for managers did not significantly predict ratings of effectiveness.

Measuring Analytical, Creative,
and Practical Intelligence Together

In the Rainbow Project (Sternberg & the Rainbow Project Collaborators, 2005, 2006), my colleagues and I investigated the extent to which
we could provide incremental validity to the SAT as an assessment for
college admissions. The participants were 1,013 students predominantly
in their first year of college or their final year of high school. Here, I discuss analyses only for college students because they were the only ones
for whom we had available college performance. The final number of
participants included in these analyses was 777. Students received tests
of creative, practical, and analytical thinking. Creative tests measured
skills such as captioning cartoons, writing fictional stories, and telling
fictional stories. Practical tests were situational judgments in which participants had to solve problems of the kinds faced by students in their
everyday academic and personal lives. The test built on the Sternberg
Triarchic Abilities Test (STAT), a multiple-choice test.

An exploratory factor analysis with Varimax rotation was conducted to explore the factor structure underlying the Rainbow measures.
Three factors were extracted with eigenvalues greater than 1, and these
accounted for 62.8% of the variation between measures. One factor represented practical performance tests. A second, weaker factor represented creative performance tests. A third factor represented multiple-
choice tests (including analytical, creative, and practical). Thus, method
variance proved to be very important in this study as in past studies
(Sternberg, Grigorenko, Ferrari, & Clinkenbeard, 1999). The results
show the importance of measuring skills using multiple formats because
method is so important in determining factorial structure.

In order to test the incremental validity provided by Rainbow measures above and beyond the SAT in predicting GPA, a series of hierarchical regressions was conducted that included the items analyzed above in
the analytical, creative, and practical assessments. In one set of hierarchical regressions, the SAT-V, SAT-M, and high school GPA were
included in the first step of the regression because these are the standard
measures used today to predict college performance. Only high school
GPA contributed uniquely to R^2. In step 2, we added the analytical
subtest of the STAT because this test is closest conceptually to the SAT.
The analytical subtest of the STAT slightly increased R^2, with a statistically significant beta weight. In step 3, the measures of practical ability
were added, resulting in a small increase in R^2. Notably, the latent variable representing the common variance among the practical performance measures and high school GPA were the only variables significantly to account for variance in college GPA in step 3. The inclusion of

the creative measures in the final step of this regression indicates that, by supplementing the SAT and high school GPA with measures of analytical, practical, and creative abilities, a total of 24.8% of the variance in GPA can be accounted for. Inclusion of the Rainbow measures in steps 2, 3, and 4 represents an increase of about 9.2% (from .156 to .248) in the variance accounted for over and above the typical predictors of college GPA. Including the Rainbow measures without high school GPA, using only SAT scores as a base, represents an increase in percentage variance accounted for of about 10.1% (from .098 to .199). Looked at in another way, this result means that the Rainbow measures almost doubled prediction versus the SAT alone.

In another set of hierarchical regressions, SAT and high school GPA were entered in the last steps. These regressions showed that SAT did not add significant incremental validity above and beyond the Rainbow measures in the penultimate step, although high school GPA did in the final step. Approximately 20.1% of the variance in college GPA could be accounted for by using Rainbow measures alone. With the addition of high school GPA in the last step, at least one task from each of the Rainbow components also contributed to the incremental prediction of college GPA above and beyond high school GPA and the SAT, significantly by the STAT-analytic and the oral stories, and marginally by the latent practical-ability measure underlying performance on the three tacit-knowledge tasks.

These multiple regression analyses pose some concern because of the large number of measures used representing each of analytical, creative, and practical skills, which risks a great deal of construct overlap. To account for this problem, a final multiple regression analysis was conducted that included only high school GPA, SAT, and one measure from each of analytical, creative, and practical skills. For analytical skills, we used the only measure available from the new measures, the $STAT_{Analytical}$. For creative skills, we used the only statistically significant predictor, the oral stories measure. For practical skills, we used the methodology that did not overlap with other methodologies in the study, namely the practical performance measures as represented by the practical performance latent variable. The results from this analysis support the claim that measuring analytical, creative, and practical skills using different methodologies can substantially improve predicting college GPA beyond using high school GPA and the SAT. All three representatives of the Rainbow measures and high school GPA maintained a statistically significant beta coefficient.

Although one important goal of the study was to predict success in college, another goal involved developing measures to reduce racial and ethnic group differences in mean levels. There are a number of ways one can test for group differences in these measures, each which involves a test of the size of the effect of race. We chose two: omega square (ω^2), and Cohen's d.

We first considered the omega-squared coefficients. This procedure involves conducting a series of one-way analyses of variance (ANOVA) considering differences in mean performance levels among the six ethnic and racial groups reported, including white, Asian, Pacific Islander, Latino, black, and Native American, for the following measures: the baseline measures (SAT-V and SAT-M), the STAT ability scales, the creativity performance tasks, and the practical-ability performance tasks. The omega-squared coefficient indicates the proportion of variance in the variables that is accounted for by the self-reported ethnicity of the participant. The omega-squared values were .09 for SAT-V, .04 for SAT-M, and .07 for combined SAT. For the Rainbow measures, omega square ranged from 0 to .03 with a median of .02. Thus, the Rainbow measures showed reduced values relative to the SAT.

The test of effect sizes using the Cohen's d statistic allows one to consider more specifically a standardized representation of specific group differences. For the test of ethnic group differences, each entry represents how far away from the mean for whites each group performs in terms of standard deviations. For the test of gender differences, the entries represent how far away women perform from men in terms of standard deviations. Differences were generally greater on the SAT for underrepresented minority groups than on the Rainbow measures.

These results indicate two general findings. First, in terms of overall differences represented by omega squared, the triarchic tests appear to reduce race and ethnicity differences relative to traditional assessments of abilities like the SAT. Second, in terms of specific differences represented by Cohen's d, it appears that the Latino students benefit the most from the reduction of group differences. The black students, too, seem to show a reduction in difference from the white mean for most of the triarchic tests, although a substantial difference appears to be maintained with the practical performance measures. Important reductions in differences can also be seen for the Native American students relative to whites. Indeed, their median was higher for the creative tests. The very small sample size, however, suggests that any conclusions about Native American performance should be made tentatively.

Although the group differences are not perfectly reduced, these findings suggest that measures can be designed that reduce ethnic and racial group differences on standardized tests, particularly for historically disadvantaged groups like black and Latino students. These findings have important implications for reducing adverse impact in college admissions.

These studies suggest that how well a person performs on a test depends very much on the testing situation. Is the test multiple-choice, essay, or performance? Is it measuring analytical, creative, or practical skills? Is it administered so as to emphasize reaction time or percentage correct? Intelligence is much more dependent on situations than conventional views admit.

CULTURE

Culture can be another situational influence on intelligence. People who are intelligent in one culture may not be intelligent in another (Laboratory of Comparative Human Cognition, 1982; Nuñes, 1994; Serpell, 2000). Studies of practical as well as academic intelligence across cultures show how large the effects of person–situation interaction can be.

One kind of evidence suggests the power of situational contexts in testing (see also Ceci, 1996; Gardner, 1983; Lave, 1988; Nuñes, Schliemann, & Carraher, 1993). For example, Carraher, Carraher, and Schliemann (1985) (see also Ceci & Roazzi, 1994; Nuñes, 1994) studied a group of children especially relevant for assessing intelligence as adaptation to the environment. The group was of Brazilian street children, who are under great contextual pressure to form a successful street business. If they do not, they risk death at the hands of "death squads," which may murder children who resort to robbing stores (or who are suspected of robbing stores if unable to earn money). The researchers found that the same children who are able to do the mathematics needed to run their street business are often little able or unable to do school mathematics. In fact, the more abstract and removed from real-world contexts the problems are, the worse the children do on them. These results suggest that differences in context can have a powerful effect on performance.

Such differences are not limited to Brazilian street children. Lave (1988) showed that Berkeley housewives who could successfully do the mathematics needed for comparison shopping in the supermarket were unable to do the same mathematics when they were placed in a classroom and given isomorphic problems presented in an abstract form. In other words, their problem was not at the level of mental processes but at the level of applying the processes in specific environmental contexts.

Ceci and Liker (1986; see also Ceci, 1996) showed that, given tasks relevant to their lives, men would show the same kinds of effects as were shown by women in the Lave studies. These investigators studied men who successfully handicapped horse races. The complexity of their implicit mathematical formulas was unrelated to their IQ. Moreover, despite the complexity of these formulas, the mean IQ among these men was only at roughly the population average or slightly below. Ceci (1996) subsequently found that the skills were quite specific; the same men did not successfully apply their skills to computations involving securities in the stock market. Now consider three more examples.

Children May Have Substantial Practical Skills That Go Unrecognized by Academic Tests

Investigations of intelligence conducted in settings outside the developed world can yield a picture of intelligence that is quite at variance with the picture one would obtain from studies conducted only in the developed world. In a study in Usenge, Kenya, near the town of Kisumu, my colleagues and I (Sternberg et al., 2001) studied school-age children's ability to adapt to their indigenous environment, via a test of practical intelligence for adaptation to the environment. The test measured children's informal tacit knowledge of natural herbal medicines that the locals believe can be used to fight various types of infections. Children in the villages use their tacit knowledge of these medicines on average once a week in medicating themselves and others. More than 95% of the children suffer from parasitic illnesses. Thus tests of how to use these medicines constitute effective measures of one aspect of practical intelligence as defined by the villagers. Note that the processes of intelligence are not different in Kenya. Children must still recognize the existence of an illness, define what it is, devise a strategy to combat it, and so forth, but the content to which the processes are applied and appropriate ways of testing these processes may be quite different.

Middle-class Westerners might find it quite a challenge to thrive or even survive in these contexts, or, for that matter, in the contexts of urban ghettos often not distant from their comfortable homes. For example, they would not know how to use any of the natural herbal medicines to combat the diverse and abundant parasitic illnesses in rural Kenya.

We measured the Kenyan children's ability to identify the medicines, where they come from, what they are used for, and how they are dosed. We also administered the Raven Coloured Progressive Matrices Test (Raven, Court, & Raven, 1992), a measure of fluid- or abstract-reasoning-based abilities, and the Mill Hill Vocabulary Scale (Raven et al., 1992), a measure of crystallized- or formal-knowledge-based abilities. In addition, we gave the children a comparable test of vocabulary in their own Dholuo language, which is spoken in the home (English is spoken in the schools).

All correlations between the test of indigenous tacit knowledge and scores on fluid-ability and crystallized-ability tests were *negative*, significantly with the tests of crystallized abilities. In other words, the higher the children scored on the test of tacit knowledge, the lower they scored, on average, on the tests of crystallized abilities (vocabulary).

This surprising result can be interpreted in various ways, but based on the ethnographic observations of the anthropologists on the team, Prince and Geissler (see Prince & Geissler, 2001), we concluded that a plausible scenario takes into account the expectations of families for their children. Many children drop out of school before graduation, for financial or other reasons, and many families in the village do not particularly see the advantages of formal Western schooling. (There is no reason they should, as the children of many families will for the most part spend their lives farming or engaged in other occupations that make little or no use of Western schooling.) These families emphasize teaching their children the indigenous informal knowledge that will lead to successful adaptation in the environments in which they will really live. Children who spend their time learning the indigenous practical knowledge of the community may not always invest themselves heavily in doing well in school, whereas children who do well in school generally may invest themselves less heavily in learning the indigenous knowledge.

The Kenya study suggests that the identification of a general factor of human intelligence may tell us more about how abilities interact with cultural patterns of schooling and society, especially Western patterns of schooling and society, than it does about the structure of human abilities. In Western schooling, children typically study a variety of subject matters from an early age and develop skills in a variety of areas. This kind of schooling prepares the children to take a test of intelligence, which typically measures skills in a variety of areas. Often, intelligence tests measure skills that children were expected to acquire a few years before taking the test. As Rogoff (1990, 2003) and others have noted, this pattern of schooling is not universal and has not even been common for much of the history of humankind. Throughout history and in many places still, schooling, especially for boys, takes the form of apprenticeships in which children learn a craft from an early age. They learn what they will need to know in order to succeed in a trade but not a lot more. They are not simultaneously engaged in tasks that require the development of the particular blend of skills measured by conventional intelligence tests. Hence, it is less likely that one would observe a general factor in their scores, much as was discovered in Kenya.

What does a general factor mean anyway? Some years back, Vernon (1971) pointed out that the axes of a factor analysis do not necessarily reveal a latent structure of the mind, but rather represent a convenient way of characterizing the organization of mental abilities. Vernon believed that there was no one "right" orientation of axes, and, mathematically, an infinite number of orientations of axes can be fit to any solution in an exploratory factor analysis. Vernon's point seems perhaps to have been forgotten or ignored by later theorists.

Just as I argue here that the so-called *g* factor may partly reflect human interactions with cultural patterns, Tomasello (2001) has argued that "modularity of mind" may also reflect in part human interactions with cultural patterns. This view is not to dismiss the importance of biology; rather, it is to emphasize its importance as it interacts with culture, rather than simply viewing it as some kind of immutable effect that operates independently, outside of a cultural context.

Children May Have Substantial Practical Skills That Go Unrecognized in Academic Tests

The partial context-specificity of intellectual performance does not apply only to countries far removed from North America or Europe. One can find the same results on these continents, as was done in the study of Yup'ik Eskimo children in southwestern Alaska (Grigorenko et al., 2004). We assessed the importance of academic and practical intelligence in rural and semiurban Alaskan communities. We measured academic intelligence with conventional measures of fluid (the Cattell Culture Fair Test of *g*; Cattell & Cattell, 1973) and crystallized intelligence (the Mill-Hill Vocabulary Scale; Raven et al., 1992). We measured practical intelligence with a test of tacit knowledge of skills (hunting, fishing, dealing with weather conditions, picking and preserving plants, and so on) as acquired in rural Alaskan Yup'ik communities (the Yup'ik Scale of Practical Intelligence [YSPI; PACE Center, 2000]). The semiurban children statistically significantly outperformed the rural children on the measure of crystallized intelligence, but the rural children statistically significantly outperformed the semiurban children on the YSPI. The test of tacit knowledge was superior to the tests of academic intelligence in predicting practical skills as evaluated by adults and peers of the rural children (for whom the test was created) but not of the semiurban ones. This study, like the Kenya study, suggests the importance of practical intellectual skills for predicting adaptation to everyday environments.

Static versus Dynamic Testing

The developing world provides a particularly interesting laboratory for testing theories of intelligence because many of the assumptions that are held dear in the developed world simply do not apply. A study my colleagues and I did in Tanzania (see Sternberg et al., 2002) points out the risks of giving tests, scoring them, and interpreting the results as measures of some latent intellectual ability or abilities. We administered to 358 schoolchildren between the ages of 11 and 13 years near Bagamoyo, Tanzania, tests including a form-board classification test, a linear syllogisms test, and a 20 Questions test, which measured the kinds of skills required on conventional tests of intelligence. We obtained scores that we could analyze and evaluate, ranking the children in terms of their supposed general or other abilities; however, we administered the tests dynamically rather than statically (Brown & Ferrara, 1985; Budoff, 1968; Day, Engelhardt, Maxwell, & Bolig, 1997; Feuerstein, 1979; Grigorenko & Sternberg, 1998; Guthke, 1993; Haywood & Tzuriel, 1992; Lidz, 1987, 1991; Tzuriel, 1995; Vygotsky, 1978). Dynamic testing is like conventional static testing in that individuals are tested and inferences about their abilities made, but dynamic tests give children some kind of feedback to help them improve their scores. Vygotsky (1978) suggested that the children's ability to profit from the guided instruction received during the testing session could serve as a measure of their zone of proximal development (ZPD), or the difference between their developed abilities and their latent capacities. In other words, testing and instruction are treated as being of one piece rather than as distinct processes. This integration makes sense in terms of traditional definitions of intelligence as the ability to learn ("Intelligence and Its Measurement," 1921; Sternberg & Detterman, 1986). A dynamic test directly measures processes of learning in the context of testing rather than indirectly as the product of past learning. Such measurement is especially important when not all children have had equal opportunities to learn in the past.

In our assessments, children were first given the ability tests. Then they were given a brief period of instruction in which they were able to learn skills that would potentially enable them to improve their scores and tested again. Because the instruction for each test lasted only about 5–10 minutes, one would not expect dramatic gains. Yet, on average, gains were statistically significant. More important, scores on the pretest showed weak although significant correlations with scores on the posttest. These correlations, at about the .3 level, suggested that when tests are administered statically to children in developing countries, they may be rather unstable and easily subject to influences of training. The reason could be that the children are not accustomed to taking Western-style tests and profit quickly even from small amounts of instruction on what is expected from them. Of course, the more important question is not whether the scores changed or correlated with each other, but how they correlated with other cognitive measures. In other words, which test was a better predictor of transfer to other cognitive performance: the pretest or the posttest? We found the posttest score to be the better predictor.

In other words, the situation in which the children were tested had an enormous impact on levels and rank orders of scores. In a static-testing situation, the data appeared quite different from the way they appeared in a dynamic-testing situation. Thus, even the situation in which one tests potentially can have a substantial impact on how "intelligently" test takers perform.

FALLACIES OF THINKING

There is another dimension to person–situation interaction: the extent to which particular situations elicit "stupid" thinking in intelligent people. For example, I edited *Why Smart People Can Be So Stupid* (2002b) on the premise that, in certain situations, people who are usually smart may act in ways that are anything but. I suggested that smart people are especially susceptible to five fallacies in their thinking (Sternberg, 2002a), detailed in the following sections.

The Unrealistic Optimism Fallacy

This fallacy occurs when one believes one is so smart or powerful that it is pointless to worry about the outcome, especially long-term, of what one does because everything will come out all right in the end—there is nothing to worry about, given one's brains or power. If one simply acts, the outcome will be fine. Bill Clinton, for example, tended to repeat behavior that, first as governor and then as president, was likely to have a bad end, but he seemed not to worry about it.

The Egocentrism Fallacy

This fallacy arises when one comes to think that one's own interests are the only ones that are important. One starts to ignore one's responsibilities to other people or to institutions. Sometimes, people in positions of responsibility may start off with good intentions but become corrupted by the power they wield and their seeming unaccountability to others. A prime minister, for example, might use his office to escape prosecution, as has happened in some European countries in recent years.

The Omniscience Fallacy

This fallacy results from having available essentially any knowledge one might want that is, in fact, knowable. With a phone call, a powerful leader can have almost any kind of knowledge made available to him or her. At the same time, people look up to the leader as extremely knowledgeable or even close to all-knowing. The leader may come to believe that he or she really is all-knowing and so may his or her staff, as illustrated by Janis (1972) in his analysis of victims of groupthink. In case after case, brilliant government officials have made the most foolish decisions, in part because they believed they knew much more than they did. They did not know what they did not know.

The Omnipotence Fallacy

This fallacy results from the extreme power one wields or believes one wields. The result is overextension and, often, abuse of power. Sometimes, leaders create internal or external enemies in order to demand more power for themselves to deal with the supposed enemies (Sternberg, in press). In the United States, the central government has arrogated more power than has been the case for any government in recent history on the grounds of alleged terrorist threats. In Zimbabwe, Robert Mugabe has turned one group against another, as has Hugo Chavez in Venezuela, each with what appears to be the goal of greatly expanding and maintaining his own power.

The Invulnerability Fallacy

This fallacy derives from the illusion of complete protection, such as might be provided by a large staff. Leaders may seem to have many friends ready to protect them at a moment's notice and may shield themselves from individuals who are anything less than sycophantic.

CONCLUSIONS

There are, no doubt, some fairly stable sources of individual differences in intelligence, but these stable sources may give intelligence a more trait-like appearance than it really has. The goal of this chapter has been to show how situations impact how intelligent a person is. People who are intelligent in one situation are not necessarily intelligent in another. We need to think of intelligence, like personality, as a person–situation interaction.

I would like to make one last personal plea, which gives special meaning to all I have said in this chapter. When I took that graduate personality course from Walter Mischel, he measured our accomplishments in his course via multiple-choice tests, on which I did not do so well. I hope this chapter has convinced you that my performance was simply a person–situation interaction. With a different form of testing, I might well have shown myself to be a superstar. But then again, maybe not.

ACKNOWLEDGMENTS

Preparation of this chapter was supported by a government grant under the Javits Act Program (Grant No. R206R000001) as administered by the U.S. Institute of Educational Sciences, U.S. Department of Education. Such support does not imply acceptance or endorsement of the ideas presented in this chapter.

REFERENCES

Bem, D. J., & Allen, A. (1974). On predicting some of the people some of the time: The search for cross-situational consistencies in behavior. *Psychological Review, 81*(6), 506–520.

Bem, D. J., & Funder, D. C. (1978). Predicting more of the people more of the time: Assessing the personality of situations. *Psychological Review, 85*(6), 485–501.

Binet, A., & Simon, T. (1916). *The development of intelligence in children.* Baltimore: Williams & Wilkins. (Original work published 1905)

Brown, A. L., & Ferrara, R. A. (1985). Diagnosing zones of proximal development. In J. V. Wertsch (Ed.), *Culture, communication, and cognition: Vygotskian perspectives* (pp. 273–305). New York: Cambridge University Press.

Budoff, M. (1968). Learning potential as a supplementary assessment procedure. In J. Hellmuth (Ed.), *Learning disorders* (Vol. 3, pp. 295–343). Seattle: Special Child.

Carraher, T. N., Carraher, D., & Schliemann, A. D. (1985). Mathematics in the streets and in schools. *British Journal of Developmental Psychology, 3,* 21–29.

Carroll, J. B. (1993). *Human cognitive abilities: A survey of factor-analytic studies.* New York: World Book.

Cattell, R. B. (1973). Personality pinned down. *Psychology Today, 7*(2), 41–46.

Cattell, R. B., & Cattell, H. E. P. (1973). *Measuring intelligence with the Culture Fair Tests.* Champaign, IL: Institute for Personality and Ability Testing.

Ceci, S. J. (1996). *On intelligence . . . more or less* (expanded ed.). Cambridge, MA: Harvard University Press.

Ceci, S. J., & Liker, J. (1986). Academic and nonacademic intelligence: An experimental separation. In R. J. Sternberg & R. K. Wagner (Eds.), *Practical intelligence: Nature and origins of competence in the everyday world* (pp. 119–142). New York: Cambridge University Press.

Ceci, S. J., & Roazzi, A. (1994). The effects of context on cognition: Postcards from Brazil. In R. J. Sternberg & R. K. Wagner (Eds.), *Mind in context: Interactionist perspectives on human intelligence* (pp. 74–101). New York: Cambridge University Press.

Costa, P. T., & McCrae, R. R. (1992a). Four ways five factors are basic. *Personality and Individual Differences, 13*(6), 653–665.

Costa, P. T., & McCrae, R. R. (1992b). "Four ways five factors are not basic": Reply. *Personality and Individual Differences, 13*(8), 861–865.

Costa, P. T., & McCrae, R. R. (1995). Domains and facets: Hierarchical personality assessment using the Revised NEO Personality Inventory. *Journal of Personality Assessment, 64*(1), 21–50.

Day, J. D., Engelhardt, J. L., Maxwell, S. E., & Bolig, E. E. (1997). Comparison of static and dynamic assessment procedures and their relation to independent performance. *Journal of Educational Psychology, 89*(2), 358–368.

Feuerstein, R. (1979). *The dynamic assessment of retarded performers: The Learning Potential Assessment Device theory, instruments, and techniques.* Baltimore: University Park Press.

Gardner, H. (1983). *Frames of mind: The theory of multiple intelligences.* New York: Basic Books.

Gardner, H. (1999). *Intelligence reframed: Multiple intelligences for the 21st century.* New York: Basic Books.

Goldberg, L. R., & Saucier, G. (1995). So what do you propose we use instead? A reply to Block. *Psychological Bulletin, 117*(2), 221–225.

Grigorenko, E. L., Meier, E., Lipka, J., Mohatt, G., Yanez, E., & Sternberg, R. J. (2004). Academic and practical intelligence: A case study of the Yup'ik in Alaska. *Learning and Individual Differences, 14,* 183–207.

Grigorenko, E. L., & Sternberg, R. J. (1998). Dynamic testing. *Psychological Bulletin, 124,* 75–111.

Guthke, J. (1993). Current trends in theories and assessment of intelligence. In J. H. M. Hamers, K. Sijtsma, & A. J. J. M. Ruijssenaars (Eds.), *Learning potential assessment* (pp. 13–20). Amsterdam: Swets & Zeitlinger.

Hall, C. S., & Lindzey, G. (1978). *Theories of personality.* New York: Wiley.

Haywood, H. C., & Tzuriel, D. (Eds.). (1992). *Interactive assessment.* New York: Springer-Verlag.

Hedlund, J., Horvath, J. A., Forsythe, G. B., Snook, S., Williams, W. M., Bullis, R. C., et al. (1998). *Tacit knowledge in military leadership: Evidence of construct validity.* (Technical Report 1080). Alexandria, VA: U.S. Army Research Institute for the Behavioral and Social Sciences.

"Intelligence and its measurement": A symposium. (1921). *Journal of Educational Psychology, 12,* 123–147, 195–216, 271–275.

Janis, I. L. (1972). *Victims of groupthink.* Boston: Houghton Mifflin.

Jensen, A. R. (1998). *The g factor: The science of mental ability.* Westport, CT: Praeger/Greenwoood.

Laboratory of Comparative Human Cognition. (1982). Culture and intelligence. In R. J. Sternberg (Ed.), *Handbook of human intelligence* (pp. 642–719). New York: Cambridge University Press.

Lave, J. (1988). *Cognition in practice.* New York: Cambridge University Press.

Lidz, C. S. (Ed.). (1987). *Dynamic assessment.* New York: Guilford Press.

Lidz, C. S. (1991). *Practitioner's guide to dynamic assessment.* New York: Guilford Press.

Lubart, T. I., & Sternberg, R. J. (1995). An investment approach to creativity: Theory and data. In S. M. Smith, T. B. Ward, & R. A. Finke (Eds.), *The creative cognition approach* (pp. 269–302). Cambridge, MA: MIT Press.

Mischel, W. (1968). *Personality and assessment.* New York: Wiley.

Mischel, W. (1969). Continuity and change in personality. *American Psychologist, 24*(11) 1012–1018.

Mischel, W. (1973). A cognitive social learning reconceptualization of personality. *Psychological Review, 80*(4), 252–253.

Nuñes, T. (1994). Street intelligence. In R. J. Sternberg (Ed.), *Encyclopedia of human intelligence* (Vol. 2, pp. 1045–1049). New York: Macmillan.

Nuñes, T., Schliemann, A. D., & Carraher, D. W. (1993). *Street mathematics and school mathematics.* New York: Cambridge University Press.

PACE Center. (2000). *The Yup'ik Scale of Practical Intelligence.* Unpublished test.

Plomin, R., DeFries, J. C., McClearn, G. E., & Rutter, M. (1997). *Behavioral genetics* (3rd ed.). New York: Freeman.

Prince, R. J., & Geissler, P. W. (2001). Becoming "one who treats": A case study of a Luo healer and her grandson in western Kenya. *Educational Anthropology Quarterly, 32,* 447–471.

Raven, J. C., Court, J. H., & Raven, J. (1992). *Manual for Raven's Progressive Matrices and Mill Hill Vocabulary Scales.* Oxford: Oxford Psychologists Press.

Rogoff, B. (1990). Apprenticeship in thinking. Cognitive development in social context. New York: Oxford University Press.

Rogoff, B. (2003). The cultural nature of human development. London: Oxford University Press.

Serpell, R. (2000). Intelligence and culture. In R. J. Sternberg (Ed.), *Handbook of intelligence* (pp. 549–580). New York: Cambridge University Press.

Spearman, C. (1904). "General intelligence," objectively determined and measured. *American Journal of Psychology, 15*(2), 201–293.

Spearman, C. (1927). *The abilities of man.* London: Macmillan.

Sternberg, R. J. (1981). Intelligence and nonentrenchment. *Journal of Educational Psychology, 73,* 1–16.

Sternberg, R. J. (1982). Natural, unnatural, and supernatural concepts. *Cognitive Psychology, 14,* 451–488.

Sternberg, R. J. (1987). The psychology of verbal comprehension. In R. Glaser (Ed.), *Advances in instructional psychology* (Vol. 3, pp. 97–151). Hillsdale, NJ: Erlbaum.

Sternberg, R. J. (1997). *Successful intelligence.* New York: Plume.

Sternberg, R. J. (1999). The theory of successful intelligence. *Review of General Psychology, 3,* 292–316.

Sternberg, R. J. (Ed.). (2000). *Handbook of intelligence.* New York: Cambridge University Press.

Sternberg, R. J. (2002a). Smart people are not stupid, but they sure can be foolish: The imbalance theory of foolishness. In R. J. Sternberg (Ed.), *Why smart people can be so stupid* (pp. 232–242). New Haven, CT: Yale University Press.

Sternberg, R. J. (Ed.). (2002b). *Why smart people can be so stupid.* New Haven, CT: Yale University Press.

Sternberg, R. J. (in press) The WICS approach to leadership: Stories of leadership and the structures and processes that support them. *The Leadership Quarterly.*

Sternberg, R. J., & Detterman, D. K. (Eds.). (1986). *What is intelligence?* Norwood, NJ: Ablex.

Sternberg, R. J., Forsythe, G. B., Hedlund, J., Horvath, J., Snook, S., Williams, W. M., Wagner, et al. (2000). *Practical intelligence in everyday life.* New York: Cambridge University Press.

Sternberg, R. J., & Gastel, J. (1989a). Coping with novelty in human intelligence: An empirical investigation. *Intelligence, 13,* 187–197.

Sternberg, R. J., & Gastel, J. (1989b). If dancers ate their shoes: Inductive reasoning with factual and counterfactual premises. *Memory and Cognition, 17,* 1–10.

Sternberg, R. J., Grigorenko, E. L., Ferrari, M., & Clinkenbeard, P. (1999). A triarchic analysis of an aptitude–treatment interaction. *European Journal of Psychological Assessment, 15*(1), 1–11.

Sternberg, R. J., Grigorenko, E. L., Ngrosho, D., Tantufuye, E., Mbise, A., Nokes, C., et al. (2002). Assessing intellectual potential in rural Tanzanian schoolchildren. *Intelligence, 30,* 141–162.

Sternberg, R. J., & Lubart, T. I. (1991). An investment theory of creativity and its development. *Human Development, 34*(1), 1–31.

Sternberg, R. J., & Lubart, T. I. (1995). *Defying the crowd: Cultivating creativity in a culture of conformity.* New York: Free Press.

Sternberg, R. J., & Lubart, T. I. (1996). Investing in creativity. *American Psychologist, 51*(7), 677–688.

Sternberg, R. J., & Nigro, G. (1980). Developmental patterns in the solution of verbal analogies. *Child Development, 51,* 27–38.

Sternberg, R. J., Nokes, K., Geissler, P. W., Prince, R., Okatcha, F., Bundy, D. A., et al. (2001). The relationship between academic and practical intelligence: A case study in Kenya. *Intelligence, 29,* 401–418.

Sternberg, R. J., & Powell, J. S. (1982). Theories of intelligence. In R. J. Sternberg (Ed.), *Handbook of human intelligence* (pp. 975–1005). New York: Cambridge University Press.

Sternberg, R. J., Powell, J. S., & Kaye, D. B. (1982). The nature of verbal comprehension. *Poetics, 11,* 155–187.

Sternberg, R. J., & Rifkin, B. (1979). The development of analogical reasoning processes. *Journal of Experimental Child Psychology, 27,* 195–232.

Sternberg, R. J., & the Rainbow Project Collaborators. (2005). Augmenting the SAT through assessments of analytical, practical, and creative skills. In W. Camara & E. Kimmel (Eds.), *Choosing students. Higher education admission tools for the 21st century* (pp. 159–176). Mahwah, NJ: Erlbaum.

Sternberg, R. J., & the Rainbow Project Collaborators. (2006). The Rainbow Project: Enhancing the SAT through assessment of analytical, practical, and creative skills. *Intelligence, 34,* 321–350.

Sternberg, R. J., & Wagner, R. K. (1993). The g–ocentric view of intelligence and job performance is wrong. *Current Directions in Psychological Science, 2*(1), 1–4.

Sternberg, R. J., Wagner, R. K., & Okagaki, L. (1993). Practical intelligence: The nature and role of tacit knowledge in work and at school. In H. Reese & J. Puckett (Eds.), *Advances in lifespan development* (pp. 205–227). Hillsdale, NJ: Erlbaum.

Sternberg, R. J., Wagner, R. K., Williams, W. M., & Horvath, J. A. (1995). Testing common sense. *American Psychologist, 50*(11), 912–927.

Tetewsky, S. J., & Sternberg, R. J. (1986). Conceptual and lexical determinants of nonentrenched thinking. *Journal of Memory and Language, 25,* 202–225.

Thurstone, L. L. (1938). *Primary mental abilities.* Chicago, IL: University of Chicago Press.

Tomasello, M. (2001). Cultural transmission: A view from chimpanzees and human infants. *Journal of Cross-Cultural Psychology, 32*(2), 135–146.

Tzuriel, D. (1995). *Dynamic-interactive assessment: The legacy of L. S. Vygotsky and current developments.* Unpublished manuscript.

Vernon, P. E. (1971). *The structure of human abilities.* London: Methuen.

Vygotsky, L. S. (1978). *Mind in society: The development of higher psychological processes.* Cambridge, MA: Harvard University Press.

Wagner, R. K. (1987).Tacit knowledge in everyday intelligent behavior. *Journal of Personality and Social Psychology, 52*(6), 1236–1247.

Wagner, R. K., & Sternberg, R. J. (1986). Tacit knowledge and intelligence in the everyday world. In R. J. Sternberg & R. K. Wagner (Eds.), *Practical intelligence: Nature and origins of competence in the everyday world* (pp. 51–83). New York: Cambridge University Press.

PARADIGM CHANGE
IN PSYCHOLOGICAL MODELS
OF HUMAN NATURE
(1950–2000–2050?)

15

Toward a Science of the Individual

Past, Present, Future?

WALTER MISCHEL

This book, featuring "contemporary efforts to build a science of the individual by studying persons in context" (Cervone, Shoda, & Downey, Chapter 1, this volume, p. 6), takes as its unifying theme and starting point my paper now more than three decades old (Mischel, 1973). The contributions in this volume happily make clear how far the authors have gone beyond 1973. I thank the authors for contributing them, and for so generously throwing bouquets in my direction. I am likewise grateful to the editors for their introductory chapter and for making this book happen. But I will not review or comment on the contributions gathered here, which all speak fully and lucidly for themselves.

My aim now is to put my 1973 paper into the context and psychological world in which it was written—a context that probably seems as remote to today's students as the first World War does to me. I will also briefly consider how the 1973 paper, "Toward a Cognitive Social Learning Reconceptualization of Personality," the *Personality and Assessment* monograph that led to it (Mischel, 1968), and the work in the long search for the locus and nature of consistency that directly followed (e.g., Mischel, 2004; Mischel & Shoda, 1995), do and do not fit into the ongoing study of personality and the larger effort to build a science of the individual to which the present volume is devoted.

THE CONTEXT IN 1968 AND 1973

I was a beginner teaching at Harvard trying to prepare a survey course on the state of personality psychology and assessment and the links between the two in 1960. The more I read, the greater the discrepancies became between what the personality theories assumed and what the findings showed, both for the trait and the psychodynamic–psycho-analytic approaches that then were dominant. Research articles and doctoral dissertations routinely concluded with the same depressing apology, attributing the failure of their personality tests to predict what people actually do in particular situation to the limitations of the tests and their own research without ever questioning their key assumptions. After months of working on a long manuscript to try to make sense of it, I shared the authors' depression and tried hard to forget it. But soon I became involved with personality assessment for selecting the first volunteers into the Kennedy administration's new Peace Corps projects (Mischel, 1965), and had to face again what I had been trying to ignore. Our findings were no different than those accumulating in the literature, motivating me again to try to make sense of the paradoxical state of personality and assessment.

On the one hand, the data persistently indicated lack of cross-situational consistency (Mischel, 1968). The gist of such findings is that the child who is aggressive at home may be less aggressive than most when in school; the man exceptionally hostile when rejected in love may be unusually tolerant about criticism of his work; the one who melts with anxiety in the doctor's office may be a calm mountain climber; the risk-taking entrepreneur may take few social risks. But on the other hand, intuition and a tradition going back to the ancient Greeks and their "Big Four" humors of personality (blood, bile, cholera, phlegm) as well as personality psychology as a field, led to the opposite conclusion.

The 1968 monograph distressed personality psychologists, not because it made clear the poor results of personality assessment research— that was already beginning to be recognized. It was traumatic because it asked for the first time: What if the problem is not just with bad methods and poor studies but also with wrong assumptions? And I concluded that for a half-century, researchers had been looking for personality guided by untenable assumptions and therefore could not find the results they expected.

At first the book was dismissed on a back page of *Contemporary Psychology*, in a brief review titled "Personality Unvanquished." But within a year, a divisive debate exploded, remarkably labeled the "person versus the situation debate." This heated confrontation filled the journals and the field's national and international meetings for more than 15 years. In this struggle, most personality psychologists condemned the book as trivializing the importance of personality and overblowing the causal power of situations, reading it as a rejection of the "existence of personality" and the "power of the person." Most social psychologists took it as proof for the "power of the situation" and the relative insignificance of individual differences in personality. The debate pitted the "power of the person" versus "the power of the situation" to see which was the bigger causal agent.

THE 1973 COGNITIVE-SOCIAL RECONCEPTUALIZATION

I wrote the 1973 piece in part to address the confusions that that were being created in the person versus situation debate. This dispute reflected the deeply entrenched traditional explanation of human behavior as due *either* to the internal character and traits of the individual *or* to the external situation in which the individual finds him- or herself, conceptualizing each as a mutually exclusive, independent cause. In this zero-sum conception of the relationship between the situation and the person, to the degree that the person was important, the situation was not, and vice versa—an exercise that, as now has often been said, seems as futile as debating which areas of a rectangle are caused mostly by its length and which by its width.

In the 1973 article I refused to ask "Is information about individuals more important than information about situations?" Put that way, the question is unanswerable and can only generate polemics in which "situations" become entities that supposedly exert either major or only minor control over behavior. Instead, I examined what situations are psychologically and how they may be mentally represented and function in the organization and expressions of social behavior and personality. That required drawing on what was happening within psychology but completely outside the personality area.

The sharp severing of personality psychology from the rest of the science began with Gordon Allport (1937), the founder of personality psychology, who made a point of splitting the two, a decision that may have been reasonable given that extreme behaviorism was then the dominant force, but that seems to persist for most of that field to this day. Thus mainstream personality psychologists continued to follow Allport's lead, ignoring the cognitive revolution that, beginning in the 1960s, was transforming psychology. But stimulated by that revolution, at least the outlines for a different conception of the mind were becoming visible, that might allow one to better understand the data on consistency and variability.

With that goal, in the 1973 *Psychological Review* I proposed that the field was searching for consistency in the wrong places: It was looking for the "personality as it is," apart from situations, treating situations as the noise or "error of measurement" that needed to be stripped out. Instead, the 1973 paper turned the standard view and practice upside-down. By including the situation as it is perceived by the person, and by analyzing behavior in this situational context, the consistencies that characterize the person, far from disappearing as had been assumed, would be found. But these individual differences would not be expressed in consistent cross-situational behavior; instead, consistency would be found in distinctive but stable patterns of *if . . . then . . .*, situation–behavior relations that form contextualized, psychologically meaningful personality signatures (e.g., "She does A when X, but B when Y").

I reasoned that the classic assumption of cross-situational consistency in behavior becomes untenable if one examines how the mind works as people attempt to adapt to diverse situations. As an alternative to the classic personality model, I proposed a constructivist, dynamic view of the person as a meaning-maker and analyzed how individuals make meaning out of the situations they encounter and use this to adapt their behavior to each situation. Because such adaptability and the ability to discriminate even among subtly different situations is essential for survival, humans could not have evolved to behave consistently across situations that vary in the challenges they pose and the solutions they require. Instead, people behave in ways that are consistent with the meanings that particular situations have for them: Individual differences arise from the distinctive ways that the person processes and understands situations, which in turn reflects the individuals' psychosocial and biological histories.

Given that different situations acquire different meanings for the same individual, the kinds of appraisals, expectations and beliefs, affects, goals, and behavioral scripts that are likely to become activated in relation to particular situations will vary. So there is no theoretical reason to expect the person to behave similarly in relation to different psychological situations unless they are functionally equivalent in meaning. On the contrary, adaptive behavior should be enhanced by discriminative facility, that is, the ability to make fine-grained distinctions among situations. And it should be undermined by broad response tendencies insensitive to context and the extremely different consequences produced by even subtle differences in behavior when situations differ in their nuance, as much subsequent research has shown (Cantor & Kihlstrom, 1987; Cheng, 2001, 2003; Chiu, Hong, Mischel, & Shoda,

1995; Mischel, 1973; Mendoza-Denton, Ayduk, Mischel, Shoda, & Testa, 2001). In short, the route to finding the invariance in personality requires taking account of the situation and its meaning for the individual, and may be seen in the stable interactions and interplay between them (e.g., Cervone & Shoda, 1999; Higgins, 1990; Kunda, 1999; Magnusson & Endler, 1977; Mischel, 1973; Mischel & Shoda, 1995).

FROM PARADIGM CRISIS TO PARADIGM SPLIT

Resurgence of the Traditional Trait Paradigm

The 1973 article was widely cited as a landmark, but I don't think it made a dent in the strong establishment reactions within traditional personality psychology against the 1968 book. After a decade of debates and discussions and plenary sessions on paradigm crises in personality, beginning in the late 1970s and early 1980s, the factor analytic approach was brought back to resuscitate the classic trait paradigm. It began with an agreement by a group of researchers to reach a consensus about the major traits needed for a comprehensive taxonomy of personality using factor analyses based on trait ratings in the form of the "Big Five factors" (e.g., Costa & McCrae, 1992). Many similar factor analytic studies and taxonomies had been done in earlier years, and their strengths and limitations had been recognized long ago (e.g., Mischel, 1968; Overall, 1964). The essence of those old critiques was similar to the current critiques of the Big Five summarized in the introduction to the present volume:

> In the psychology of personality, the Big Five model of personality traits energized the field in the 1980s and 1990s (e.g., Goldberg, 1993) but soon was shown to be limited as a model of the individual person in two significant respects: (1) the five factors, being merely latent variables that summarize variation in the population at large, could not be assumed to explain psychological functioning at the level of the individual (Borsboom, Mellenberg, & van Heerden, 2003; also see Sternberg, Chapter 14, this volume) and (2) the factor structure was found to replicate in populations of nonhuman animals (Gosling & John, 1999), which means that it did not capture unique psychological features of persons. (Cervone et al., Chapter 1, this volume, p. 4)

In the same vein, more than 40 years earlier Overall (1964) had demonstrated that factor analyses of the physical dimensions of books revealed that there is no necessary correspondence between the factors obtained and the primary conceptual dimensions of the object (Mischel, 1968). Such concerns were swept away in a massive forgetting of the field's history when advocates of the Big Five reached decided on the five factors that they proclaimed captured "the basic structure of personality." Traits were declared "alive and well" (Epstein, 1977), and the old approach was back with renewed exuberance (e.g., Goldberg, 1993). In this spirit, for many years the field's flagship *Journal of Personality and Social Psychology* described the mission of its personality section as devoted to contributions on "personality psychology as traditionally defined"—a statement that might surprise anyone who believes that a science encourages ideas and findings that could challenge and upend its traditional definitions.

The mainstream reaction within personality psychology to the field's paradigm crisis (usually dated to my 1968 book) was to embrace the Big Five and the "aggregation" approach originally advocated by Epstein (1979). In that view, the data on context effects and the variability of were seen as simply reflecting the noise and error of measurement. Lip service was given to the self-evident importance of situations (people weep more at funerals than at parades), and the low correlations in the individual's behavior found from situation to situation were acknowldged (Epstein, 1979). The proposed soulution (a rediscovery of the classic Spearman–Brown formula) was to increase reliability by aggregating the individual's behavior on a given dimension (e.g., conscientiousness, sociability) over many different situations to estimate an overall "true score" (as discussed in Epstein, 1979, 1980; Mischel & Peake, 1982; Pervin, 1994). These correlations, document that people differ significantly on virtually any dimension, documenting what was never disputed: On the whole, some people are more friendly than others, some are more open-minded, some are more punctual, and so on. Such aggregate information is useful for many goals, and its strengths as well as its limitations have been extensively described (e.g., Mischel & Shoda, 1998).

PERSONALITY COHERENCE
IN THE PATTERN OF VARIABILITY

Although most personality psychologists continued to treat the situation as the error term and to eliminate its effects by aggregating it out, Yuichi Shoda, Jack Wright, Phil Peake, our students and colleagues, and I, went the opposite way: We searched for the invariance in personality not by removing the situation but by incorporating it into the conception and assessment of personality. We were driven by the idea that the person's variability across situations, the ups and downs in the stream of natural behavior, is not simply error variance but a key to finding the structure of coherence in the individual's patterns of behavior. If the pattern or profile of variability still proved to be stable after the random noise of measurement is removed, thus contradicting the expectations of classic personality trait theory, it also might open a window into the underlying system that produced it (Mischel, 2004). While the 1973 paper suggested much of the interpretation, it lacked the empirical evidence to evaluate its claims.

Equipped now with video cameras and computers as they became available in the early 1980s, we conducted a massive field study to get such evidence within a summer camp called Wediko. In this residential camp setting and treatment program for children with a variety of behavioral problems, particularly aggression and self-regulation, one could directly observe the participants over many hours and weeks. We collected diverse measures and dense data across multiple situations and repeated occasions, under conditions that assured high reliability among well-trained observers (e.g., Mischel, Shoda, & Mendoza-Denton, 2002; Shoda, Mischel, & Wright, 1993a, 1993b, 1994). The results provided probably the thickest data archive to date for fine-grained analyses of the consistency and variability of directly observed social behavior across situations and over time.

Consistent with the findings in Mischel (1968), we saw that individual differences (rank order positions) in behavior with regard to such dimensions as physical and verbal aggression were relatively inconsistent across different types of psychological situations (e.g., "when teased or provoked by peers" vs. "when warned by adults" or "when approached positively by peers"). As expected, aggressive behavior in one type of situation did not strongly predict the individual's behavior in a different type of situation. The exciting news was that we discovered that individuals with similar average levels of a type of behavior (e.g., their overall aggression) nevertheless differ predictably in the types of situations in which their aggressiveness occurs. A youngster characterized by a pattern of becoming exceptionally aggressive when peers approach him to play, but less aggressive than most other children when chastised by an adult for misbehaving, is psychologically very different from one who shows the opposite pattern, even if both have similar overall levels of total aggressive behavior. Particularly exciting about these behavioral signatures, therefore, is that they open a window onto the underlying motivations, goals, and processing dynamics of the individual (Mischel & Shoda, 1995).

In summary, the results showed that when closely observed, individuals are characterized by stable, distinctive, and highly meaningful patterns of variability in their actions, thoughts, and feelings across different types of situations. These *if . . . then . . .* situation–behavior relationships revealed, as anticipated in the 1973 article, form a kind of "behavioral signature of personality" that identifies the individual distinctively, is relatively stable, maps on to the impressions formed by observers about what they are like, and opens a window onto the personality organization and dynamics that underlie the signatures (Shoda et al., 1993a, 1994). Although the camp findings gave clear and strong evidence for the stability of *if . . . then . . .* behavioral signatures, data from other studies (e.g., Vansteelandt & Van Mechelen, 1998) are consistently showing that such reliable patterns of behavior variability characterize individuals distinctively as a rule, rather than an exception, and in diverse domains, measured in all sorts of different ways (e.g., Andersen & Chen, 2002; Borkenau, Riemann, Spinath, & Angleitner, 2006; Cervone & Shoda, 1999; Fournier, Moskowitz, & Zuroff, 2007; Shoda & LeeTiernan, 2002).

This type of stability in patterns of variability contradicts traditional assumptions about the consistency and structure of dispositions and their behavioral expressions. In the classical psychometric conception of behavioral dispositions, the person's "true score" on the behavioral dimension, relative to normative levels in each situation, should remain constant. Because the deviations from the true score observed in each situation are assumed to reflect measurement noise or random fluctuation, if the data are standardized and rescaled relative to the typical level of behaviors expected in each situation, the "shape" of the profile should be random over multiple times and observations. The stable *if . . . then . . .* patterns that were found directly contradict this classic assumption and reveal a second type of within-person consistency that needs to be assessed and explained in the search for personality invariance. There are clear and strong regularities in behavior that characterize each individual in the form of stable, distinctive patterns of variability, and they are found by incorporating the situation into the search for consistency, not by eliminating it. Both types of stability coexist as two aspects of the expressions of coherence, reflected in the elevation (Type 1), and shape (Type 2), of behavioral signatures (e.g., Mischel, Shoda, & Ayduk, in press). Each is informative and both need to be taken into account and predicted in a comprehensive theory of personality.

THE CAPS MODEL: EXPLAINING THE VARIABILITY

The next challenge was to develop the kind of model that could account for the findings revealed by the Wediko research and anticipated at least in broad terms by the 1973 paper. The CAPS (Cognitive–Affective Personality System) model that Yuichi Shoda and I proposed was intended to be a meta-theory, a general framework that spells out a possible underlying structure that can produce both stable and distinctive behavioral signatures of the sort we found, as well as the average differences overall between individuals on which traditional trait theories focus (Mischel & Shoda, 1995). While developing this general model we were influenced by the zeitgeist in psychology in the late 1980s that suggested a more brain-like or neural network information-processing architecture. In such architecture, the basic principle of operation is not logical decisions, but more the pattern of associations that governs which mental representations become activated. A guiding idea in CAPS is that the pattern of associations, the network, among the units within it, underlies complex information processing in a personality system. That requires taking account not just of individual differences in the availability of different units but also, and most important, of the organization of their interconnections within the system.

We designed CAPS as an alternative to the traditional trait model, with the hope that it would help in the building of a personality science linked to cognitive–affective science, drawing on developments in connectionist and neural network theories in cognitive psychology as well as in social cognition and other disciplines. It was grounded in heavy empiricism and supported by Shoda's elegant computer simulations. But what mattered most to me was that CAPS seemed to be a step toward a view of the person that, in psychological terms and with scientific methods, could begin to capture the richness of human character, conveyed in the "rounded" humans found in the best literature, and in our own lives, but missed in the flat, simplistic, static portraits offered by psychology's trait theories, and bemoaned in my 1968 and 1973 critiques of the field.

The CAPS model is idiographic in the sense that it is about each person's distinctive organization and how it is expressed in interactions with the social world. But it is not limited to $N = 1$. It lends itself easily to the nomothetic study of types of people who share common *if . . . then . . .* behavioral signatures and similar underlying processing dynamics generated by similarities in their CAPS networks. For example, it is currently being used to identify the behavioral signatures of individuals high in the tendency to activate anxious expectations of interpersonal rejection (e.g., Pietrzak, Downey, & Ayduk, 2005).

THE OTHER SIDE OF CONTEXTUALISM: COGNITIVE–AFFECTIVE REAPPRAISAL OF SITUATIONS

The other side of the argument about the need to incorporate the meaning for the person of the particular context into the conceptualization of personality and its expressions is the recognition that individuals are able, at least sometimes, to transform the impact of situations by changing their meaning (Mischel, 1973). Evidence for this side of contextualism came from the discovery of the psychological mechanisms that allow people to delay immediate gratification and resist the pull of the immediate situational temptations and pressures for the sake of more valued future consequences.

Beginning in the late 1960s and early 1970s, my students and I demonstrated that the crucial determinant of the young child's willingness and ability to delay immediate gratification and resist temptation was not the objective rewards faced in the situation, as earlier theories had suggested, but how the rewards were mentally represented. Delay behavior and self-control could be changed readily and dramatically by modifying how the objects of gratification were cognitively appraised (Mischel, 1974a, 1974b; Mischel, Shoda, & Rodriguez, 1989): The preschool child could wait for otherwise unbearable delay periods for tempting treats such as a marshmallow by focusing on its nonconsummatory "cool" qualities (e.g., its shape), or yield immediately to the temptation by focusing on its consummatory "hot," or arousing features (e.g., its yummy, sweet, chewy taste). Thus while situations influence what the person does and becomes, persons also have the ability, under some conditions, to transform what "hot," compelling situations do, overcoming stimulus control and automatic responding, allowing at least some self-direction and choice.

To identify those conditions, in the experimental studies we specified how cognitive appraisals and attention deployment during the effort to delay immediate gratification influence the ability to do so and make waiting or working for delayed rewards either predictably easy or impossibly difficult for the young child (Mischel et al., 1989). We also identified the diagnostic laboratory conditions in which the child's spontaneous delay-of-gratification behavior and attention control turned out to be remarkably predictive of a wide range of developmental outcomes over many decades (Mischel, Shoda, & Peake, 1988). We followed these children into adulthood and showed that seconds of delay time in these situations waiting for such treats as two little pretzels later or one now, at age 4, predicted long-term outcomes that range from their SAT scores and ratings of their adaptive social and cognitive functioning in adolescence to effective goal pursuit, positive self-concepts, well-being, and less cocaine and other drug use in adulthood.

These findings indicated considerable temporal stability in self-regulatory competencies that in turn can lead to a wide variety of correlated positive outcomes in life trajectories. Individuals who are able to delay gratification and exert effortful self-control and adhere to planned behavior in light of long-term goals are likely to have an advantage in dealing with the frustrations and challenges of life, reflected in distinctive life trajectories and characterized with such outcomes as higher educational achievement, better attainment of difficult but important goals that require effortful persistence, and greater resistance to drug abuse and other high health-risk behaviors.

Thus self-regulatory competencies provide another source of long-term stability and coherence within individuals. On the other hand, the ability to self-regulate, and its utilization in different contexts, are not necessarily highly correlated. A notable example, by no means rare, is a recent U.S. president who was famous for his inability (or unwillingness) to delay gratification in some interpersonal situations, although distinguished in his ability to do so effectively in other domains.

The work on self-regulation made it possible to extend the CAPS model to encompass two interacting subsystems: a cool, cognitive, reflective "know" system, and a hot, reflexive, impulsive, automatic, emotional "go" system (Mischel & Ayduk, 2004; Metcalfe & Mischel, 1999). The interactions between these systems have turned out to enable the prediction of long-term developmental outcomes, not only of goal-directed delay of gratification but also of cognitive and emotional self-regulation in contexts that range from drug addiction and impulse disorders to economic decision-making, to conflict in interpersonal relationships (Mischel, Ayduk, & Mendoza-Denton, 2003; Mischel, 2004). In retrospect, although the research on delay of gratification proved to be highly consequential in its own right, it was essential for the reconceptualization of personality, and indeed human nature, by providing the early experimental support for some of its most basic assumptions about the cognitive appraisal of situations.

THE FUTURE? APPLYING OUR SCIENCE TO THE INDIVIDUAL

It is gratifying to see that the core ideas and themes presented in the 1973 paper, proposing a contextualized approach to the assessment and conceptualization of persons, continue to be relevant to a wide range of new research contributions in diverse directions, as the outstanding examples in this volume illustrate, and as the introductory chapter summarizes. I deeply appreciate the contributions to this volume by my many colleagues and friends. The contributors and editors are gracious in honoring the role I, and particularly the 1973 paper, have played in their work, and in some cases in their professional lives. The situation, however, is fully reciprocal: I have greatly benefited from theirs, and will always appreciate their invaluable work and colleagueship in helping to build the science of persons to which we share a commitment.

Science, like life, moves in mostly unpredictable ways, and the default predictions of the future are that it will be different from what we expect. But the groundwork for a science of persons is extremely promising (e.g., Cervone & Mischel, 2002), and more than that, as the contributions in this volume illustrate, it is vigorously under construction. Especially important, and again well-sampled in this volume, is that these developments bridge the classic partitioning most unnatural and destructive to the building of a cumulative science of the individual—the one that split the person apart from the situation, treating each as an independent cause of behavior. At the time of the "person *versus* situation" debate this splitting (amazingly) threatened to make personality the discipline that studies people apart from situations, and social psychology the neighbor that studies situations apart from people. Fortunately, that debate is long past, and the changes in the past decade or two seem especially noteworthy.

The contributions in this volume, in my view, are major steps in overcoming the original Allportian divorce of personality psychology and the study of individuals from the larger science. The scientific study of persons in contexts now seems well on its way to becoming a discipline without closed borders, open to, and interacting with, the relevant advances of science, eager to cut nature at its natural joints, regardless of outdated subdiscipline turf divisions and local graduate training programs (Mischel, 2005). If that is the case, given the robustness of our larger science, and the dramatic progress addressing basic questions of mind–brain–behavior links, the prospects to me seem as exciting as they are unpredictable.

REFERENCES

Allport, G. W. (1937). *Personality: A psychological interpretation.* New York: Holt, Rinehart & Winston.

Andersen, S. M., & Chen, S. (2002). The relational self: An interpersonal social-cognitive theory. *Psychological Review, 109,* 619–645.

Borkenau, P., Riemann, R., Spinath, F. M., & Angleitner, A. (2006). Genetic and environmental influences on person situation profiles. *Journal of Personality, 74,* 1451–1480.

Borsboom, D., Mellenbergh, G. J., & Van Heerden, J. (2003). The theoretical status of latent variables. *Psychological Review, 110,* 203–219.

Cantor, N., & Kihlstrom, J. F. (1987). *Personality and social intelligence.* Englewood Cliffs, NJ: Erlbaum.

Cervone, D., & Mischel, W. (Eds.). (2002). *Advances in personality science.* New York: Guilford Press.

Cervone, D., & Shoda, Y. (1999). Social-cognitive theories and the coherence of personality. In D. Cervone & Y. Shoda (Eds.). *The coherence of personality: Social-cognitive bases of consistency, variability, and organization* (pp. 3–33). New York: Guilford Press.

Cheng, C. (2001). Assessing coping flexibility in real-life and laboratory settings: A multimethod approach. *Journal of Personality and Social Psychology, 80,* 814–833.

Cheng, C. (2003). Cognitive and motivational processes underlying coping flexibility: A dual-process model. *Journal of Personality and Social Psychology, 84,* 425–438.

Chiu, C., Hong, Y., Mischel, W., & Shoda, Y. (1995). Discriminative facility in social competence: Conditional versus dispositional encoding and monitoring-blunting of information. *Social Cognition, 13,* 49–70.

Costa, P. T., Jr., & McCrae, R. R. (1992). Normal personality assessment in clinical practice: The NEO Personality Inventory. *Psychological Assessment, 4,* 5–13.

Epstein, S. (1977). Traits are alive and well. In D. Magnusson & N. Endler (Eds.), *Personality at the crossroads: Current issues in interactional psychology* (pp. 83–98). Hillsdale, NJ: Erlbaum.

Epstein, S. (1979). The stability of behavior: I. On predicting most of the people much of the time. *Journal of Personality and Social Psychology, 37,* 1097–1126.

Epstein, S. (1980). The stability of behavior: II. Implications for psychological research. *American Psychologist, 35,* 790–806.

Fournier, M. A., Moskowitz, D. S., & Zuroff, D. C. (2007). *Integrating dispositions, signatures, and the interpersonal domain.* Manuscript under review.

Goldberg, L. R. (1993). The structure of phenotypic personality traits. *American Psychologist, 48,* 26–34.

Gosling, S. D., & John, O. P. (1999). Personality dimensions in non-human animals: A cross-species review. *Current Directions in Psychological Science, 8,* 69–75.

Higgins, E. T. (1990). Personality, social psychology, and person–situation relations: Standards and knowledge activation as a common language. In L. A. Pervin (Ed.), *Handbook of personality: Theory and research* (pp. 301–338). New York: Guilford Press.

Kunda, Z. (1999). *Social cognition: Making sense of people.* Cambridge, MA: MIT Press.

Magnusson, D., & Endler, N. (Eds.). (1977). *Personality at the crossroads: Current issues in interactional psychology.* Hillsdale, NJ: Erlbaum.

Mendoza-Denton, R., Ayduk, O., Mischel, W., Shoda, Y., & Testa, A. (2001). Person × situation interactionism in self-encoding (*I am . . . when . . .*): Implications for affect regulation and social information processing. *Journal of Personality and Social Psychology, 80,* 533–544.

Metcalfe, J., & Mischel, W. (1999). A hot/cool-system analysis of delay of gratification: Dynamics of willpower. *Psychological Review, 106,* 3–19.

Mischel, W. (1965). Predicting the success of Peace Corps volunteers in Nigeria. *Journal of Personality and Social Psychology, 1,* 510–517.

Mischel, W. (1968). *Personality and assessment.* New York: Wiley.

Mischel, W. (1973). Toward a cognitive social learning reconceptualization of personality. *Psychological Review, 80,* 252–283.

Mischel, W. (1974a). Cognitive appraisals and transformations in self-control. In B. Weiner (Ed.), *Cognitive views of human motivation* (pp. 33–39). New York: Academic Press.

Mischel, W. (1974b). Processes in delay of gratification. In L. Berkowitz (Ed.), *Advances in experimental social psychology* (Vol. 7, pp. 249–292). New York: Academic Press.

Mischel, W. (2004). Toward an integrative science of the person [prefatory chapter]. *Annual Review of Psychology, 55,* 1–22.

Mischel, W. (2005). Alternative futures for our science. *American Psychological Society Observer, 18,* 15–19.

Mischel, W., & Ayduk, O. (2004). Willpower in a cognitive-affective processing system: The dynamics of delay of gratification. In R. F. Baumeister & K. D. Vohs (Eds.), *Handbook of self-regulation: Research, theory, and applications* (pp. 99–129). New York: Guilford Press.

Mischel, W., Ayduk, O., & Mendoza-Denton, R. (2003). Sustaining delay of gratification over time: A hot/cool systems perspective. In G. Loewenstein, D. Read, & R. Baumeister (Eds.), *Time and decision: Economic and psychological perspectives on intertemporal choice* (pp. 175–200). New York: Sage.

Mischel, W., & Peake, P. K. (1982). In search of consistency: Measure for measure. In M. P. Zanna, E. T. Higgins, & C. P. Herman (Eds.), *Consistency in social behavior: The Ontario Symposium* (Vol. 2, pp. 187–207). Hillsdale, NJ: Erlbaum.

Mischel, W., Shoda, Y., & Mendoza-Denton, R. (2002). Situation–behavior profiles as a locus of consistency in personality. *Current Directions in Psychological Science, 11,* 50–54.

Mischel, W., & Shoda, Y. (1995). A cognitive-affective system theory of personality: Reconceptualizing situations, dispositions, dynamics, and invariance in personality structure. *Psychological Review, 102,* 246–268.

Mischel, W., & Shoda, Y. (1998). Reconciling processing dynamics and personality dispositions. *Annual Review of Psychology, 49,* 229–258.

Mischel, W., Shoda, Y., & Ayduk, O. (in press). *Introduction to personality: Toward an integrative science of the person* (8th ed.). New York: Wiley.

Mischel, W., Shoda, Y., & Peake, P. K. (1988). The nature of adolescent competencies predicted by preschool delay of gratification. *Journal of Personality and Social Psychology, 54,* 687–696.

Mischel, W., Shoda, Y., & Rodriguez, M. L. (1989). Delay of gratification in children. *Science, 244,* 933–938.

Overall, J. (1964). Note on the scientific status of factors. *Psychological Bulletin, 61,* 270–276.

Pervin, L. A. (1994). A critical analysis of trait theory. *Psychological Inquiry, 5,* 103–113.

Pietrzak, J., Downey, G., & Ayduk, O. (2005). Rejection sensitivity as an interpersonal vulnerability. In M.W. Baldwin (Ed.), *Interpersonal Cognition* (pp. 62–84). New York: Guilford Press.

Shoda, Y., & LeeTiernan, S. J. (2002). What remains invariant? Finding order within a person's thoughts, feelings, and behaviors across situations. In D. Cervone & W. Mischel (Eds.), *Advances in personality science* (pp. 241–270). New York: Guilford Press.

Shoda, Y., Mischel, W., & Wright, J. C. (1993a). Links between personality judgments and contextualized behavior patterns: Situation-behavior profiles of personality prototypes. *Social Cognition, 4,* 399–429.

Shoda, Y., Mischel, W., & Wright, J. C. (1993b). The role of situational demands and cognitive competencies in behavior organization and personality coherence. *Journal of Personality and Social Psychology, 56,* 41–53.

Shoda, Y., Mischel, W., & Wright, J. C. (1994). Intra-individual stability in the organization and patterning of behavior: Incorporating psychological situations into the idiographic analysis of personality. *Journal of Personality and Social Psychology, 67,* 674–687.

Vansteelandt, K., & Van Mechelen, I. (1998). Individual differences in situation-behavior profiles: A triple typology model. *Journal of Personality and Social Psychology, 75,* 751–765.

Toward a Cognitive Social Learning Reconceptualization of Personality

WALTER MISCHEL

Diverse data challenge the central assumptions of the traditional trait approach to personality. The implications for conceptions of individual differences and situations in the study of personality are examined. The issued discussed include the nature of behavioral "specificity," the acquired meaning of stimuli, the uses and misuses of traits, and the construction of personality. To move toward a more adequate theoretical approach to persons, the following cognitive social learning variables are proposed as basic units for the study of individuals: cognitive and behavioral construction competencies, encoding strategies and personal constructs, behavior–outcome and stimulus–outcome expectancies, subjective stimulus values, and self-regulatory systems and plans. The specific interactions between these and person variables and psychological situations are analyzed within the framework of a cognitive social learning approach.

There has been a curious—indeed alarming—bifurcation between progress in theories regarding complex social behavior and cognition on the one hand, and in conceptualizations regarding the basic nature of personality on the other. Many of the therapeutic implications of social learning (social behavior) theories have become evident in the last few years. There have been notable advances in treatment techniques as well as significant reconceptualizations of the treatment process itself (e.g., Bandura, 1969). These developments are just starting to he accompanied by comparable parallel developments in personality theory. In a second direction, there has been vigorous progress in cognitive psychology (e.g.,

This chapter originally appeared in *Psychological Review,* Vol. 80, No. 4, 1973. Copyright 1973 by the American Psychological Association. Reprinted by permission.

Neisser, 1967). But while cognitive and symbolic processes have received increasing attention both in the laboratory and in therapeutic applications, their implications for personality psychology have not yet been thoroughly explored and their impact on the basic traditional assumptions of personality psychology until recently has been limited.

During the last 50 years, when basic concepts were changing rapidly in most fields of psychology, the most fundamental assumptions about the nature of personality seem to have been retained with few substantial modifications. Of course there have been many changes in the names and particular characteristics of the trait dispositions advocated by different theoreticians and personality researchers in the last few decades. But in spite of the heterogeneity of hypothesized dimensions or structures, perhaps the most fundamental assumptions about them have remained almost monolithic until very recently. This paper briefly reviews the central assumptions of global dispositional approaches to personality, considers some of the main misconceptions, issues, and implications arising from recent challenges to those assumptions, and finally attempts a reconceptualization of person variables in the light of concepts from the study of cognition and social learning.

GLOBAL DISPOSITIONAL APPROACHES TO PERSONALITY

Assumptions of Traditional Trait Approaches

It has generally been assumed that personality dispositions or traits—the basic units of personality study—are relatively stable, highly consistent attributes that exert widely *generalized* causal effects on behavior. Whether one uses the language of factors, or of habits, or of basic attitudes, or of dynamics and character structure, this fundamental assumption has been shared: personality comprises broad underlying dispositions which pervasively influence the individual's behavior across many situations and lead to consistency in his behavior (e.g., Allport, 1937).[1] These dispositions are not directly observed but are inferred from behavioral signs (trait indicators), either directly or indirectly (Mischel, 1968). Guided by this assumption, personality research has been a quest for such underlying broad dimensions, for basic factors, or for pervasive motives, or for characteristic life styles. In personality assessment the trait assumptions regarding structure are seen in the existence of hundreds of tests designed to infer dispositions and almost none to measure situations. The same belief in global traits that manifest themselves pervasively is perhaps best seen in the projective test assumption that responses to vague or minimal stimuli will reveal individual differences in fundamental generalized dispositions (MacFarlane & Tuddenham, 1951).

Empirical Status of Assumptions

Given the pervasiveness of the consistency assumption of dispositional personality theory, its empirical status becomes especially important. There have been several recent reviews of that evidence (e.g., Mischel, 1968, 1969, 1971; Peterson, 1968; Vernon, 1964). The data cannot be summarized adequately here, but several themes emerge. To recapitulate briefly, impressive consistencies often have been found for intellective features of personality and for behavior patterns such as cognitive styles and problem-solving strategies that are strongly correlated with intelligence (e.g., Witkin, 1965). Consistency also is often high when people rate their own traits, as in questionnaires and other self-reports (e.g., E. L. Kelly, 1955). Temporal continuity also has been demonstrated often when the individual's behavior is sampled at different time periods but in similar situations. When one goes beyond cognitive variables to personality dimensions and when one samples personality by diverse methods and not just by self-report questionnaires, the data change and undermine the utility of inferring global personality dispositions from behavioral signs, as has been documented in detail (Mischel, 1968):

> Response patterns even in highly similar situations often fail to be strongly related. Individuals show far less cross-situational consistency in their behavior than has been assumed by trait–state theories. The more dissimilar the evoking situations, the less likely they are to produce similar or consistent responses from the same individual. Even seemingly trivial situational differences may reduce correlations to zero. Response consistency tends to be greatest within the same response medium, within self-reports to paper-and-pencil tests. for example, or within directly observed non-verbal behavior. Intra-individual consistency is reduced drastically when dissimilar response modes are employed. Activities that are substantially associated with aspects of intelligence and with problem solving behavior—like achievement behaviors, cognitive styles, response speed—tend to be most consistent. (p. 177)

Psychodynamic Approach to Consistency

Recognizing both the specificity and complexity of behavior, psychodynamic theorists long ago rejected the idea of broad overt behavioral consistencies across situations. Instead, psychodynamic theories emphasize that behavior varies, but diverse behavioral patterns serve the same enduring and generalized *underlying* dynamic or motivational disposi-

tions. The search for dispositions thus rests on a distinction between surface behaviors ("signs" or "symptoms") and the motives that they serve.
This involves the familiar distinction between the "phenotypic" and the
"genotypic" and entails an indirect, rather than a direct measurement
model (Mischel, 1968). Indeed, the most common argument for personality consistency in the face of seeming behavioral specificity is the distinction between the phenotypic and the genotypic. Granted that overt
behavior is not highly consistent, might it not be useful to posit
genotypic personality dispositions that endure, although their overt
response forms may change? This genotypic–phenotypic model has been
at the crux of dynamic dispositional theories of personality (Mischel,
1969). The psychodynamic model construes behaviors as highly *indirect*
signs of the dispositions that underlie them, because defenses are
hypothesized to distort and disguise the true meaning of the observed
behaviors. If basic motives express themselves only indirectly after being
distorted by defensive maneuvers, then their overt behavioral manifestations have to be interpreted symbolically as indirect signs. Thus, for
example, using the white space of an inkblot in a percept may be taken
as a sign of negativistic tendencies, or saying the inkblot looks like blood
may be interpreted as a sign of a psychopathic personality. The psychodynamic approach thus shares with the trait approach a disinterest in
behaviors except as they serve as signs—albeit more indirect signs—of
generalized dispositions.

While inherently logical, the utility of the indirect sign approach to
dispositions depends on the value of the inferences provided by the clinical judge. Consequently, the reliability and validity of clinicians' judgments become crucial. The extensive empirical studies on this issue have
investigated in detail the value of clinicians' efforts to infer broad dispositions indirectly from specific symptomatic signs and to unravel dis-
guises in order to uncover the motivational dispositions that might be
their roots. As is now generally recognized, the accumulated findings
give little support for the utility of clinical judgments, even when the
judges are expert psychodynamicists working in clinical contexts and
using their favorite techniques. Reviews of the relevant research generally show that clinicians guided by concepts about underlying genotypic
dispositions have not been able to predict behavior better than have the
person's own direct self-report, simple indices of directly relevant past
behavior, or demographic variables (e.g., Mischel, 1968, 1971, 1972).

MISCONCEPTIONS AND ISSUES

The findings on the specificity–consistency of personality traits and the
implications of social behavior theory for the psychology of personality

may be leading to a paradigm crisis in the field (e.g., Fiske, 1973), and hence it is not surprising that they are easily misunderstood. These misunderstandings are evident in repeated critiques (e.g., Adelson, 1969; Adinolfi, 1971; Alker, 1972; Craik, 1969; Dahlstrom, 1970; Wachtel, 1973) aimed at applications of social behavior theory to the domain of personality (e.g., Mischel, 1968, 1969) and particularly to the issue of the specificity–generality of behavior. The thrust of these reactions is that social behavior theory, especially in its emphasis on the discriminativeness ("specificity") of behavior, implies a "personalityless" view of man.

Common Misconceptions

The position developed in Mischel's (1968) *Personality and Assessment* has been widely misunderstood to imply that people show no consistencies, that individual differences are unimportant, and that "situations" are the main determinants of behavior (e.g., Bowers, 1972). For example, Alker (1972) has thoroughly distorted the basic issues (as Bem, 1972, has shown), guarding the traditional personality paradigm against evidence that "behavior varies from situation to situation." But the fact that behavior varies across different situations is not questioned by anyone, including classical trait theorists. More serious issues, instead, are the consistency–specificity with which the same person reacts to situations that ostensibly are relatively *similar* (i.e., that are selected to evoke the same trait), and most important, the utility of predictions based on global trait inferences (Mischel, 1968). In the same vein, Wachtel (1973) defended psychodynamic theory against being forever consigned to a "scientific Valhalla" by emphasizing that psychodynamic theories in fact recognize people's responsiveness to variations in stimulus conditions. Unfortunately, he ignored the data and challenges that are relevant, most notably the failure of the psychodynamically oriented clinician to demonstrate the utility of the indirect sign approach when compared to more parsimonious alternatives (Mischel, 1968, 1972, 1973b).

Evidence for the lack of utility of inferring hypothesized global trait dispositions from behavioral signs should not be misread as an argument for the greater importance of situations than persons (Bowers, 1972). Is information about individuals more important than information about situations? The author has persistently refrained from posing this question because phrased that way it is unanswerable and can serve only to stimulate futile polemics. Moreover, in current debates on this topic, "situations" are often erroneously invoked as entities that supposedly exert either major or only minor control over behavior, without specifying what, psychologically, they are or how they function (Alker, 1972; Bowers, 1972; Wallach & Leggett, 1972). But while some situations may be powerful determinants of behavior, others are likely to be exceedingly trivial. The relative importance of individual differences will depend on the situation selected, the type of behavior assessed, the particular individual differences sampled, and the purpose of the assessment. In later sections of this article, an attempt will be made to consider in detail how cognitive social learning person variables interact with conditions and how "situations" function psychologically. But first it is necessary to review further, and hopefully to clarify, some of the main issues and misconceptions regarding the status of global traits.

Moderator Variables and Person–Situation Interactions

Several recent trait studies have investigated the relative separate quantitative contributions of persons and situations as well as the variance accounted for by the interaction of the individual and the environment (e.g., Argyle & Little, 1972; Endler & Hunt, 1966, 1968, 1969; Endler, Hunt, & Rosenstein, 1962; Moos, 1968, 1969). The essential method consists of sampling the behavior of individuals (by questionnaire and/or by observation) across a series of situations and through various response modes. On the whole, these studies have indicated that the sampled individual differences, situations, and response modes when considered separately tend to account for less variance than does their interaction.

The overall results suggest, as Endler and Hunt (1969, p. 20) noted with regard to their own findings for anxiety, that behavior "is idiosyncratically organized in each individual . . ." A similar conclusion emerges from Moos's (1968) studies of self-reported reactions by staff and patients to various settings. Consider, for example, his obtained interactions between persons and nine settings with regard to "sociable, friendly, peaceful" versus "unsociable, hostile, angry" behavior. The results revealed that although different individuals reacted differently to the settings, a given person might be high on the dimension in the morning but not at lunch, high with another patient but not when with a nurse, low in small group therapy, moderate in industrial therapy, but high in individual therapy, etc. An entirely different pattern might characterize the next person. These results and interpretations are totally congruent with the conclusions emerging from earlier reviews that emphasize the idiosyncratic organization of behavior within individuals (Mischel, 1968, p. 190).

It would be wasteful to create pseudocontroversies that pit person against situation in order to see which is more important. The answer must always depend on the particular situations and persons sampled; presumably, studies could be designed to demonstrate almost any outcome. The interaction studies correctly demonstrated that the question of whether individual differences or persons are more important is a fruitless one that has no general answer. The views of Moos (1972, personal communication) regarding the limits of the kinds of interaction studies that he and Endler and Hunt pioneered seem extremely sensible. Moos recognized that these studies can be designed so that:

> any result is possible. I think that all one can say is that given relatively real life situations (e.g., patients on wards or in outpatient psychotherapy, or your delay of gratification studies) that the major proportion of the variance simply does not appear to be accounted for by individual difference variables. One could certainly, however, easily design studies in which the major portion of the variance would be accounted for by individual difference variables. Frankly this is why I have stopped doing studies of this sort. It seems to me that the point has now been amply demonstrated, and it is time to get on with other matters.

It is encouraging that recent research on dispositions has started to recognize seriously the extraordinary complexity of the interactions found between subject variables and conditions. The concept of "moderator variables" was introduced to trait theory to refer to the fact that the effects of any particular disposition generally are moderated by such other variables as the subject's age, his sex, his IQ, the experimenter's sex, and the characteristics of the situation (Wallach, 1962). When one examines closely the interactions obtained in research on the effects of dispositions and conditions, the number of moderator variables required to predict behavior and the complexity of their interrelationships (e.g., McGuire, 1968) tend to become most formidable. For example, to predict a subject's voluntary delay of gratification, one may have to know how old he is, his sex, the experimenter's sex, the particular objects for which he is waiting, the consequences of not waiting, the models to whom he was just exposed, his immediately prior experience—the list gets almost endless (Mischel, 1973a). This seems to be another way of saying in the language of moderator variables and interaction terms that what a person does tends to be relatively specific to a host of variables, and that behavior is multiply determined by all of them rather than being the product of widely generalized dispositions. Some psychologists may find these interpretations more palatable if they are not phrased as reflecting the specificity of the acquired meanings of stimuli and the resulting specificity of behavior patterns (Mischel, 1968). Instead, they may prefer to construe the data as highlighting the uniqueness and complexity of personality. To say that what a person thinks, and does, and feels—and hence what he is at any moment—depends on many subject and condition variables is also to underline the complexity and uniqueness of his behavior.

The foregoing discussion does not imply that predictions cannot be made from subject variables to relevant behaviors, but it does suggest severe limits on the range and level of relationships that can be expected. Consider, as a representative example, a recent effort to relate individual differences in young children's expectancies about locus of control to their behavior in theoretically relevant situations (Mischel, Zeiss, & Zeiss, 1974). To explore these interactions, the Stanford Preschool Internal–External Scale was developed as a measure of expectancies about whether events occur as a consequence of the child's own action ("internal control") or as a consequence of external forces ("external control"). Expectancies about locus of control were measured separately for positive and negative events so that scores reflect expectancies for degree of internal control of positive events (I+), of negative events (I–), and a sum of these two (total I). Individual differences in I+, I–, and total I then were correlated with the children's ability to delay gratification under diverse working and waiting conditions. The results provided highly specific but theoretically meaningful patterns of relationships. To illustrate, relationships between total I and overall delay behavior were negligible, and I+ was unrelated to I–. As expected, I+ (but not I–) was found to be related to persistence in three separate situations where instrumental activity would result in a *positive* outcome; I– (but not I+) was related to persistence when instrumental activity could prevent the occurrence of a *negative* outcome.

The overall findings showed that individual differences in children's beliefs about their ability to control outcomes are partial determinants of their goal-directed behavior, but the relationships hinge on extremely specific moderating conditions, both with regard to the type of behavior and the type of belief. If such moderating conditions had not been considered and all indices of "delay behavior" had been combined regardless of their positive or negative valence, the actual role of the relevant individual differences would have been totally obscured. While the results were of considerable theoretical interest, the number and mean level of the achieved correlations were not appreciably higher than those typically found in correlational personality research. Moreover, the ability of these correlations to survive cross-validation remains to be demonstrated.

The more moderators required to qualify a trait, the more the "trait" becomes a relatively specific description of a behavior–situation unit. That is, the more highly circumscribed, "moderated," and situation specific the trait, the more it becomes indistinguishable from a specific behavior–situation description. At its extreme, when many strings of hyphenated moderator variables are required, the behavioral "signs" from which the disposition is inferred may become equivalent to the inferred disposition and make the inference gratuitous. As we increasingly qualify the description of a person to specify the exact response modes and conditions in which a particular behavior will occur, we move from characterizing him with generalized traits to describing his behavior in particular forms and under particular conditions.

The language of "interactions" and "moderator variables" provides simply another way of talking about the idiosyncratic organization of behavior and its dependence upon specific conditions unless (as Bem, 1972, p. 21, has noted) one can *"predict* on a priori grounds which moderators are likely to divide up the world into useful classes. . . ." Demonstrations that both subject and situational moderators can be used predictively, not merely to partial out the variance from each source post hoc, are especially important in light of the negative conclusions reached by Wallach, one of the main formulators of the moderator variable strategy in personality research. Commenting on the extensive results from his decade of work on the problem:

> Further analyses and additional data collection by us and others suggest that not only are findings ungeneralizable from one sex to the other, but even when, within sex, one simply tries to duplicate the results of a given study, such attempts do not pan out. . . . we cannot say that use of moderators has successfully pinpointed subgroups for whom consistency among diverse tests will be predictable. . . . The empirical basis for recommending moderators as the answer to the search for consistency thus seems more apparent than real. (Wallach & Leggett, 1972, p. 313)

In regard to this last issue, the interaction studies of the sort conducted by Endler and Hunt and Moos, unfortunately, leave perhaps the most important question unanswered: once an individual's idiosyncratic pattern has been identified, can it be used accurately to *predict* consistencies in his subsequent behavior later in the same or (even more interestingly) in similar settings? While the interaction studies have demonstrated the existence of extensive Person × Situation interactions, they have not yet addressed themselves to the challenge of demonstrating that useful predictions can be made a priori about individual consistencies across a set of specified conditions. Such demonstrations are particularly necessary in light of the frequent failures to achieve replications in this domain (e.g., Averill, Olbrich, & Lazarus, 1972; Wallach & Leggett, 1972, pp. 313–314). Moreover, the interaction studies have not in any sense explained the nature of the obtained interactions. Later sections of this paper attempt to analyze the psychological bases for "interaction";

in the absence of such an analysis, an emphasis on interaction is in danger of being little more than the proclamation of a truism.

In sum, when interpreting the meaning of the data on Person × Situation interactions and moderator variables, it has been tempting to treat the obtained interactions as if they had demonstrated that people behave consistently in predictable ways across a wide variety of situations. But demonstrations of the predictive utility of the moderator variable–interaction strategy still lie in the future (e.g., Bem, 1972). The available data on this topic now merely highlight the idiosyncratic organization of behavior within individuals, and hence the uniqueness of stimulus equivalences and response equivalences for each person. Such data provide encouragement for idiographic study (Allport, 1937) but not for the predictive utility of "common" (nomothetic) personality traits.

"Specificity" or Discriminative Facility?

Viewed from the perspective of the traditional personality paradigm, the "specificity" and "inconsistency" found in behavior constitute an embarrassment that is generally attributed to methodological flaws and faulty measurements. Thus empirical evidence concerning the specificity of the relations between social behavior and conditions usually has been interpreted as due to the inadequacies of the tests and measures, faulty sampling, and the limitations of the particular raters or clinical judges. These and many other similar methodological problems undoubtedly are sources of error and seriously limit the degree of consistency that can be observed (e.g., Block, 1968; Emmerich, 1969).

An alternative interpretation, however, and one favored by a specific interaction theory of social behavior, is that the "specificity" so regularly found in studies of noncognitive personality dimensions accurately reflects man's impressive discriminative facility and the inadequacy of the assumption of global dispositions, and not merely the distortions of measurement (Mischel, 1968). The term "discriminative facility" seems to fit the data better than "specificity" and avoids the unfortunate negative semantic connotations of specificity when applied to persons (e.g., the implications of inconsistency, insincerity, fickleness, unreliability; see also Gergen, 1968).

Whereas discriminative facility is highly functional (Gibson, 1969) diminished sensitivity to changing consequences (i.e., indiscriminate responding) may be a hallmark of an organism coping ineffectively. In fact, indiscriminate responding (i.e., "consistent" behavior across situations) tends to be displayed more by maladaptive, severely disturbed, or less mature persons than by well-functioning ones (Moos, 1968). For example, on the basis of their studies of hyperaggressive children undergoing therapeutic treatment, Raush, Dittman, and Taylor (1959) reported: "there appears to be a trend for social behavior to become more related to situational influences with ego development . . . the children seem to have gained in the ability to discriminate between different situations" (p. 368). Yet although relatively more "indiscriminate behavior" tends to be found in more immature and/or severely abnormal persons, its extent should not be exaggerated. Even extremely autistic behavior, for example, is highly discriminative when closely analyzed (e.g., Lovaas, Freitag, Gold, & Kassorla, 1965).

Discrimination, Generalization, and Idiosyncratic Stimulus Meanings

The discriminativeness found in behavior is *not* so great that we cannot recognize continuity in people. It is also not so great that we lime to treat each new behavior from a person as if we never saw anything like it from him before. But the findings remind us that what people do in any situation may be changed dramatically even by relatively trivial alterations in their prior experiences or by slight modifications in the particular features of the immediate situation. Rather than argue about the existence of "consistency," it would be more constructive to analyze and study the cognitive and social learning conditions that seem to foster— and to undermine—its occurrence.

If expected consequences for the performance of responses across situations are largely uncorrelated, the responses themselves should not be expected to covary strongly, as they indeed do not in most empirical studies. When the probable reinforcing consequences to the person for cheating, waiting, or working differ widely across situations depending on the particular task or circumstances, the behavior of others, the likelihood of detection, the probable consequences of being caught, the frustration induced, the value of success, etc., impressive generality will not be found. Conversely, when similar behaviors are expected and supported in numerous situations, consistency will be obtained.

Because most social behaviors produce positive consequences in some situations but negative ones in other contexts, the relatively low associations found among an individual's response patterns even in seemingly similar situations should not be surprising. Consider, for example, the intercorrelations among measures intended to sample dependent behaviors, such as "touching, holding, and being near." If a child has been rewarded regularly at nursery school for "touching, holding, and being near" with his teacher but not with his father at home, a high correlation between dependency measured in the two situations will not be found and should not be expected.

The consequences for similar content expressed in different response modes also tend to be drastically different. If on a projective test a person tells stories full of aggressive themes, he mould be judged to have a healthy fantasy life, but he would be jailed if he enacted those themes in his relations with other people. It therefore should not be surprising that when different response modes are used to sample the individual's behavior (e.g., data from questionnaires, from behavior observation), consistency is even harder to demonstrate (Mischel, 1968).

To the degree that idiosyncratic social learning histories characterize each person's life, idiosyncratic (rather than culturally shared) stimulus equivalences and hence idiosyncratic behavior patterns may be expected. As was noted earlier (Mischel, 1968, p. 190, italics added):

> The phenomena of discrimination and generalization lead to the view that behavior patterns are remarkably situation-specific on the one hand, while also evokable by diverse and often seemingly heterogeneous stimuli on the basis of generalization effects. *The person's prior experiences with related conditions and the exact details of the particular evoking situation determine the meaning of the stimuli*, i.e., their effects on all aspects of his life. Usually generalization effects involve relatively *idiosyncratic* contextual and semantic generalization dimensions and are based on more than gradients of physical stimulus similarity . . . *one must know the properties or meaning that the stimulus has acquired for the subject.* If the history is unknown, the response has to be assessed directly.

Idiosyncratic histories produce idiosyncratic stimulus meanings. In clinical assessment of the individual, it is apparent, for example, that seemingly heterogeneous stimuli may come to elicit similar intense approach or avoidance patterns accompanied by strong arousal (Mischel, 1968). Because the conditions under which stimuli acquire their meaning and power are often both adventitious and unique, and because the dimensions of stimulus and response generalization tend to be idiosyncratic, it may be futile to seek common underlying dimensions of similarity on the basis of which diverse events come to evoke a similar response pattern for all persons. Especially when the individual's prior learning history is unknown, and when he is exposed to multiple and exceedingly complex stimuli as in virtually all life situations, it becomes important to assess the effective stimuli, or "stimuli as coded," which regulate his responses in particular contexts. These stimuli as coded should not be confused with the totality of objective physical events to which he is exposed. It is hardly novel now to assert that the objective distal stimulus impinging on sense organs does not necessarily correspond to the "effective" stimulus; organisms respond selectively to particular aspects of the objective stimulus event (Lawrence, 1959).

The meaning and impact of a stimulus can be modified dramatically by *cognitive transformations*. Such transformations are illustrated in research on the determinants of how long preschool children will actually sit still alone in a chair waiting for a preferred but delayed outcome before they signal with a bell to terminate the waiting period and settle for a less preferred but immediately available gratification (e.g., Mischel, Ebbesen, & Zeiss, 1972). We have been finding that the same child who on one occasion may terminate his waiting in less than half a minute may be capable of waiting by himself for long times on another occasion a few weeks earlier or later, if cognitive and attentional conditions are appropriate (Mischel, 1973a).

For example, if the child is left during the waiting period with the actual reward objects (e.g., pretzels or marshmallows) in front of him, it becomes extremely difficult for him to wait for more than a few moments. But through instructions he can cognitively transform the reward objects in ways that permit him to wait for long time periods (e.g., Mischel & Baker, 1973). If he cognitively transforms the stimulus, for example, by thinking about the pretzel sticks as little brown logs or by thinking about the marshmallows as round white clouds or as cotton balls, he may wait much longer than our graduate student experimenters. Conversely, if the child has been instructed to focus cognitively on the consummatory qualities of the reward objects, such as the pretzel's crunchy, salty taste or the chewy, sweet, soft taste of the marshmallows, he tends to be able to wait only a short time. Similarly, through instruction the children can easily transform the real objects (present in front of them) into a "color picture in your head," or they can transform the picture of the objects (presented on a slide projected on a screen in front of them) into the "real" objects by pretending in imagination that they are actually there on a plate in front of them (Mischel & Moore, 1973b).

The results clearly show that what is in the children's heads—not what is physically in front of them—determines their ability to delay. Regardless of the stimulus in their visual field, if they imagine the real objects as present, they cannot wait long for them. But if they imagine pictures (abstract representations) of the objects, they can wait for long time periods (and even longer than when they are distracting themselves with abstract representations of objects that are comparable but not relevant to the rewards for which they are waiting). Through instructions (administered before the child begins to wait) about what to imagine during the delay period, it is possible to completely alter (indeed, to reverse) the effects of the physically present reward stimuli in the situation and to cognitively control delay behavior with considerable precision. But while in experiments the experimenter provides instructions (which our subjects obligingly followed) about how to construe the stimulus situation, in life the "subject" supplies his own instructions and may transform the situation in many alternative (unpredictable) ways. The ability of individuals to cognitively transform the meaning and impact of stimuli in any given situation (e.g., by self-instructions) makes it even more unlikely that the assessor will discover a priori broad equivalence classes of stimulus meanings for many individuals across many situations, unless they all transform the stimuli in the same way.

Recognition of the idiosyncratic organization of behavior in each person suggests that individually oriented assessments are bound to have very limited success if they try to label a person with generalized trait terms, sort him into diagnostic or type categories, or estimate his average position on average or modal dimensions (Mischel, 1968).[2] Instead, it may be more useful for the clinician to assess the exact conditions that regularly covary with increments or decrements in the problem-producing behaviors for the particular person. For this purpose in a behavioral analysis, one attempts to sample directly the individual's relevant cognitions and behaviors in relation to the conditions of particular current concern:

> In this sense, behavioral assessment involves an exploration of the unique or idiographic aspects of the single case, perhaps to a greater extent than any other approach. Social behavior theory recognizes the individuality of each person and of each unique situation. This is a curious feature when one considers the "mechanistic S-R" stereotypes not infrequently attached by critics to behavioral analyses. *Assessing the acquired meaning of stimuli is the core of social behavior assessment.* . . . (Mischel, 1968, p. 190, italics added)

The above point is often misunderstood. For example, Adinolfi (1971, p. 174) asked: "How then does the social–behavioral critic of current clinical and personality theory propose to determine the stimulus conditions to which the observed is responding?" The answer to this question comes from actively enrolling the "observed" person in the assessment process (Mischel, 1968). In collaboration with the assessor the individual provides hypotheses about the conditions that lead to increases and decreases in his own problematic behaviors. To elaborate, verify, or modify these hypotheses, the stimulus conditions are introduced and systematically varied, and their impact on the person is assessed from his self-report and from other changes in his behavior. In this manner, one can analyze how changes in the particular stimulus conditions are correlated with changes in the behavior of interest. The acquired meanings of a stimulus can only be known by determining what the person does with it verbally and behaviorally, when it is introduced and varied in sampled situations. To reveal the acquired meanings of stimuli, one must assess what the individual says and does when they occur in symbolic form (e.g., when discussed in interviews) and more realistically when presented in hypothetical, role-playing or life situations, as has been discussed in detail (Mischel, 1968). Considerable evidence suggests that in this assessment enterprise, direct information from the person is the best source of data (Mischel, 1972).

Some of the clearest examples of the analysis of stimulus conditions influencing behavior are found in efforts to construct subjective anxiety hierarchies (e.g., Wolpe, 1961). In collaboration with the assessor, the individual can identify the specific conditions that generate fear in him and arrange them on a gradient of severity from least to most intense. For one client, items such as "thinks I only did an hour's work today," "sitting at the movies," "going on a casual stroll," and "staying in bed during the day (even though ill)" were some of the events arranged on a subjective continuum of "guilt"-producing stimuli. Such individually oriented assessments lead naturally to the design of individually oriented treatments intended to provide the best possible conditions for achieving each individual's objectives (Bandura, 1969). In the case of the client suffering from guilt, for example, after the subjective hierarchy of guilt-inducing stimuli had been identified, conditions could be arranged to help him make new responses incompatible with anxiety when the problem-producing stimuli are presented cognitively through thought-inducing instructions.

Uses and Misuses of Traits

In sum, obviously behavior is not entirely situation specific; we do not have to relearn everything in every new situation, we have memories, and our past predisposes our present behavior in critically important and complex ways. Obviously people have characteristics and overall "average" differences in behavior between individuals can be abstracted on many dimensions and used to discriminate among persons for many purposes. Obviously knowing how a person behaved before can help predict how he will behave again in similar contexts. Obviously the impact of any stimulus depends on the organism that experiences it. No one suggests that the organism approaches every new situation with an empty head, nor is it questioned by anyone that different individuals differ markedly in how they deal with most stimulus conditions. What has been questioned (Hunt, 1965; Mischel, 1968) is the utility of inferring broad dispositions from behavioral signs as *the* bases for trying to explain the phenomena of personality and for making useful statements about individual behavior. The available data do *not* imply that different people will not act differently with some consistency in different classes of situations; they *do* imply that the particular classes of conditions must be taken into account far more carefully than in the past, tend to be much narrower than traditional trait theories have assumed, and for purposes of important individual decision making, require highly individualized assessments of stimulus meanings (Mischel, 1968, pp. 235–280). The data also suggest that inferences about global underlying traits and dispositions tend to have less utility for most assessment efforts to predict or therapeutically modify individual behavior than do more economical, alternative analyses based on more direct data such as the person's past behavior in similar situations or his direct self-report.

A critique of traits as inadequate causal explanations and an indictment of the utility of indirect trait inferences for many individually oriented assessment and clinical purposes (Mischel, 1968) does not imply a rejection of their other possible uses. The layman as well as the trait psychologist generates and employs trait constructs. The question becomes not "do traits really exist?" but "when are trait constructs invoked and what are their uses and misuses?"

Research on the layman's attribution of causation to dispositional versus situational factors helps to clarify when person variables and individual differences are used in the everyday formation of impressions. Person (trait) explanations are invoked when the individual's behavior is "distinctive" (Kelley, 1967), that is, when it deviates from others' behavior in the same situation. Thus, behaviors that are at variance with relevant group norms (e.g., success when others fail, failure when others succeed) are attributed to the person or to "internal causes" (e.g., Frieze & Weiner, 1971; Weiner & Kukla, 1970). Conversely, when a person's behavior is consistent with the norms in the situation (when the person succeeds when others succeed, or fails when others fail), his performance is attributed to situational factors such as task difficulty (Weiner et al., 1971).

Traits are constructs which are inferred or abstracted from behavior. When the relations between the observed behavior and the attributed trait are relatively direct, the trait serves essentially as a summary term for the behaviors that have been integrated by the observer. People emit behaviors and these are perceived, integrated, and categorized by those who observe them, including those who emit them. The process of integrating the observed information is receiving much study but is still not completely understood (e.g., Anderson, 1971, 1972). Regardless of the exact genesis of trait impressions, trait labels may serve as summaries (essentially arithmetic averages) for categories of observed behavior (e.g., "dependent on peers," "physically aggressive with siblings"). For purposes of global characterizations of salient personal qualities, broad, highly abstract categories may be useful with minimal moderators or specific situational qualifiers. But for purposes of more specific communication and for prediction of specific behavior in relation to specific conditions, careful discriminative limits must be included.

Estimates of mean past behavior often are the best predictors of future behavior in similar situations, especially when there are no other bases for prediction (Mischel, 1968, 1972). The predictive limitations of traits become evident, however, when one attempts to predict from past behavior to behavior in different new situations. Moreover, when observers categorize an individual's behavior in trait terms, the "salient" (central, mean, primary) features of the behavior may become *the* basis for the categorization, so that the person becomes labeled as "anxious," for example, even if that term accurately characterizes only a small portion of his total social behavior. Then the "moderators" become omitted and the situation-free trait abbreviations that remain may serve more as global stereotypes and broad character sketches than as accurate bases for the prediction of specific behaviors.

When the consistency issue is viewed in terms of the *utility* of inferring broad response tendencies and not in terms of the more metaphysical question of the existence or validity of personality dispositions, it becomes evident that the answer must depend on the particular objective or purpose for which the inference is made. For example, while global trait inferences may have little utility for the prediction of the subject's specific future behavior in specific situations or for the design of specific treatment programs, they may have value for the person himself—for instance, when he must abstract attributes to answer such everyday questions as: Is your assistant reliable? or What kind of person is my psychotherapist? or Might this stranger lurking on the next corner be a murderer? or What are *you* like? Similarly, an indictment of the relative lack of utility of inferring broad dispositions for purposes of predicting and/or therapeutically modifying the individual's behavior does not deny the utility of using such inferences for many other purposes—such as for gross initial screening decisions or for studying average differences between groups of individuals in personality research (Mischel, 1968).

The limitations of traditional personality theories which invoke trait constructs as the psychologist's explanations for behavior should not deflect attention from the importance of the layman's everyday use of trait categories. How do trait categorizations function for the layman? Do they serve him well? For what purposes might they be used? In our research my students and I are asking such questions now. For example, we find that when required to predict a person's behavior and given a choice of how to categorize the available behavioral information, subjects overwhelmingly preferred to organize data in terms of traits rather than settings (Jeffrey & Mischel, 1973). But when the perceiver's purpose was structured as memorizing as much information as possible, setting categories were used. Clearly the functions of trait constructs for the layman deserve serious attention and hopefully will inform us further about the psychological uses and abuses of trait categorization.

From Behavior to the Construction of Personality

As Heider (1958) has noted, in the psychology of common sense the subject goes quickly from act to global internalized disposition. While behavior often may be highly situation specific, it seems equally true that in daily life people tend to construe each other as if they were highly consistent, constructing consistent personalities even on the basis of relatively inconsistent behavioral fragments.

This discrepancy may reflect in part that people go rapidly beyond the observation of *some* consistency which does exist in behavior to the attribution of greater perceived consistencies which they construct (e.g., Mischel, 1969; Schneider, 1973). After these construction systems have been generated, they may be adhered to tenaciously even in the face of seemingly disconfirmatory data (Mischel, 1968, 1969).

Many processes contribute to the construction and maintenance of consistent impressions of others. Tversky and Kahneman (1971), for example, contended that both sophisticated scientists and naive subjects intuitively but often erroneously interpret small samples of observations as if they were highly representative. Moreover, after an initial impression of a person has been formed, observations of his subsequent behavior are biased toward consistency with the initial impression (Hayden & Mischel, 1973). Like the clinician (e.g., Chapman & Chapman, 1969), the layman's impressions may perpetuate consistent but invalid "illusory correlations." There even seems to be a substantial bias of memory for the attributes of behavior in the direction of preexisting cognitive structures or implicit personality theories (D'Andrade, 1970, 1973). Consequently, recall-based trait ratings may yield data that are systematic but unrelated to results based on direct observation of ongoing behavior as it occurs (Shweder, 1972).

The overattribution of consistency may be something people do unto others more than to themselves. Jones and Nisbett (1971) noted that when explaining *other* people's behavior we invoke their consistent personality dispositions: Steve is the sort of person who puts bumper stickers on his car; Jill tripped because she's clumsy. But when asked to explain our *own* behavior we consider specific conditions: "AAA sent me this catchy bumper sticker in the mail" or "I tripped because it was dark." Thus Jones and Nisbett (1971, p. 58) on the basis of some promising preliminary data theorized that "actors tend to attribute the causes of their behavior to stimuli inherent in the situation while observers tend to attribute behavior to stable dispositions of the actor." Jones and Nisbett analyzed many possible reasons for this seemingly paradoxical state of affairs, including the tendency to treat every sample of behavior we observe from another person as if it were modal or typical for him. It thus seems as if traits may be the consistent attributes that *other* people have. When describing other people, we seem to act more like trait theorists, but when we attempt to understand ourselves we function more like social behaviorists. Might there be a warning here for clinicians? Do we pin our clients with consistent dispositional labels and trait explanations more than we do ourselves? If that is true it may be because we have more information about ourselves and the multiplicity, variety, and complexity of the situations we encounter in our own lives, whereas we know others in only limited contexts and therefore tend to over-generalize from their behavior in those instances.

Traits as Causes versus Traits as Summary Labels

According to the traditional trait paradigm, traits are the generalized dispositions in the person that render many stimuli functionally equivalent and that cause the individual to behave consistently across many situations (Allport, 1937). The present view, in contrast, construes the individual as generating diverse behaviors in response to diverse conditions; the emitted behaviors are observed and subsequently integrated cognitively by the performer, as well as by others who perceive him, and are encoded on semantic dimensions in trait terms. Thus while the traditional personality paradigm views traits as the intrapsychic *causes* of behavioral consistency, the present position sees them as the *summary terms* (labels, codes, organizing constructs) applied to observed behavior. In the present view, the study of global traits may ultimately reveal more about the cognitive activity of the trait theorist than about the causes of behavior, but such findings would be of great value in their own right.

COGNITIVE SOCIAL LEARNING
PERSON VARIABLES

The previous sections have considered the limitations of the basic assumptions of traditional global dispositional theories of personality and some of the main misconceptions and issues arising from recent challenges to those assumptions. Progress in the area of personality will require more than criticism of existing positions and hinges on the development of an alternative conceptualization. In this section therefore a set of person variables is proposed, based on theoretical developments in the fields of social learning and cognition.

Given the overall findings on the discriminativeness of behavior and on the complexity of the interactions between the individual and the situation, it seems reasonable in the search for person variables to look more specifically at what the person *constructs* in particular conditions, rather than trying to infer what broad traits he generally *has,* and to incorporate in descriptions of what he does the specific psychological conditions in which the behavior will and will not be expected to occur. What people do, of course, includes much more than motor acts and requires us to consider what they do cognitively and affectively as well as motorically.

The proposed cognitive social learning approach to personality shifts the unit of study from global traits inferred from behavioral signs to the individual's cognitive activities and behavior patterns, studied in relation to the specific conditions that evoke, maintain, and modify them and which they, in turn, change (Mischel, 1968). The focus shifts from attempting to compare and generalize about what different individuals "are like" to an assessment of what they do—behaviorally and cognitively—in relation to the psychological conditions in which they do it. The focus shifts from describing situation-free people with broad trait adjectives to analyzing the specific interactions between conditions and the cognitions and behaviors of interest.

Personality research on social behavior and cognition in recent years has focused mainly on the processes through which behaviors are acquired, evoked, maintained, and modified (e.g., Bandura, 1969; Mischel, 1968). Much less attention has been given to the psychological products within the individual of cognitive development and social learning experiences. Yet a viable psychology of personality demands attention to person variables that are the products of the individual's total history and that in turn mediate the manner in which new experiences affect him.

The proposed person variables are a synthesis of seemingly promising constructs in the areas of cognition and social learning. The selections should be seen as suggestive and open to progressive revision rather than as final. These tentative person variables are not expected to provide ways to accurately predict broadly cross-situational behavioral differences between persons: the discriminativeness and idiosyncratic organization of behavior are facts of nature, not limitations unique to trait theories. But these variables should serve to demonstrate that a social behavior approach to persons does not imply an empty organism.

They should suggest useful ways of conceptualizing and studying specifically how persons mediate the impact of stimuli and generate distinctive complex molar behavior patterns. And they should help to conceptualize person–situation interactions in a theoretical framework based on contributions from both cognitive and behavioral psychology.

The proposed cognitive social learning person variables deal first with the individual's *competencies* to construct (generate) diverse behaviors under appropriate conditions. Next, one must consider the individual's *encoding* and *categorization* of events. Furthermore, a comprehensive analysis of the behaviors a person performs in particular situations requires attention to his *expectancies* about outcomes, the *subjective dues* of such outcomes, and his *self-regulatory systems and plans*. The following five sections discuss each of these proposed person variables. While these variables obviously overlap and interact, each may provide distinctive information about the individual and each may be measured objectively and varied systematically.

Cognitive and Behavioral Construction Competencies

Through direct and observational learning the individual acquires information about the world and his relationship to it. As a result of observing events and attending to the behavior of live and symbolic models (through direct and film-mediated observation, reading, and instruction) in the course of cognitive development the perceiver acquires the potential to generate vast repertoires of organized behavior. While the pervasive occurrence and important consequences of such observational learning have been convincingly demonstrated (e.g., Bandura, 1969; Campbell, 1961), it is less clear how to conceptualize just what gets learned. The phenomena to be encompassed must include such diverse learnings as the nature of sexual gender identity (e.g., Kohlberg, 1966), the structure (or construction) of the physical world (e.g., Piaget, 1954), the social rules and conventions that guide conduct (e.g., Aronfreed, 1968), the personal constructs generated about self and others (e.g., G. Kelly, 1955), and the rehearsal strategies of the observer (Bandura, 1971a). Some theorists have discussed these acquisitions in terms of the products of information processing and of information integration (e.g., Anderson, 1972; Bandura, 1971a; Rumelhart, Lindsey, & Norman, 1971), others in terms of schemata and cognitive templates (e.g., Aronfreed, 1968).

The concept of *cognitive and behavioral construction competencies* seems sufficiently broad to include the vast array of psychological acquisitions of organized information that must be encompassed. The term "constructions" also emphasizes the constructive manner in which information seems to be retrieved (e.g., Neisser, 1967) and the active organization through which it is categorized and transformed (Bower, 1970; Mandler, 1967, 1968). It has become plain that rather than mimicking observed responses or returning memory traces from undisturbed storage vaults, the observer selectively *constructs* (generates) his renditions of "reality." Indeed, research on modeling effects has long recognized that the products of observational learning involve a novel, highly organized synthesis of information rather than a photocopy of specific observed responses (e.g., Bandura, 1971b; Mischel & Grusec, 1966). The present concept of construction competencies should call attention to the person's cognitive activities—the operations and transformations that he performs on information—rather than to a store of finite cognitions and responses that he "has."

Although the exact cognitive processes are far from clear, it is apparent that each individual acquires the capacity to construct a great range of potential behaviors, and different individuals acquire different behavior construction capabilities. The enormous differences between persons in the range and quality of the cognitive and behavioral patterns that they can generate is evident from even casual comparison of the construction potentials of any given individual with those, for example, of an Olympic athlete, a Nobel Prize winner, a retardate, an experienced forger, or a successful actor.

The person's behavior construction potential can be assessed readily by introducing incentives for the most complete constructions that he can render on particular performance tasks. In a sense, the assessment conditions here are identical to those in achievement testing (Wallace, 1966). The same strategy can be used to assess what subjects "know" (i.e., the cognitive constructions they can generate, for example, about abstract and physical properties and relationships as in mathematics and geography) and what they are capable of doing (enacting) in the form of social behaviors. For example, to assess what children had acquired from observing a model, attractive rewards later were offered to them contingent upon their reproducing the model's behaviors (e.g., Bandura, 1965; Grusec & Mischel, 1966). The results showed that the children had acquired a great deal of information from observation of the model which they could reconstruct elaborately but only when given appropriate incentives.

For many purposes, it is valuable to assess the quality and range of the cognitive constructions and behavioral enactments of which the individual is capable. In this vein, rather than assess "typical" behavior, one assesses *potential* behaviors or achievements. One tests what the person *can* do (e.g., Wallace, 1966) rather than what he "usually" does. Indeed one of the most recurrent and promising dimensions of individual differences in research seems to involve the person's *cognitive and behavioral (social) competencies* (e.g., White, 1959; Zigler & Phillips, 1961, 1962). These competencies presumably reflect the degree to which the person can generate adaptive, skillful behaviors that will have beneficial consequences for him. Personality psychology can profit from much greater attention to cognitive and intellectual competencies since these "mental abilities" seem to have much better temporal and cross-situational stability and influence than most of the social traits and motivations traditionally favored in personality research (e.g., Mischel, 1968, 1969).

The relevance of cognitive-intellective competencies for personality seems evident in light of the important, persistent contributions of indices of intelligence to the obtained networks of personality correlations (Campbell & Fiske, 1959; Mischel, 1968). In spite of extensive efforts to minimize or "partial out" the role of intelligence in personality studies, for example, cognitive competencies (as tested by "mental age" and IQ tests) tend to be among the very best predictors of later social and interpersonal adjustment (e.g., Anderson, 1960). Presumably, brighter, more competent people experience more interpersonal success and better work achievements and hence become more positively assessed by themselves and by others on the evaluative "good–bad" dimension which is so ubiquitous in trait ratings (e.g., Vernon, 1964). Cognitive achievements and intellective potential, as measured by mental age or IQ tests, also are receiving a central place in current cognitive–developmental theories (e.g., Kohlberg, 1969) and presumably are an important ingredient of such concepts as "ego strength" and "ego development." Indeed, it is tempting to speculate that the pervasive and substantial "first factor" found on tests like the MMPI (Block, 1965), often labeled with terms connoting "adjustment" at the positive end and maladaptive character structure at the negative end, reflects to a considerable degree the individual's level of cognitive-social competence and achievement. To the degree that certain demographic variables (e.g., socioeconomic class, high school graduation) reflect the individual's construction capacities and achievements, they also may be expected to predict "adjustment" and interpersonal competencies, as they often do (e.g., Robbins, 1972). The assessment of competence in response to specific problematic situations in the direct manner developed by Goldfried and D'Zurilla (1969) seems especially promising.

The relative stability of the person's construction capacities may be one of the important contributors to the impression of consistency in personality. The fact that cognitive skills and behavior-generating capacities tend to be relatively enduring is reflected in the relatively high stability found in performances closely related to cognitive and intellectual variables, as has been stressed before (Mischel, 1968, 1969). The individual who knows how to be assertive with waiters, for example, or who knows how to solve certain kinds of interpersonal problems competently, or who excels in singing, is *capable* of such performances enduringly.

Encoding Strategies and Personal Constructs

From the perspective of personality psychology, an especially important component of information processing concerns the perceiver's ways of encoding and grouping information from stimulus inputs. As discussed in earlier sections, people can readily perform *cognitive transformations* on stimuli (Mischel & Moore, 1973a), focusing on selected aspects of the objective stimulus (e.g., the taste versus the shape of a food object): such selective attention, interpretation, and categorization substantially alter the impact the stimulus exerts on behavior (see also Geer, Davison, & Gatchel, 1970; Schachter, 1964). Likewise, the manner in which perceivers encode and selectively attend to observed behavioral sequences greatly influences what they learn and subsequently can do (Bandura, 1971a, 1971b). Clearly, different persons may group and encode the same events and behaviors in different ways. At a molar level, such individual differences are especially evident in the personal constructs individuals employ (e.g., Argyle & Little, 1972; G. Kelly, 1955) and in the kinds of information to which they selectively attend (Mischel, Ebbesen, & Zeiss, 1973).

The behaviorally oriented psychologist eschews inferences about global dispositions and focuses instead on the particular stimuli and behaviors of interest. But what are "the stimuli and behaviors of interest?" Early versions of behaviorism attempted to circumvent this question by simplistic definitions in terms of clearly delineated motor "acts" (such as bar press) in response to clicks and lights. As long as the behaviors studied were those of lower animals in experimenter-arranged laboratory situations, the units of "behavior" and "stimuli" remained manageable with fairly simple operational definitions. More recent versions of behavior theory, moving from cat, rat, and pigeon confined in the experimenter's apparatus to people in exceedingly complex social situations, have extended the domain of studied behavior much beyond motor acts and muscle twitches; they seek to encompass what people do cognitively, emotionally, and interpersonally, not merely their arm, leg, and mouth movements. Now the term "behavior" has been expanded to include virtually anything that an organism does, overtly or covertly, in relation to extremely complex social and interpersonal events. Consider, for example, "aggression," "anxiety," "defense," "dependency," "self-concepts," "self-control," "self-reinforcement." Such categories go considerably beyond self-evident behavior descriptions. A category like aggression involves inferences about the subject's intentions (e.g., harming another versus accidental injury) and abstractions about behavior, rather than mere physical description of actions and utterances.

A focus on behavior must not obscure the fact that even the definition and selection of a behavior unit for study requires grouping and categorizing. In personality research, the psychologist does the construing, and he includes and excludes events in the units he studies, depending on his interests and objectives. He selects a category—such as "delay of gratification," for example—and studies its behavioral referents. In personality assessment, however, it becomes quickly evident that the subject (like the psychologist) also groups events into categories and organizes them actively into meaningful units. The layman usually does not describe his experience with operational definitions: he categorizes events in terms of his *personal constructs* (G. Kelly, 1955), and these may or may not overlap either with those of the psychologist or of other individuals. As previously noted (Jeffery & Mischel, 1973), observers tend to group information about persons with dispositional categories (such as "honest," "intolerant," "freaky," "do gooder"). Skepticism about the utility of traditional trait constructs regarding the subject's broad dispositions in no way requires one to ignore the subject's constructs about his own and others' characteristics. People invoke traits and other dispositions as ways of describing and explaining their experience and themselves, just as professional psychologists do, and it would be strange if we tried to define out of existence the personal constructs and other concepts, perceptions, and experiences of the individuals whom we are studying. The study of personal construct systems (e.g., Little & Stephens, 1973), of implicit personality theories (e.g., Hamilton, 1971; Schneider, 1973), and of self-concepts (e.g., Gergen, 1968) promises to illuminate an important set of still poorly understood person variables.

Cognitive consistency tends to be enhanced by selective attention and coding processes that filter new information in a manner that permits it to be integrated with existing cognitive structures (e.g., Norman, 1969). Cognitive processes that facilitate the construction and maintenance of perceived consistency (e.g., D'Andrade, 1970; Hayden & Mischel, 1973) have been mentioned earlier and are elaborated elsewhere (Mischel, 1968, 1969). After information has been integrated with existing cognitive structures and becomes part of long-term memory, it remains available enduringly and exerts further stabilizing effects. For example, the individual's subjective conception of his own identity and continuity presumably rests heavily on his ability to remember (construct) subjectively similar behaviors on his part over long time periods and across many situations. That is, the individual can abstract the common elements of his behavior over time and across settings, thereby focusing on his more enduring qualities.

There is considerable evidence that people categorize their own personal qualities in relatively stable trait terms (e.g., on self-ratings and self-report questionnaires). These self-categorizations, while often only complexly and tenuously related to nonverbal behavior, may be relatively durable and generalized (Mischel, 1968, 1969). Such stable styles of self-presentation and self-description may be reflected in personality test "response sets" like social desirability (Edwards, 1957), and in tendencies to depict oneself in relatively positive or negative terms found in the behavior of so-called "repressers" versus "sensitizers" on the Byrne (1961) Repression–Sensitization Scale (Mischel, Ebbesen, & Zeiss, 1973). While traditional personality research has focused primarily on exploring the correlates of such self-categorizations, in the present view they comprise merely one kind of person variable.

Behavior–Outcome and Stimulus–Outcome Expectancies

So far the person variables considered deal with what the individual is capable of doing and how he categorizes events. To move from potential behaviors to actual performance, from construction capacity and constructs to the construction of behavior in specific situations, requires attention to the determinants of performance. For this purpose, the person variables of greatest interest are the subject's expectancies. While it is often informative to know what an individual *can* do and how he construes events and himself, for purposes of specific prediction of behavior in a particular situation it is essential to consider his specific expectancies about the consequences of different behavioral possibilities in that situation. For many years personality research has searched for individual differences on the psychologist's hypothesized dimensions while neglecting the subject's own expectancies (hypotheses). More recently, it seems increasingly clear that the expectancies of the subject are central units for psychology (e.g., Bolles, 1972; Estes, 1972; Irwin, 1971; Rotter, 1954). These hypotheses guide the person's selection (choice) of behaviors from among the enormous number which he is capable of constructing within any situation.

On the basis of direct experience, instructions, and observational learning, people develop expectancies about environmental contingencies (e.g., Bandura, 1969). Since the expectancies that are learned within a given situation presumably reflect the objective contingencies in that situation, an expectancy construct may seem superfluous. The need for the expectancy construct as a person variable becomes evident, however, when one considers individual differences in response to the same situational contingencies due to the different expectancies that each person brings to the situation. An expectancy construct is justified by the fact that the person's expectancies (inferred from statements) may not be in agreement with the objective contingencies in the situation. Yet behavior may be generated in light of such expectancies, as seen, for example, in any verbal conditioning study when a subject says plural nouns on the erroneous hypothesis that the experimenter is reinforcing them.

In theories based on lower animal behavior, the expectancy construct has served as a limited heuristic (e.g., Bolles, 1972), since rats and pigeons cannot tell us their expectancies. Fortunately, humans are not so handicapped and under appropriate assessment conditions are willing and able to externalize their expectancies. Hence the expectancy construct applied to human rather than animal learning leads readily to measurement operations and to research strategies that can take account directly of the subject's hypotheses. Empirically, since direct self-reports seem to be one of the best data sources about the individual (Mischel, 1968, 1972), it should be possible to fruitfully assess behavior–outcome expectancies by asking the subject.

One type of expectancy concerns *behavior–outcome relations* under particular conditions. These *behavior–outcome expectancies* (hypotheses, contingency rules) represent "the if___; then___" relations between behavioral alternatives and probable outcomes anticipated with regard to particular behavioral possibilities in particular situations. In any given situation, the person will generate the response pattern which he expects is most likely to lead to the most subjectively valuable outcomes (consequences) in that situation (e.g., Mischel, 1966; Rotter, 1954). In the absence of new information about the behavior–outcome expectancies in any situation the individual's performance will depend on his previous behavior–outcome expectancies in similar situations. This point is illustrated in a study (Mischel & Staub, 1965) which showed that presituational expectancies significantly affect choice behavior in the absence of situational information concerning probable performance–outcome relationships. But the Mischel and Staub study also showed that new information about behavior–outcome relations in the particular situation may quickly overcome the effects of presituational expectancies, so that highly specific situational expectancies become the dominant influences on performance.

When the expected consequences for performance change, so does behavior, as seen in the discriminative nature of responding which was elaborated in earlier sections and documented elsewhere (Mischel, 1968). But in order for changes in behavior–outcome relations to affect behavior substantially, the person must recognize them. In the context of operant conditioning, it has become evident that the subject's awareness of the behavior–outcome relationship crucially affects the ability of response consequences (reinforcements) to modify his complex performances (e.g., Spielberger & DeNike, 1966). As previously stressed, the essence of adaptive performance is the recognition and appreciation of new contingencies. To cope with the environment effectively, the individual must recognize new contingencies as quickly as possible and reorganize his behavior in the light of the new expectancies. Strongly established behavior–outcome expectancies with respect to a response pattern may constrain an individual's ability to adapt to changes in contingencies. Indeed, "defensive reactions" may be seen in part as a failure to adapt to new contingencies because the individual is still behaving in response to old contingencies that are no longer valid. The "maladaptive" individual is behaving in accord with expectancies that do not adequately represent the actual behavior–outcome rules in his current life situation.

In the present view, the effectiveness of response-contingent reinforcements (i.e., operant conditioning) rests on their ability to modify behavior–outcome expectancies. When information about the response pattern required for reinforcement is conveyed to the subject by instructions, "conditioning" tends to occur much more readily than when the subject must experience directly the reinforcing contingencies actually present in the operant training situation. For example, accurate instructions about the required response and the reinforcement schedule to which subjects would be exposed exerted far more powerful effects on performance than did the reinforcing contingencies (Kaufman, Baron, & Kopp, 1966). Presumably, such instructions exert their effects by altering response–outcome expectancies. To the extent that information about new response–reinforcement contingencies can be conveyed to motivated human beings more parsimoniously through instructions or observational experiences than through operant conditioning procedures (e.g., Kaufman et al., 1966), an insistence upon direct "shaping" may reflect an unfortunate (and wasteful) failure to discriminate between the animal laboratory and the human condition.

A closely related second type of expectancy concerns *stimulus–outcome relations*. As noted previously in the discussion of generalization and discrimination, the outcomes expected for any behavior hinge on a multitude of stimulus conditions that moderate the probable consequences of any pattern of behavior. These stimuli ("signs") essentially "predict" for the person other events that are likely to occur. More precisely, the individual learns (through direct and observational experiences) that certain events (cues, stimuli) predict certain other events.

This concept of *stimulus–outcome expectancy* is similar to the S–S* expectancy representing stimulus–outcome contingencies proposed by Bolles (1972) in the context of animal learning.

Stimulus–outcome expectancies seem especially important person variables for understanding the phenomena of classical conditioning. For example, through the contiguous association of a light and painful electric shock in aversive classical conditioning the subject learns that the light predicts shock. If the product of classical conditioning is construed as a stimulus–outcome expectancy, it follows that any information which negates that expectancy will eliminate the conditioned response. In fact, when subjects are informed that the "conditioned stimuli" will no longer be followed by pain-producing events, their conditioned emotional reactions are quickly eliminated (e.g., Grings & Lockhart, 1963). Conversely, when subjects were told that a particular word would be followed by shock, they promptly developed conditioned heart-rate responses (Chatterjee & Eriksen, 1962). In the same vein, but beyond the conditioning paradigm, if subjects learn to generate "happy thoughts" when faced by stimuli that otherwise would frustrate them beyond endurance, they can manage to tolerate the "aversive" situation with equanimity (Mischel, Ebbesen, & Zeiss, 1972). Outside the artificial confines of the laboratory in the human interactions of life, the "stimuli" that predict outcomes often are the social behaviors of others in particular contexts. The meanings attributed to those stimuli hinge on a multitude of learned correlations between behavioral signs and outcomes.

Just as correlational personality research yields a host of validity associations between behavioral "signs" from persons in one context and their behavior in other situations, so does the perceiver's learning history provide him with a vast repertoire of meaningful signs. For example, as research on person perception suggests, "shifty eyes," "tight lips," "lean and hungry looks," obese body build, age, sex, and an enormous number of even subtler behavioral cues (e.g., regarding the status and power of others) come to predict for observers other correlated behaviors. If it were possible to compute them, many of these correlations probably would not average more than the .30 "personality coefficient" (Mischel, 1968) typically found in correlational personality research, but that may be sufficiently accurate (especially on an intermittent schedule) to assure their persistent use. Some of these stimulus–outcome associations presumably reflect the perceiver's idiosyncratic learning history and his own evolving personal rules about stimulus meanings. Many of these associations, however, are likely to be widely shared by members of a common culture and probably depend importantly on the transcultural semantic associations discussed by D'Andrade (1970) and Shweder (1971, 1972). An adequate study of stimulus–outcome expectancies therefore would require attention to the rule system of the individual as well as to the shared "sign" grammar of the culture and of the transcultural lexicon structure.

Both behavior–outcome and stimulus–outcome expectancies depend on inferences about the *intentions* motivating behavior (i.e., its perceived causes). For example, a person's reactions to a physical blow from another will crucially depend on whether it was perceived as accidental or deliberate. Similarly, whether praise and attention produces in the recipient a warm glow (and "conditioning" of his preceding behaviors) or suspicion (and a rebuff) depends on whether the behaviors are perceived as sincere or as ingratiating (Jones, 1964). Extremely subtle social and interpersonal cues affect the interpretation of the motivation (and hence the impact) of these complex human behaviors.

Although expectancy constructs often have been proposed, some of the main formulations have been based entirely on animal research (e.g., Bolles, 1972) which makes their relevance for human personality remote. Rotter's (1954) "subjective expectancy" construct was an important and theoretically influential exception. However, it deals only with one type of expectancy (similar to the present "behavior–outcome expectancies"); it does not consider stimulus–outcome expectancies. Moreover, Rotter's formulation focuses on "generalized expectancies" which are functionally similar to generalized traits and are not posited in the present approach.

In the present view, the person's expectancies mediate the degree to which his behavior shows cross-situational consistency or discriminativeness. When the expected consequences for the performance of responses across situations are not highly correlated, the responses themselves should not covary strongly (Mischel, 1968). As previously noted, since most social behaviors lead to positive consequences in some situations but not in other contexts, highly discriminative specific expectancies tend to be developed and the relatively low correlations typically found among a person's response patterns across situations become understandable (Mischel, 1968). Expectancies also will not become generalized across response modes when the consequences for similar content expressed in different response modes are sharply different, as they are in most life circumstances (Mischel, 1968). Hence expectancies tend to become relatively specific, rather than broadly generalized. Although a person's expectancies (and hence performances) tend to be highly discriminative, there certainly is some generalization of expectancies, but their patterning in the individual tends to be idiosyncratically organized to the extent that the individual's history is unique. (See the earlier section in this paper on generalization, discrimination, and idiosyncratic stimulus meanings.)

While behavior–outcome and stimulus–outcome expectancies seem viable person variables, it would be both tempting and hazardous to transform them into generalized trait-like dispositions by endowing them with broad cross-situational consistency or removing them from the context of the specific stimulus conditions on which they depend. At the empirical level, "generalized expectancies" tend to be generalized only within relatively narrow, restricted limits (e.g., Mischel & Staub, 1965; Mischel, Ebbesen, & Zeiss, 1973). As was noted before in this paper, for example, the generality of "locus of control" is in fact limited, with distinct, unrelated expectancies found for positive and negative outcomes and with highly specific behavioral correlates for each (Mischel, Zeiss, & Zeiss, 1974). If expectancies are converted into global trait-like dispositions and extracted from their close interaction with situational conditions, they are likely to become just as useless as their many theoretical predecessors. On the other hand, if they are construed as relatively specific (and modifiable) "if ___, then___" hypotheses about contingencies, it becomes evident that they exert important effects on behavior (e.g., Mischel & Staub, 1965).

SUBJECTIVE STIMULUS VALUES

Even if individuals have similar expectancies, they may select to perform different behaviors because of differences in the *subjective values* of the outcomes which they expect. For example, given that all persons expect that approval from a therapist depends on verbalizing particular kinds of self-references, there may be differences in the frequency of such verbalizations due to differences in the perceived value of obtaining the therapist's approval. Such differences reflect the degree to which different individuals value the response-contingent outcome. Therefore it is necessary to consider still another person variable: the subjective (perceived) value for the individual of particular classes of events, that is, his stimulus preferences and aversions. This unit refers to stimuli that have acquired the power to induce positive or negative emotional states in the person and to function as incentives or reinforcers for his behavior. The subjective value of any stimulus pattern may be acquired and modified through instructions and observational experiences as well as through direct experiences (Bandura, 1969).

Stimulus values can be assessed by measuring the individual's actual choices in life-like situations as well as his verbal preferences or ratings (e.g., Mischel, 1966 ; Mischel & Grusec, 1966). Verbal reports (e.g., on questionnaires) about values and interests also may supply valuable information about the individual's preferences and aversions, and appear to provide some of the more temporally stable data in the domain of personality (E. L. Kelly, 1955; Strong, 1955). Alternatively, subjects may be asked to rank-order actual rewards (Rotter, 1954), or the reinforcement value of particular stimuli may be assessed directly by observing their effects on the individual's performance (e.g., Gewirtz & Baer, 1958).

Reinforcement (incentive) preferences may also be assessed by providing individuals opportunities to select the outcomes they want from a large array of alternatives, as when patients earn tokens which they may exchange for objects or activities: the "price" they are willing to pay for particular outcomes provides an index of their subjective value (e.g., Ayllon & Azrin, 1965). The concept that any behavior which has a high natural frequency of occurrence can serve as a reinforcer for other less likely behaviors (Premack, 1965) also suggests that subjective reinforcers may be discovered by assessing the individual's naturally occurring high frequency behaviors in particular situations (Mischel, 1968).

A comprehensive assessment of stimulus values must include attention to stimuli that have acquired strong emotion-eliciting powers, as in the conditioned autonomic reactions seen in intense fears. For this purpose, specific self-report inventories, physiological measures, and direct behavior sampling of approach and avoidance behavior in response to the real or symbolically presented emotional stimulus may all be useful (Mischel, 1968).

The measurement operations for assessing stimulus values require considerable specificity. Just as the probable consequences of any behavior pattern hinge on a host of specific moderating considerations, so does the affective value (valence) of any stimulus depend on the exact conditions—in the person and in the situation—in which it occurs. The many variables known to affect the emotional meaning and valence of a stimulus include its context, sequencing, and patterning (e.g., Helson, 1964); social comparison processes (e.g., Festinger, 1945); and the cognitive labels the person assigns to his own emotional arousal state (Schachter & Singer, 1962). Thus, like instrumental responses, emotional reactions also tend to become far more discriminative than dispositional theories have assumed. Lazarus (1963), for example, has noted the specificity of sexual fears in frigid women. For instance, one woman could calmly imagine herself engaged in certain sexual caresses, but only if they occurred in the dark. Or consider the pilot who became debilitatingly anxious when flying, but only when his plane was higher than 9,000 feet (White, 1964), or the young woman who had asthmatic attacks mostly after she had contacts with her mother (Metcalf, 1956). Good illustrations of the analysis of stimulus conditions influencing emotional responses come from attempts to create subjective anxiety hierarchies (e.g., Wolpe, 1961).

Self-Regulatory Systems and Plans

While behavior is controlled to a considerable extent by externally administered consequences for actions, the individual also regulates his own behavior by self-imposed goals (standards) and self-produced consequences. Even in the absence of external constraints and social monitors, persons set performance goals for themselves and react with self-criticism or self-satisfaction to their behavior depending on how well it matches their expectations and criteria. The concept of self-imposed achievement standards is seen in Rotter's (1954) "minimal goal" construct and in more recent formulations of self-reinforcing functions (e.g., Bandura, 1971c; Kanfer, 1971; Kanfer & Marston, 1963; Mischel, 1968, 1973a).

The essence of self-regulatory systems is the subject's adoption of *contingency rules* that guide his behavior in the absence of, and sometimes in spite of, immediate external situational pressures. Such rules specify the kinds of behavior appropriate (expected) under particular conditions, the performance levels (standards, goals) which the behavior must achieve, and the consequences (positive and negative) of attaining or failing to reach those standards. Each of these components of self-regulation may be different for different individuals, depending on their unique earlier histories or on more recently varied instructions or other situational information.

Some of the components in self-regulation have been demonstrated in studies of goal setting and self-reinforcement (e.g., Bandura & Whalen, 1966; Bandura & Perloff, 1967; Mischel & Liebert, 1966). Perhaps the most dramatic finding from these studies is that even young children will not indulge themselves with freely available immediate gratifications but, instead, follow rules that regulate conditions under which they may reinforce themselves. Thus, children, like adults, far from being simply hedonistic, make substantial demands of themselves and impose complex contingencies upon their own behavior. The stringency or severity of self-imposed criteria is rooted in the observed standards displayed by salient models as well as in the individual's direct socialization history (e.g., Mischel & Liebert, 1966), although after they have been adopted, the standards may be retained with considerable persistence.

After the standards (terminal goals) for conduct in a particular situation have been selected, the often long and difficult route to self-reinforcement and external reinforcement with material rewards is probably mediated extensively by covert symbolic activities, such as praise and self-instructions, as the individual reaches subgoals. When individuals imagine reinforcing and noxious stimuli, their behavior appears to be influenced in the same manner as when such stimuli are externally presented (e.g., Cautela, 1971). These covert activities serve to maintain goal-directed work until the performance matches or exceeds the person's terminal standards (e.g., Meichenbaum, 1971). Progress along the route to a goal is also mediated by self-generated distractions and cognitive operations through which the person can transform the aversive "self-control" situation into one which he can master effectively (e.g., Mischel et al., 1972; Mischel & Moore, 1973a, 1973b). While achievement of important goals leads to positive self-appraisal and self-reinforcement, failure to reach significant self-imposed standards may lead the individual to indulge in psychological self-lacerations (e.g., self-condemnation). The anticipation of such failure probably leads to extensive anxiety, while the anticipation of success may help to sustain performance, although the exact mechanisms of self-regulation still require much empirical study.

Self-reactions and self-regulation also are influenced by the person's affective state. Following positive experiences, individuals become much more benign both toward themselves and others than after negative experiences. For example, after success experiences or positive mood inductions, there is greater selective attention to positive information about the self (Mischel et al., 1973), greater noncontingent self-gratification (e.g., Mischel, Coates, & Raskoff, 1968; Moore, Underwood, & Rosenhan, 1973), and greater generosity (e.g., Isen, Horn, & Rosenhan, 1973).

In conceptualizing the organization of complex self-regulatory behavior, it will be necessary to consider the individual's "priority rules" for determining the *sequencing* of behavior and "stop rules" for the *termination* of a particular sequence of behavior. The ideas concerning "plans" as hierarchical processes which control the order in which an organism performs a sequence of operations, proposed by Miller, Galanter, and Pribram (1960), seem relevant. Subjectively, we do seem to generate plans, and once a plan is formed (to go on a trip, to marry, to move to a new job, to write a paper) a whole series of sub-routines follows. While intuitively plausible, the concept of plans has not yet stimulated the necessary personality-oriented cognitive research. Promising steps toward the study of plans are the concepts of behavioral intentions (Dulany, 1962), intention statements, and contracts (e.g., Kanfer, Cox, Greiner, & Karoly, 1973). Although self-instructions and intention statements are likely to be essential components of the individual's plans and the hierarchical organization of his self-regulatory behavior, at present these topics provide perhaps the largest void and the greatest challenge in personality psychology.

To summarize, a comprehensive approach to person variables must take account of the individual's self-regulatory systems. These systems include: the rules that specify goals or performance standards in particular situations; the consequences of achieving or failing to achieve those criteria; self-instructions and cognitive stimulus transformations to achieve the self-control necessary for goal attainment; and organizing rules (plans) for the sequencing and termination of complex behavioral patterns in the absence of external supports and, indeed, in the face of external hindrances.

Overview of Personal Variables

In sum, individual differences in behavior may reflect differences in each of the foregoing person variables and in their interactions, summarized in Table 16.1. First, people differ in their *construction competencies*. Even if people have similar expectancies about the most appropriate response pattern in a particular situation and are uniformly motivated to make it, they may differ in whether or not (and how well) they *can* do it, that is, in their ability to construct the preferred response. For example, due to differences in skill and prior learning, individual differences may arise in interpersonal problem solving, empathy and role taking, or cognitive–intellective achievements. Response differences also may reflect differences in how individuals *categorize* a particular situation (i.e., in how they encode, group, and label the events that comprise it)

TABLE 16.1. Summary of Cognitive Social Learning Person Variables

1. Constuction competencies: ability to construct (generate) particular cognitions and behaviors. Related to measures of IQ, social and cognitive (mental) maturity and competence, ego development, social–intellectual achievements and skills. Referes to what the subject knows and *can* do.

2. Encoding strategies and personal constructs: units for categorizing events and for self-descriptions.

3. Behavior–outcome and stimulus–outcomes expectancies in particular situations.

4. Subjective stimulus values: motivating and arousing stimuli, incentives, and aversions.

5. Self-regulatory systems and plans: rules and self-reactions for performance and for the organization fo complex behavior sequences.

and in how they construe themselves and others. Differences between persons in their performance in any situation depend on their behavior–outcome and stimulus–outcome *expectancies*, that is, differences in the expected outcomes associated with particular responses or stimuli in particular situations. Performance differences also may be due to differences in the subjective *values* of the outcomes expected in the situation. Finally, individual differences may be due to differences in the *self-regulatory systems* and plans that each person brings to the situation.

COGNITIVE SOCIAL LEARNING VIEW OF INTERACTION

In this final section, some issues in current theorizing about personality will be reconsidered and interpreted in light of the proposed cognitive social learning person variables. These issues concern the role of individual differences and the specific interaction of person variables and situations.

When Do Individual Differences Make a Difference?

From the present viewpoint, the conditions or "situational variables" of the psychological environment provide the individual with information which influences the previously discussed person variables, thereby affecting cognitive and behavioral activities under those conditions. "Situations" thus affect behavior insofar as they influence such person variables as the individual's encoding, his expectancies, the subjective value of stimuli, or the ability to generate response patterns. In light of the proposed set of person variables, it is now possible to return to the question of when situations are most likely to exert powerful effects and, conversely, when person variables are likely to be most influential.

Psychological "situations" and "treatments" are powerful to the degree that they lead all persons to construe the particular events the same way, induce *uniform* expectancies regarding the most appropriate response pattern, provide adequate incentives for the performance of that response pattern, and instill the skills necessary for its satisfactory construction and execution. Conversely, situations and treatments are weak to the degree that they are not uniformly encoded, do not generate uniform expectancies concerning the desired behavior, do not offer sufficient incentives for its performance, or fail to provide the learning conditions required for successful construction of the behavior.

Individual differences can determine behavior in a given situation most strongly when the situation is ambiguously structured (as in projective testing) so that subjects are uncertain about how to categorize it and have no clear expectations about the behaviors most likely to be appropriate (normative, reinforced) in that situation. To the degree that the situation is "unstructured," the subject will expect that virtually *any* response from him is equally likely to be equally appropriate (i.e., will lead to similar consequences), and variance from individual differences will be greatest. Conversely, when subjects expect that only *one* response will be reinforced (e.g., only one "right" answer on an achievement test, only one correct response for the driver when the traffic light turns red) and that no other responses are equally good, and all subjects are motivated and capable of making the appropriate response, then individual differences will be minimal and situational effects prepotent. To the degree that subjects are exposed to powerful treatments, the role of individual differences will be minimized. Conversely, when treatments are weak, ambiguous, or trivial, individual differences in person variables should exert significant effects.

There have been several empirical demonstrations of these points. Mischel and Staub (1965) examined some of the conditions determining the interaction and relative importance of individual differences and situations. Adolescent subjects were assessed on a measure of their expectancies for success in ability areas. Three weeks later, they worked on a series of problems and in one treatment obtained success, in a second, failure, and in a third, no information. Next, they had to make many choices, including one between a noncontingent but less preferred reward and a more preferred reward whose attainment was contingent upon their successful performance on a task similar to the one on which they had previously either succeeded, failed, or received no information. On this choice, situational success and failure had the expected effects: subjects who had succeeded chose much more often to work for the contingent preferred reward than did those who had failed. The effects of situational success and failure were so strong that they wiped out the role of individual differences in preexperimental expectancy for success. But in the "no-information" condition (in which subjects obtained no feedback about their performance quality in the situation) preexperimental expectancy was a highly significant determinant of their choice to work for contingent rewards. Thus situational manipulations which provided new expectancies minimized the effects of relevant preexisting individual differences, but when situational variables were weak or ambiguous (the no-information about-performance condition) the expectancies that persons brought to the situation affected their behavior. Similar conclusions come from a recent study investigating the influence of success and failure experiences on subsequent selective attention to information about the self (Mischel et al., 1973).

The complex social settings of life also may be construed as varying in the degree to which they prescribe and limit the range of expected and acceptable behavior for persons in particular roles and settings and hence permit the expression of individual differences (e.g., Barker, 1966). In some settings the rules and prescriptions for enacting specific role behaviors impose narrow limits on the range of possible behaviors (e.g., in church, at school, in a theatre, at a conference), while in others the range of possible behaviors is broad and often the individual can select, structure, and reorganize situations with minimal external constraints. Because in particular settings certain response patterns are reinforced while others are not, different settings become the occasion for particular behaviors in different degrees. Raush (1965), for example, found that in a sample of normal American boys, friendly acts led to unfriendly responses in 31% of the instances in game situations but in only 4% of the time at mealtimes.

Person–condition interactions are never static, but environmental stabilities can be identified which help to account for continuities in behavior and permit useful predictions (e.g., Mischel, 1968). While it would be bizarre to ignore the person in the psychology of personality, behavior often may be predicted and controlled efficaciously from knowledge about relevant stimulus conditions, especially when those conditions are powerful (Mischel, 1968). The potency of predictions based on knowledge of stimulus conditions is seen, for example, in predictive studies regarding posthospital prognosis for mental patients. Of special interest are studies which revealed that the type, as well as the severity, of psychiatric symptoms depended strikingly on whether the person was in the hospital or in the community, with little consistency in behavior across changing situations (Ellsworth, Foster, Childers, Gilberg, & Kroeker, 1968). Moreover, accurate predictions of posthospital adjustment hinged on knowledge of the environment in which the ex-patient will be living in the community, such as the availability of jobs and family support, rather than on any measured person variables or in-hospital behavior (e.g., Fairweather, 1967). In another context, predictions of intellectual achievement are greatly improved if they take account of the degree to which the child's environment supports (models and reinforces) intellectual development (Wolf, 1966). Finally, when powerful treatments are developed, such as modeling and desensitization therapies for phobias, predictions about outcomes are best when based on knowing the treatment to which the individual is assigned (e.g., Bandura, Blanchard, & Ritter, 1969). On the other hand, when relevant situational information is absent or minimal, or when predictions are needed about individual differences in response to the same conditions, or when treatment variables are weak, information about person variables becomes essential.

Specific Interactions between Behavior and Conditions

Traditionally, trait research has studied individual differences in response to the "same" situation. But some of the most striking differences between persons may be found not by studying their responses to the same situation but by analyzing their selection and construction of stimulus conditions. In the conditions of life outside the laboratory the psychological "stimuli" that people encounter are neither questionnaire items, nor experimental instructions, nor inanimate events, but they involve people and reciprocal relationships (e.g., with spouse, with boss, and with children). The person continuously influences the "situations" of his life as well as being affected by them in a mutual, organic two-way interaction. These interactions reflect not only the person's reactions to conditions but also his active selection and modification of conditions through his own cognitions and actions.

As the analysis of complex social interactions illustrates (e.g., Patterson & Cobb, 1971), the person continuously selects, changes, and generates conditions just as much as he is affected by them. The mutual interaction between person and conditions (so easily forgotten when one searches for generalized traits on paper-and-pencil tests) cannot be overlooked when behavior is studied in the interpersonal contexts in which it is evoked, maintained, and modified.

Generally, changes in behavior toward others tend to be followed by reciprocal changes in the behavior of those others (Raush et al., 1959). In Raush's (1965) studies of naturalistic interactions, for example, "the major determinant of an act was the immediately preceding act. Thus if you want to know what child B will do, the best single predictor is what child A did to B the moment before" (p. 492). Construed from the viewpoint of child A, this means that A's own behavior determines B's reactions to him. In that sense, the person is generating his own conditions. Such subject variables as the person's expectancies, self-regulatory rules, plans, and constructs presumably guide the situations which he selects, generates, and structures for himself.

The proposed cognitive social learning approach to person variables emphasizes most strongly the need to study the individual's behavior in specific interaction with particular conditions. Indeed, the conceptualization of behavior, whether psychologist defined (as in research) or subject defined (as in clinical, individually oriented assessment) must be embedded in relation to the specific conditions in which the behavior occurs. Rather than talk about "behavior," it may he more useful to conceptualize *behavior–contingency units* that link specific patterns of behavior to the conditions in which they may be expected. Accurate descriptions require specifying as precisely as possible the response mode of the behavior as well as the contingencies in which it is expected to be of high or low frequency, as was discussed in earlier sections on situational moderator variables. Thus rather than describe a person as "aggressive," it would he necessary to qualify the mode of aggressive behavior (e.g., verbal insults but not physical attacks) and the specific contingencies (e.g., when criticized for poor athletic performance on playground but not in class). Such cumbersome, hyphenated descriptions (e.g., Mischel, 1969) would lack the "thumbnail sketch" appeal of global trait portraits. But they would remind us of the discriminativeness and complexity of the individual's behavior, its idiosyncratic organization, its dependence on conditions, and the hazards of attempting to abbreviate it grossly.

The previously discussed person variables should make it plain that a cognitive social learning approach does not construe the individual as an empty organism buffeted entirely by situational forces. Yet it should be equally apparent that the nature and effects of these person variables depend on specific interactions between the individual and the psychological conditions of his life. Construction capacities cannot be adequately understood without linking them to the cognitive social learning conditions through which they develop and are maintained and to the behaviors which they yield. Similarly, the study of expectancies must not lose sight of their roots in the individual's direct and vicarious experiences and of their ready modifiability in the light of changes in behavior–outcome and stimulus–outcome relationships. While subjective stimulus values and the individual's preferences and aversions may have a greater degree of stability, their meaning and impact also hinge on the specifics of the conditions in which they occur. Self-regulatory rules, standards, and plans serve to impose additional continuity and consistency upon behavior and guide the individual in the absence of immediate situational forces. Yet such standards, rules, and plans also are not situation free, and their flexibility in response to changing conditions provides further testimony to human adaptiveness.

Perhaps substantial immunity to situational changes is shown by some of the individual's personal constructs. The "theories" formed about behavior (as in the subject's implicit personality theories about self and others) may be some of the most stable and situation-free constructions. That has double-edged consequences; the person's constructs provide a measure of perceived stability in an otherwise excessively complex, disorganized, and unstable world, but they also may become hard to disconfirm. Yet even in the realm of constructs, consistency is far from pervasive. For example, Gergen's (1968) findings reveal that contrary to the popular belief, when it comes to their self-perceptions people do not have a consistent, unitary self-concept. Indeed, he concludes with regard to the phenomena of self-concepts that "inconsistency" rather than "consistency" seems to be the natural state of affairs.[3]

The proposed approach to personality psychology emphasizes the interdependence of behavior and conditions, mediated by the constructions and cognitive activities of the person who generates them, and recognizes the human tendency to invent constructs and to adhere to them as well as to generate subtly discriminative behaviors across settings and over time. It emphasizes the crucial role of situations (conditions) but views them as informational inputs whose behavioral impact depends on how they are processed by the person. It focuses on how such information processing hinges, in turn, on the prior conditions which the individual has experienced. And it recognizes that the person's behavior changes the situations of his life as well as being changed by them. The term "personality psychology" need not be preempted for the study of differences between individuals in their consistent attributes: it fits equally well the study of the individual's cognitive and behavioral activities as he interacts with the conditions of his life.

Three Perspectives in Personality Study

The study of persons may be construed alternatively from three complementary perspectives. Construed from the viewpoint of the psychologist seeking procedures or operations necessary to produce changes in performance, it may be most useful to focus on the environmental *conditions* necessary to modify the subject's behavior and therefore to speak of "stimulus control," "operant conditioning," "classical conditioning," "reinforcement control," "modeling," and so on. Construed from the viewpoint of the theorist concerned with how these operations produce their effects in the subject who undergoes them, it may be more useful to speak of alterations in processed information and specifically in constructs, expectancies, subjective values, rules, and other theoretical *person variables* that mediate the effects of conditions upon behavior. Construed from the viewpoint of the experiencing subject, it may be more useful to speak of the same events in terms of their *phenomenological impact* as thoughts, feelings, wishes, and other subjective (but communicable) internal states of experience. Confusion arises when one fails to recognize that the same events (e.g., the "operant conditioning" of a child's behavior at nursery school) may be alternatively construed from each of these perspectives and that the choice of constructions (or their combinations) depends on the construer's purpose. Ultimately, conceptualizations of the field of personality will have to be large enough to encompass the phenomena seen from all three perspectives. The present cognitive social learning approach to persons hopefully is a step in that direction.

ACKNOWLEDGMENTS

Parts of this manuscript are based on the Address of the Chairman, Section III, Division 12, American Psychological Association, Washington, DC, September 3, 1971. Preparation of this manuscript was facilitated by National Institute of Mental Health Grant M-6830 and National Science Foundation Grant GS-32582. Constructive comments have been received from more colleagues and students than can be listed here; the author is grateful for their help.

NOTES

1. In social psychology, the "attitude" has been the unit endowed with properties parallel to those assigned to the trait in the field of personality, and it appears to be suject to very similar criticisms and problems (e.g., Abelson, 1972).
2. It is possible that for each individual there are unique but broad classes of subjective stimulus equivalences, but these cannot be assessed by comparing individuals in situations that are construed as equivalent by the assessor. Such subjective equivalences certainly merit attention, but so far the clinician has not demonstrated his ability to find them reliably (Mischel, 1968).
3. In the same vein, in their analysis of sources of variance in personal constructs, Argyle and Little (1972) found that the average variation attributable to persons was only 16.1% whereas the percentages for situations and interaction were 43.6 and 40.2, respectively.
4. All references have been updated in the reprinting of this article.

REFERENCES[4]

Abelson, R. (1972). Are attitudes necessary? In B. T. King & E. McGinnies (Eds.), *Attitudes, conflict, and social change*. New York: Academic Press.

Adelson, J. (1969). Personality. *Annual Review of Psychology, 20,* 217–252.

Adinolfi, A. A. (1971). Relevance of person perception research to clinical psychology. *Journal of Consulting and Clinical Psychology, 37,* 167–176.

Alker, H. A. (1972). Is personality situationally specific or intrapsychically consistent? *Journal of Personality, 40,* 1–16.

Allport, G. (1937). *Personality: A psychological interpretation.* New York: Holt.

Anderson, J. (1960). The prediction of adjustment over time. In I. Iscoe & H. Stevenson (Eds.). *Personality development in children.* Austin: University of Texas Press.

Anderson, N. H. (1971). Integration theory and attitude change. *Psychological Review, 78,* 171–206.

Anderson, N. H. (1972). *Information integration theory: A brief survey* (Tech. Rep. No. 24). La Jolla: University of California at San Diego, Center for Human Information Processing.

Argyle, M., & Little, B. R. (1972). Do personality traits apply to social behavior? *Journal of Theory of Social Behavior, 2,* 1–35.

Aronfreed, J . (1968). *Conduct and conscience: The socialization of internalized control over behavior.* New York: Academic Press.

Averill, J. R., Olbrich, E., & Lazarus. R. S. (1972). Personality correlates of differential responsiveness to direct and vicarious threat: A failure to replicate previous findings. *Journal of Personality and Social Psychology, 21,* 25–29.

Ayllon, T., & Azrin, N. H. (1965). The measurement and reinforcement of behavior of psychotics. *Journal of the Experimental Analysis of Behavior, 8,* 357–383.

Bandura, A. (1965). Influence of model's reinforcement contingencies on the acquisition of imitative responses. *Journal of Personality and Social Psychology, 1,* 589–595.

Bandura, A. (1969). *Principles of behavior modification.* New York: Holt, Rinehart & Winston.

Bandura, A. (1971a). Analysis of modeling processes. In A. Bandura (Ed.), *Psychological modeling: Conflicting theories.* Chicago: Aldine-Atherton.

Bandura, A. (1971b). *Social learning theory.* New York: General Learning Press.

Bandura, A. (1971c). Vicarious and self-reinforcement processes. In R. Glaser (Ed.), *The nature of reinforcement.* New York: Academic Press.

Bandura, A., Blanchard, E. B., & Ritter, B. (1969). Relative efficacy of desensitization and modeling approaches for inducing behavioral, affective, and attitudinal changes. *Journal of Personality and Social Psychology, 13,* 173–199.

Bandura, A., & Perloff, B. (1967). Relative efficacy of self-monitored and externally imposed reinforcement systems. *Journal of Personality and Social Psychology, 7,* 111–116.

Bandura, A., & Whalen, C. K. (1966). The influence of antecedent reinforcement and divergent modeling cues on patterns of self-reward. *Journal of Personality and Social Psychology,* 373–382.

Barker, R. (1966). *The stream of behavior.* New York: Appleton-Century-Crofts.

Bem, D. J. (1972). Constructing cross-situational consistencies in behavior: Some thoughts on Alker's critique of Mischel. *Journal of Personality, 40,* 17–26.

Block, J. (1965). *The challenge of response sets.* New York: Appleton-Century-Crofts.

Block, J. (1968). Some reasons for the apparent inconsistency of personality. *Psychological Bulletin, 70,* 210–212.

Bolles, R. C. (1972). Reinforcement, expectancy, and learning. *Psychological Review, 79,* 394–409.

Bower, G. H. (1970). Organizational factors in memory. *Cognitive Psychology, 1,* 18–46.

Bowers, K. (1972). Situationism in psychology: On making reality disappear. *Research Reports in Psychology,* No. 37, University of Waterloo, Ontario, Canada.

Byrne, D. (1961). The repression-sensitization scale: Rationale, reliability, and validity. *Journal of Personality, 29,* 334–349.

Campbell, D. T. (1961). Conformity in psychology's theories of acquired behavioral dispositions. In I. A. Berg & B. M. Bass (Eds.), *Conformity and deviation.* New York: Harper.

Campbell, D., & Fiske, D. W. (1959). Convergent and discriminant validation. *Psychological Bulletin, 56,* 81–105.

Cautela, J. R. (1971). Covert conditioning. In A. Jacobs & L. B. Sachs (Eds.). *The psychology of private events.* New York: Academic Press.

Chapman, L. J., & Chapman, J. P. (1969). Illusory correlations as an obstacle to the use of valid psycho-diagnostic signs. *Journal of Abnormal Psychology, 74,* 271–280.

Chatterjee, B. B., & Eriksen, C. W. (1962). Cognitive factors in heart rate conditioning. *Journal of Experimental Psychology, 64,* 272–279.

Craik, K. C. (1969). Personality unvanquished. *Contemporary Psychology, 14,* 147–148.

Dahlstrom, W. C. (1970). Personality. *Annual Review of Psychology, 21,* 1–48.

D'Andrade, R. G. (1970, August 16–21). *Cognitive structures and judgment.* Paper prepared for T.O.B.R.E. Research Workshop on Cognitive Organization and Psychological Processes, Huntington Beach, CA.

D'Andrade, R. G. (1973). *Memory and the assessment of behavior.* Unpublished manuscript, University of California at San Diego, Department of Anthropology.

Dulany, D. H. (1962). The place of hypotheses and intentions: An analysis of verbal control in verbal conditioning. *Journal of Personality, 30,* 102–129.

Edwards, A. L. (1957). *The social desirability variable in personality assessment and research.* New York: Dryden.

Ellsworth, R. B., Foster, L., Childers, B., Gilberg, A., & Kroeker, D. (1968). Hospital and community adjustment as perceived by psychiatric patients, their families, and staff. *Journal of Consulting and Clinical Psychology, 32*(5, Pt. 2).

Emmerich, W. (1969, March 27). *Models of continuity and change.* Paper presented at the meeting of the Society for Research in Child Development, Santa Monica, California.

Endler, N. S., & Hunt, J. McV. (1966). Sources of behavioral variance as measured by the S–R inventory of anxiousness. *Psychological Bulletin, 65,* 336–346.

Endler, N. S., & Hunt, J. McV. (1968). S–R inventories of hostility and comparisons of the proportions of variance from persons, responses, and situations for hostility and anxiousness. *Journal of Personality and Social Psychology, 9,* 309–315.

Endler, N. S., & Hunt, J. McV. (1969). Generalizability of contributions from sources of variance in the S–R inventories of anxiousness. *Journal of Personality, 37,* 1–24

Endler, N. S., Hunt, J. McV., & Rosenstein, A. J. (1962). An S–R inventory of anxiousness. *Psychological Monographs, 76*(17, Whole No. 536).

Estes, W. K. (1972). Reinforcement in human behavior. *American Scientist, 60,* 723–729.

Fairweather, G. W. (1967). *Methods in experimental social innovation.* New York: Wiley.

Festinger, L. (1945). A theory of social comparison processes. *Human Relations, 7,* 117–140.

Fiske, D. W. (1973). *The limits of the conventional science of personality.* Unpublished manuscript, University of Chicago.

Frieze, I., & Weiner, B. (1971). Cue utilization and attributional judgments for success and failure. *Journal of Personality, 39,* 591–605.

Geer, J. H., Davison, G. C., & Gatchel, R. K. (1970). Reduction of stress in humans through nonveridical perceived control of aversive stimulation. *Journal of Personality and Social Psychology, 16,* 731–738.

Gergen, K. J. (1968). Personal consistency and the presentation of self. In C. Gordon & K. J. Gergen (Eds.), *The self in social interaction.* New York: Wiley.

Gewirtz, J. L., & Baer, D. M. (1958). Deprivation and satiation of social reinforcers as drive conditions. *Journal of Abnormal and Social Psychology, 57,* 165–172.

Gibson, E. J. (1969). *Principles of perceptual learning and development.* New York: Appleton-Century-Crofts.

Goldfried, M. R., & D'Zurilla, T. J. (1969). A behavioral-analytic model for assessing competence. In C. D. Spielberger (Ed.), *Current topics in clinical and community psychology. Vol. 1.* New York: Academic Press.

Grings, W. W., & Lockhart, R. A. (1963). Effects of anxiety-lessening instructions and differential set development on the extinction of GSR, *Journal of Experimental Psychology, 66,* 292–299.

Grusec, J., & Mischel, W. (1966). Model's characteristics as determinants of social learning. *Journal of Personality and Social Psychology, 4,* 211–215.

Hamilton, D. L. (1971, September). *Implicit personality theories: Dimensions of interpersonal cognition.* Paper presented at the meeting of the American Psychological Association, Washington, DC.

Hayden, T., & Mischel, W. (1973). Maintaining trait consistency in the resolution of behavioral inconsistency: The wolf in sheep's clothing. Unpublished manuscript, Stanford University.

Heider, F. (1958). *The psychology of interpersonal relations.* New York: Wiley.

Helson, H. (1964). *Adaptation-level theory.* New York: Harper & Row.

Hunt, J. McV. (1965). Traditional personality theory in the light of recent evidence. *American Scientist, 53,* 80–96.

Irwin, F. W. (1971). *Intentional behavior and motivation.* New York: Lippincott.

Isen, A., Horn, N., & Rosenhan, D. (1973). Effects of success and failure on children's generosity. *Journal of Personality and Social Psychology, 27,* 239–247.

Jeffrey, K., & Mischel, W. (1973). *The layman's use of traits to predict and remember behavior.* Unpublished manuscript, Stanford University.

Jones, E. E. (1964). *Ingratiation: A social psychological analysis.* New York: Appleton-Century-Crofts.

Jones, E. E., & Nisbett, R. E. (1971). The actor and the observer: Divergent perceptions of the causes of behavior. In E. E. Jones et al. (Eds.), *Attribution: Perceiving the causes of behavior.* McCaleb-Seiler.

Kanfer, F. H. (1971). The maintenance of behavior by self-generated stimuli and reinforcement. In A. Jacobs & L. B. Sachs (Eds.), *The psychology of private events*. New York: Academic Press.

Kanfer, F. H., Cox, L. E., Greiner, J. M., & Karoly, P. (1973). *Contracts, demand characteristics, and self-control*. Unpublished manuscript, University of Cincinnati.

Kanfer, F. H., & Marston, A. R. (1963). Determinants of self-reinforcement in human learning. *Journal of Experimental Psychology, 66,* 245–254.

Kaufman, A., Baron, A., & Kopp, R. E. (1966). Some effects of instructions on human operant behavior. *Psychonomic Monograph Supplements, 1,* 243–250.

Kelley, H. H. (1967). Attribution theory in social psychology. In D. Levine (Ed.), *Nebraska Symposium on Motivation: 1967*. Lincoln: University of Nebraska Press.

Kelly, E. L. (1955). Consistency of the adult personality. *American Psychologist, 10,* 659–681.

Kelly, G. (1955). *The psychology of personal constructs*. New York: Basic Books.

Kohlberg, A. A (1969). A cognitive-developmental analysis of children's sex-role concepts and attitudes. In E. E. Maccoby (Ed.), *The development of sex differences*. Stanford, CA: Stanford University Press.

Kohlberg, L. (1969). Stage and sequence: The cognitive-developmental approach to socialization. In D. A. Goslin (Ed.), *Handbook of socialization theory and research*. Chicago: Rand McNally.

Lawrence, D. H. (1959). The nature of a stimulus: Some relationships between learning and perception. In S. Koch (Ed.), *Psychology: A study of a science*. New York: McGraw-Hill.

Lazarus, A. A. (1963). The treatment of chronic frigidity by systematic desensitization. *Journal of Nervous and Mental Disease, 136,* 272–278.

Little, B. R., & Stephens, E. D. (1973). Psychological construing and selective focusing on content versus expressive aspects of speech. *Journal of Consulting and Clinical Psychology*.

Lovaas, O. I., Freitag, G., Gold, V. J., & Kassorla, I. C. (1965). Experimental studies in childhood schizophrenia: I. Analysis of self-destructive behavior. *Journal of Experimental Child Psychology, 2,* 67–84.

Macfarlane, J. W., & Tuddenham, R. D. (1951). Problems in the validation of projective techniques. In H. H. Anderson & G. L. Anderson (Eds.), *Projective techniques*. New York: Prentice Hall.

Mandler, G. (1967). Organization and memory. In K. W. Spence & J. T. Spence (Eds.), *The psychology of learning and motivation: Advances in research and theory*. New York: Academic Press.

Mandler, G. (1968). Association and organization: Facts, fancies and theories. In T. R. Dixon & D. L. Horton (Eds.), *Verbal behavior and general behavior theory*. Englewood Cliffs, NJ: Prentice Hall.

McGuire, W. J. (1968). Personality and susceptibility to social influence. In E. F. Borgatta & W. W. Lambert (Eds.), *Handbook of personality theory and research*. Chicago: Rand McNally.

Meichenbaum, D. H. (1971). *Cognitive factors in behavior modification: Mod-*

ifying what clients say to themselves (Research Report No. 25). Waterloo, Ontario, Canada: University of Waterloo.

Metcalf, M. (1956). Demonstration of a psychosomatic relationship. *British Journal of Medical Psychology, 29,* 63–66.

Miller, G. A,, Galanter. E., & Pribram, K. H. (1960). *Plans and the structure of behavior.* New York: Holt, Rinehart & Winston.

Mischel, W. (1966). Theory and research on the antecedents of self-imposed delay of reward. In B. A. Maher (Ed.), *Progress in experimental personality research* (Vol. 3). New York: Academic Press.

Mischel, W. (1968). *Personality and assessment.* New York: Wiley.

Mischel, W. (1969). Continuity and change in personality. *American Psychologist, 24,* 1012–1018.

Mischel, W. (1971). *Introduction to personality.* New York: Holt, Rinehart & Winston.

Mischel, W. (1972). Direct versus indirect personality assessment: Evidence and implications. *Journal of Consulting and Clinical Psychology, 38,* 319–324.

Mischel, W. (1973a). Processes in delay of gratification. In L. Berkowitz (Ed.), *Advances in social psychology* (Vol. 7). New York: Academic Press.

Mischel, W. (1973b). On the empirical dilemmas of psychodynamic theory: Issues and alternatives. *Journal of Abnormal Psychology, 82,* 335–344.

Mischel, W., & Baker, N. (1973). *Cognitive appraisals and transformations in delay behavior.* Unpublished manuscript, Stanford University.

Mischel, W., Coates. B., & Raskoff, A. (1968). Effects of success and failure on self-gratification. *Journal of Personality and Social Psychology, 10,* 381–390.

Mischel, W., Ebbesen, E. B., & Zeiss, A. R. (1972). Cognitive and attentional mechanisms in delay of gratification. *Journal of Personality and Social Psychology, 21,* 204–218.

Mischel, W., Ebbesen, E. B., & Zeiss, A. R. (1973). Selective attention to the self: Situational and dispositional determinants. *Journal of Personality and Social Psychology, 27,* 129–142.

Mischel, W., & Grusec, J. (1966). Determinants of the rehearsal and transmission of neutral and aversive behaviors. *Journal of Personality and Social Psychology, 3,* 197–205.

Mischel, W., Grusec, J., & Masters, J. C. (1969). Effects of expected delay time on the subjective value of rewards and punishments. *Journal of Personality and Social Psychology, 11,* 363–373.

Mischel, W., & Liebert, R. M. (1966). Effects of discrepancies between observed and imposed reward criteria on their acquisition and transmission. *Journal of Personality and Social Psychology, 3,* 45–53.

Mischel, W., & Moore, B. (1973a). Effects of attention to symbolically presented rewards upon self-control. *Journal of Personality and Social Psychology, 28,* 172–179.

Mischel, W., & Moore, B. (1973b). *Cognitive transformations of the stimulus in delay of gratification.* Unpublished Manuscript, Stanford University.

Mischel, W., & Staub, E. (1965). Effects of expectancy on working and waiting for larger rewards. *Journal of Personality and Social Psychology, 2,* 625–633.

Mischel, W., Zeiss, R., & Zeiss, A. R. (1974). Internal–external control and persistence: Validation and implications of the Stanford Preschool I–E Scale. *Journal of Personality and Social Psychology, 29,* 265–278.

Moore, B. S., Underwood, B., & Rosenhan, D. L. (1973). Affect and altruism. *Developmental Psychology, 8,* 99–104.

Moos, R. H. (1968). Situational analysis of a therapeutic community milieu. *Journal of Abnormal Psychology, 73,* 49–61.

Moos, R. H. (1969). Sources of variance in response to questionnaires and in behavior. *Journal of Abnormal Psychology, 74,* 405–412.

Neisser, U. (1967). *Cognitive psychology.* New York: Appleton-Century-Crofts.

Norman, D. A. (1969). *Memory and attention.* New York: Wiley.

Patterson, G. R., & Cobb, J. A. (1971). Stimulus control for classes of noxious behaviors. In J. F. Knutson (Ed.), *The control of aggression: Implications from basic research.* Chicago: Aldine.

Peterson, D. R. (1968). *The clinical study of social behavior.* New York: Appleton-Century-Crofts.

Piaget. J. (1954). *The construction of reality in the child.* New York: Basic Books.

Premack, D. (1965). Reinforcement theory. In D. Levine (Ed.), *Nebraska Symposium on Motivation: 1965.* Lincoln: University of Nebraska Press.

Raush, H. L. (1965). Interaction sequences. *Journal of Personality and Social Psychology, 2,* 487–499.

Raush, H. L., Dittman, A. L., & Taylor, T. J. (1959). The interpersonal behavior of children in residential treatment. *Journal of Abnormal and Social Psychology, 58,* 9–26.

Robbins, L. N. (1972, February 19). *Dissecting the "broken home" as a predictor of deviance.* Paper presented at the NIMH Conference on Developmental Aspects of Self-Regulation, La Jolla, California.

Rotter, J. B. (1954). *Social learning and clinical psychology.* Englewood Cliffs, NJ: Prentice Hall.

Rumelhart, D. E., Lindsey, P. H., & Norman, D. A. (1971). *A process model for long-term memory* (Tech. Rep. No. 17). La Jolla: University of California at San Diego, Center for Human Information Processing.

Schachter, S. (1964). The interaction of cognitive and physiological determinants of emotional state. In L. Berkowitz (Ed.), *Advances in experimental social psychology* (Vol. 1). New York: Academic Press.

Schachter, S., & Singer. J. E. (1962). Cognitive, social, and physiological determinants of emotional state. *Psychological Review, 69,* 379–399.

Schneider, D. J. (1973). Implicit personality theory: A review. *Psychological Bulletin, 79,* 294–309.

Shweder, R. A. (1971). *Is a culture a situation?* Unpublished manuscript, Harvard University, Department of Social Relations.

Shweder, R. A. (1972). Semantic structures and personality assessment. Unpublished doctoral dissertation. Harvard University, Department of Social Relations.

Spielberger, D. C., & Denike, L. D. (1966). Descriptive behaviorism versus cognitive theory in verbal operant conditioning. *Psychological Review, 73,* 306–326.

Strong, E. K., Jr. (1955). *Vocational interests 18 years after college.* Minneapolis: University of Minnesota Press.

Tversky, A., & Kahneman, D. (1971). Belief in the law of small numbers. *Psychological Bulletin, 76,* 105–110.

Vernon, P. E. (1964). *Personality assessment: A critical survey.* New York: Wiley.

Wachtel, P. L. (1973). Psychodynamics, behavior therapy, and the implacable experimenter: An inquiry into the consistency of personality. *Journal of Abnormal Psychology, 82,* 324–334.

Wallace. J. (1966). An abilities conception of personality: Some implications for personality measurement. *American Psychologist, 21,* 132–138.

Wallach, M. A. (1962). Commentary: Active–analytical versus passive–global cognitive functioning. In S. Messick & J. Ross (Eds.), *Measurement in personality and cognition.* New York: Wiley.

Wallach, M. A., & Leggett, M. I. (1972). Testing the hypothesis that a person will be consistent: Stylistic consistency versus situational specificity in size of children's drawings. *Journal of Personality, 40,* 309–330.

Weiner, B., Frieze, I., Kukla, A., Reed, L., Rest, S., & Rosenbaum, R. M. (1971). *Perceiving the causes of success and failure.* New York: General Learning Press.

Weiner, B., & Kukla, A. (1970). An attributional analysis of achievement motivation. *Journal of Personality and Social Psychology, 15,* 1–20.

White, R. W. (1959). Motivation reconsidered: The concept of competence. *Psychological Review, 66,* 297–333.

White, R. W. (1964). *The abnormal personality.* New York: Ronald Press.

Witkin, H. A. (1965). Psychological differentiation and forms of pathology, *Journal of Abnormal Psychology, 70,* 317–336.

Wolf, R. (1966). The measurement of environments. In A. Anastasi (Ed.), *Testing problems in perspective.* Washington, DC: American Council on Education.

Wolpe, J. (1961). The systematic desensitization treatment of neuroses. *Journal of Nervous and Mental Disease, 132,* 189–203.

Zigler, E., & Phillips, L. (1961). Social competence and outcome in psychiatric disorder. *Journal of Abnormal and Social Psychology, 63,* 264–271.

Zigler. E., & Phillips, L. (1962). Social competence and the process-reactive distinction in psychopathology. *Journal of Abnormal and Social Psychology, 65,* 215–222.

17

From Homunculus to a System

Toward a Science of the Person

YUICHI SHODA

For the last half-century, a quiet paradigm shift has been taking place in how individuals are conceptualized in psychology. Behavior variation across contexts—once considered measurement noise that obscured a clear view of the person—is now seen as reflecting the essence of the person. Delay of gratification—once considered a test of willpower to resist tempting situations—is now understood to reflect individuals' knowledge of the effect of situations and their ability to harness it. People, in their everyday task of understanding other people's behavior, were once considered to make the same error as psychologists, considering behavior as primarily reflecting forces internal to the person, such as their "personality" and "willpower," and overlooking situational context. Now, such a tendency has been shown to reflect the intuitive conception of human behavior in cultures of Western European origin, rather than universal human nature. Even in Western culture, people are found, under some conditions, to be able to invoke a more complex understanding of human behavior that takes situations into account.

In short, in the last few decades, a shift seems to be taking place in the understanding of human nature, from one that focuses almost exclusively on the factors internal to a person, like a homunculus, to one that views human behaviors as reflecting systems, intraindividual as well as interpersonal.

A paradigm shift is supposed to be invisible while it is occurring, so this chapter is an attempt to step back and think about what the process of paradigm shift might look like from the point of view of those who participate in one.

Here is an illuminating passage in a history book by Bruce Moran (2005), titled *Distilling Knowledge:*

> If you were young and inquisitive in 1597, because you were born into a world familiar with the earth-moving astronomical theories of Nicolaus Copernicus (1473–1543), you might have read the dazzling defense of Copernican astronomy just published by Johannes Kepler (1571–1630) called the *Cosmographic Mystery* (1596). You might also have known of a terrific book printed in that year that historians of later time would revere as the first real textbook in the history of chemistry. . . . Although hard to read in Latin, it would have taught you how to prepare a variety of chemical substances and how to make them purer by means of fire. . . . The author made plain how chemical changes followed from combining different substances, . . . and gave precise instructions about how to build and use a variety of laboratory vessels. . . . You would have found a wonderfully pragmatic and logical guide to the useful, empirical, and theoretical parts of an art long discussed by scholars. My guess is that you would have been excited by all of this and would not have been the least bit put off, disappointed, or confused by the book's title, namely, *Alchemy* (Libavius, 1597). (p. 8)

I am not for a moment suggesting that what psychology has achieved so far resembles alchemy, in the sense of a belief in the mystical, the magical, or the occult. But I do wonder if there might not be certain similarity between psychology now and chemistry then in how confusing the world must have looked. For 16th-century chemists, the world had been making sense, more or less, for centuries, ever since Aristotle (around 350 B.C.E.) stated what was then already a fairly well-established theory, that all matter consists of combinations of four elementary properties or qualities, forming two pairs of opposites: hot and cold, wet and dry. When combined, they were believed to give rise to the four fundamental simple bodies, or elements, namely earth, air, fire, and water (see Figure 17.1). Hovering above these elements was a fifth element— Aristotle called it ether, the element of the stars.

Similarly, behaviors of all the heavenly objects had seemed to move in a nice circular orbit around the Earth, following the predictions like clockwork. Except sometimes it was not true. For example, some heavenly objects (planets) seem to stall in the middle of their orderly procession and even go backwards for a while. This observation, of course, led to a world view that is drastically different from the prevailing one— namely, that if we assume that the Earth goes around the sun, rather

FIGURE 17.1. The Four Elements, based on a diagram from Isidore of Seville, *Liber de responsione mundi* (Augsburg, 1472). Original in the Huntington Library.

than the other way around, and if we assume the same for all other planets, then what was a previously troubling anomaly is no longer one. It is not noise, but a key ingredient of a new conception of the universe.

The world of human behavior also made pretty good sense, for the most part, for a long time, and the way it made sense resembled the Aristotelian view of the physical world. Just as the Earth was considered the center of the universe, so was the person. The person was the figure, and the world surrounding the person was ground. Just as matter consisted of Aristotelian elements, so did personality, consisting of four humors, the qualities sanguine, melancholy, choleric, and phlegmatic.

To illustrate, let us examine the question of how people resist temptations in pursuit of goals, one of the central questions Walter Mischel's work focused on. It is quite natural to attribute people's ability to resist temptation to the person. When people were asked what is it that allows one to keep an unwavering eye on the prize and resist temptations, a popular answer was willpower, which, according to Webster's dictionary, is "the power of control over one's own actions or emotions." That begs the question: what determines willpower? Perhaps ego strength. Then "What determines *that*?" and on and on, down the path of infinite regress, approaching, but never reaching, the *mythical homunculus*.

Walter Mischel's work presented a challenge to this view. He found that children who clenched their teeth and summoned their willpower to stare down tempting marshmallows actually ended up ringing a bell to end the delay pretty quickly (summarized in Mischel, 1974). They did so much sooner than those children who knew that they were, to a great extent, at the mercy of the situation. When asked, these children would say that if they looked at the marshmallows, they would want to eat them, so they covered their eyes, turned around, and thought about fun things. Those who were resigned to the realization that one is powerless in the face of temptation actually had more power over the temptation (e.g., Mischel, 1983). In discovering this Zen-like paradox, Mischel was subtly shifting the worldview with regard to willpower. The person, the homunculus inside the person, and the homunculus inside the homunculus inside the person are no longer necessary as the seat of willpower.

He found that this result was not limited to his experiments with young children. Some of his earliest work was a field study on the island of Trinidad (e.g., Mischel, 1958). There, he saw that a person dancing happily at a carnival, who at first might have seemed like a happy-go-lucky type with minimal willpower, actually engaged in amazingly long-term, planful, goal-driven pursuits. It would have been simple to understand if lazy people were lazy, and conscientious folks were the ones who made and carried out painstaking plans, but that was not the case. The possibility that the world of personality and individual differences wasn't quite as orderly as one hoped was backed up by his study of Peace Corps volunteers, which gave him systematic, indisputable evidence that something was awry (Mischel, 1965). All sorts of tests and assessment of volunteers' ability to succeed in Nigeria, provided by a panel of well-trained psychologists and psychiatrists, did not do much to predict the actual performance of the volunteers in Africa. This discovery led to an even more systematic survey of what other researchers were finding, and to everyone's surprise, there were many instances in which the best personality assessment techniques were not predicting actual behaviors, as summarized by Mischel's seminal volume (1968).

Did this mean that all the observations that supported the old view were wrong? No, before and after the publication of Mischel's 1968 book that challenged the basic assumptions behind personality assessment, it remained the case that there were large and reliable individual differences in most behaviors. It also remained the case that these individual differences were not always consistent across situations, so that, for example, a person who is never late for a meeting at work may often be a no-show for a dental checkup. Is she a conscientious person or not? The problem was not the data, but the basic worldview about how persons and their behaviors are conceptualized—namely, that persons reliably differ in their disposition toward certain behaviors and that the variances in disposition accounted for individual differences in behavior.

We now view things differently. Before, the expectation was that conscientious people engage in more conscientious behaviors, and people with greater willpower more effectively resisted temptations to pursue goals. Stated more abstractly, the relationship between personal characteristics and behaviors was that of isomorphism—conscientious person, conscientious behavior; stronger willpower, stronger resistance to temptation. But the emerging new conception inspired by Mischel's work does not assume such isomorphism.

Interestingly, isomorphism and a lack of it between the phenomena and the constructs that explain them, is one of the key differences between the Aristotelian view of matter and modern chemists' view. In contemporary chemistry, if litmus paper turns red when exposed to lemon juice, it reflects the fact that lemon juice is acidic. Modern chemistry allows us to understand this phenomenon without resorting to hypothesizing lemon juice's latent redness. Rather, chemistry accounts for the phenomenon by the acidity of lemon juice, which it in turn understands in terms of the abundance of hydrogen ions in a solution.

Similarly, before the late–20th-century shift in the conception of a person, if a person behaved in a conscientious way, that was because the person was conscientious. Now, if a person behaves in a conscientious way in a given situation, it's not because she has more of the element of "conscientiousness" but because of the way her psychological system responds to the particular situation she is in. Conscientiousness happens. It is an emerging phenomenon, which itself does not exist in the person herself or in the situation. Similarly, willpower happens. It doesn't exist in the person, nor is it the characteristic of the homunculus that resides in the person. It is an emerging phenomenon that reflects the interplay among the components of the system that is a person.

REFERENCES

Mischel, W. (1958). Preference for delayed and immediate reinforcement: An experimental study of a cultural observation. *Journal of Abnormal and Social Psychology, 56,* 57–61.

Mischel., W. (1965). Predicting the success of Peace Corps volunteers in Nigeria. *Journal of Personality and Social Psychology, 1,* 510–517.

Mischel, W. (1968). *Personality and assessment.* New York: Wiley.

Mischel, W. (1974). Processes in delay of gratification. In L. Berkowitz (Ed.), *Advances in experimental social psychology* (Vol. 7, pp. 249–292). New York: Academic Press.

Mischel, W. (1983). The role of knowledge and ideation in the development of delay capacity. In L. S. Liben (Ed.), *Piaget and the foundations of knowledge* (pp. 201–229). Hillsdale, NJ: Erlbaum.

Moran, B. T. (2005). *Distilling knowledge: Alchemy, chemistry, and the scientific revolution, New Histories of Science, Technology, and Medicine.* Cambridge, MA: Harvard University Press.

Index